SOCIAL COGNITION, INFERENCE, AND ATTRIBUTION

SOCIAL COGNITION, INFERENCE, AND ATTRIBUTION

ROBERT S. WYER, JR.
University of Illinois at Urbana-Champaign

DONAL E. CARLSTON
University of Iowa

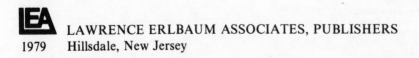 LAWRENCE ERLBAUM ASSOCIATES, PUBLISHERS
1979   Hillsdale, New Jersey

DISTRIBUTED BY THE HALSTED PRESS DIVISION OF
JOHN WILEY & SONS
New York   Toronto   London   Sydney

ALBRIGHT COLLEGE LIBRARY

Lawrence Erlbaum Associates, Inc., Publishers
365 Broadway
Hillsdale, New Jersey 07642

Distributed solely by Halsted Press Division
John Wiley & Sons, Inc., New York

Library of Congress Cataloging in Publication Data

Wyer, Robert S.
  Social cognition, inference, and attribution.

  Bibliography: p.
  Includes indexes.
  1. Social perception. 2. Attribution (Social
psychology) 3. Cognition. I. Carlston, Donal E.,
joint author. II. Title.
HM132.W93   301.1   79-18402
ISBN 0-470-26850-6

Printed in the United States of America

Contents

Preface

This book developed out of a series of general discussions between the authors on research and theory in person perception and attribution phenomena. During the course of this discussion, two things became clear. First, many of the traditional approaches to investigating these phenomena, made popular during the past decade by the advent of algebraic models of information integration, were not providing answers to several fundamental questions concerning the manner in which social stimulus information is interpreted, organized, and stored in memory, and the factors that affect its retrieval and use in making judgments of the people and events to which it is relevant. Indeed, the methodology typically used in these areas required conceptualizations that interfered with the identification of these questions. Second, many fundamental issues associated with the processing of social stimulus information were relevant to phenomena investigated in a variety of traditionally segregated areas (e.g., impression formation, attribution, social comparison, interpersonal attraction, belief and opinion change, etc.). However, these commonalities were rarely identified. This appeared to result from a tendency to focus on microtheoretical formulations developed to account for a circumscribed set of phenomena, without considering these phenomena within a broader conceptual framework.

This book is an attempt to respond to these various deficiencies. We present an approach to conceptualizing and investigating fundamental processes of interpreting, storing and retrieving information about social stimuli and, when necessary, identifying and combining its implications to arrive at judgments of these stimuli. In doing so, we have not attempted to construct a single theoretical formulation from which all social phenomena can be predicted. Rather, we have tried to develop a perspective that helps one to understand where the implications of existing theory and research potentially fit into a general conceptualization of social cognition, and where theoretical and empirical holes exist that need filling. In this regard, our approach has been to concentrate on basic processes of dealing with social stimulus information, introducing existing theory and research in the context of discussing these processes.

The book is organized around three aspects of social stimulus information processing. The first concerns the interpretation of new information, its organization and storage in memory, and its retrieval for use in making judgments. The second focuses on the characteristics of information that affect perceptions of its implications and the processes whereby its implications are construed. Finally, we consider the processes of combining the implications of different pieces of information to arrive at judgments and the conditions in which these processes are likely to be invoked. The latter section may appear to be a return to some of the traditional approaches against which this book is ostensibly a reaction. However, we hope to provide a fresh perspective on information integration phenomena that permits them to be understood in relation to other, equally important phases of social information processing.

In the course of our discussion, many existing formulations will be considered, although often from a different point of view and in a different theoretical context than those in which they are usually evaluated. As a result, issues are raised that are frequently overlooked when viewing the formulations from more traditional vantage points. In addition, several new and untested theoretical analyses are brought to bear upon many of the issues to be addressed. In the absence of empirical support for these formulations, our presentation of them here may seem premature. However, we consider the contribution of this book to be more heuristic than definitive. That is, we hope to plant the seeds of an integrated conceptual approach to social information processing that will stimulate additional research and theorizing about the phenomena of concern. Such efforts would inevitably lead to refinements and modifications of many if not all of the theoretical analyses proposed here, while retaining the more general conceptual framework within which they are housed. If this work is in fact stimulated by the material in this volume, our primary objectives will be accomplished.

Both authors have contributed equally to the preparation of this volume and the concepts and ideas presented herein. The order of authorship is therefore not intended to convey the relative magnitude of these contributions. Many other groups and individuals have contributed in many different ways to the preparation of this volume. The major portion of the original research reported in this volume, as well as the writing of much of the manuscript, was supported by National Science Foundation grants GS

29241, GS 39938, SOC 73-0568, and BMS 76-24001 to the first author, and by University of Illinois and National Science Foundation fellowships to the second author. Without this support, the book would not have been possible. Additional work in preparing the manuscript was performed during the first author's tenure as a guest professor at Sonderforschungsbereich 24 of the University of Mannheim, Germany. Their assistance in providing facilities and materials associated with this work is gratefully acknowledged.

Numerous colleagues read and commented extensively on sections of this book or individual chapters, as well as previous manuscripts related to it. Of these, we are particularly indebted to Dieter Frey, Harry F. Gollob, Jon Hartwick, Reid Hastie, Tory Higgins, Thomas Ostrom, Steven J. Sherman, Edward Shoben, Thomas Srull, and Harry S. Upshaw for exceptionally penetrating comments and criticisms, as well as for more general discussions of the issues related to it that have substantially affected our thinking about the issues of concern over the course of the past several years. In addition, many students have contributed, both as assistants and colleagues, to much of the research upon which aspects of this volume are based, and the conceptualizations underlying them. While these persons are too numerous to acknowledge here, the contributions of Jon Hartwick, Marilyn Henninger, Ronald Hinkle, and Thomas Srull have been particularly invaluable, and the work of Bradford Groff, Cathy Morris, Gail Nottenburg and Michael Wolfson has also been greatly appreciated.

In this regard, the graduate students at the University of Illinois during the authors' tenure there have been a constant source of stimulation to us both, that has contributed to our thinking enormously. This stimulation has been personally gratifying and professionally invaluable, and it is to them that we dedicate this volume.

Robert S. Wyer, Jr.
Donal E. Carlston

INTRODUCTION

1 Overview and Basic Concepts

Inference-making is a fundamental and pervasive human process. Nearly every interaction we have, and every decision we make, is likely to involve one or more inferences about ourselves or aspects of our social environment. The variety of these inferences and the conditions in which they occur are nearly limitless. We may infer our own needs, abilities, personality characteristics, moods, and feelings about other persons and events. Similarly, we may infer the traits, abilities, and feelings of others. We may infer how we or others will act in certain situations, and what the consequences of these actions will be. We infer that certain events taking place in our environment are desirable or undesirable, or that they are caused by this or that factor. Moreover, before using information we receive to make other kinds of inferences, we may estimate the likelihood that this information is true.

In each case, these judgments are based upon certain information the inference maker has available. However, the types and sources of this information are as diverse and manifold as the inferences that are based upon it. For example, people's traits may be inferred from other traits they are thought to possess, from the behaviors they manifest, from others' behavior toward them, or from the traits, attitudes and abilities of their associates. Inferences about people's behavior may be based on information about their general traits, their past behaviors, the traits and behaviors attributed to persons in general, knowledge about external pressures to engage in the behavior, or the possible consequences of the behavior for the actor or for others. Moreover, information may vary along more general dimensions. For example, it may be present in the situation, or it may be previously acquired information that the judge recalls from memory; it may be either verbal or nonverbal, either ambiguous or clear, and either consistent or inconsistent in its implications.

It is therefore hardly surprising that a general concern with social inference processes pervades much contemporary research and theory in social psychology, in areas such as impression formation (Anderson, 1968a, 1971a), attribution theory (Bem, 1972; Jones & Davis, 1965; Kelley, 1967), interpersonal attraction (Berscheid & Walster, 1969; Clore, 1975; Heider, 1958), social comparison theory (Festinger, 1954; Latané, 1966), social judgment (Sherif & Hovland, 1961; Upshaw, 1969), and belief and opinion change (for a review, see McGuire, 1968c). However, perhaps because of the great diversity of both the types of judgments that people make and the types of information used in making them, most current theoretical formulations have concentrated upon restricted types of inferences and have considered the effects of only a few types of information. As a consequence, little attention has been given to more general cognitive processes that pervade social judgmental phenomena, and to general theoretical and empirical issues concerning these processes that are common to many types of inferences.

In this book, we will identify many of these general processes and the issues surrounding them, and will explore their role in inference making. Our discussion will not only conceptually integrate many issues that are seldom associated in contemporary social psychological theory and research, but will also raise presently unanswered (and often unasked) questions that are fundamental to an understanding of inference phenomena. As a result, we hope to provide new insights into the possible nature of these phenomena and to stimulate research designed to test the implications of our discussion for a variety of judgments and information types.

When a person (or "judge," as we will typically refer to him[1] in this book) is called upon to infer something about himself or his social environment, he must first identify information that is relevant to this judgment. This information may come in part from the immediate situation in which the judgment is made. However, equally important sources of information are concepts (or instances of concepts) that the judge has stored in memory. This recalled material may have three functions. First, it may have direct implications for the judgment to be made. (For example, the concept that people are generally honest may be used as a basis for inferring that a

---

[1]Here and elsewhere in this volume, "the judge" will be referred to by the masculine form of the third person pronoun. The authors are aware of the possible sex bias that this may seem to imply. However, the ideas to be communicated in this volume are complex, and continual qualifications of the judge's sex (or in some instances, use of the plural form) may seriously tax the reader's processing capacity, thereby increasing his (her) difficulty in understanding these ideas. We therefore hope that he (she) will forgive us for this intentional but unavoidable breach of social etiquette.

particular person is honest.) Second, it may be used to encode or interpret the new information presented. Finally, it may be used to construe the implications of newly encoded information for the judgment to be made. Thus, a clear understanding of judgmental processes requires knowledge of the encoding, organization, and storage of social information in memory.

Questions also arise concerning the nature of the judgmental process itself. Different processes may be involved at different times, depending upon the nature of the information presented, the nature of the judgment to be made, and the situational conditions surrounding the judgment. In some cases, a judge may base his inference on the similarity of the total configuration of information he is considering to configurations he has encountered in the past. (For example, I may infer that a new graduate student will make a good research assistant because her blend of personality characteristics and abilities reminds me of a star student I knew in my own graduate school days.) In other cases, the judge may consider the separate implications of several different pieces of information, and may use abstract, higher order rules to combine these implications into an overall judgment.

This book will be devoted to an analysis of these and other questions that are fundamental to a general understanding of social inference. In this effort, we will consider several areas of theory and research that until recently have not been of central interest to most social psychologists. While more traditional areas of investigation will also be covered in some detail, they will often be discussed in different terms, and from a different perspective, than that to which the typical reader may be accustomed.

To provide a perspective for our discussion, we will now consider more formally the various components of the inference situation and the inference process. We will first state more precisely what we mean by an inference. Then we will identify the classes of elements about which judgments are made, and will circumscribe both the nature of the "information" relevant to these judgments and the ways in which it is used. This discussion will anticipate many issues to be addressed in considerably more detail in the chapters to follow. Finally, we will attempt to show the relation of the concerns of this volume to specific theories and research areas in contemporary social psychology.

1.1 COMPONENTS OF THE JUDGMENTAL SITUATION

The basic elements of a judgmental situation consist of (a) the judgment (or inference) itself, (b) the thing being judged (the object of judgment), (c) the information that directly or indirectly bears upon this judgment, and (d) the judge. Let us consider each in turn.

The Nature of Inferences

A judgment or *inference* about an object may be conceptualized as the assignment of the object to a verbal or nonverbal concept, or cognitive category (Wyer, 1973a, 1974b). In many instances, this assignment will be based upon the similarity of the object's attributes to those the judge uses to define the concept or to characterize its exemplars. Thus, a judge's inference that a particular object is a tree may be based upon prior inferences that the object has those attributes that he uses to define membership in the category "tree" (e.g., that the object is "leafy," "wooden," "growing in the ground," etc.). Alternatively, his inference that Italians are intelligent or likeable may be based upon evidence that instances of the cateogry "Italians" have the particular subsets of attributes that define "intelligent" and "likeable." If an object were known to possess all of the attributes necessary for inclusion in a category, it would presumably be judged to belong to this category with complete certainty. More typically, however, certain relevant attributes of the object are not known. In these cases, the object will be assigned to the category with less certainty or, alternatively, with a subjective probability of less than one.

It is often important to distinguish between the *cognitive* categories that a judge uses to classify stimuli and the *response* categories that he uses to communicate this judgment to others. This distinction and its implications have been elaborated elsewhere (Wyer, 1974b; see also Parducci, 1965; Upshaw, 1969). The labels (if any) attached to cognitive categories and those assigned to response categories are not necessarily the same. Thus, when a person is asked to make a judgment, he must not only identify the cognitive category to which the object belongs, but must also decide how to communicate this classification in a language that others will understand and correctly interpret. In an experiment, this language may be not of the judge's choosing, but rather may be assigned to him by the experimenter. Then, the uncertainty with which a judge reports his inference may be attributable in part to his uncertainty about the meaning of the response alternatives given him as well as to his uncertainty about the cognitive category to which the object belongs. For simplicity we will generally assume that cognitive and response categories are isomorphic, but the reader should recognize that this is an oversimplification, and that in practice the distinction between the two may often be important.

Two general procedures are typically used in experiments to assess judges' inferences. In one, the judge is given a category name (e.g., "intelligent" or "tree"), and asked to estimate the likelihood that the object in question belongs to this category (e.g., the likelihood that "Italians" are "intelligent"). Such an estimate may be interpreted as a *probability* estimate, or alternatively a *belief* (Fishbein & Ajzen, 1975; Wyer, 1974b). In the second procedure, the judge is given a set of alternative categories, such as those comprising a numerical response scale, and is asked to assign the object to the category to which it is most likely to belong. These latter inferences are often assumed to be *magnitude* estimates. Although judgments made using the two procedures may appear to be quite different things, both probably involve the mapping of cognitive categories onto available response categories. Thus, suppose a judge is asked to consider the intelligence of an Italian. The judge may possess several cognitive categories pertaining to intelligence. These categories may or may not have verbal labels (e.g., "stupid," "ignorant," "smart," "brilliant," etc.), but each presumably has some defining criteria for membership. Based upon his knowledge of Italians, the judge may infer an Italian to belong to several categories with some probability. Assume that the distribution of these probabilities is that shown in Fig. 1.1a. Now, first imagine that the judge is asked to estimate the likelihood that the Italian is "intelligent". In this case, he must first decide which subset of his cognitive categories should be included in the general *response* category "intelligent" and which should not. This decision may be based not only upon the judge's own interpretation of "intelligent," but also upon how he expects the word to be used by the person to whom he is communicating. Once this decision is made, the judge may then map the distribution of his beliefs into two dichotomous response categories (intelligent or not intelligent) as shown in Fig. 1.1b. His response would then represent the overall probability associated with membership in the subset that fall in the range of "intelligent" (i.e., .65).

Now suppose that the judge is asked instead to rate the Italian's intelligence along a 7-category scale from –3 to +3. Here again, he may first position the response categories given him so as to include the alternative cognitive categories he assumes are relevant to the judgment, and may map the underlying distribution of his beliefs into these categories, as shown in Fig. 1.1c. His ratings would then correspond to the response category he perceives to be most representative of this underlying distribution. This category might be a "subjective expected value" of the object along the scale in question (for empirical evidence supporting this assertion, see Wyer, 1973a). That is,

$$J_o = \Sigma p_i V_i$$

where V_i is the value assigned to category i and p_i is the judge's belief that the object belongs to this category. In our example,

$$J_o = .05\,(-2) + .10\,(-1) + .20\,(0) + .25\,(1) + .25(2) + .15(3) = 1.00$$

Here the judge would assign the Italian an intelligence rating of +1, reflecting his judgment that this rating most closely corresponds to his implicit beliefs concerning Italians.

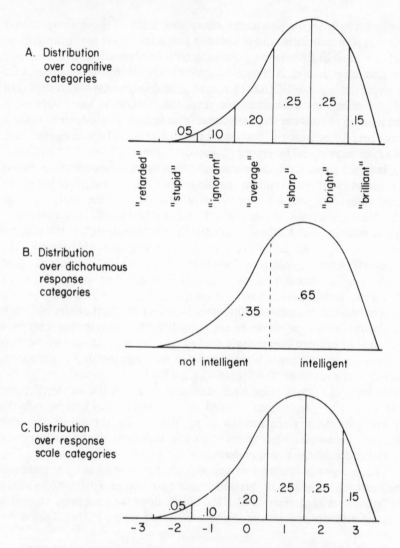

A. Distribution
   over cognitive
   categories

.05 .10 .20 .25 .25 .15

"retarded" "stupid" "ignorant" "average" "sharp" "bright" "brilliant"

B. Distribution
   over dichotumous
   response
   categories

.35   .65

not intelligent   intelligent

C. Distribution
   over response
   scale categories

.05 .10 .20 .25 .25 .15

-3   -2   -1   0   1   2   3

FIG. 1.1.   Hypothetical distributions of beliefs about a person's membership
in (a) cognitive categories pertaining to intelligence, (b) the dichotomous
response categories "intelligent" and "not intelligent", and (c) categories along
a response scale of intelligence.

Thus, if these mapping processes adequately characterize the processes
underlying each kind of judgment, each would reflect the same underlying
distribution of beliefs about object membership in relevant cognitive
categories. Despite their surface differences in appearance, the cognitive
demands and the implications of the two kinds of judgments would be similar.

Evaluative versus Nonevaluative Inferences. A distinction is often made between nonevaluative judgments of an object (e.g., the inference that Italians are "religious") and evaluative judgments (e.g., the inference that Italians are "good," or that one "likes Italians"). The latter judgments are often assumed to reflect attitudes toward the object. From the perspective we are proposing, however, there is no fundamental difference between the two types of judgments; each involves the assignment of an object to a cognitive category ("religious," or "persons I like") on the basis of certain criteria assumed to define the category. The primary difference may lie in the nature of these criteria. For example, an object's membership in an evaluative category may be based *in part* upon information about one's emotional reactions to the object, while its membership in a nonevaluative category may not be. (We consider the use of emotional reactions as information relevant to a judgment in more detail in Chapter 6.)

The Object of Judgment and Characteristics to be Judged

The discussion in this volume will focus upon five general classes of elements about which information may be available or about which judgments may be made. These elements comprise a prototypic social interaction situation in which one person or group responds in some fashion to another person, group, or object. These elements, and the aspects of these elements that are most often judged, are as follows:

1. *The actor.* Judgments of the actor may pertain to physical characteristics (age, beauty, etc.), personality traits, abilities, motives, social groups to which he belongs, or social and vocational roles that he may occupy.

2. *The actor's behavior.* This behavior may be either overt (e.g., offering help, advocating a certain position, studying for an exam) or subjective emotional reactions (fear, anger, liking for another). Judgments typically refer either to the desirability of a behavior, its magnitude or intensity, or its likelihood of occurrence.

3. *The recipient, or object of the behavior.* When the object is another person, inferences about it may be of the same type as those about the actor.

4. The *consequences* of the actor's behavior for either the actor himself or for the object. Judgments of consequences typically refer either to their desirability or their likelihood of occurrence.

5. The *situational context* in which the actor's behavior occurs. Judgments of situational factors may concern the general pleasantness of the situation, its probability of occurrence, the pressures bearing upon the actor's behavior (in the form of coercion, incentives to manifest the behavior, etc.), and the responsibility of these pressures for the behavior actually manifested.

Sources and Types of Information

The five elements we have described may not only be the object of judgments, but may also be a source of information for judgments about other elements or different aspects of the same element. (For example, an actor's honesty may be used as a basis for judging his intelligence, in predicting whether he will cheat on exams, and determining whether his associates are honest.) The information may vary along dimensions similar to those along which judgments are made (see above). However, certain more general characteristics of information, of particular relevance to our discussion in later chapters, may be worth mentioning at this time.

First, information may be either verbal or nonverbal. Moreover, it may be either new (that is, presented in the immediate situation in which the judgment is made) or previously acquired (that is, stored in memory). For example, new verbal information might consist of a written or oral communication or a descriptive statement about an object or event, while previously acquired verbal information might consist either of a semantic representation of the contents of such a communication or statement received in the past, or a semantically encoded previous experience that is relevant to the judgment to be made. New nonverbal information may come from a judge's direct observations of a person, object, or event, and may pertain either to the appearance or behavior of these elements, or to the situational context in which they are found. Such information could also consist of the judge's emotional reaction to one or more of these elements, or to the situation as a whole. Previously acquired nonverbal information may consist of a visual image of past experiences relevant to the judgment to be made or to recalled emotional reactions to these experiences.

Verbal and nonverbal information are obviously interrelated. For example, aspects of a visual or emotional experience may be assigned verbal labels at the time the experience occurs; these labels may then be stored in long-term memory, and may subsequently be recalled for use in making inferences. On the other hand, semantically encoded information, acquired either in the past or in the immediate situation, may be used to construct a visual representation of an object or event, or may elicit an emotional reaction, that may then be used as the basis for one's judgment. The interrelatedness of visual and semantic memory systems is an issue of both theoretical and empirical interest (Abelson, 1976; Kosslyn & Pomerantz, 1977; Paivio, 1971; Pylyshyn, 1973). We consider these matters in more detail in Chapter 2.

Information may also vary in generality. For example, information about a person may describe a specific act in a specific situation (e.g., "Joe picked up the brown alley-cat and threw it against the barn door"), or may describe more general behavioral or dispositional tendencies ("Joe hurts animals,"

"Joe is sadistic," etc.). Moreover, the level of generality at which information is ultimately encoded and stored may differ from that at which it is presented. Thus, a judge's observation of Joe throwing a cat against the door may be semantically encoded at a more general level and stored in memory as "Joe hurts animals" or "Joe is sadistic"; alternatively, the general statement that Joe hurts animals may elicit a prototypic image of Joe engaging in particular aggressive acts toward a cat. Moreover, the detail with which a given piece of information is stored may depend upon its novelty, its consistency with other previously acquired information, and the amount of this prior information. These issues will also be considered in later chapters.

The foregoing discussion points out an obvious but important distinction between the physical stimulus information presented and the informational *cues,* constructed from this material by the judge, upon which the judge's inference is based. Stimulus material may be encoded or interpreted in several ways. Moreover, when several pieces of information are presented simultaneously, the judge may not only treat each piece as a separate cue of relevance to the judgment to be made, but may respond to two or more pieces in combination as a *configural* cue, the implications of which may differ from the implications of each individual piece considered separately. Thus, to use an example we will elaborate later in this chapter, suppose a judge receives information that an actor has opposed women's liberation in a speech to another person who favors this concept. The actor's behavior and his audience's opinion could each be used as separate cues. On the other hand, the two pieces in combination could be interpreted as a configural cue, "the actor publicly disagrees with his audience." This cue could have implications for judgments that differ from those of each piece considered in isolation.

Indirect Uses of Information.   In addition to its direct implications for the judgment to be made, information may have indirect effects on this judgment. For example, one piece of information may provide a context for interpreting other pieces. Or, one piece may distract the judge's attention from other information. Finally, information may have a directive influence. That is, if a piece of information is novel or if its implications are unclear, it may stimulate the judge to seek additional information that will help him to understand these implications, and this latter information may consequently have more effect on his judgments than it would otherwise. These and other indirect effects are discussed in Chapter 6.

The Judge

Characteristics of the judge and his relation to the judgmental situation may vary along several dimensions. For example, the judge may either be a participant in the situation about which inferences are made or a disinterested observer. Moreover, when the judge is a participant, his inference may be either about other objects and events in the situation or about himself. These factors may have a variety of effects (cf. Jones, 1976; Jones & Nisbett, 1971; Monson & Snyder, 1977). For example, a judge's perspective when witnessing a situation may affect the specific information he extracts from this situation, and thus the information he uses to make inferences about it or its participants. The subset of previous experience a judge brings to bear upon his inference may also depend upon whether the judge is a participant or observer. Finally, a participant in a situation may experience various subjective emotional reactions unknown to the observer that could either provide information relevant to the judgment or affect the interpretation of other available information (cf. Zanna & Cooper, 1976). A more detailed discussion of these matters is provided in Chapter 2 and in subsequent chapters of this volume.

1.2. INFERENCE PROCESSES

An inference based on new or old information involves several interrelated steps. First, the information must be encoded or interpreted. Second, its potential implications for the judgment to be made must be identified. Third, when there is more than one possible implication of the information, the alternative implications must be combined or integrated into a single judgment that is considered most representative of the set of alternatives.[2] The three major sections of this book will focus in some detail on each of these processes. However, some brief comments may be in order at this time.

Encoding and Interpretation.   A judge who is asked to make an inference on the basis of information about a social situation must first encode and organize this information in terms of previously formed concepts about persons and events. This encoding may involve either specific aspects of the information received or clusters of this information. The encoding may occur in several stages. For example, a configuration of information about an unfamiliar person (e.g., a description of the person as blonde, beautiful, and obnoxious) may first be interpreted in terms of the verbal or nonverbal concepts defined by each label separately. However, once this is done, the

---

[2]A fourth subprocess is also involved. That is, the judge who communicates his judgment to another must often select a label for reporting this judgment that he believes the recipient will understand. This response selection process is of considerable importance, both practically and theoretically. However, since it has been discussed extensively elsewhere (Wyer, 1974a; see also Ostrom & Upshaw, 1968; Upshaw, 1969), it will not be dealt with extensively in this already lengthy volume.

configuration of concepts may elicit a representation of a particular person one has known who has this cluster of attributes, or the stereotype of a class of persons with these attributes. Similarly, a person who witnesses an interaction between two acquaintances may initially encode specific characteristics of the event involving particular behaviors, utterances and facial expressions, but may ultimately encode it as a unit (i.e., "another one of Bob's and Mary's nasty arguments over having children"). It is the result of this encoding that we refer to in this volume as an "informational cue".

Identification of Implications. Once information is encoded and organized, the judge must then construe its implications for the judgment to be made. He typically does this by invoking certain assumptions derived from his past experience with other instances of the involved concepts, or by deriving conclusions from other information that logically bears upon these concepts. For example, consider a judge who has encoded a person's behavior as "helping someone out on an examination" and who is asked how well he would like this person. The judge may infer that he probably would like the person, based on the assumption that people who help others are typically kind and friendly and that kind and friendly people are apt to be likeable. Three things are apparent from this simple example, however. First, the assumptions that are used to construe the implications of a piece of information depend upon its initial encoding. If the person's behavior in the example had been encoded as "cheating on an exam" rather than "helps another out," the assumptions brought to bear might have been quite different. Second, the perceived implications of an event depend in part upon the extent to which the judge believes that the event reflects a general characteristic of the person being judged. This belief may in turn be based upon assumptions concerning the generalizability of the event over situations, and over other people requiring help. (Certainly, if the judge assumed that this was the only time the actor had ever helped someone out on an exam, and that anyone would have helped the person out under the same conditions, his belief that the behavior reflects a general attribute of the actor would be less strong.) Finally, note that the process of evaluating the implications of the information implicitly involves something akin to syllogistic reasoning (i.e., "the person is kind and friendly; if a person is kind and friendly, he is likeable; therefore..."). Understanding these processes may thus require a more precise analysis of this type of reasoning and its general role in inference phenomena.

Integration of Implications. In many conditions, the information presented may be perceived to have several different implications for the judgment to be made. For example, certain aspects of the information may imply that the person is honest, while other aspects may imply that he is dishonest; some information may suggest that he favors a given position on foreign aid, while other information may imply that he holds a different opinion. In such instances, the judge must combine these various implications in some way to arrive at an overall judgment, using a rule or principle that he deems appropriate. This rule may depend on the type of information to be combined and the type of judgment to be made.

An Example. The type of assumptions that underlie the use of information to make judgments in a social situation are potentially manifold, and their implications are often diverse. To give a concrete example of these assumptions and their implications, suppose a female actor delivers a speech opposing women's liberation to an audience for $10 pay. Moreover, suppose that the audience is initially in favor of women's liberation, but changes this opinion after hearing the actor's speech. A witness to this situation might then make inferences about the actor's attitude toward women's liberation, and also about more general attributes of the actor such as friendliness. In doing so, he might treat the information about each element in isolation as a different information cue, and evaluate the implications of each cue on the basis of assumptions developed as a result of past social experience. Table 1.1 summarizes one informational cue associated with each element, an assumption that might underlie the use of that cue in inferring the actor's attitude, and the implications of this assumption for the inference to be made.

In addition, two or more pieces of information may combine to form a configural cue. One such cue, consisting of the combination of the actor's behavior and the other's opinion, is also noted in the table. However, an even more configural response is possible. For example, the information presented in combination may have many characteristics in common with a prototypic situation the judge has encountered in the past. The judge may therefore recall this situation and its participants, and use them as a basis for his judgment. (E.g., "The person in this situation reminds me of Susan Schwartz, who was a very effective speaker and worked her way through college making speeches for conservative political organizations. However, she never believed a word of what she was saying, and I suspect this person probably doesn't either.") This sort of configural response, which is similar to that postulated by Abelson (1976; see also Schank & Abelson, 1977) in his theory of script processing, may in fact be very common in social inference situations outside the experimental laboratory. We will elaborate upon this possibility and its implications in Chapter 2.

Several things are made salient by the summary in Table 1.1. First, the particular informational cues available depend upon the manner in which information is encoded. Thus, in this example, the judge encoded the actor as "female." Another judge, or this same judge under other circumstances, might

TABLE 1.1

Summary of Informational Cues Used in Inferring an Actor's Attitude Toward Women's Liberation

Source of Information	Informational Cue	Assumption Underlying Use of Cue	Implication for Actor's Attitude Toward Women's Liberation (WL)
Actor	"female"	"Women typically favor women's liberation"	pro-WL
Behavior	"delivers a speech opposing women's liberation"	"People believe what they say"	anti-WL
Other (audience)	"favors women's liberation"	"People are similar to those with whom they associate (birds of a feather flock together)"	pro-WL
Situation	"$10 is given as an incentive to oppose women's liberation"	"People who have to be paid a lot to say something probably don't want to say it"	pro-WL
Consequences for actor	"pay of $10"	"People who receive pay for doing something increase their liking for it"	anti-WL
Consequences for other	"decreased belief in women's liberation"	"People who are able to convince others of a position are likely to be sincere"	anti-WL
Behavior and other	"(actor) disagrees publically with views of others"	"People who are willing to disagree publically with others are likely to believe what they are saying"	anti-WL
All elements	"female gets paid to deliver speech opposing women's liberation"	"This person is like Susan Schwartz, who got paid to make speeches for conservative political organizations and who never believed what she was saying"	pro-WL

15

instead have encoded the actor simply as a "person," and relied on the assumption that "most persons are ambivalent about women's liberation."

Second, the same piece of information may function as two different informational cues, depending upon how it is interpreted. Moreover, the implications of each cue may differ. Thus, the pay of $10 may be interpreted as a situational constraint (i.e., an inducement to deliver the speech), in which case it may have positive implications for the actor's attitude toward women's liberation. However, it may also be interpreted as a consequence of the actor's behavior, in which case it would have negative implications for this attitude. Third, when pieces of information are contained in a configural cue, their implications cannot be predicted from the implications of each piece considered in isolation. In this regard, the assumptions underlying the use of the cues described in Table 1.1., and thus the relative magnitude of their contributions, are apt to vary with the attribute being judged. For example, suppose the judge is asked to infer the actor's friendliness rather than her attitude toward women's liberation. The configural cue "disagrees with audience" may also contribute to this judgment, based upon the assumption that persons who disagree publicly with another are not very friendly. However, the actor's behavior alone, or the audience's opinion alone, have less obvious implications for the actor's friendliness. Thus, the relative contributions of the three cues to judgments of the actor's friendliness may differ from their relative contributions to judgments of her beliefs in women's liberation.

Finally, it is important to note that the assumptions underlying the use of these various cues or configurations of information are not mutually exclusive. Several could be used simultaneously in arriving at a judgment. In these conditions, the judge is required to combine the possibility different implications of these cues to arrive at an overall judgment. A higher order combinatorial rule may be required to do this. The nature of such rules, and the contingencies where they may be applied, will be considered in the last section of this book.

1.3 RELEVANCE TO EXISTING FORMULATIONS OF SOCIAL INFERENCE

Although the example we constructed for use in describing social inference phenomena concerned judgments of the actor, the considerations outlined are obviously relevant to inferences about any element of the social interaction situation. A general formulation of inference processes that incorporates these considerations would therefore be of considerable value in predicting and interpreting a variety of specific inference phenomena. This potential value is increased by the fact that much existing research and theory may be conceptualized in terms of inferences about one of the elements in our prototypic situation as a function of information pertaining to the same or different elements. A few concerns of particular relevance to issues discussed in this book are summarized below.

Stereotyping and Halo Effects. Stereotyping may be viewed as a tendency to infer a person's attributes from information about his social or vocational role, or his ethnic group membership. It thus is reflected in particular encodings of the actor in terms of social, vocational, or ethnic categories, and in the use of these encodings as informational cues in judgment processes. A related phenomenon, generally referred to as a "halo effect," is a tendency to infer some characteristics of a person from other characteristics on the basis of the similarity of their evaluative implications (favorableness). Both tendencies may reflect the nature of judges' "implicit personality theories" about how attributes are interrelated (Rosenberg & Sedlak, 1972; Schneider, 1973). In each case, the inference of concern may be conceptualized as judgments of an actor or object on the basis of other information about this same element.

Attribution Processes. Research and theory on social attribution has been principally concerned with the effects of either a person's behavior, or the consequences of this behavior, on judgments of this person or the object toward which the behavior is directed (cf. Bem, 1972; Jones & Davis, 1965; Kelley, 1967; Weiner, Freize, Kukla, Reed, Rest, & Rosenbaum, 1971). Research on these phenomena has taken several directions, depending upon whether the judge is the actor himself or an external observer, and whether the judgment pertains to a belief or attitude of the actor or to a more general attribute (e.g., competence). Moreover, two types of judgments have been considered. One, a *trait* attribution, is simply an inference about the characteristics of an actor or object on the basis of information about the actor's behavior and its situational context. A second type, referred to as a *causal* attribution, is an inference of the extent to which these characteristics are responsible for the actor's behavior.

A related body of theory and research has focused on the effect of the consequences of an action. One concern has been with the effects of information about the outcomes of an actor's achievement task performance (success or failure) on inferences of the actor's ability or effort, or the difficulty of the task (cf. Weiner et al., 1971). A second concern has been with the effects that the consequences of an accident may have upon the assignment of responsibility for this accident, and on judgments of either the perpetrator or the victim (Lerner & Simmons, 1966; Walster, 1966). The concern here is basically with judgments of either an actor, an object or a situation, based on information about the consequences of an action or event. These matters are addressed more fully in Chapter 6.

Impression Formation and Interpersonal Attraction. Research on the determinants of one person's liking for another has also taken many directions. Substantial work during the past decade and a half has focused upon the effect of personality adjectives describing a hypothetical person on predictions of how well one would like this person. In terms of our present analysis, an ambiguity arises in interpreting the referent of judgments made in this research. That is, the judgments could refer either to the actor's behavior (i.e., his subjective affective reaction to the object), or to a general attribute of the person being described (i.e., his general likeableness). This distinction may be more than academic; a judge's criteria for inferring a person's general likeableness may differ from his criteria for predicting how he would personally react to the person. Certain of these differences are suggested by Kelley's (1967, 1971) work, to be discussed in Chapter 5. (The area of research as a whole is considered in detail in Chapter 8.)

A second approach to the study of interpersonal attraction has been taken by Byrne and his colleagues (Byrne, 1969, 1971; Byrne & Nelson, 1965). The major portion of this work has concentrated on the hypothesis that one's liking for a person is a function of the perceived similarity of this person to oneself, either in attitudes, values, or general personality. More recent work by the Byrne group has been concerned with perceiver variables (information about the actor) that affect attraction (for a summary, see Clore, 1975), while still other research has considered environmental variables that affect these reactions (e.g., Griffitt & Veitch, 1971). In the latter case, it is sometimes unclear whether these environmental factors have direct informational effects upon judgments, whether they affect the judge's mood or emotional state which is then used as information relevant to the judgment, or whether they make salient different subsets of previously formed cognitions about persons that provide a basis for the inference. These possibilities are considered in more detail in Chapter 6.

Expectancy Theory. Several authors have been implicitly or explicitly concerned with the prediction of behavior or the intention to engage in behavior. Such behavioral predictions are implicitly assumed to underlie people's decisions about how they will respond in conflict resolution situations, where the outcome of one's behavior depends in part upon the other's behavior (cf. Wyer, 1969b, 1971; for a review, see Nemeth, 1972). In much of this research, however, the determinants of these expectancies have not been investigated directly or systematically analyzed (for one exception, see Kelley & Stahelski, 1970). A more explicit formulation of the determinants of behavioral intent has been proposed by Fishbein and Ajzen (1975), who hypothesize that a person's estimate of the likelihood he will manifest a given behavior is a function of both the intrinsic desirability of the consequences of this behavior (weighted by the belief that these consequences will occur), and the normative sanctions on this behavior.

Social Comparison Processes. Social comparison theory (Festinger, 1954) and research (Latané, 1966) has been concerned with the tendency for persons to use characteristics of others as information about themselves. Much of the research performed within this theoretical framework has been concerned with conditions under which persons will seek information about others rather than with the process of *making* judgments based upon that information. However, other research and theory, such as comparison level theory (Thibaut & Kelley, 1959), assimilation–contrast theory (Sherif & Hovland, 1961), and reference scale formulations such as Upshaw's (1969) are relevant to this latter concern. Certain considerations related to these comparative processes are noted in Chapter 6.

The foregoing summary gives a general feel for the range of theoretical and empirical issues that may potentially be brought together by a general conceptualization of social inference processes. Certain aspects of the summary should be noted in this regard. First, nearly all of the research and theory described above may be viewed in terms of the effect of only one type of information upon only one type of judgment, often by only a particular type of judge. Thus, this tabulation makes salient many gaps in our existing knowledge. On the other hand, the theoretical and empirical issues investigated in these rather-restricted-content domains may often have potential implications for inference phenomena in general. We will attempt to demonstrate this in the pages that follow.

1.4 A PREVIEW OF THINGS TO COME

The following chapters will address the general issues we have noted briefly above, as well as several not yet mentioned. The book is divided into three major sections which correspond roughly to the three phases of information processing we have identified: encoding and interpretation of information, identification of the information's implications for judgments, and integration processes. This correspondence is shown in Fig. 1.2.

The next section, Basic Processes in Social Inference, begins with a conceptualization of inference phenomena based upon Abelson's script-processing theory (1976), which provides a general framework for much of our subsequent discussion. The next two chapters deal with more specific questions raised by a script-processing analysis: Chapter 3 presents a

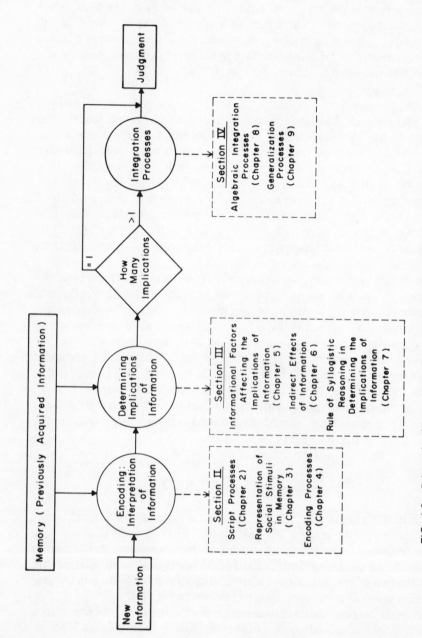

FIG. 1.2. Schematic diagram of the processes underlying judgments and their relation to material covered in this volume.

theoretical formulation of the manner in which information about persons is organized and stored in memory, and of the processes by which it is retrieved for use in making judgments. Chapter 4 considers in detail the manner in which information is encoded, and the effects of this encoding on inferences based upon that information.

Part III, Identifying the Implications of Information for Judgments, consists of three chapters that examine (a) the factors affecting the perception of information's implications for a judgment and (b) the processes of identifying and evaluating these implications. Chapter 5 focuses on specific characteristics of both presented information and information acquired through past experience that may affect the implications drawn from presented information. Chapter 6 is concerned with the indirect effects that information may have upon judgments, with particular emphasis upon (a) the effects of internal emotional reactions on the selection and interpretation of other information, and (b) the use of information about other persons as a basis for interpreting information about oneself. Finally, Chapter 7 analyzes the role of syllogistic reasoning in identifying the implications of information. This chapter attempts to establish a link between these processes and considerations raised in earlier chapters concerning the use of previously acquired information in the encoding and interpretation of information.

The last section, Integration Processes, is concerned with general principles that judges may use to combine the implications of information to form a judgment. Chapter 8 considers the role of algebraic inference rules, while Chapter 9 explores the role of inductive and deductive reasoning in the acceptance of general propositions about behavioral events.

While the primary issues of concern in this volume are not restricted to specific types of judgments based upon specific types of information, the reader will find that much contemporary research and theory on these matters is incorporated into our discussion. Moreover, new theoretical treatments of several specific facets of inference making are often proposed. As a result, we hope to provide a general understanding of social inference phenomena that will enable many current issues in the field to be considered from a common theoretical perspective, and which will suggest many new avenues of empirical investigation on problems of general theoretical importance.

A Note on Theory. Since much of our discussion in this volume is theoretically based, a few comments on the role of theory in social cognition are perhaps in order. Despite a variety of formulations of social inference phenomena of the sort noted in the preceding section, we presently have very little theoretical or empirical understanding of the fundamental processes involved in making judgments. This is in part due to the traditional unwillingness of many theorists to stray too far beyond the data available to them—that is, the observed relations between input (stimuli) and output (responses). However, an acceptable theory of social cognition must ultimately postulate, at some level of abstractness, the cognitive processes that account for these relations.

In principle, a number of alternative inference processes could be hypothesized to account for input–output relations of the sort investigated in social inference research. Without a direct observation of these processes, the theoretical formulations that postulate them can never be demonstrated to be "true"; we can only evaluate these formulations in terms of their consistency with the available data. However, there are additional criteria for evaluating a theory. A theoretical formulation should be internally consistent. It should be parsimonious; that is, it should permit us to comprehend a variety of empirical events in terms of a smaller number of general processes. It should be stated with sufficient precision to allow the clear derivation of predictions. At the same time, it should be capable of modification or refinement in specific ways as new evidence accumulates. Finally, a theory should have heuristic value, in that it stimulates research that will not only lead to modification of the theory itself, but will also lead to the identification and elaboration of uncharted areas of empirical investigation. The general framework we will propose in this book, as well as more specific theoretical analyses of phenomena falling within the scope of this framework, will hopefully meet some if not all of these criteria.

II

BASIC PROCESSES IN SOCIAL INFERENCE

Given its ostensible concern with cognitive processes, much past research and theory on social inference is surprisingly easy to interpret from a stimulus–response perspective. This is because the primary emphasis has been on the identification of characteristics of informational stimuli that evoke different patterns of inferential responses. Relatively little attention has been paid to what inference-makers actually do with the information they receive: that is, with how they identify relevant aspects of this information, encode it in the context of previously formed concepts, organize and store it in memory, and retrieve it for use in making judgments. One consequence has been a general lack of understanding of how individual differences in the processing of information may result in different inferences. Perhaps the most obvious example of this orientation has been the extensive work on "impression formation" (e.g., Anderson, 1968a, 1971a), which is actually concerned with the ways different characteristics of personality adjectives are related to different patterns of evaluative responses, and not with the formation of person impressions per se. However, it is true even of theories of social attribution (e.g., Jones & Davis, 1965; Kelley, 1967), which might be better termed theories of informational characteristics that affect judgments (see Chapter 5). It is often difficult

23

to understand from this research why there is any variability at all in judges' responses to a given configuration of stimulus information.

But there are of course individual differences in the treatment of stimulus information, and something is going on in the judges' heads during the course of inference making that may account for these differences. In the next three chapters, we will consider what these things may be. In this discussion, we will often employ terms and concepts that are fundamental to research and theory in the area of cognitive psychology, but which until recently have been quite foreign to the area of social inference. For example, we will be concerned with processes of concept identification, information encoding, associative processes, and human memory. In discussing these processes, we will invoke several conceptualizations that have seldom been applied to social judgment, but will help to integrate the disparate lines of theory and research that bear upon social inference phenomena.

In Chapter 2, we will outline a general conceptualization of social cognition, based upon Abelson's (1976) formulation of script processing. The formulation, as we will present it, is not a formal theory from which specific hypotheses are rigorously derived. Rather, it is intended primarily to provide a general conceptual perspective for many more specific issues to be discussed in later chapters. The formulation not only enables much existing research and theory to be conceptually integrated, but raises several important theoretical and empirical questions fundamental to an understanding of social inference phenomena. The next two chapters are devoted to certain of these questions. Chapter 3 will delve more formally and rigorously into the ways in which stimulus information is organized in memory and recalled by inference-makers for use in judgments. Chapter 4 deals with the encoding of information and the consequences of this encoding for subsequent inferences. The concerns of Chapters 3 and 4 obviously overlap considerably in their application and implications. However, they provide alternative perspectives on highly interrelated cognitive processes that, in combination, provide a useful and heuristic approach to an understanding of social cognition.

2

Scripts, Schemata and Implicational Molecules: A Conceptualization of Complex Information Processing

In this chapter, we will outline an approach to complex information processing that will provide a perspective for conceptualizing and integrating much of the research and theory to be discussed in later chapters. This approach is stimulated by Abelson's (1976) formulation of script processing (for details, see Schank & Abelson, 1977). As noted previously, this formulation (as we will describe it) *is not a tightly constructed set of principles from which specific hypotheses can be derived.* However, it provides a way of conceptualizing social cognition that not only allows much of the current theory and research on social inference to be integrated, but suggests many new and intriguing avenues of investigation. (More rigorous theoretical analyses of phenomena made salient by a script-processing conceptualization are presented in subsequent chapters.)

Before discussing this formulation, however, it may first be worthwhile to consider its simpler ancestor, implicational molecule theory (Abelson & Reich, 1969). Many assumptions underlying the two formulations are similar, and the inference processes implied by them have much in common. Moreover, implicational molecule theory is of interest in its own right, since many existing formulations of social inference and attribution may be viewed as special cases of more general phenomena to which the theory is relevant. Thus, the theory enables these more circumscribed formulations to be conceptually interrelated, and allows possible similarities in the processes they imply to be identified.

2.1 IMPLICATIONAL MOLECULE THEORY

Theoretical Principles

Abelson and Reich (1969) postulate the existence of sets of generalizations about persons, objects, and events that are "bound together by psychological implication." In combination, the generalizations in each set form a *molecule* or general concept. To use one of Abelson and Reich's examples, the idea that people do things to achieve desired ends may be formalized in the three-sentence "purposive behavior" molecule [A wants Y; X causes Y; A does X], where A is a class of persons, X is a class of acts or behaviors, and Y is a class of outcomes or events. A second idea, that people are forced to behave as others wish them to, might be embodied in the three-sentence "servitude" molecule [B bosses A; B wants X; A does X]. Still another idea, that people do things they like, would be represented in the two-sentence "hedonic" molecule [A likes X; A does X].

Each molecule of the sort described above can be used to interpret information about specific persons and events and make inferences about them. Abelson and Reich hypothesize that this is done according to a *completion principle.* This principle states that if the information a judge receives about specific persons and events is consistent with all but one generalization in a given molecule, the judge will tend to infer a relation between these specific instances that is consistent with the remaining generalization. Thus, suppose a judge is told that a particular person, Alan, studies for exams and that studying for exams produces good grades. Suppose further that the judge considers Alan to be an exemplar of the general category A, "studying for exams" to be an exemplar of X, and "good grades" to be an exemplar of Y. Then, this information would be consistent with two of the three generalizations in the purposive behavior molecule (i.e., the generalizations "A does X" and "X causes Y"). The judge might therefore apply this molecule and infer a relation between Alan and "good grades" that is consistent with the third generalization contained in it ("A wants Y"); that is, he would infer that Alan wants good grades. Alternatively, if the judge is told that Alan wants good grades and that studying for exams produces good grades, he might again apply this molecule and infer that Alan studies for exams.

When the information available about specific instances is relevant to only one generalization in a three-sentence molecule, a judge may often make inferences consistent with the other two. For example, if a judge is told that a particular member of class A does X, he may infer that X produces some unspecified outcome in class Y that the member of A considers desirable. In some cases, the nature of this outcome may be obvious to the judge from his previous experience. (Certainly in our example, it is unlikely that a judge would need to be told that studying produces good grades to infer that Alan wants good grades from information that Alan studies.) In other cases, however, more than one instance of a class might plausibly complete a molecule. For example, a judge who is told that Alan wants good grades could infer either than Alan studies or that he cheats, since both behaviors would be instances of behavior (X) that produces good grades. A particular generalization may often be contained in more than one molecule. In this case, a judge who encounters a specific instance of this generalization may consider the implications of several of the molecules in which it is contained. If the information available contradicts a generalization described in one of these molecules, that molecule will presumably be rejected as inapplicable. However, if more than one molecule remains plausible, the judge may infer that each is applicable with some subjective probability.

Thus, suppose a judge receives information that Arthur (a member of class A) has delivered a speech on communism (a behavior representative of class X), and is asked why this occurred. This information describes an instance of the generalization "A does X," which is contained in all three molecules described above: that is, [A wants Y; X causes Y; A does X], [B bosses A; B wants X; A does X], and [A likes X; A does X]. In the absence of any other information, the judge may be uncertain about which molecule applies; that is, he may infer that either (a) delivering the speech causes something that Arthur wants, that (b) someone with influence over Arthur wants him to deliver the speech, or that (c) Arthur thinks that speaking about communism is intrinsically enjoyable. Without additional evidence to help him evaluate the correctness of these alternatives, the judge is apt to assume that each has some likelihood of being correct, based upon his a priori expectancies about how often each sort of event occurs. However, suppose the judge has additional information that Arthur was paid $10 to deliver the speech. The evidence that the speech produced a particular outcome ($10) is apt to increase the judge's perception that the purposive behavior molecule is applicable, and thus to increase his belief that Arthur gave the speech because he wanted $10. While the other two molecules still provide possible explanations for Arthur's behavior, they are less apt to be invoked given this additional evidence bearing directly on elements of the purposive behavior molecule (i.e., Y). On the other hand, suppose the judge has information that Arthur delivered the speech without pay, and that people with influence over Arthur would have preferred that he *not* deliver the speech. Since this information renders both the purposive behavior molecule and the servitude molecule inapplicable, it increases by default the likelihood that the third, hedonic molecule applies. In other words, the information should increase the judge's inference that Arthur intrinsically desires to speak about communism.

In some instances, two or more molecules may be relevant to an inference but their implications for the inference may differ. For example, suppose a judge is asked to predict whether a person's speech will favor or oppose welfare on the basis of information that (a) the person favors welfare, but that (b) the person needs money and has been offered $10 to speak against welfare. Here, the hedonic molecule would imply that the person will advocate welfare in his speech, whereas the purposive behavior molecule would imply that he will oppose it. In such instances, the judge would need to invoke a higher order process in order to integrate the implications of the two molecules. Certain of these possible processes will be considered in Chapter 8.

Relation to Existing Theories

As we have described it, implicational molecule theory unfortunately provides no guidelines for predicting a priori which molecules may exist in a judge's cognitive system and which are apt to be brought to bear on judgments in a given situation. However, much theoretical and empirical work in contemporary social psychology can be interpreted as concerned with a priori hypotheses about the existence of specific molecules and the conditions in which they are invoked. For example, our analysis in the above example is obviously consistent with implications of social attribution theory (Heider, 1958; Jones & Davis, 1965; Kelley, 1967). That is, an actor (a member of class A) is less likely to be attributed a general disposition consistent with his behavior (e.g., a positive attitude toward performing the task) when external situational factors can account for this behavior. In Abelson and Reich's terms, this means that a judge is less apt to invoke a hedonic molecule to explain an actor's behavior if a purposive behavior molecule is also applicable. This proposition may be derived from the more general (and somewhat obvious) hypothesis that judges are less apt to invoke a given molecule to explain or interpret behavior if alternative molecules also apply.

Other contemporary conceptualizations may be interpreted similarly. For example, the "just world" hypothesis (Lerner & Simmons, 1966) is implicitly based upon the notion that judges typically believe people get what is coming to them, and thus have "just desserts" molecules of the form [A is bad; bad things befall A] and [A is good; good things befall A]. In applying these molecules, judges should infer that a member of class A is good (or bad) on the basis of information that something good (or bad) happens to him. Another possible molecule, implicitly postulated by Byrne (1969) as well as by balance theory (Heider, 1958), is the "similarity–attraction" molecule, which has the form [A likes X; B likes X; A likes B]. In addition, "competition" and "jealousy" molecules may also exist, of the form [A wants X; B wants X; A dislikes B] and [A wants X; B has X; A dislikes B], respectively. Finally, many of the assumptions underlying the use of informational cues of the sort considered in Chapter 1 may also be viewed as being based upon implicational molecules.

Aside from its integrative function, a conceptualization of these theoretical principles in terms of implicational molecules may not seem to add much to existing theories. However, two things should be noted. First, the completion principle, which implies that any relation in a molecule may be inferred from information bearing on the other relations, increases the range of inference phenomena beyond those of primary concern to other theories. For instance, a judge may use a "just desserts" molecule not only to infer that a particular person is bad on the basis of information that something unpleasant has befallen him, but also to infer that something unpleasant has or will befall a person who is bad. Similarly, a judge may invoke a jealousy molecule to infer that one person dislikes another because he knows that the other has something the first person wants; however, he may also infer that a person wants a particular object because he knows that the person dislikes someone who has it.

In another sense, however, implicational molecule theory is more restrictive than other formulations. For example, the applicability of the formulation to conditions in which balance or similarity-attraction theories are often invoked (e.g., conditions in which the molecule [A likes X; B likes X; A likes B] is relevant) is limited to situations in which the two persons involved are exemplars of classes A and B and the object is an instance of the class X. The former theories make few, if any, explicit assumptions about the nature of these classes. Moreover, they make few distinctions between alternative expressions of positive feelings that might underlie the relations being pedicted. For example, balance theory predicts that if two people have a positive sentiment toward X, they will be inferred to like one another. However, note that "A likes X," "A wants X" and "A has X" are all manifestations of a positive sentiment or attitude relation between A and X. A balance principle would therefore seem to predict that instances of A and B will be believed to like one another, regardless of whether they both like X, they both want X, or one has X and the other wants it. In contrast, implicational molecule theory calls attention to the possibility that other molecules (e.g., the jealousy or competitiveness molecules) may be called into play in the latter two cases, leading to inferences opposite to those predicted by balance (and similarity-attraction) theory. This again emphasizes the need to determine, either theoretically or empirically, the configurations of categories to which alternative molecules are considered relevant, and thus the conditions in which these molecules are apt to be used. Thus, while the theory does not in itself provide many guidelines concerning the nature of specific molecules and the conditions in which they are used, it at least calls attention to the empirical need to circumscribe more clearly the applicability of existing formulations that fall within its purview.

Effects of Encoding of Information.   One related consideration underlying the application of implicational molecule theory is worth noting. To invoke a particular molecule, one must first identify the general classes to which elements belong and to which the molecule applies. Particular persons, objects and events may belong to several classes of varying degrees of abstractness. The use of a particular molecule, and the type of inference made, will depend partly upon the salience of these different classes to the judge at the time he makes his inference. Suppose a judge is told that Alice likes Beethoven sonatas and Bob likes the Rolling Stones. If the judge interprets "Beethoven sonatas" and "the Rolling Stones" as instances of the general category "music" (X), he may invoke the "similarity–attraction" molecule and infer that Alice likes Bob. However, if the judge interprets Beethoven sonatas and the Rolling Stones to be in a different categories (e.g., "classical music" and "rock," respectively), he may consider that molecule to be inapplicable, and not make this inference. While this particular example may not be very exciting, the possibility that inferences about specific persons and events depend upon the cognitive categories to which they are assigned is of considerable importance. We will explore this possibility further in Chapter 4.

2.2 SCRIPT-PROCESSING THEORY

An implicational molecule may often be conceptualized as a verbal description of a main character (an actor) and an event or situation that occurs in his life. Abelson's more recent formulation of cognitive scripts (Abelson, 1976; see also Schank & Abelson, 1977) may be viewed as an extension of this basic notion, which takes into account the possibility of a related series of such episodes, and broadens the conceptualization of their cognitive representation. The hypothesized uses of scripts and implicational molecules in inference making are similar in many respects, as we will see.

General Concepts

Abelson (1976) defines a script as a "coherent sequence of events expected by the individual, involving him either as participant or observer." Scripts are presumably acquired throughout the individual's lifetime, either through direct experience with people and events or indirectly, through various communications media (conversations with others, reading, television, etc.). Thus, scripts, like implicational molecules, may often be idiosyncratic to an individual, resulting from his unique past history. On the other hand, many situations and experiences are sufficiently common to our culture that the essential features of some scripts are apt to be widely shared.

A script is theoretically composed of a series of *vignettes*. Each vignette is a verbal and/or nonverbal representation of an event, often involving an actor, his behavior, an object of this behavior, and its situational context. It generally consists of both an image and a conceptual representation of the event and the elements involved (Abelson, 1976). Although Abelson likens a vignette to a "picture plus caption," the modality of both the image and its representation is unrestricted. For example, the image may be visual, but may also involve other sense modalities and the affective or emotional reactions of the judge. Moreover, the conceptual representation of the image may not necessarily be verbal. Thus, the conception of a vignette is very broad, and is potentially able to incorporate a variety of more specific notions about how verbal and nonverbal information are represented in memory.

In combination, the vignettes comprising a script tell a story. A simple script may consist of two frames, one of which sets up a situation (e.g., a child writing on the walls of his room) and the second of which resolves it (e.g., the child getting spanked). The conceptual representations, or "captions," of the vignettes themselves are much richer than such sentences. For example, the vignette of a child writing on the wall may consist of an image of a blonde 3-year-old (perhaps one's own child), crayon in hand, decorating the wall by his bed with large red and black circles. This image may be accompanied by feelings of anger, fear, or humor, depending upon whether the vignette is held by the child's parent, the child himself, or a disinterested observer.

A vignette of an actor's behavior (e.g., a professor's drinking beer with a student) may often be viewed as a set of related complex concepts, or *schemata*. Each schema ("professor," "student," etc.) has a name and consists of a configuration of attributes. For example, the attributes comprising schemata about persons may consist of physical characteristics, general mannerisms, personality traits, social groups and certain typical behaviors. The nature of these attributes may vary with the vignette. Thus, the attributes associated with a professor in the above beer-drinking vignette differ from those associated with a professor in a class-lecture vignette. Some of the attributes associated with a particular schema may be inherent in the vignette in which it is contained (e.g., the professor in the beer-drinking vignette is obviously a beer drinker). However, others may be entirely unrelated (e.g., the professor may have a moustache and wear glasses.) When different visual representations of the professor schema are invoked by different vignettes, the perceiver may view the professor involved in one vignette as an entirely different type of person from that involved in other vignettes in which a professor is represented.

Abelson distinguishes between scripts and vignettes at different levels of abstractness. A vignette at the most concrete, or *episodic*, level may relate to a specific experience one has had or observed. In addition, similar experiences may be placed into more general conceptual groupings. At this latter, *categorical,* level, the vignettes comprising a script are more abstract, and consist of general features of the prototypic situations to which they refer. The "child writing on the wall and getting spanked" script, described earlier, was episodic. In contrast, a categorical script might contain vignettes about more general events such as doing a bad thing or getting punished. Scripts at these two levels may be interrelated. For example, the captions of vignettes in the categorical script described above are analogous to the generalizations contained in the "just desserts" molecule [A is bad; bad things will befall A], while the captions of vignettes in the episodic script are analogous to specific instances of these generalizations.

The analogy between categorical scripts and implicational molecules can be carried a step further. Just as a generalization may be contained in several different molecules, a categorical vignette may be a component of more than one script. In such instances, accessing the vignette may invoke fairly complex cognitive processes that can lead to different alternative inferences. To borrow another example from Abelson (1976), suppose a child has a categorical vignette captioned "doing a bad thing." This vignette may be contained in three scripts, with vignettes that are captioned as follows:

Script 1:   (a) doing a bad thing; (b) parents finding out; (c) getting punished severely.

Script 2:   (a) doing a bad thing; (b) parents finding out; (c) making it look as if brother did it; (d) brother getting punished.

Script 3:   (a) doing a bad thing; (b) parents finding out; (c) sweet-talking mother; (d) mother pacifying father; (e) getting a mild scolding.

These scripts are interrelated schematically in the manner described in Fig. 2.1. Given this configuration of vignettes, access to the "doing a bad thing" vignette might stimulate a rather complex cognitive process that would be represented verbally as follows: "My doing a bad thing could lead to my getting punished severely if my parents found out about it (unless I could make it look like my brother did it), but if I could sweet-talk my mother and she could get around my father, then maybe I'd just get a mild scolding."

A script may be accessed at any vignette, and an inference then made by progressing either forward or backward in the sequence. Thus, script processing may be invoked not only to predict future events but also to infer the nature of past events, and to explain present events in terms of the antecedent conditions that may have produced them. For example, information that someone is an accomplished musician may access an "outcome" vignette of a script that is then used to infer that the person's parents made him practice for three hours daily from the age of 6, that the person has never seen a baseball game, and that he went through four years of college without a date.

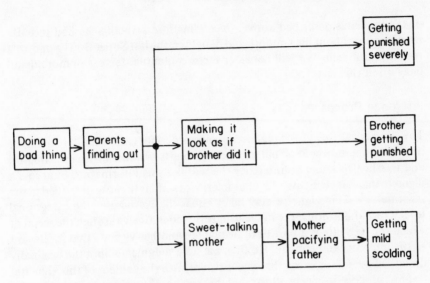

FIG. 2.1.   Series of vignettes contained in three alternative scripts associated with doing a bad thing.

In addition, scripts may be used routinely to interpret verbal information about situations. To borrow an example used by R. C. Anderson, Reynolds, Schallert and Goetz (1976), consider the following three sentences:

The baby kicked the ball.
The punter kicked the ball.
The golfer kicked the ball.

The predicate, "kicked the ball," is the same in each sentence. However, the interpretations of the sentences differ in ways reflecting differences in the scripts they are likely to evoke. For example, the first sentence may elicit a vignette of an infant in a crib jabbing awkwardly at a light rubber ball; the second, a vignette of a football player getting off a fourth-down punt in the face of onrushing tacklers; and the third, a vignette of a disgusted duffer knocking his golf ball out of the rough. These vignettes differ not only in the referent of "kicked the ball" but also in the implied mood and intentions of the actors. These examples make an important point: *the interpretation of verbal information is extremely context-defined.* In the absence of more specific information, the context is constructed by the judge himself through access to a script or vignette that happens to be salient to him at the time the information is received. Thus, to pursue our example, a judge who hears the statement "the person kicked the ball" might interpret it by accessing any one of the vignettes described above, depending upon whether he had recently been thinking about his 1-month-old daughter, the last Super Bowl game, or a recent golf match. We will consider these contextual factors in more detail later on in this chapter.

Inference Processes

The theoretical role of scripts in inference processes is very similar to that of implicational molecules. That is, when a judge is presented with information and is asked to make an inference, he will use this information to access a vignette that has elements with characteristics similar to those described in the information. This vignette may be at either the episodic or the categorical level. Once this is done, the judge progresses cognitively through the script of which this vignette is a part until he reaches another vignette that is relevant to the inference to be made. He then makes a judgment about the originally described person or event that is consistent with the content of this vignette.

This process is nicely illustrated by yet another example provided by Abelson (1976). Suppose a judge is asked to evaluate a candidate for admission to graduate school on the basis of information in his application folder. The first step in this inference process is to match features of the candidate's application with those comprising the schema of a participant in either an episodic or categorical vignette. At the episodic level, this participant might be a particular student the judge has known. At the categorical level, it might be a prototypic person whose characteristics correspond to those described in the application. In each case, after accessing the vignette, the judge may progress through the script to another vignette that describes the person's fate in graduate school. A verbal analog of accessing and drawing inferences on the basis of an episodic script might be: "This candidate reminds me very much of Paul Kolodny, who hung around for eight years never writing his dissertation. Let's not get into that again." The verbal analog corresponding to a categorical script with similar implications might be "He seems to be one of those guys who writes all about that existential stuff and winds up wanting to be a clinician."

Other examples are easy to construct. For instance, suppose a man who meets a woman for the first time is trying to decide how to behave, or whether to seek any further interaction with her. To make these decisions, he may match the aspects of the information he has acquired in this initial encounter with aspects of a vignette in a script that helps him to evaluate the likelihood of a satisfying future relationship (e.g., "This girl reminds me of Susan Smith who smiled a lot but talked only about herself and wanted to do nothing but neck.") The woman may in turn access a script in the process of deciding whether or not to respond to the man's overtures ("This is the sort of guy who, given any encouragement at all, winds up trying to monopolize all of your time and who can't keep his hands off you for 30 seconds."). In addition to scripts about others, judges are often apt to invoke "self-scripts" pertaining to their own behavior or reactions (e.g., "The last time I had a date with a person like this, I got so uptight that I couldn't utter a complete sentence and wound up feeling like a fool."). Indeed, it is conceivable that a major component of many scripts about other people, and thus the major bases for judgments of them, may be one's own personal reactions to these people during interactions with them. For example, the aspects of a vignette I use to judge a colleague's intelligence may consist less of his behavior than of my feelings of intellectual intimidation during conversations with him. Alternatively, my judgment that a woman is warm and friendly may be based more on my recall of how I felt in her presence than upon any particular behavior she manifested.

The particular vignettes and scripts that a judge accesses probably depend upon (a) the type of judgment he wishes to make and (b) the aspects of the information presented that happen to attract his attention. These factors are interrelated; a judge who is making graduate admissions decisions will presumably focus on different aspects of available information than a judge who is searching for a roommate. Different vignettes and scripts may be accessed even when the *same* information is attended to, depending upon the perspective of the judge. We will return to this matter shortly. Chance factors probably play a role as well. For example, a judge who fortuitously notices that a graduate school applicant grew up on the South Side of Chicago and got Ds in physical education may access his "self-script" and predict the candidate's progress through graduate school to be similar to his own. On the other hand, if the judge fails to notice this information, he may access a very different script, and thus draw very different conclusions.

Construction of New Scripts and Vignettes. While the preceding discussion has focussed on the access and use of previously formed scripts in interpreting new information and making predictions, the implications of this process for the construction of new scripts should not be ignored. This constructive process is implicit in the examples given above. That is, a judge who is required to evaluate a graduate school applicant, or who must decide how to respond to someone in a social interaction, essentially constructs a hypothetical script of this person and his behavior based upon previously formed categorical or episodic scripts he has acquired about others. This new script, once constructed, presumably becomes stored in memory, and is therefore available for use in making subsequent inferences about the person to which it pertains at some future time. This raises the possibility that hypothetical scripts that are initially constructed to predict or interpret a person's behavior may have enduring effects on inferences about the person that may persist independently of the original considerations that led the scripts to be constructed. We will elaborate on this possibility in a later section of this chapter.

Limitations on the Occurrence of Script Processing

Abelson speculates that script processing often plays a predominant role in social judgment and decision making. However, conditions do arise when script processing is unlikely to occur to the exclusion of other processes.

1. In some instances, the configuration of information presented may not adequately match an existing vignette. For example, not every graduate school application is likely to elicit a script of a particular student one has known in the past, or even a prototypic student. In such cases, a judge who is asked to evaluate the application may subjectively compile a list of academic credentials (GRE scores, grade point average, mathematics background, etc.) that he considers "ideal," and base his evaluation upon the similarity of the applicant's credentials to those contained in this list. Alternatively, he may weight the separate implications of the applicant's individual characteristics by some subjective index of their importance and then combine them in pseudo-algebraic fashion to arrive at a judgment. In these cases, the judgment may not be mediated by any integrated impression of the candidate as a person at all.

2. Abelson (1976) speculates that when judges are required to make a large number of similar decisions in a short period of time, each based upon a different set of information, they are less apt to engage in the multifaceted cognitive activity involved in script processing, but are more apt to resort to simpler, perhaps mechanistic rules for dealing with this information.

3. When a vignette is contained in several different scripts, each script may have a different implication for the judgment to be made. For example, suppose the person whose cognitive system is described in Fig. 2.1 wishes to predict the likelihood that the child will be punished for doing something bad. Each of the alternative scripts initiated by the vignette "doing something bad" has implications for the judgment. However, the nature of these implications may differ. In predicting the overall likelihood that the child will be punished, the person must therefore resort to some higher order process in which these various implications are combined to form a single judgment. Each implication may be weighted differently, depending upon the perceived likelihood of the events leading up to it. The nature of the possible integration processes involved in such cases will be considered in Chapters 7 and 8.

Other factors undoubtedly also affect the use of script processing, but the exact nature of these effects is less obvious on a priori grounds. One such factor may be the amount of information presented. On one hand, it seems reasonable to suppose that as the amount of information presented increases, the number of pieces of this information that may correspond to aspects of a previously formed vignette may also increase, and therefore the more likely it is that this vignette will be used as a basis for judgments. However, by the same token, the number of pieces that do *not* correspond to aspects of the vignette may also increase with the total amount of information presented, thus decreasing the likelihood of a match between the information and this vignette. Therefore, when a large amount of information is available, several different vignettes may be accessed, each stimulated by a different subset of the information presented. Still another possibility is that an increase in the amount and complexity of the information presented may tax the judge's processing capabilities, leading him to ignore some of the information, or possibly to resort to rules for combining the information that are simpler than those implied by script processing. These possibilities require systematic empirical investigation.

The above contingencies in the use of script processing have methodological as well as theoretical implications. Research in the area of "impression formation" (e.g., Anderson, 1965; Birnbaum, 1974; Wyer, 1974b) provides a useful illustration. In this research, judges typically estimate their liking for each of a large number of persons on the basis of a set of personality adjectives describing these persons. Sets are constructed so that the adjectives in them vary systematically over several levels of favorableness. The design enables individual differences in response scale usage to be minimized, and the independent and interactive effects of the information to be identified. However, this design is not apt to elicit script processing for at least two of the reasons noted above. First, many of the adjective sets may not describe a meaningful person. Second, judges are required to make a large number of judgments in succession. It is precisely under these conditions that script processing is unlikely to occur. This suggests that the rigorous methodological techniques often applied in studying impression formation may be washing out the baby with the bath-water. We will consider this possibility in more detail in Chapter 8.

Selecting Among Alternative Scripts

To use script-processing notions to make a priori predictions of judgmental phenomena, one must understand not only when scripts are used in responding to information, but also *which* scripts are likely to be accessed when more than one is applicable. The use of particular scripts is apt to depend on the relative salience of various schemata making up these scripts. This possibility will be discussed in some detail in the next chapter. However, two factors that may affect script salience are worth noting at this time: the order in which information is presented, and the extent to which scripts with implications for the interpretation of this information have been activated in the recent past.

Order of Presentation of Information

If information is presented in sequence, the first information may often stimulate access to a script that is then used to interpret later-occurring information. While no direct evidence of this effect is available, a series of studies by Langer and Abelson (1972) is suggestive. In one study, a woman who had ostensibly injured her knee approached people in a shopping center and asked them to do her a favor. Although the content of her remarks was always the same, in some cases the request for help preceded the expression of need (e.g., "Would you do something for me? Please do me a favor and call my husband and ask him to pick me up? My knee is killing me. I think I sprained it."), while in other cases, the expression of need occurred first ("My knee is killing me. I think I sprained it. Would you do something for me? Please do me a favor . . ."). A second pair of conditions was similar, except that here, the request was made to appear less legitimate; specifically, people were asked to call the victim's employer to tell him she would be late.

It seems reasonable to expect that the first order condition, which places initial emphasis upon the request for aid, will typically stimulate subjects to access a "social responsibility" self-script (i.e., a script of oneself as a person who generally helps others). To this extent these requests may lead to helping independently of the legitimacy of the request. However, the second order condition, in which the statement of need occurs first, may stimulate access to a victim-oriented script. Such a script is apt to evoke empathy, and thus helping, if the request is legitimate, but to evoke irritation, and refusal to help, if the request is illegitimate. Based upon this reasoning, the authors hypothesized that the second order would be more effective than the first order when the request was legitimate, but less effective than the first when the request was illegitimate. This was in fact the case.

There are undoubtedly other explanations for these findings that do not require recourse to script-processing notions. However, the results suggest that the sequence in which information is presented does lead to different interpretations of the information and therefore to different behavioral decisions, even when the total amount of information is small.

Similarly order effects may occur in other situations. For example, Jones, Rock, Shaver, Goethals and Ward (1968) found that observers attribute higher ability to a performer who succeeds early in a series of performance tasks and fails on later tasks than they do to one who fails initially and succeeds later on. This finding is readily interpretable from a script-processing perspective. The observers may attempt to explain performance during the early trials by constructing a vignette that incorporates the performance outcome with the actor's attributes. For instance, a typical vignette in the early success condition might be paraphrased as, "Actor develops high ability; actor succeeds on performance tasks." (The comparable vignette in early failure conditions would of course be, "Actor lacks ability; actor fails on performance tasks.") When information about the actor's subsequent performance becomes available, the observer must find a script that incorporates the initial vignette with this new information. (Such a script in the early success condition might be, "Actor develops high ability; actor succeeds on performance tasks; actor becomes bored and quits trying; actor fails on performance tasks.") Since the initial vignette becomes a component of the complete explanatory script, the ability attributions made initially are likely to remain a part of the actor schema, with additional factors (e.g., changes in effort or task difficulty) incorporated to explain changes in performance. Hence, differences in the information available at the time the first vignette is constructed will be reflected in different explanatory scripts and therefore will lead to different interpretations of the information to follow.[1]

"Priming" Effects: Previous Use of Scripts for Other Purposes

We noted previously that many situations exist where more than one explanatory script may apply. In such cases, judges are likely to use the script that happens to be most easily accessible to them to explain the situation and make inferences about it. Thus, the use of a script to explain one event, involving either the judge or someone else, should increase the likelihood that the script will be used in explaining subsequent events. While the cognitive processes underlying these "priming" effects are discussed in more detail in Chapters 3 and 4, a recent study by Carlston provides an interesting demonstration of these effects.

For a task that ostensibly involved an analysis of high-school basketball teams, subjects were provided with team records for the first ten games of a season, and then were asked to make a number of inferences about the team's talent, movitation, and future performance. In all conditions, the target teams had the same overall won–lost records. However, some subjects received records showing a general improvement in performance over the ten games, while others received records showing a general decline. To manipulate the salience of different scripts that might be used to explain these changes,

---

[1]Note that this example implies that the observer's initial inference of a performer's ability, made in the course of forming his initial script, becomes itself a piece of evidence that is integrated with other evidence and brought to bear on subsequent inferences. This implication will be considered in more detail in Chapter 4.

subjects received a bogus newspaper story for use as background information. Although the article consisted primarily of various useless informational tidbits, it did include a description of the improvement or decline of another team during an earlier season, along with an explanation for that team's performance in terms of changes in either its ability, its effort, luck, or task difficulty. For example, the explanation for team improvement in terms of luck went something like this:

> Readers will remember that last year, Mount Ivy got off to a terrible start, dropping their first three games because of bad officiating calls, bad breaks, and bad luck... In the game against Dimsville, a half dozen questionable foul calls put the game out of Mount Ivy's reach before halftime... But luck tends to even out in the end, and by midseason, it was Mount Ivy that was getting all the breaks...

Under control conditions, the improvement or decline of another team was also described in detail, but without explanatory commentary.

It was possible to explain the target team's performance in terms of scripts involving changes in luck, effort, task difficulty, and even ability over the course of the ten games played. However, the manipulation of script salience was expected to affect which type of explanation was actually used, despite the fact that the information eliciting the script had nothing objectively to do with the team being judged. Results were consistent with these expectations. For example, subjects who were primed with "effort" scripts judged improving teams to have experienced a greater increase in motivation, and deteriorating teams to have experienced a greater decline in motivation, than did either control subjects or subjects who were primed with other explanatory scripts. Additional data added further clarification of this phenomenon. Specifically, subjects' explanations for a second team's pattern of wins and losses, which was different from the first team's, were minimally affected by the primed explanations, although the same factor (motivation, luck, ability, etc.) could still in principle have been involved. On the other hand, explanations for a third team's performance, which *was* comparable to the first team's, were again affected by the script manipulation, even though the background information presented in this case was completely neutral. The persisting effects of the first-trial salience manipulation during the third trial suggests that subjects accessed and used the primed scripts even when there were no implicit demands to take into account the particular background information accompanying the team being judged. At the same time, the lack of effects on the second trial indicates that subjects were not simply influenced to apply the primed explanatory dimensions indiscriminately. Instead, they did so only when the performance pattern of the team being judged was one that matched the script made salient to them.

Not all of the results obtained in the study were entirely predictable from knowledge of the script being primed in each condition. For example, improving teams were judged to have had a greater increase in motivation than declining teams, regardless of the script condition, even though luck and task difficulty scripts seemingly implied no changes in motivation. This reintroduces the possibility that judges may utilize several scripts simultaneously, perhaps making probabilistic judgments based upon perceptions of the likelihood that each script is applicable.

The Role of Visual Imagery

An aspect of the script-processing formulation that distinguishes it from many other formulations of cognitive functioning is its explicit recognition of the role of visual imagery in social judgment. While it is intuitively evident that people can construct visual images of situations they have experienced in the past, and also of hypothetical persons and events, imagery has only recently been considered seriously as an important mode of cognitive functioning (for early explications of this role, see Paivio, 1971; Bower, 1972). Indeed, the nature of this role is subject to continuing debate (cf. Kosslyn & Pomerantz, 1977; Pylyshyn, 1973). We will not enter into the details of this debate here. Rather, we will attempt to conceptualize the possible role of imagery in cognitive functioning, both alone and in combination with verbally encoded material, and we will cite some research concerning these matters. While this research has not used social stimuli, its implications for social inference processes are readily apparent.

General Concepts

Kosslyn and Pomerantz (1977) conceptualize an image as a "spatial representation like that underlying the experience of seeing an object during visual perception." However, they point out the importance of distinguishing between an image, which is a representation of experience that exists in one's head, and a picture, or concrete object that exists in the outside world. This distinction is much the same as that between a verbal statement that one reads or hears and a verbally coded idea that one generates internally during thought processes. At the same time, there are similarities between the processing of information contained in an image and the processing of information contained in a picture or real sense experience of an external event, much as there are similarities between the processing of externally presented and internally generated verbal material.

A particular experience may often be represented either verbally or using imagery. However, the manner in whch these representations are used to make judgments may differ. An image is a spatial representation of information that is apt to be responded to configurally. In contrast, a verbal representation is apt to consist of a series of discrete propositions that may be operated upon linguistically, using principles of inductive or deductive reasoning. However, the two types of representations are obviously not independent. Certainly we often verbally encode aspects of our sensory experience, including visual perceptions. Moreover, we generate images from verbal stimulus information. In principle, a system of verbally coded propositions may be constructed to represent any desired configuration (Kosslyn & Pomerantz, 1977). Indeed, it may be reasonable to postulate that both images and verbal encoding of experiences may be generated from a common underlying abstract representation. Which type of representation is generated in any given instance may depend in part upon the type of judgment and the type of information relevant to it. To evaluate a female graduate student's likelihood of performing well as a research assistant, I may generate information about the student in a propositional form that I can operate on inductively (e.g., "Mary got an A from me in the graduate lab course I taught, wrote an interesting master's thesis, and is a great computer programmer. These are certainly qualities I find make good assistants; therefore, I suspect Mary would do pretty well.") However, to decide whether Mary would be a good date for a friend, I may be more apt to generate a visual representation of Mary's appearance and her behavior toward members of the opposite sex, and to base my judgment on a comparison of this representation with the one that I have constructed for a prototypic "good date." Of course, I may ultimately encode this representation verbally in order to *communicate* the basis for my judgment. However, this verbal encoding might occur after the decision, thus reflecting the judgment but not determining it.

Empirical Evidence

Judges may extract information from visual images in much the same way that they extract information from their direct sense experience. Two programs of research have focussed on this possibility. In one, conducted by Shepard (Cooper & Shepard, 1973a, b; Shepard & Metzler, 1971), a judge is asked to decide whether a test figure (e.g., a letter, or geometrical shape) is the same as a standard. When the test figure is rotated to one of several orientations relative to the standard, the time required to make a decision is a direct function of the degree of physical rotation of the test figure from the standard. In other words, it is a function of the time required to rotate the figure mentally back to a position that would allow direct visual comparison of the two stimuli. Spontaneous verbal reports by judges that they do in fact "solve" the problems by mentally rotating the test figure add strength to this interpretation.

A series of studies by Kosslyn, using a quite different approach, is also noteworthy. In one study (Kosslyn, 1975), judges were instructed to imagine a target animal (e.g., a rabbit) standing beside either (a) a fly or (b) an elephant. After forming an image, they were presented a property name (e.g., "ears") and asked whether it was a feature of the target animal in the image they had formed. Kosslyn argued that images of the target animal in the context of a fly would be very large, and therefore the feature to be verified would be very prominent. However, images of the target in the context of the elephant should be very small, and its features should therefore be difficult to verify without mentally "walking in" to get a closer look, much as one would have to do if he were actually exposed to the two animals from the distance represented in the image. This "walk" should take time to perform, and therefore more time should be required to verify the feature in this case than in the former one. Results were consistent with this prediction.

As Kosslyn and Pomerantz (1977) note, the results described above could be explained in terms of a propositional representation of the information as well as in terms of an imagery representation. However, this would require very cumbersome and intuitively implausible assumptions. An indication that propositional representations of information are in fact often more difficult to process than images was obtained by Kosslyn (1973). Subjects were presented pictures of familiar objects (an airplane, a speedboat, etc.) along with names of these objects. Then, they were presented the name of each object alone and asked to verify one of its features under one of four conditions. In *whole image* conditions, they were told to form an image of the original object as a whole during the five-second interval between the presentation of its name and the request to verify one of its properties. In a second, *focussed image* condition, they were also told to form a visual image of the picture when its name was presented, but this time to focus on a particular end of the imagined object "as if they were staring at that place in the picture". In a third, *whole verbalization* condition, subjects were told to begin describing the named picture verbally to themselves until the property to be verified was presented. Finally, in *focussed verbalization* conditions, subjects were told that when the name of the object was presented, they should begin describing a specified end of the picture verbally until the property word was presented.

The time required to verify properties under each condition is shown in Fig. 2.2 as a function of the position of the property. Two aspects of these data are of interest. First, verification time was generally longer in verbalization conditions than in imagery conditions. Second, although verification time in both "focussed" conditions increased with the spatial distance between the property and the end of the picture that subjects were asked to focus upon, the magnitude of this increase was greater under verbalization conditions than under image conditions.

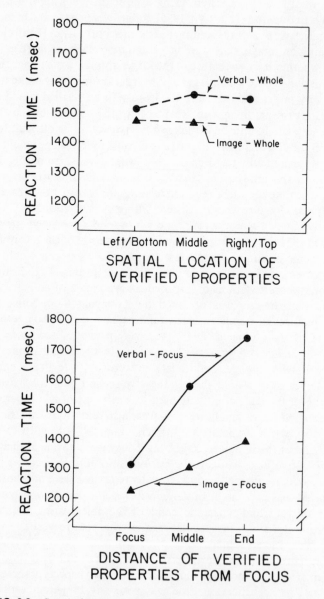

FIG. 2.2. Speed of verification of picture properties as a function of spatial distance and location from the point of focus (reprinted from Kosslyn, 1973, p. 92).

The increases in verification time with greater spatial distances is understandable in terms of either mode of processing. Just as visual processors must visually search the imaged object, verbal processors may need to work their way verbally across the object (e.g., "The flag is on the bow of the ship, and next to it is an anchor, and standing next to the anchor is a funny little man..."). When the focal point is further from the target property, there will be more verbally encoded properties and property-relations for the judge to talk his way through. However, the important result is that the increase in verification time was less when judges were asked to encode the information visually rather than verbally. Assuming that judges followed instructions, this suggests that pictorially presented material is more easily searched on the basis of visual encodings than verbal ones.

More recent research by Kosslyn (1976) bears directly on the speculation that both verbal and visual representations of information may be formed, and that the effect of these representations may differ. In one experiment (Kosslyn, 1976), judges were asked to verify features of animals (e.g., "bear") that were either (a) small in size but strongly associated with the animal ("claws") or (b) large in size but weakly associated with the animal (e.g., "legs"). The time required to make these verifications was assessed under each of two conditions. In one, no mention was made of imagery; judges were simply asked to respond as quickly as possible. In this condition, response time was less for features that were semantically associated with the target animal, but small in physical size. In the second condition, judges were asked to base their judgments on visual images of the animals described. In this case, response time was less for features that were large in size, but low in their semantic association to the object. These results indicate that, in fact, the type of mediating process differs as a function of instructional set, and that the use of imagery in making judgments is under cognitive control.

A final study, by Kosslyn, Holyoak, and Huffman (1976), has implications for the interdependence of the two modes of processing. Subjects were asked to learn 12-item lists of concrete nouns under four conditions. In one (*verbal-verbal*) condition, they learned all 12 words by rehearsing their names verbally as they were presented. In a second (*imagery-imagery*) condition, subjects learned the words by forming a visual image of each object as the noun describing it was presented. In the other two conditions (*imagery-verbal* and *verbal-imagery*), subjects learned the first 6 words using one strategy and the last 6 words using the other strategy. After the entire list was presented in each condition, subjects were asked to recall the words they had been presented.

The recall of items in the second half of each list was better in the two mixed-strategy conditions than in the two single-strategy conditions, suggesting that when two different processes are used to encode material, more of this material can be assimilated. However, the recall of items in the first half of the list was greatest under imagery–verbal conditions, but poorest in verbal–imagery conditions. There is a good reason for this. Kosslyn et al. point out that in forming images of verbally described objects, judges must process the information verbally before they can generate a visual image of its referent. In other words, the strategy used under imagery conditions requires *both* verbal and imagery processing. In the imagery–verbal condition, judges may discard the verbal labels of the imaged words in the first half of the list once the images are formed, and therefore may be free to learn the second half of the list without interference from these verbal labels. In the verbal–imagery condition, however, the preliminary verbal encoding of the second-half words may infere with the verbal labels learned in the first half of the list, thus decreasing recall. Note that if this interpretation is correct, analogous effects should occur when the original stimuli are pictures of objects rather than names of objects. In this case, however, interference should be greater under imagery–verbal conditions than under verbal–imagery conditions, and so recall should be *poorer* in the former case.

Visual vs. Verbal Encoding of Social Stimuli

Kosslyn's work suggests strongly that visual imagery plays an important role in information processing. It seems particularly likely to play a role in the acquisition of information about social stimuli in nonlaboratory situations, since much of this information is apt to be nonverbal. In the representation of complex situations, verbal encodings and imagery may supplement one another, much as implied by Abelson's conceptualization of a script or vignette.

As we have noted, information can either be transformed from the visual mode to the propositional mode or vice versa before it is operated upon to arrive at an inference. These translation rules must ultimately be understood. We also need to circumscribe the conditions in which verbal or nonverbal information processing is most apt to occur, and to determine means of establishing empirically the different manifestations of processing in each mode. These matters have rarely (if ever) been explored in research on social inference phenomena.

One determinant of the way information in encoded and processed may simply be the form in which it is initially received. A judge who acquires information about a person's appearance and behavior through direct contact is apt initially to encode this information nonverbally, whereas a judge who receives comparable information in the form of a written description may encode it verbally. Additional factors must also be considered. First, certain verbal descriptions of a person are inherently likely to elicit nonverbal reactions in a judge, either in the form of visual images, emotional responses, or both. (For example, consider one's immediate reaction to the verbal description of someone picking his nose at the dinner table.) Second, one's encoding of information may depend upon the type of judgment to be made. Certain judgments may be made more easily on the basis of visually encoded representations than others. For example, one may be more likely to construct a visual representation in judging people's effectiveness in interpersonal relations (e.g., what they would be like on a date, or whether they would make good roommates) than in judging their effectiveness in areas to which personal contact is irrelevant (e.g., their ability to master complex mathematical concepts).

The role of nonverbal cues in social judgment has only recently begun to be investigated empirically. (Some examples are provided later in this chapter and also in Chapter 6.) The possibility that these cues may be acquired, stored, and subsequently recalled for use in making a judgment without any mediating verbal encoding whatsoever is of methodological as well as theoretical importance in research on social interference. Among other things, it suggests that studies using verbal stimulus information may be considering only one basis, and perhaps not the most important basis, for judgments of persons and events outside the laboratory.

2.3. IMPLICATIONS FOR SOCIAL INFERENCE AND ATTRIBUTION

A script-processing formulation makes salient several issues of considerable interest and importance to a general understanding of social inference phenomena. These issues include (a) context effects on the impressions formed of persons and events, (b) the role of perspective on the acquisition and recall of information, and (c) the relative effects of concrete and abstract information on judgments. These topics will be examined in the following sections.

Context Effects on Impressions of Persons and Events

As conceptualized earlier in this chapter, a vignette consists of a complex schema or set of schemata about an event and the persons or objects involved in it. However, the information that stimulates the use of a particular vignette may not describe completely the many detailed features of its various elements. When this occurs, unmentioned features of the situation may be "filled in" in a manner consistent with the vignette that is elicited. For example, a person who establishes that a given object is a desk lamp may subsequently infer that the lamp had an on/off switch even if the switch was not actually present. This inference is presumably made on the basis of a general concept, or schema, of desk lamps that contains "on/off switch" as an attribute.

While the above example is somewhat mundane, the general phenomenon it exemplifies has important implications for social inference. For one thing, it suggests that inferences about a person may often be made not only on the basis of information directly describing the person, but also on the basis of contextual factors that do not pertain directly to the person's characteristics at all. Consider three sets of sentences, the first borrowed from an example used by Schank and Abelson (1977), and the others slight variations of the first:

1. John knew his wife's operation would be expensive. There was always Uncle Harry... John reached for the suburban telephone book.
2. John could not face that thought of asking a friend to take out his ugly sister. There was always Uncle Harry... John reached for the suburban telephone book.
3. John knew his wife's operation would be expensive. There was always Uncle Harry... John reached for the .32-calibre revolver he kept beside his bed.

In each of the examples, information is provided about the situation confronting John and about John's behavior, but no direct information is given about Uncle Harry. Nevertheless, if a judge were asked to describe Uncle Harry, it seems likely that his description would differ substantially in the three cases. The context of each reference to Uncle Harry would presumably elicit a different script in each case, and the representation (schema) of Uncle Harry in each script would probably differ markedly.

To the extent that visual imagery plays a role in script processing, the physical characteristics of the persons and events elicited on the basis of verbal material are also likely to be influenced by context. Thus, "Uncle Harry" may be ascribed different physical attributes as well as different personality traits under the three context conditions described above. Anecdotal evidence suggests that strong visual impressions are often formed of people one has never met but has heard about, written to, or spoken to on the telephone—impressions that are, of course, often grossly in error. It is somewhat disconcerting to meet a psychologist with a rich, literary writing style, a penchant for abstract mathematical concepts, and a record of influential research and theory-building, and find him to resemble the lead singer in a rock group. Presumably the content and style of a person's writing or speaking elicits a vignette consisting of a visual image of the person as well as an impression of his personality. The specific cues that give rise to different visual impressions of persons, and the effects of these impressions upon subsequent inferences about the person and his behavior, are barely understood.

On the other hand, we obviously do not always form images of everyone from whom we receive a letter or whose journal article we happen to read. Such imagery is most likely to occur only after a period of continued contact with the person's writing. There may be several reasons for this. One is simply that a great deal of information may be necessary to construct an episodic vignette, or to fit the person into a previously formed categorical vignette. A second is that script processes may not often be invoked unless they are stimulated by an anticipated or desired interaction with the person to be judged. A judge who thinks about interacting with someone may construct a script of their hypothetical interaction, and in the course of this construction may ascribe physical as well as behavioral characteristics to this person. In other circumstances, where interaction with the person is not contemplated, script processing may not occur. Thus, for example, script processing may be less apt to underlie judgments of a person one believes to be hypothetical than judgments of a person one believes is real and expects to meet at some future time. For similar reasons, the activation of script processing may depend upon the objectives of the judge at the time information is presented, and upon the type of judgment to be made. For example, a judge may be less apt to invoke script processing to estimate a person's intelligence (a judgment that does not necessarily involve a consideration of interpersonal relations) than to decide whether he would like to date the person or to have the person for a roommate.

The above hypotheses are difficult to test directly. However, certain strategies seem reasonable. For example, suppose a judge is presented with verbal information about a person, and is then asked to predict other attributes of the person (e.g., personality and physical characteristics) under conditions that might lead to script information. It should take a judge less time to make these inferences if he has already formed a vignette of the person than if he has not. The use of response-time procedures to test certain hypotheses concerning the cognitive representation of information will be considered in more detail in later chapters.

Verbal Context Effects on the Recall and Interpretation of Information

Several recent studies of the role of context in interpreting and recalling new information are at least indirectly relevant to the general hypothesis that scripts and vignettes mediate the interpretation and storage of information. Particularly intriguing is research by Bransford and his associates (Bransford, Barclay & Franks, 1972; Bransford & Johnson, 1973). In one study

(Bransford & Johnson, 1973), subjects were asked to learn sets of sentences that appeared nonsensical out of context (e.g., "The notes were sour because the seam was split"; "The haystack was important because the cloth ripped"; etc.) In some cases, however, these sentences were preceded by a cue (in the above examples, "bagpipe" and "parachute," respectively). Recall of the sentences was consistently greater in the latter condition than when no context words were presented. It seems likely that in each case the cue elicited a vignette that enabled the sentence to be interpreted and remembered (e.g., an image of a Scotsman playing discordant music on his defective bagpipes, or of a parachutist landing in a pile of hay).

The contextual bases for interpreting information may not only be provided by information in the stimulus situation itself, but may also be a result of past experiences that lead different scripts to be called to mind and applied. A graphic demonstration of this was constructed by R. C. Anderson et al., (1976). Subjects read a paragraph that could be interpreted in either of two ways. For example, one paragraph was as follows:

> Every Saturday night, four good friends get together. When Jerry, Mike and Pat arrived, Karen was sitting in her living room writing some notes. She quickly gathered the cards and stood up to greet her friends at the door. They followed her into the living room but as usual they couldn't agree on exactly what to play. Jerry eventually took a stand and set things up. Finally, they began to play. Karen's recorder filled the room with soft and pleasant music. Early in the evening, Mike noticed Pat's hand and the many diamonds. As the night progressed the tempo of play increased. Finally, a lull in the activities occurred. Taking advantage of this, Jerry pondered the arrangement in front of him. Mike interrupted Jerry's reverie and said, "Let's hear the score." They listened carefully and commented on their performance. When the comments were all heard, exhausted but happy, Karen's friends all went home. [pp. 10–11]

The above paragraph is typically interpreted as being about a group of friends getting together to play cards. However, it can also be interpreted as being about a rehearsal session of a woodwind ensemble. A second ambiguous paragraph was also constructed that was typically interpreted as being about a convict planning his escape from prison, but could also describe a wrestler trying to break the hold of his opponent. After reading one of these paragraphs, subjects answered a series of multiple choice questions, each of which had two correct answers, depending upon the interpretation given the paragraph. For example, a question pertaining to the paragraph described above was:

> What did the four people comment on?
> a. The odds of having so many high cards.
> b. The sound of their music.

c. The high cost of musical instruments.
d. How well they were playing cards. [p. 11]

Subjects in the study were either female students planning a career in music education or students from weight-lifting classes in physical education. It seems reasonable to suppose that the music students would be more likely than the physical education students to interpret the music/card playing paragraph by constructing a "music" script, but should be less likely to interpret the prison escape/wrestling paragraph by constructing a "wrestling" script. Results were consistent with these expectations. That is, subjects with a music background gave more music-correct answers to questions about the first paragraph, but fewer wrestling-correct answers to questions about the second paragraph, than did subjects with the physical education background. This study again suggests that scripts and schemata play a role in the interpretation of information. Moreover, it indicates that individual differences in the scripts constructed for interpretation may be predictable from general background factors that affect the salience of concepts related to these scripts.

Once a person has constructed a script to interpret a body of information, he may subsequently be unable to distinguish easily between details of the original stimulus material and details that were not contained in this material but were inferred on the basis of the script. Thus, a judge who is told that John pounded a nail into the wall will interpret this by constructing a script of John banging away at the nail with a hammer, and therefore may subsequently recall the hammer as having actually been mentioned in the original communication (Johnson, Bransford & Solomon, 1973). Other evidence also suggests that subjects who reconstruct an event by inferring missing details are subsequently apt to recall these details as having actually been contained in the original stimulus information (Loftus & Loftus, 1974; Loftus & Palmer, 1974).

The Role of Nonverbal Context Information in Interpreting Verbal Communications

When scripts and vignettes consist of both verbal and nonverbal information, the nonverbal aspects may affect the interpretation of the verbal ones. Some provocative work bearing on this possibility has been conducted by Robert Krauss and his colleagues (Krauss, 1977; Krauss, Geller & Olson, 1976; Streeter, Krauss, Geller, Olson & Apple, 1977). This research has focused on the use of nonverbal cues in detecting deception, and suggests some useful procedures for investigating the interaction between nonverbal and verbal cognitive representations.

In an initial study (Krauss, et al., 1976), judges interviewed others about matters concerning politics, religion, personal values, and so forth. In some (*face-to-face*) conditions, the interviewer could both see and hear the interviewee, while in other (*intercom*) conditions, he could only hear the interviewee's responses. (In all cases, however, the complete interview was recorded for future use.) The interviewee was instructed to lie in response to questions on some topics and to tell the truth in response to questions on other topics, and the interviewer's task was to infer whether the respondent was or was not telling the truth in answering each question.

Several empirical findings are of intrinsic interest. (For example, females were more accurate in distinguishing lying in one another than were males. As the authors point out, this could mean either that females are more sensitive than males to nonverbal indications of lying, or that they are relatively poorer deceivers.) However, the central finding of concern here is that detection accuracy was greater when interviewers only had access to the interviewee's auditory responses than when they were face-to-face with the interviewee. The authors hypothesize three possible factors to account for this result, all of which could contribute simultaneously to the phenomenon observed. One, the *information overload* hypothesis, is that interviewers who receive both visual and auditory information may process this information ineffectively, and therefore may be less sensitive to the critical cues embedded in this information. A second, the *distracting cue* hypothesis, is that visual cues are less diagnostic, and therefore distract interviewers from the more relevant auditory cues. The third, the *feedback* hypothesis, is that under face-to-face conditions, the deceiver has access to cues elicited by the interviewer as well as vice versa. Therefore, the deceiver may gain information from the interviewer's reactions that helps him/her to lie successfully.

To help clarify matters, a second study was run in which judges were not themselves involved in the interview situation, but were shown segments of the interviews taped during the first experiment. In one condition, both the video portion (which focussed on the interviewee alone) and the audio portion were shown; in a second, only the audio was shown; and in a third, only the video was presented. The segments were drawn from both the face-to-face and the intercom conditions of the original study. The results, shown in Fig. 2.3, are quite provocative. When the tape segments were taken from the original face-to-face conditions, accuracy in distinguishing lying from truth-telling was relatively low, and did not depend upon whether the information presented was visual, auditory or both. This suggests that interviewees who could monitor the interviewer actually did a very good job of suppressing all indicants of deception, consistent with the feedback hypothesis. However, when the original tape was drawn from intercom conditions, where the interviewer did not see the interviewee, judges were most accurate when they could see the interviewee but could not hear what he

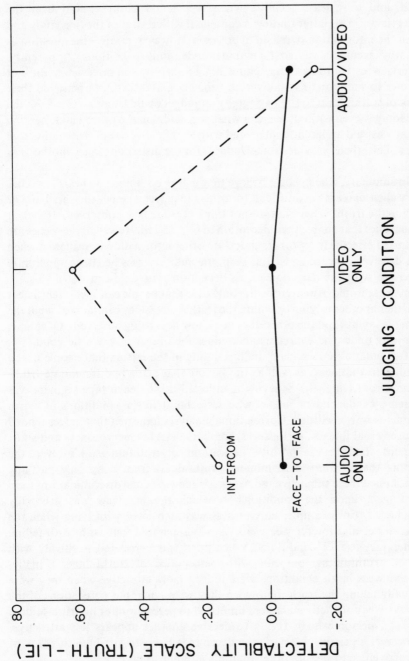

FIG. 2.3. Accuracy of detecting truth-telling and lying as a function of the type of information available (audio only, video only or both) and conditions in which the original interview was conducted (reprinted from Krauss, 1977).

said, and were least accurate when they could both see and hear the interviewee. This latter finding is consistent with results of the first study and with the information overload hypothesis. However, it raises the question as to why accuracy was so high under video-only conditions. Apparently, interviewees who knew they could not be seen by the interviewer did not bother to monitor their nonverbal behaviors, and therefore betrayed their lack of truthfulness to such a degree that judges could later detect it from the videotapes even without hearing what was said. On the other hand, hearing what was said apparently interfered with the effective use of these nonverbal cues. This, then, provides some support for the distracting cue hypothesis as well.

In summary, when people believe they will be both seen and heard, the cues they elicit make it very difficult for others to detect whether they are lying or telling the truth. When they do not think they are being observed, they elicit visual cues that enable their deception to be detected. However, these cues are not used effectively by others unless no other information is available; when the deceiver is heard as well as seen, the auditory cues he elicits apparently interfere with the detection of his deception. The implications of this are somewhat ironic. Apparently, the only time that people can accurately detect whether another is lying or telling the truth is when they cannot hear what the other is saying (and the other does not know he is being observed). Of course, knowing under these circumstances does the observer very little good.

To obtain a more precise understanding of the factors that people use to predict truthfulness, as well as the factors that actually differentiate truth-telling from lying, the behavior manifested during each tape segment was coded by independent judges who were blind to the conditions in which segments were recorded. Correlational analyses indicated that judges tended to use verbal fluency, seriousness, emphaticness, low nervousness and short response latencies as positive indications of truthfulness. However, the factors that *actually* discriminated truthfulness from lying only partially overlapped these subjective indicants. Moreover, actual discriminations were contingent upon the conditions in which the interview was originally conducted. For example, nervousness was associated with lying when the interviewer and interviewee were visually separated, but with truth-telling under face-to-face conditions. Voice pitch was correlated positively with actual truthfulness, but not with perceptions of truthfulness. Finally, interviewees in all conditions were judged more attractive when they were actually telling the truth than when they were lying, but perceptions of the interviewee's attractiveness were unrelated to perceptions of his truth-telling. Thus, a person who is trying to deceive another appears less attractive. However, a person observing the deceiver is likely to attribute this lack of attractiveness to factors other than his attempt to deceive.

Implications for Script Processes.   The research by Krauss et al. (1976) has many implications for the manner in which scripts may be constructed from information of the sort acquired in many-social interactions. For example, the data clearly indicate that nonverbal cues are used in the interpretation of statements that people make about themselves, and therefore in the scripts and vignettes that are presumably formed of these persons. Moreover, the evidence that judges are often less able to distinguish lying from truth-telling when both visual and auditory cues are available suggests that scripts formed on the basis of large amounts of information may not be as accurate in portraying others as scripts formed on the basis of fewer cues. Finally, the indication that actual truth-telling affects judgments of attractiveness, whereas perceived truth-telling is unrelated to perceived attractiveness, suggests that the vignettes constructed of persons on the basis of their behavior may sometimes affect judgments of a wide variety of otherwise unrelated characteristics.

Effects of Perspective on Information Processing

General Considerations.

The manner in which a judge remembers a situation is apt to depend in large part upon the vantage point from which he views this situation. That is, a judge is most likely to form a visual representation of those aspects of the situation that fall within his field of vision. Moreover, vignettes may involve sense experiences in other modalities that are unique to the judge experiencing the sensations. Consequently, the vignette of behavior is apt to contain different information when it is formed by the actor than when it is formed by the person toward whom the behavior is directed, or by a disinterested observer not involved in the interaction.

More interesting perhaps is the possibility that judges who receive verbal information about *hypothetical* situations may construct scripts and vignettes that contain visual and sensory as well as verbal components, and that these components may be affected by the perspective adopted by the judge. Judges who imagine themselves as participants in a hypothetical situation may form vignettes similar to those that would be formed by the actual participants in the situation. These vignettes would therefore differ from those formed by judges who imagine themselves as observers of the situation being described. The two sets of judges should consequently recall the situation differently, and perhaps make different inferences about it.

This possibility is suggested in a study reported by Abelson (1976). Judges were read a lengthy story about a character leaving a hotel and walking down the street, encountering a variety of events along the way. While listening to the story, some judges were told to imagine themselves as the character in the story, while others were told to imagine themselves watching the situation from a fourth-floor hotel balcony. The story contained (a) far visual details, which would best be seen from a distance; (b) near visual details (i.e., a wrist watch) which would normally be viewed at close range; and (c) "body sensation" details (e.g., a sore arm, a wire fence feeling cold to the touch). If judges interpret the story by constructing series of vignettes, the nature of these vignettes should depend upon the judge's perspective. For example, if the main chacter is described running his hand along a cold wire fence, a judge with the character's perspective may construct a vignette that includes the sensation of touching the wire, while a judge whose imagined vantage point is the balcony is more likely to construct a vignette that includes the image of the actor touching the wire, but not the actor's subjective reactions. More generally, the judge with the actor's perspective may be more likely to construct vignettes consisting of body sensation details, while the judge with the observer's perspective may be more apt to construct vignettes consisting of visual details. These differences should be reflected by differential recall of the information presented. Results supported this hypothesis. Specifically, body sensation details were recalled 17.6% better by judges with the actor's perspective than by judges with the observer's perspective; however, far visual details were recalled 15% better by judges with the balcony observer's perspective than by judges with the actor's perspective. No differences occurred in the recall of near visual details, contrary to expectations that these details, like body sensation details, should be recalled better by judges with the actor's perspective. Perhaps, as Abelson points out, people with the "balcony" perspective "zoom in" to pick up near visual details, much as in a movie, so that near visual details as well as distant ones are included in their scripts.

A study with somewhat similar implications was performed by Pichert and R. C. Anderson (1976). In this study, subjects read a paragraph describing two boys playing hookey from school. In the scenario, the boys wandered through the yard of a house, the garage, and the house itself, noting various details of both the house and its contents (e.g., the stereo, a leaky roof) and the surrounding area. Before reading the story, however, judges were asked to imagine themselves in the role of either a prospective homebuyer or a prospective burglar. After reading the story and working on an interpolated task, they were asked to recall as much of the story as they could. (A conceptual replication was also run involving a story of two gulls frolicking on a remote island, where judges were given the perspective of either a florist or a shipwrecked sailor.) As anticipated, subjects recalled more details of the story that were important from their particular perspective (as determined by normative data) than details that were important from other perspectives.

While the above studies are preliminary, they are important for several reasons. First, Abelson's study suggests once again that visual and sensory imagery play a role in the processing and recall of information. Second, both studies demonstrate that the nature of the recalled information may be a function of the judge's subjective perspective at the time the information is received and organized, as well as his physical perspective in relation to the objects and events involved in the situation.

However, an important question arises in interpreting the results of these studies. In both studies, perspectives were instilled in judges before information was presented. It is therefore unclear whether differences in recall obtained in these studies were the result of differences in input (i.e., in selective attention to information as it was received) or to differences in the reconstruction of information during its retrieval. It is conceivable that all of the presented information becomes assimilated and stored in memory, and that the scripts induced by these perspectives function as retrieval strategies that help in reconstructing the situation and recalling its characteristics. The use of such retrieval strategies is intuitively evident in other domains. For example, anyone who tries to recall the names of the fifty United States is likely to find that states that are unretrievable using some strategies (recalling by geographical location) come to mind using other strategies (e.g., recalling by first letter). It would be interesting to know whether similar results would be obtained in the studies cited above if perspectives were induced *after* the information was received rather than before. If they were, this would suggest that the effects of perspectives on recall have more to do with the post hoc reorganization of stored information than with attentional or perceptual differences that occur during information acquisition. While either process may be usefully characterized in terms of script construction, the approximate timing of these constructions is of obvious theoretical importance.

Actor-Observer Differences in Judgments

Script-processing theory implies that differences in perspective, either actual or imagined, should produce differences not only in the recall of situational information embodied in scripts, but also in judgments to which this information is relevant. A similar hypothesis was suggested by Jones and Nisbett(1971) to explain differences in the judgments made by actors and observers. Specifically, these authors speculated that when interpreting information about a given situation, judges typically focus upon aspects of the situation that fall within their perceptual field. While an actor and his behavior in a situation are very prominent to an outside observer, they are not particularly prominent to the actor himself, whose vantage point leads him to focus on characteristics of his environment. Thus, actors should generally be less likely to use their own behavior as information in inferring their personal characteristics than observers of that behavior would be. Similarly, if they are asked to explain this behavior, actors should be less likely than observers to attribute it to their personal characteristics, and more likely to explain it in terms of external, situational factors.

Results consistent with this general hypothesis have been obtained in several studies where judges' actual perspectives have differed. For example, Wyer, Henninger and Hinkle (1977) found that an actor's behavior of delivering a speech had less influence on the actor's own belief in the position advocated than it had on observers' judgments of this belief; in contrast, the opinion of the person to whom the actor was ostensibly communicating had (nonsignificantly) *more* influence on the actor's self-judgments of his belief than on observers' judgments. A study by Storms (1973) which directly manipulated judges' perspectives is also noteworthy. In this study, both actors and observers were shown a video tape of a previous "get-acquainted" conversation between the actor and another person. In *normal perspective* conditions, each type of judge viewed a tape of the conversation filmed from a vantage point appropriate to that perspective; that is, the actor viewed a tape showing the other person to whom he was communicating, and the observer viewed a tape showing the actor. In the *reverse perspective* condition, however, the actor was shown a tape of himself, and the observer was shown a tape of the other person. Then all judges were asked whether the actor's behavior during the course of the conversation was attributable to the actor's dispositional characteristics (personality, mood, personal style, etc.) or to characteristics of the situation (the fact that it was an experiment, the behavior of the other participant, etc.). In normal perspective conditions, actors attributed their behavior more to situational factors, and less to their own dispositions, than did observers. However, in reverse perspective conditions, actors attributed their behavior relatively more to their own dispositions, while observers attributed it relatively more to situational factors. These data support the hypothesis that judges base their inferences upon scripts containing those aspects of the situation within their direct perceptual field.

Perhaps a more interesting question is whether similar differences in judgments can be produced by simply asking judges to *imagine* themselves viewing the situation from different perspectives. In fact, this appears to be the case. Regan and Totten (1975) showed judges a videotape of a "get-acquainted" conversation involving two other people. The judges were instructed either to observe the target person (the actor) or to "empathize" with this person. In all cases, the same information was available to observers in both conditions. Consistent with expectations, observers who empathized with the actor subsequently attributed his behavior more to situational factors and less to the actor than did observers who were not given this set.

These data, like those reported by Abelson, suggest that judges who imagined themselves having the perspective of the actor constructed scripts containing information that would be salient to them from this perspective, and based their subsequent judgments upon these scripts.

Differences in a judge's perspective may often depend on his personal objectives in viewing a situation and on the sort of information he wishes to obtain. For example, observers who expect someday to occupy a role similar to the actor's may be more inclined to construct a representation of the situation from the actor's perspective than those who do not have this expectation. Their judgments should therefore be relatively more similar to those the actor himself would make about the situation. Wolfson and Salancik (1977) report data consistent with this hypothesis. Specifically, observers watched an actor perform an achievement task. Some observers expected to engage in the task themselves later in the study while others did not. As predicted, observers who anticipated performing the task themselves attributed the actor's performance more to situational factors (task characteristics) and less to the actor's dispositional characteristics (ability or effort) than did observers who did not expect to perform the task.

The Relative Influence of Scripts and Abstract Verbal Information

Abelson hypothesizes that in most realistic situations involving actual social stimuli, script processes are likely to take priority over other possible types of processes in arriving at judgments. This hypothesis has at least two important implications. First, information that is likely to activate a previously formed script, or that readily precipitates the construction of a new script, is more apt to affect inferences than is other available information that does not elicit a script. Second, once a script is accessed in order to interpret new information, its effects may persist independently of the information that led to its construction. Some avenues of research bearing on these possibilities are described below.

Use of Generalizeability Information

Scripts should normally be easier to form on the basis of concrete anecdotal information about an individual person than on a basis of abstract information about a group of people. This is particularly likely when the implications of the abstract information are discrepant from past experience, making a categorical script about people in general difficult to construct. Therefore, anecdotal information may often have more influence on judgments than abstract information, even when the latter is ostensibly more reliable.

A series of studies bear on this hypothesis and help to circumscribe the conditions under which it is valid . In an initial study by Nisbett and Borgida (1975), judges read verbal descriptions of one of two actual psychology experiments (Nisbett & Schachter, 1966; Darley & Latané, 1968) in which subjects' actual behavior differed considerably from that expected by college students. In the described Nisbett & Schachter study (1966), participants volunteered to receive a series of increasingly intense shocks, and the dependent variable was the amount of shock they were willing to tolerate before withdrawing. (Shock levels were classified verbally in terms of the physical reaction induced by the shock: tingling fingers, a jolt felt throughout the hand, a jerk of the entire hand and forearms, etc.) In the original experiment, most subjects actually tolerated considerable shock, often the maximum amount administered. In the Darley and Latané (1968) experiment, subjects were exposed to conditions in which another person manifested increasing degrees of distress, and the dependent variable was the level of distress necessary to induce subjects to help. Here, actual subjects typically failed to help regardless of the level of distress.

After reading a description of one of these experiments, Nisbett and Borgida's judges received one of several types of information:

1. Consensus Information—Judges were given a distribution showing subjects' actual behaviors in the original experiment (e.g., the number of subjects who withdrew after each shock level, or who administered aid at each level of distress). This "base-rate" information therefore indicated that subjects typically manifested behavior that deviated from judges' a priori expectations. In addition, judges were shown videotaped interviews of two "randomly selected" participants in the experiment (target subjects). The interviews covered such material as the target's major in college, grade point average, career plans, and parents' occupations, but contained no information about the target's behavior in the experiment.

2. No Consensus Information—Judges were shown the interviews with the two "randomly selected" targets but received no base-rate information.

3. Target Information—Judges were shown the interviews with the two target participants and told that each had manifested the most extreme and unexpected behavior (e.g., had received the maximum amount of shock administered). However, no base-rate information was provided.

After judges received one of these sets of information, they predicted the number of participants in the original study who had manifested each type of behavior (e.g., the number who withdrew at each shock level, or the number who offered help at each distress level). Under Consensus and No Consensus Information conditions, they also predicted the behavior of the target participants whose interviews they had heard. Several aspects of the results obtained are of interest.

1. The distribution of behaviors predicted by judges who did not receive the actual base-rate distribution was quite different from actual base rates, confirming that in the absence of any information, judges expected subjects to manifest different behaviors than they actually did.

2. Judges who were given the base-rate distribution recalled it accurately, indicating that they understood its implications. Nevertheless, the probabilities they estimated for the behaviors of the two target subjects were quite dissimilar to the actual base rate distribution. Instead, they were similar to the base-rate distributions estimated by judges who were not given base-rate information. This suggests that judges ignored the implications of the actual base-rate information in predicting the targets' behaviors.

3. On the other hand, judges who were told that the individual target subjects had each been willing to receive the maximum amount or shock (or, alternatively, had been unwilling to help under any circumstances) predicted that the actual base-rate distributions would be consistent with these behaviors. This occurred despite the fact that judges were given no indication that the target subjects were representative of the group as a whole.

The above results are quite consistent with the implications of a script-processing formulation. The base-rate information provided in this study was deviant from judges' a priori expectancies for how persons would behave in the situations described. Moreover, it implied that the behavior manifested had undesirable consequences, either for the actor himself or for others. These factors may have made it difficult for judges to construct a categorical script to summarize and explain why the behavior typically occurred. Therefore, to predict targets' behavior, they may have constructed an episodic self-script describing how they personally would be apt to behave in the situations. This may generally occur when the target appears to be similar to the judge in general background and values (e.g., a college student). On the other hand, when information about a particular target subject's behavior was presented, judges appear to construct an episodic script about this person, and to use this, rather than their self-script, to predict the behavior of people in general. As a result, anecdotal information about an individual person had considerable influence upon predictions of the behavior of people in general, while information about the behavior of people in general had little impact on the prediction of an individual's behavior.

The above interpretation, if correct, has even further implications. For one thing, it implies that if judges could more easily construct a categorical script in order to explain the base-rate distribution, they would be more apt to use this information in making subsequent inferences. To investigate this possibility Zuckerman (1978) essentially replicated the Darley and Latané condition of Nisbett and Borgida's experiment, but added conditions in which the alleged base-rate distribution was the reverse of the actual distribution. That is, it indicated that most subjects in the experiment offered to help very quickly, rather than not at all (see Fig. 2.4). Judges should be more easily able to form a script about subjects engaging in the socially desirable behavior (helping) than the socially undesirable behavior (not helping), and therefore should use the consensus information more in the first case than in the second. A second factor considered by Zuckerman was whether judges were given background information about the target individual whose behavior was to be predicted (similar to the procedure used by Nisbett and Borgida). It seems reasonable that judges who received this

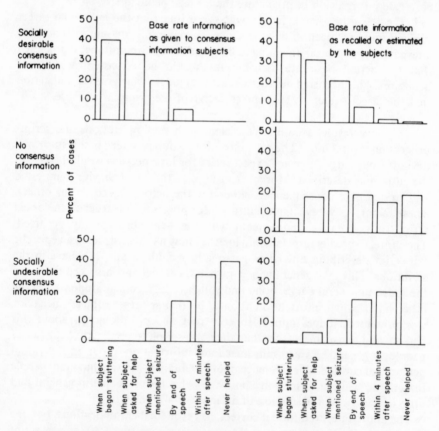

FIG. 2.4.   Base-rate (consensus) information about participants helping behavior received and recalled by subjects under different consensus information conditions (reprinted from Zuckerman, 1978, p. 167).

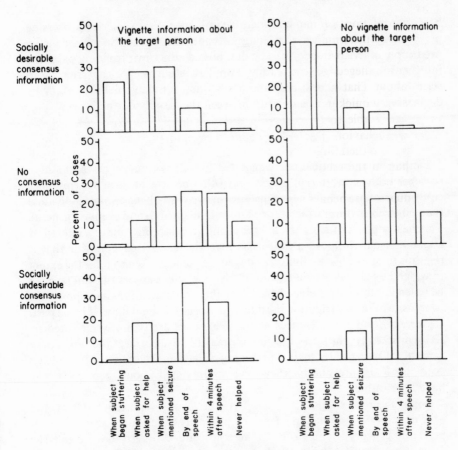

FIG. 2.5.   Distribution of predictions of target person's behavior as a function of base-rate (consensus) information and availability of vignette (reprinted from Zuckerman, 1978, p. 168).

background information, which described a typical student like themselves, could more easily identify with the target. They might therefore be more apt to use their self-script in predicting the target's behavior than they would otherwise. Results shown in Fig. 2.4 and 2.5 were consistent with these expectations. Judges who received the different base-rate distributions recalled them accurately (Fig. 2.4). Moreover, they ignored these distributions in predicting the target subjects' behavior *only* under the conditions originally run by Nisbett and Borgida; that is, they ignored the base-rate information only when this information implied that most subjects had not helped *and* a background vignette of the target was provided. When either the base-rate information implied that the majority of subjects offered help immediately or no background information about the target was given, the base-rate information had considerable influence. From a script-processing perspective, this implies that judges' tendencies to apply self-scripts in predicting others' behavior can be diminished either by providing base-rate information that judges can readily assimilate into a categorical script (i.e., a script about socially desirable and easily understandable behaviors), or by decreasing the apparent similarity between the target and the judge.

Determinants and Effects of Self-Judgments

Despite the qualifications suggested by Zuckerman's research, it is reasonable to suppose that judges may often be able to form a script more easily on the basis of a concrete instance or event involving a single individual than on the basis of abstract information about persons and events in general. This has implications for the effects of information on a judge's inferences about himself. Suppose a judge has recently manifested behavior that is relevant to one of his attributes, and is subsequently asked to infer the extent to which he has this attribute. Intuitively, one might expect this inference to be based less upon the judge's behavior in this single situation than upon some composite of the information the judge has acquired about himself in the past. However, if judges' inferences about themselves are typically mediated by script processing, the script they invoke may be based in large part upon their "anecdotal" experience in the preceding situation, and the more abstract "summary" of information they have accumulated about themselves may have little influence.

Some indirect support for this hypothesis was reported by Bem and McConnell (1970) in a study designed primarily to test implications of self-perception theory (Bem, 1972). In this study, judges agreed to write an essay opposing a position they initially favored. Once judges had engaged in this attitude-relevant behavior, they not only inferred their post-behavior attitudes to be consistent with the implications of the behavior, but incorrectly recalled their pre-behavior attitudes as also consistent with these implications. These data suggest that judges may have constructed an episodic script based upon the "anecdotal" information about their behavior in the situation, and subsequently used this script both to infer their present attitudes and to infer what their attitudes must have been before participating in the situation. There are, of course, other interpretations of these findings (cf. Bem, 1972). However, the consistency of these results with a script-processing formulation is noteworthy.

An assumption underlying our script-processing interpretation of Nisbett and Borgida's study is that judges often invoke self-scripts as bases for making judgments about others. This possibility, which was also noted by Abelson (1976), is similar in its implications to that of the "false consensus" bias postulated by Ross (1977). Ross argues that people have a general tendency to infer that others will behave as they do themselves. Therefore, a judge who is induced to manifest a given behavior, and who bases it on a script concerning the behavior's determinants and consequences, will invoke the same script in predicting others' behavior in the same circumstances. Evidence consistent with this hypothesis was obtained by Ross, Greene and House (cited in Ross, 1977). Judges first considered a scenario in which they were asked if they would permit themselves to be filmed for a television commercial, and predicted the response they would make. Then, after making their prediction, they were asked to predict what others would do in the same circumstances. Judges who said they personally would comply with the request predicted that 75% of others would also comply, whereas judges who said they would not comply predicted that only 57% of others would comply. In a conceptually similar study, students who agreed to wear a sandwich-board sign around campus for 30 minutes predicted that 62% of other students would also agree to wear the sign, whereas those who refused predicted that only 33% of other students would agree to do so. These results are consistent with the hypothesis that the self-script involved in making decisions may often be used subsequently to predict others' decisions. There is, of course, an obvious alternative interpretation. That is, when subjects in the above experiments were asked whether they would personally comply with the request, they may first have constructed a categorical script of how others would behave in that situation, and then conformed to this behavior. Thus, predictions of others' behavior may have been a *determinant* of their own decisions rather than an effect of these decisions. Despite this ambiguity, the general hypothesis raised by Ross is provocative and worth pursuing more rigorously.

Persisting Effects of Scripts on Social Judgments

A final indication of the power of scripts in information processing lies in the suggestion that once a script is elicited by certain stimulus information, it may remain salient and affect judgments even after the information that stimulated it is found to be invalid. In a study of Ross, Lepper and Hubbard (1975), judges were first asked to distinguish between real and bogus suicide notes. Then, some judges were falsely told that they had done quite well on the task, while others were falsely told that they had done badly. Later, all judges were told the truth, that the feedback was determined using a table of random numbers and bore no relation to their true performance. They were then asked to predict their performance on a future judgment task of a similar nature. Despite the debriefing, judges who had originally received positive feedback predicted that they would do better on the second task than did those who had originally received negative feedback. Thus, the script that judges formed to explain their past performance appeared to be used as a basis for predicting their future performance, despite the fact that the information upon which the script was based was rendered invalid. An earlier series of studies by Valins (1966, 1974) may be interpreted similarly. Here, judges received false information about their heart rate as they viewed slides of nude females. They subsequently judged photographs as more attractive if the photos had been accompanied by high heart-rate feedback than if they had been accompanied by normal heart-rate feedback. Moreover, the effects of this feedback persisted even after subjects had been told that the heart-rate information they had received was false, and bore no relation to their true re-actions. It is interesting to speculate that judges formed scripts of themselves in interaction with the females portrayed in the photographs in order to explain their apparent emotional reactions, and that these scripts served as a basis for their subsequent judgments even after they found that the reactions eliciting these scripts were bogus.

A study by Ross, Lepper, Strack and Steinmetz (cited in Ross, 1977) is also relevant to this general hypothesis. Here, judges were first given a clinical description of a person and asked to explain one of two quite different future events on the basis of this information (either that the person committed suicide, or that he donated money to the Peace Corps). In some instances, judges were told at the outset that the behavior they would explain was hypothetical. In other cases, they were first led to believe that the behavior had actually occurred, but were then told that the experimenter actually had no idea about the person's future behavior. Judges then estimated the likelihood that the target would engage in a variety of behavior, including the one they had previously explained. In each case, it was clear to judges that the behavior they had explained was hypothetical. Nevertheless, they predicted this behavior to be more likely to occur in the future than behaviors they had not attempted to explain. There are again alternative interpretations of this finding.[2] However, its consistency with the results obtained in other studies cited above, and with the script-processing formulation, is noteworthy. Subjects may have created scripts to explain the behavior they considered, and then subsequently used these scripts to make predictions independently of the information they originally received about the target person and despite the knowledge that the event they had used as a basis for constructing the script was hypothetical.

---

[2]For example, judges may have inferred from the experimenter's request to explain the target's behavior that he personally expected the target to be likely to manifest this behavior, and therefore may have conformed to this implicit experimental demand.

2.4 CONCLUDING REMARKS

Abelson's general formulation of script processing is intuitively appealing. However, very few of the research findings described in this chapter are directly implied by this formulation. In several instances, other formulations are equally capable of accounting for the results obtained. In general, the theory is not sufficiently precise to permit the derivation and empirical test of many clear hypotheses. In order to do this, one must be able to determine in advance the scripts that are likely to be accessed and used in any given instance, particularly under conditions where more than one is potentially applicable. Moreover, one must develop criteria for distinguishing empirically the overt manifestations of script processing from those of other types of processes that might be invoked in judgmental situations.

Nevertheless, the script-processing formulation, along with its ancestor, implicational molecule theory, provide a conceptual perspective from which research and theory on social inference and attribution may be interpreted and evaluated. This general perspective will be reflected in much of our discussion in the remainder of this book. Moreover, considering social inference phenomena from a script-processing point of view raises several general questions that are fundamental to understanding judgmental processes. For example, a detailed understanding is required of the manner in which information about social stimuli is organized and stored in memory, and the factors that determine when and how it is accessed for use in making judgments. Of particular concern is the relation between the representation of information contained in schemata about particular persons and events (of the sort contained in episodic scripts) and the representation of information in schemata about more general classes of stimuli (of the sort comprising categorical scripts). An additional question involves the manner in which information is encoded at the time it is initially received, and the effects of this encoding on the subsequent retrieval and use of information in making judgments. These issues are addressed in the next two chapters. Finally, there are conditions in which script processes are unlikely to be used, either because they are irrelevant to the judgment, or because they are insufficient, and higher order integration and inference processes may be required. The nature of these processes, and the conditions in which they occur, must also be understood. These matters will be considered in Chapters 8 and 9.

3 A Preliminary Model of Person Memory

In Chapter 2 we described a vignette as a complex representation of an event (e.g., Professor Smith telling John to get out of his office), each component of which (Professor Smith, John and the behavioral act) was a schema, or configuration of verbally and nonverbally encoded attributes. A temporally-related sequence of events was defined as a script. The representation in memory of schemata, vignettes, and scripts, and the processes of accessing them for use in making inferences, are obviously complex. For one thing, the nature of a schema and the attributes comprising it may depend very heavily upon the nature of other schemata in the vignette in which the schema is contained. Several models have been proposed to describe the organization and use of scripts, most notably by Schank and Abelson (1977). Although a discussion of these models is beyond the scope of this volume, it is nevertheless desirable to consider in some detail the possible cognitive organization of information about social stimuli, and the processes involved in retrieving this information for use in making judgments.

In this chapter, therefore, we propose a set of postulates concerning the representation of social stimuli in memory, and how this representation affects judgments. The formulation is stimulated in part by existing theories of semantic and episodic memory, notably those proposed by Collins and Quillian (1969; see also Collins & Loftus, 1975), Smith, Shoben and Rips (1974), and J. R. Anderson and Bower (1973). However, it takes into account some of the factors uniquely associated with the organization and use of information about persons. In its present form, the formulation we will propose does not pretend to account for all phenomena uncovered in research on semantic and episodic memory, or for all the effects of cognitive organization on the interpretation of new information. Because of this, its presentation in this volume may seem premature. However, our intent is to provide a framework within which a variety of social inference processes can be conceptualized and which will suggest new avenues of empirical investigation. Such research may not only help to refine the model, but may provide more general insights into social inference phenomena that are of importance in their own right.

In the discussion to follow, we will focus primarily on the nature of person schemata and their interrelations, and will consider the effects of these schemata on three different types of inferences that judges are often called upon to make. However, the model we propose is not restricted to any given type of schema, and could apply in principle to script processing of the type described in Chapter 2. (The application of the formulation to certain script processes will be suggested later in this chapter.)

Although we will consider some experimental investigations of phenomena related to the proposed formulation, research bearing upon many implications of this formulation for social judgment is quite limited. Consequently, this chapter refers much less frequently to existing research than do other chapters in this book. Rather, we will illustrate the issues to which the formulation is potentially relevant, and will demonstrate the heuristic value of this approach we have taken through a number of specific and empirically testable hypotheses suggested by the model we propose.

3.1 THE ORGANIZATION OF SOCIAL CONCEPTS

The Representation of Concepts in Memory

The components of memory we will consider are concepts at various levels of generality. Each concept has a nominal representation (often a verbal label, such as "honest," "Republican," "Charles de Gaulle," "breaks the window," etc.), and is typically associated with other concepts that in combination serve to define its "meaning." Two different concepts may have the same name. For example, "recorder" labels both a component of one's audio tape system and a musical instrument; alternatively, "dog" may have different referents when it is used in the contexts of "playing with children" and "frightening strangers."

The association between concepts may differ in strength. That is, "doctor" is more strongly associated with "nurse" than with "chorus girl," and "warm" is more closely associated with "friendly" than with "intelligent." The basis for these associations will be considered presently. It seems reasonable to suppose that the stronger the association between two concepts, the more likely it is that making one of the concepts salient will lead the other to become salient as well.

Three basic considerations have led to the development of several "network" models of memory (e.g., Anderson & Bower, 1973; Collins & Loftus, 1975). We will adopt a similar approach here, although some of the specific assumptions and postulates we will make are different from those of existing models. Very briefly, we will propose a model in which concepts in memory are connected by pathways of different widths, and in which the activation of one concept may lead to activation of a second as a result of "excitation" that travels through these pathways. The greater the width of a given pathway connecting two concepts, the more excitation can be transmitted along it, and therefore the more quickly one concept will activate a second. In order to develop these ideas more rigorously, and convey their implications, we will present the model in terms of a series of formal postulates. The first four postulates, to be presented in this section, concern the structure of memory. The remaining postulates concern the processes whereby concepts are activated and used as a basis for inferences.

Our first postulate simply reiterates more formally an assumption noted above:

> Postulate 1.   The organization of concepts in memory may be represented in terms of a network of interconnected nodes. Each concept is represented by a node. The relation between any two concepts is represented by a path connecting the nodes pertaining to these concepts.

A path may connect either single concepts or configurations of concepts. For example, the concept "businessmen" may be associated with the configuration "like Republican presidents," which is composed of the concepts "like," "Republican," and "president." It seems reasonable that in many instances, these configurations function as single units, the meaning of which differs from the sum of its parts. Certainly the meaning of "like" in the configuration "like Republican presidents" differs from its meaning in the configuration "likes strawberry jam" (that is, the associates of "like" differ in the two cases). Moreover, the referent and associates of "Republican presidents" may be different in the configuration "like Republican presidents" than in the configuration "bribe Republican presidents."

It may ultimately be useful to distinguish between "verb" and "object" concepts, particularly when considering the organization of scripts and vignettes. However, for simplicity, we will forego this distinction in our present discussion. Thus, the statements "businessmen like Republican presidents" and "businessmen bribe Republican presidents" are interpreted as statements conveying relations between the concept "businessmen" and each of two other configural concepts, "like Republican presidents" and "bribe Republican presidents," rather than as two different relations between the concepts "businessmen" and "Republican presidents."

Concept nodes may be associated with memory either directly, through a direct pathway connecting them, or indirectly, through a series of intermediate nodes. For example, Chicago aldermen may be associated with corruptness either through a direct pathway connecting "Chicago aldermen" to "corrupt" or, indirectly , through pathways from "Chicago alderman" to "politicians" and from "politicians" to "corrupt." This leads to a second postulate:

Postulate 2. The strength of association between two concept nodes in memory is (a) an inverse function of the number of intermediate pathways required to connect them; and (b) a positive function of the diameter of these pathways.

In making this postulate, we assume that the length of each direct path connecting two concept nodes is the same, and that therefore the diameter of the path (and thus the amount of excitation that can flow through it in any given time interval) is the critical factor. This assumption distinguishes our model from previous formulations that invoke a "spreading excitation" concept (cf. Collins & Loftus, 1975; Meyer & Schvaneveldt, 1976). An alternative assumption might seem intuitively to be that strength of association is a function of pathway length rather than width. However, our representation has several advantages, which will become clear as we elaborate our formulation. For one thing, it provides for the possibility that entire configurations of connected concepts may sometimes be accessed as a unit (when the pathways connecting them are all wide). On the other hand, it also allows for the possibility that in other instances, two related concepts may both individually be activated as a result of excitation from other sources without the activation of one leading to activation of the second.

Postulate 3. The diameter of a path connecting two concept nodes is a function of both the frequency with which excitation has been transmitted along it, and the recency with which excitation has been transmitted along it.

Thus, a pathway is like an artery that expands with constant use, strengthening the association of the concepts it connects. However, if two concepts that at one time were strongly associated are no longer often thought about, the pathway will contract, and therefore their association will weaken.

The frequency of transmission of excitation along a path is presumably a function of the frequency with which the two concepts it connects have been related in the judge's previous experience. This experience may be gained either from reading or hearing about the concepts, or from direct encounters with exemplars of these concepts. The association of two concepts may also be a function of the frequency with which the judge has "rehearsed" the association between them. Thus, the diameter of the path connecting "businessman" to "Republican" would be greater than the path connecting "businessman" to "athlete" if the judge has either heard or thought about the fact that businessmen are Republicans more often than he has heard or thought about the fact that businessmen are athletes. Similarly, the path connecting a particular person node, "Mary," to "professor" would be wider than that connecting "Mary" to "feminist" to the extent that Mary has been referred to as a professor more often than as a feminist.

It is important to note that the strength of association between two concepts in memory does not necessarily reflect the true (objective) association between them. Two classes of objects may be highly related in the real world, but concepts pertaining to them may still be far apart in memory. For example, professors are almost invariably college graduates; however, the concepts "professor" and "college graduate" may not be strongly associated in memory, since the relation between them is rarely considered. Alternatively, an uncommon or surprising relationship may be thought about quite frequently, and the path connecting the concepts involved may therefore be very wide.

Postulate 4. A path between two nodes is directed. Its direction reflects the order in which the concepts have occurred in the relation as it has been encountered.

Thus, if the judge has typically learned that Mary is a professor rather than that a professor is Mary, the path connecting the two concepts involved would be directed from "Mary" to "professor." In some instances, the relations have been experienced in both directions; for example, the judge may often encounter the notion that Republicans are businessmen as well as the notion that businessmen are Republicans. In such cases, two paths may exist between the concepts, one in each direction. These paths need not be the same width.

Most directed paths in a network, and the ones of primary concern in this chapter, can be interpreted as "is" or "are" relations. That is, a path between "businessmen" and "Republicans" represents the relation conveyed by the statement "businessmen [are] Republicans," whereas the path between "businessmen" and "like Republicans" represents the relation conveyed by the statement "businessmen [are persons who] like Republicans," etc. However, some paths may exist by virtue of the simple juxtaposition of two concepts in one's experience. For example, the concepts "bread" and "butter," or "men" and "women," may be closely associated because they frequently co-occur either in verbal communication or in one's personal contact with exemplars of the concepts. Many personality traits ("honest," "trustworthy," "friendly," etc.), may be connected for similar reasons.

Basic Structure

Given the four postulates described above, the organization of information about persons may be conceptualized in terms of three interconnected networks, or structures:

1. a *superstructure,* consisting of schemata about individual persons or categories of persons and the relations among them;
2. a set of *schema substructures,* each pertaining to a particular schema in the superstructure, and consisting of concepts about attributes and behaviors that are associated with this schema;
3. a *semantic* structure, consisting of attributes and behaviors that, while used to characterize persons, are associated on the basis of their semantic similarity, independently of any particular person or group they may describe.

Let us consider each type of structure, and the relations between them, in more detail.

The Superstructure

The schemata or concepts contained in the superstructure may be at varying levels of abstractness. They may refer to general classes of persons ("professor," "feminist," etc.) or to particular instances ("Richard Nixon," "Mary Smith"). Moreover, they may be either temporally and situationally independent, as in the above examples, or time- and situation-specific ("Richard Nixon in 1960"; "Richard Nixon in 1972"; "Mary Smith working at the office"; "Mary Smith eating dinner with me last Saturday evening"). These latter, more specific schemata may be considered to be *subschemata* of a more general concept ("Richard Nixon" or "Mary Smith"). A fragment of a hypothetical judge's superstructure might be represented as shown in Fig. 3.1. In this diagram, as in others we will present, no distinction is made between a concept itself and the verbal label or name attached to it. In practice, however, this distinction may be of considerable importance, as we point out later in this chapter (cf. J. R. Anderson & Hastie, 1974).

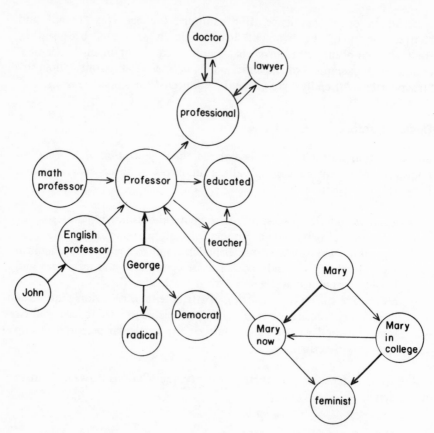

FIG. 3.1.   Hypothetical superstructure of schemata. Arrows denote direction of pathways.

Schema Substructures

Each schema or subschema in the superstructure consists of attributes. These attributes may be verbally or nonverbally coded physical characteristics ("brown-eyed," "long-haired"), general traits and behaviors ("intelligent," "talks a lot"), or specific behaviors manifested toward particular objects in particular situations ("stole the psychology midterm exam from my office last Friday"). These attribute concepts may be represented in memory by nodes, each of which is connected to the central node in the superstructure.

The substructure of a hypothetical subschema, "Mary in college," might resemble that shown in Fig. 3.2. As in the superstructure, the paths may differ in width. However, in this case, all paths are typically directed from the central node outward, reflecting the manner in which the relations are most

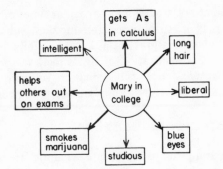

FIG. 3.2.   Hypothetical substructure of schema pertaining to "Mary in college." Arrows denote direction of pathways connecting schema node to concept nodes in the substructure.

apt to be learned. (For example, one is more apt to learn that Mary is intelligent, or that a professor writes books, than that an intelligent person is Mary, or that someone who writes books is a professor.) This does not, of course, preclude the possibility of pathways in both directions. However, even when this occurs, the outward-directed path is likely to be the dominant (wider) one.

Certain general differences seem likely to exist between the substructures of schemata about individual persons and the substructures of schemata about general categories of persons. The information one receives about classes of persons is more apt to pertain to general characteristics ("professors are intelligent, absent-minded, and underpaid"). However, information about particular persons is often acquired through direct contact with them, and thus is more apt to pertain to physical attributes of these persons and to specific behaviors they have manifested. It therefore seems reasonable to suppose that, in general, the majority of concepts connected directly to a "categorical" schema node are apt to pertain to general traits and attributes, whereas concepts connected to a schema node representing an individual person are more likely to concern specific behaviors or physical characteristics. However, there are undoubtedly exceptions to this rule. For example, the schema substructure of "basketball player" may contain the general physical attributes "tall" and "well coordinated." Moreover, the schemata of particular acquaintances may contain general traits as a consequence of prior judgments or descriptions using these traits, which a person has made or overheard. These possibilities will be described in more detail presently.

The representation in Fig. 3.2 is oversimplified in at least two respects. First, characteristics of a person may be represented visually and therefore may be organized spatially (Kosslyn & Pomerantz, 1977). To this extent, it may be somewhat misleading to represent the relation of each characteristic to the central schema node by a different path rather than treating the characteristics as a configuration that is connected to the schema node by a single path. Second, we have noted that a general schema may be composed of subschemata of a person at particular times or in particular situations, and that the sets of attributes comprising these subschemata may differ. We will discuss the implications of this latter possibility later in this chapter, when we consider the organization of the vignettes in more detail. Meanwhile, our temporary avoidance of these matters will help us to convey more easily the processes we postulate to govern inference phenomena.

The Semantic Structure

The assumption of a separate semantic structure pertaining to traits and behaviors is based in part upon research by d'Andrade (1965). This research suggests that the interrelatedness of traits may be based upon purely semantic considerations, and may not depend upon the presence of these traits in particular persons or groups of persons. For example, judges may not always infer that an honest person is trustworthy because they have learned about persons described as "honest" who also meet the criteria for inclusion in the category "trustworthy." Rather, they may make this inference because "honest" and "trustworthy" have similar semantic features (Smith et al., 1974), independently of any particular persons who possess these traits in combination.

In a multidimensional analysis of trait similarity ratings, Rosenberg, Nelson, and Vivekananthan (1968) identified three dimensions of "meaning" along which personality traits are presumed to vary. The organization of traits along these dimensions is described in Fig. 3.3. Note that this organization appears to be based in large part upon the general principle that good things go with good things and bad things with bad. However, there are both social and intellectual dimensions of "goodness." The distance between any two traits in multidimensional space is an indication of their difference in semantic meaning. It seems reasonable to assume that the relations among traits could be represented in a network similar to that used to represent the superstructure and schema substructures. Each trait would be represented by a node, and the width of each path connecting a pair of nodes could be a function of the semantic distance between traits in the multidimensional space shown in Fig. 3.3.

Judges are also apt to have implicit "theories" about what behaviors go together (Triandis, 1964), and about what behaviors are implied by different traits. These relations may also be semantic in nature. For example, we learn that telling that truth is honest, and that helping someone is kind, without considering particular persons or classes of persons who manifest these behaviors. In principle, these trait–behavior relations could also be incorporated into a semantic structure of the sort identified by Rosenberg and Sedlak. Concepts in this structure would be highly interconnected. For example, not only may a given trait category ("honest") be connected to more

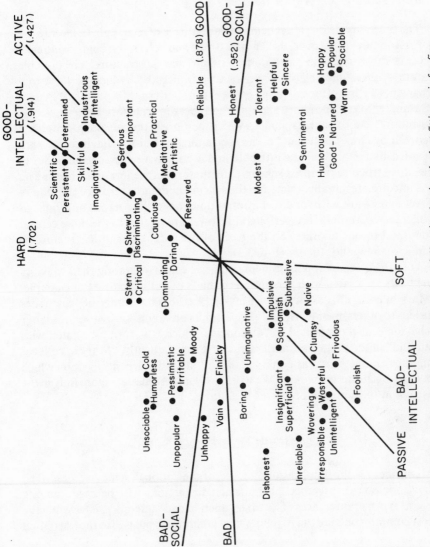

FIG. 3.3. Two-dimensional configuration of 60 traits showing the best-fitting axis for five properties. Each number in parentheses indicates the multiple correlation between projections on the best-fitting axis and property values (reprinted from Rosenberg & Sedlak, 1972, p. 252).

than one behavior ("returning lost property," "reporting someone who cheated on an exam"), but a behavior (e.g., "helping someone solve a difficult problem") may be related to more than one trait ("kind" and "intelligent").

Interrelations Among Structures

The central node in each schema substructure is of course also a node in the superstructure. Moreover, the features (traits and behaviors) comprising each schema substructure are also nodes in the semantic structure. The possible nature of these interrelations may be seen in Fig. 3.4,[1] which pertains to a fragment of a hypothetical judge's concepts of both specific persons ("Peter," "Susan," "Mary in college," etc.) and person categories ("professor," "feminist," etc.). Schema nodes, which comprise the superstructure, are denoted by circles. Attribute nodes (pertaining to traits, behaviors, etc.) are denoted by rectangles. The attribute nodes directly tied to schema nodes in the superstructure comprise schema substructures of the sort described in Fig. 3.2, and are presumably related to the schema nodes as a result of the judge's direct experience with, or direct information about, the persons or groups to which they pertain. More peripheral features are related to the more central ones (and to one another) on the basis of the judge's semantic structure or implicit personality theory (Fig. 3.3).

Note that certain apparent inconsistencies can arise among the behaviors and traits associated with persons on the basis of this structure. For example, "Mary in college" is associated with "kind," through the intermediate nodes "listens to others' problems" and "helps others on exams." However, the latter behavior is also connected to "dishonest," which is in turn associated with "unkind" in the judge's semantic structure. Consequently, "Mary in college" might be characterized as either "kind" or "unkind," depending upon which set of associations is invoked. We will consider these matters more fully in the discussion of inference processes to follow.

3.2 INFERENCE PROCESSES

In considering the implications of the organizational structure described above for social inference phenomena, distinctions will be made among several types of inferences. The first, "open-ended" inference, is possibly the most common outside the psychological laboratory, but is also the least often

---

[1]Certain peripheral features, such as "kind," occur more than once in the diagram. This does not indicate the existence of more than one node with the same label, but rather the impossibility of representing a multidimensional structure in two dimensions. In this diagram, different nodes with the same labels should be considered identical.

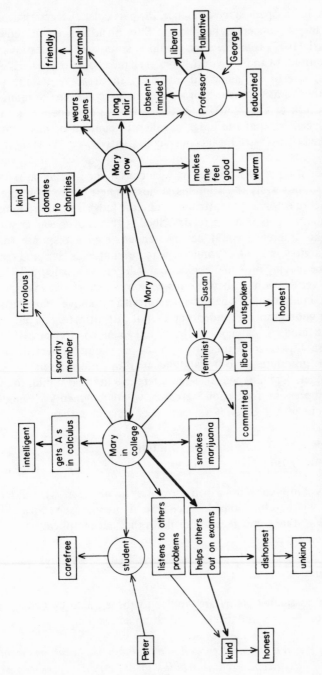

FIG. 3.4. Hypothetical section of a judge's cognitive network associated with an acquaintance, Mary. Circles denote schema nodes; rectangles denote concept nodes in schema substructures or in the semantic structure. (Concept nodes directly connected to schema nodes comprise the substructure of the schema involved. Other nodes connected to the substructure nodes are contained in the judge's semantic structure.)

studied inside. In an open-ended inference, the particular characteristic to be inferred (the "target" concept) is unspecified. Such an inference, referred to by Clark and Clark (1977) as *production,* would be stimulated by questions like, "What do you think of today's youth?" or, "Tell me about your sister." Such inferences might also be generated internally in decision making (e.g., deciding whether to ask someone for a date). In a second type of inference, *verification* (Clark & Clark, 1977), both a stimulus concept and a target concept are specified, and the judge is asked to confirm or disconfirm a relation between them ("Are businessmen conservative?" or, "Is Mary Smith unkind?").

Two additional types of inference may be considered special cases of the first two. Here, however, the stimulus is not a single concept. Rather, it consists of a set of categories or attributes, and the judge is required to make an inference about a person or object described by the set of characteristics as the whole. This inference could be open-ended (e.g., a response to the question, "what do you think of someone who never attends class and spends most of his time playing pinball machines but still gets As in calculus?"). Or it could involve verification of the stimulus person's membership in a specific category (e.g., a judgment of whether a person with the above characteristics would make a good graduate student) or a set of categories (e.g., a judgment of this person along a category scale of likeableness). Certain of these inferences were illustrated in the script-processing examples describing the evaluation of graduate school candidates from information in their application folders (see Chapter 2). Such inferences are also similar to those involved in "impression formation" research, where judgments are made of fictitious persons on the basis of adjective sets describing them.

General Processes: A Spreading-Excitation Model of Memory Search

The three types of inferences described above may involve somewhat different processes. We will therefore consider each type of inference separately. First, however, we will state some general postulates that have implications for all three types of inference.

Basic Postulates

Most of the postulates below are similar to those made by Collins and Loftus (1975) in their formulation of spreading activation.

Postulate 5. When a judge is exposed to a stimulus that contains the name of a concept, excitation builds up at the node representing this concept. When this excitation reaches a certain minimal activation threshold, the concept node is activated. (That is, the judge thinks of the concept.)

Postulate 6. When one concept node is activated, excitation emanates from this node along the paths connecting it to other nodes. Excitation may be transmitted along a path in either direction. However, in any given period of time, less excitation can be transmitted through a narrow pathway than through a wide one, and less excitation can be transmitted in the reverse direction than in the forward direction.

Thus, the time required for a given amount of excitation from one node to reach a second, and thus the likelihood that activation of the first concept will lead the second to be activated as well, is a function of both the strength of association between the two concepts (as reflected by the width of the paths connecting them) and the direction of these paths. Moreover, we noted earlier that two paths may often exist between two concepts, one in each direction, and that these paths may differ in diameter, depending upon the frequency and recency with which the concepts have been associated in each direction. In such cases, excitation may of course be transmitted along both paths simultaneously, although at possibly different rates.

We have drawn an analogy between pathways and arteries that expand or contract. Pursuing this analogy, the effect of directionality may be represented in terms of filters in the artery that regulate the flow of energy in each direction. Regardless of directionality, however, any particular filter will allow greater flow of excitation when the path is large than when it is small. Therefore, an increased frequency of transmission in *either* direction increases the strength of the association of the two concepts being related in *both* directions. (Thus, repeated exposure to information that businessmen are conservative will not only increase the likelihood that the activation of "businessmen" will lead to the activation of "conservative," but will increase the likelihood that the activation of "conservative" will lead to the activation of "businessman.") This possibility is of course empirically testable. For example, one might build up different degrees and direction of association between nonsense words, and determine differences in the effects of these differences on reaction times and/or error rates in a word association paradigm.

Postulate 7. The total amount of excitation emanating from an activated concept node is the same, regardless of the number of paths connected to it.

Consequently, the amount of excitation transmitted along any given path from an activated node will be inversely related to the number of other paths connected to the node. More precisely, the amount of excitation transmitted along path P from concept A will be a function of the ratio of (a) the potential excitation transmitted along P to (b) the sum of the potential amounts of excitation transmitted along all paths connected to A. The potential excitation transmitted along P is proportional to the quantity $b_P W_P$, where W_P is the width of pathway P and b_P is a coefficient of resistance that is either high or low, depending upon whether transmission is in the forward or reverse direction. Hence, the amount of excitation transmitted along P, or E_P may be represented as

$$E_P = f\left(\frac{b_P W_P}{\Sigma b_i W_i}\right) \tag{3-1}$$

This formulation has several intriguing implications. For one thing, it implies that the likelihood that activating one concept, A, will activate a second, B (i.e., that thinking of A will lead the judge to think of B), will increase as (a) the strength of A's association with B increases; as (b) the total number of concepts associated with A decreases; and as (c) the strength of A's association with concepts other than B decreases.

A possible problem with Equation 1 should be noted, however. If P were the only path connecting the two concepts A and B, the expression on the right of the equation would reduce to unity. In such a case, the likelihood that thinking of A will activate B is independent of path width, or in other words, of the strength of the association between them. The validity of this prediction seems intuitively questionable, and suggests the possible need to modify Equation 1 in a way that will eliminate this problem. However, since the determinants of W_i are theoretically specified by the model (see Postulate 3), the implication is empirically verifiable.

Postulate 8. Excitation will continue to emanate from a concept node as long as this concept is processed (i.e., as long as the judge continues to think about the concept).

Postulate 9. When excitation from an activated node (A) reaches an unactivated node (B), it will accumulate at this node. When the excitation that has accumulated reaches activation threshold, this node (B) will also be activated (see Postulate 4).

That is, the judge will think of the concept to which the node pertains. Once this node is activated, excitation will then spread from it to others that are connected to it, and so on, as implied by Postulates 5–7.

Postulate 10. Only a limited number of concept nodes will remain activated at any given time.

A judge is obviously able to think about only a limited number of things at once. Thus, the activation of one node may often be accompanied by deactivation of certain others, perhaps including the concept node from which excitation was first transmitted. (Put more simply, a judge who begins thinking about new concepts is likely to stop thinking about old ones, sometimes including the one that initially stimulated his cognitive activity.) However, a judge is assumed to have some control over what he thinks about, and therefore over which concepts he continues to activate at times of processing overload. Thus, a judge who is asked to describe an acquaintance may continue to process the node pertaining to this acquaintance until the description is provided.

Postulate 10 also helps to explain how differing rates of transmission may affect the activation of concepts. While a certain minimal level of excitation must accumulate at a particular node before this node is activated, the attainment of that level does not insure activation. It seems reasonable to suppose that at any given time, the subset of nodes activated will be those at which the greatest amount of excitation has built up, provided this excitation is above threshold. Thus, the activation of a concept depends not only upon whether the excitation accumulated at the node is above threshold, but also upon its level of excitation in relation to that of other concepts at the same point in time.

Postulate 11. Once a node has been deactivated (i.e., once the judge no longer thinks about the concept to which it pertains), *the excitation that has accumulated at the node decays over time.*

Although the precise nature of this decay function is unclear, it seems reasonable to assume that the residual excitation at a deactivated node decreases more rapidly initially than later on. However, it may take a substantial amount of time before this excitation dissipates entirely. To the extent that some residual excitation exists at the node as a result of its prior activation, it will require less additional excitation for the node to be reactivated. The implications of this are important, as we shall see.

In combination, Postulates 5–11 imply that the activation of one concept, B, may result from activation of a second, A, that is directly or indirectly related to it. Moreover, the likelihood that B is activated, and the speed with which it occurs, will be greater to the extent that:

1. The path connecting A and B is wide (the two concepts are strongly associated).
2. The direction of the path connecting the concepts is from A to B rather than from B to A (e.g., the judge has previously learned that "A is B" rather than that "B is A").
3. Few concepts other than B are connected to A.

4. Concept A is continually processed, or thought about, for an extended period of time (and therefore the excitation accumulating at B is more likely to *reach* threshold).
5. Few concepts other than A and B are activated.
6. Concept B, or concepts related to B, have been activated in the recent past (and thus the additional excitation required to activate B is less).

It is evident from this summary that several alternative explanations can be given for the same phenomenon, not all of which are easy to verify independently. For example, suppose a judge thinks of "liberal" more quickly when he is asked to describe a "professor" than he thinks of "professor" when he is asked to characterize liberals. This could be accounted for in several ways. First, the directed path from "professor" to "liberal" may be wider than the directed path from "liberal" to "professor." Second, excitation may in both cases be transmitted along a path from "professor" to "liberal," but may be transmitted more quickly in the forward direction than in the reverse. Third, fewer paths may be connected to "professor" than are connected to "liberal." (Consequently, a greater proportion of the total excitation is transmitted along each of the former paths, leading to more rapid activation of the nodes connected to it.) Finally, "liberal" may have been thought about more frequently in the past than has "professor." (Thus, relatively more residual excitation may have existed at the "liberal" node, and relatively less additional excitation was required to reactivate it.) The first two of these explanations would be particularly difficult to distinguish without knowledge of the factors that are postulated to affect pathway width and directionality (e.g., the frequency and recency with which the concepts have been activated in the past, and the direction of these relations). Nevertheless, the assumptions underlying both appear necessary when considered in a broader context. That is, the relations between some pairs of concepts are certainly experienced in both directions, and these associations are apt to differ in strength. At the same time, it seems likely that judges who have considered a relation between A and B in only one direction (e.g., that Lou Gehrig was a Yankee first-baseman who went to Columbia University) can nevertheless generate A in response to the stimulus B (i.e., they can identify Gehrig if asked to name the person who has the above characteristics).

Effects of Activating Concepts on Cognitive Organization and Change

According to our formulation, the activation of a particular schema, or network of concepts, may alter that schema in several ways. First, it causes residual excitation to build up at particular concept nodes, thus increasing the likelihood that these concepts will be accessed in the future. Second, it causes the activated pathways to expand, facilitating future associations between the concepts they connect. Hence, entire schemata, or configurations of concepts, may become more accessible as a result of prior use. The subsequent stimulation of particular concepts will thus be more likely to cause activation of the schemata of which they are a part. This, of course, is consistent with assumptions underlying the activation and use of scripts for interpreting stimulus events. By the same token, the nonuse of pathways inhibits their use in the future; that is, concept nodes lose their residual excitation, and pathways contract, during periods of nonuse.

The postulation of facilitating and inhibiting changes in pathways as well as in node characteristics has important implications for memory processes. For example, it implies that the association between two concepts may be weak, even though the concepts, considered individually, are quite salient. In this regard, since the expansion or contraction of pathways and the accumulation and decay of excitation at concept nodes reflect different aspects of the associative process, the effects of changes in these characteristics may occur at different rates. Suppose that pathways contract fairly rapidly with nonuse, while concepts lose their excitation slowly. If this were true, two concepts that at one time were strongly related may become dissociated over a period of time, even though each individual concept can still be activated easily by excitation from other sources. There are, in fact, numerous suggestions of such dissociations between concepts in memory. One of the most interesting concerns the apparent dissociation of ideas from their source. It is reasonable to suppose that associations between a source and an idea will not be used or rehearsed as frequently as the associations between the concepts comprising the idea, and between this idea and others contained in memory. Thus, people should often be able to recall ideas even after they have forgotten where the ideas originally came from. There is evidence that after a period of time, subjects cannot recall whether they learned or inferred certain aspects of a situation (Bransford, Barclay & Franks, 1972), whether events were observed or were suggested after the fact (Loftus & Palmer, 1974), or whether arguments were presented by a credible or an incredible source (Kelman & Hovland, 1953). Hence this implication of the formulation appears to have empirical support.

The proposed formulation leads to several other interesting hypotheses, certain of which will be considered in later sections.

Empirical Support

A construct of spreading excitation may seem rather remote from the actual memory processes of humans. However, indirect support for the implications of such a formulation has been obtained in a series of studies by Meyer and his associates on "priming" effects: that is, the effects of activating one concept on the accessibility of related concepts (for a summary, see Meyer & Schvaneveldt, 1976). These studies have typically employed stimuli of little relevance to person perception. For example, they have used familiar words (bird, canary, bread, butter, etc.) that are associated on the basis of semantic considerations rather than on the basis of direct experience with the persons and objects involved. Moreover, in many of these studies, the nature of the association is universally agreed upon, whereas in social stimulus domains, such consensus does not exist. (For example, everyone would agree that canaries are birds, whereas not everyone would agree that liberals are kind, or that businessmen are Republicans.) However, while these considerations suggest that individual differences may exist in memory structures pertaining to social concepts, the cognitive processes involved in dealing with these concepts may be similar to those considered by Meyer and his colleagues.

In one study (Meyer & Schvaneveldt, 1971), judges were presented with pairs of letter strings that were either words or nonwords. Moreover, in some instances the pair consisted of two semantically related words (BREAD–BUTTER, NURSE–DOCTOR) and in other cases of two unrelated words (BREAD–DOCTOR, NURSE–BUTTER). In each case, judges were asked to indicate whether both letter strings in the pair were words by pressing a button. Of particular relevance to the spreading excitation formulation is a comparison of the time required to respond to semantically related word pairs with the time required to respond to unrelated word pairs. To decide on the appropriate response, the judge presumably determines initially whether the first letter string is a word. If it is, he then considers the second string. In each case, verification requires activation of the concept node to which the word pertains. However, if the second word is related to the first (and thus the path connecting them is wide), some of the excitation required to verify the first word will spread to the node corresponding to the second. The additional excitation required to activate this latter node will therefore be less, and the second word will be verified more quickly. The overall time to determine that the two letter strings are words should consequently be less when the words are related than when they are not. This hypothesis was confirmed.

Meyer and Schvaneveldt note an alternative interpretation of the above finding. When a judge has accessed a particular location in memory, it may simply take less time for him to shift to and "read out" of other locations in memory that are close to it than locations that are further away. However, there is an interesting difference between the implications of the two interpretations. Suppose judges are presented with sets of *three* letter strings, two of which are related words (e.g., BREAD and BUTTER) and the third of which is unrelated to either of the others (STAR). Moreover, suppose the strings are presented in either the order STAR–BREAD–BUTTER or the order BREAD–STAR–BUTTER. The spreading–excitation hypothesis would not predict much difference in the overall time to respond to the two sets, since the excitation that has been transmitted from the "bread" node to the "butter" node is unlikely to decrease appreciably during the short time required to verify that STAR is a word. On the other hand, a simple "location-shifting" interpretation would imply that in the second case (BREAD–STAR–BUTTER), judges would have to shift from the location of "bread" to a location remote from it in memory ("star") and then back again (to "butter"), whereas in the first case (STAR–BREAD–BUTTER), only one major shift (from "star" to "bread") is required. Thus, according to this interpretation, response time should be greater in the second order condition than in the first. Schvaneveldt and Meyer (1973) tested this hypothesis using procedures similar to those used in the first experiment. In fact, differences in response time under the two order conditions were negligible, while response time was less in both conditions than when none of the words were related. Thus, of the two alternative interpretations, the spreading-excitation notion seems most consistent with data.

The interpretation of these results is not without ambiguities. For example, despite the similar response times obtained under the two critical conditions in the second study, more errors of identification occurred when the unrelated word was interpolated between the two related ones than when it was not. Also, the "priming effects" obtained in the word identification task used by Meyer have not been consistently replicated using other paradigms (Shoben, 1976). Nevertheless, Meyer's work is of interest in the present context for both methodological and theoretical reasons. First, it suggests a useful research paradigm for diagnosing the organization of person information in memory. Second, the evidence suggests that priming effects may also affect social judgments in many real-life situations, and that these effects may persist despite the interpolated activation of cognitions that are not related either to the judgment to be made or to the concepts being primed. Examples of such effects will be noted presently. However, first let us consider in more detail each of the three types of inferences described earlier in this section, and evaluate the implications of the above assumptions for the nature of these inferences and the factors that may affect them.

Open-Ended Inferences (Production)

Open-ended inferences are typically made about existing concepts in the superstructure. The hypothetical processes underlying such inferences are conveyed in the following postulate, which is derivable from the more basic postulates described above.

Postulate 12. When a judge is asked to make an open-ended inference about a concept, he activates the node pertaining to this target concept. The excitation at this node then spreads to others

> *along the paths connecting them. When sufficient excitation has accumulated at another node for it to be activated, the judge will output the contents of the node as a description of the target concept.*

Note that the longer the time a target concept is processed, the more nodes are likely to be activated, and thus the more detailed the description is apt to be. Under some circumstances, the order in which these descriptive concepts are reported may reflect the relative strength of their association with the stimulus concept. However, this order also depends upon how recently these related concept nodes have been activated in the past, and therefore how much residual excitation exists at these nodes at the time the inference is made. Moreover, the length of time spent processing a target concept is often rather limited. That is, the concept will only be processed until a number of features are identified that the judge considers sufficient for answering the question confronting him, or for attaining other objectives to which the information is relevant. In these instances, the factors noted above may have considerable influence on the particular subset of features included in the description being generated.

Thus, suppose the judge whose cognitive network is represented in Fig. 3.4 is asked to describe Mary when she was in college. This request will presumably lead the judge to activate the "Mary in college" node. If no excitation has accumulated at other nodes in the network prior to the activation of "Mary in college," the excitation spreading from this node will first activate the nodes directly connected to it by the widest paths; that is, the judge will report that she "gets As in calculus," "helps others out on exams," "smokes marijuana," and "listens to other persons' problems." Alternatively, if the judge believes that the person to whom he is communicating wants a more general description of Mary, he may wait until other, more general features connected to these behavioral characteristics are activated ("intelligent," "kind," "dishonest," etc.). If processing continues for a still longer period of time, the "student" and "feminist" concept nodes will be activated, and ultimately, features associated with them, leading the judge to describe Mary as "committed," "liberal," "outspoken," "carefree," etc.

In constructing Fig. 3.4, we assumed that specific behaviors and concrete physical attributes are more closely associated with schema nodes referring to individual persons (Mary in college, Peter, etc.), whereas more abstract traits are more closely connected to schema nodes referring to groups of persons (professor, feminist, etc.). If this were generally the case, open-ended descriptions of individual persons should more typically consist of concrete, behavioral or physical characteristics, and less often of general traits, than should descriptions of groups or classes of persons. However, there are two reasons why this may not always be true. One of these has already been mentioned briefly, while the other requires an additional postulate.

Priming Effects

First, suppose in the above example that some residual excitation exists at certain peripheral nodes ("feminist," "student," etc.) at the time the judge is asked to describe Mary in college. In such circumstances, these general category nodes, and traits associated with them, might be reactivated more quickly than behaviors, despite the fact that the behaviors are more closely associated with the schema node.

In this regard, Postulate 12 implies that descriptions of a person may be systematically manipulated by priming concepts to which different sets of attributes are related. Thus, suppose the judge is asked to describe either Peter or Susan before describing Mary in college. His judgment of Peter would presumably involve the activation "student" whereas his judgment of Susan would involve the activation of "feminist." Therefore, he would be more likely to describe Mary in college using traits associated with "student" (e.g., "carefree") in the first case, and with "feminist" ("committed," "liberal," etc.) in the second.

While the above discussion has focussed upon the hypothetical example described in Fig. 3.4, it suggests more general hypotheses concerning the situational factors that lead judges to use traits or behaviors in describing others. One hypothesis is simply a direct implication of the assumption that traits are more closely associated with schema nodes pertaining to groups, while behaviors are more closely associated with schema nodes pertaining to single persons. Two others derive from this assumption in conjunction with Postulate 12.

Hypothesis 1. Open-ended descriptions of individual persons are generally more likely to consist of behaviors and concrete physical characteristics, and less likely to consist of abstract traits, than are open-ended descriptions of groups of persons.

Hypothesis 2. The tendency to use general traits rather than behaviors to describe an individual target person will be greater if the judge has recently met or thought about another member of a group or category of persons to which the target also belongs.

Hypothesis 3. The tendency to use the specific traits associated with a general category of persons to describe an individual member of this category will be greater if the judge has recently met or thought about another member of the category.

An additional implication of this line of reasoning follows from our assumption that the judge will output only those concepts that are connected to the stimulus concept node by paths directed away from this node.[2] This assumption implies that if the judge in our example were asked to describe Mary in college, he would ultimately generate characteristics typical of feminists (committed, liberal, outspoken, etc.). However, asking him to describe a feminist would *not* lead him to describe general characteristics specific to Mary. (This would not occur unless the judge had established a path from "feminist" to "Mary in college," perhaps as a result of being told that most feminists are similar to Mary.) We have assumed that paths are less often directed from a general category node to an exemplar (or subcategory) node than from an exemplar node to a superordinate category node. If this assumption is correct, individual persons should be described by attributes associated with a group to which they belong more often than groups are described in terms of attributes of their individual members. This line of reasoning has implications for stereotyping phenomena. Specifically, it suggests that judges are more apt to apply traits associated with a stereotype to instances of the stereotype than they are to modify their descriptions of the stereotype to take into account characteristics of individual instances. Finally, with respect to priming effects, the following hypothesis is suggested:

Hypothesis 4. Calling the judge's attention to individual members of a group will have less effect on his description of the group as a whole than calling his attention to a group will have on his descriptions of its individual members.

Establishment of New Paths

A second reason why individual persons may be described in terms of general traits, despite the fact that the information initially acquired about them is in terms of concrete behaviors and physical attributes, is related to a more general consideration raised by J. R. Anderson and Hastie (1974). They postulate that once two concepts are associated as a result of an inference made about their relation, a direct path is established between the concepts that can be used in subsequent judgments. Thus, for example, the judge whose structure is represented in Fig. 3.4 may describe Mary in college as dishonest as a result of the indirect path connecting these concepts through "helps

---

[2]The general need for this assumption is seen with reference to Fig. 3.4. That is, if the restriction were not made, it would be possible for the activation of "Mary in college" to activate "Peter" through the intermediate node "student," or "Susan" through the intermediate activation of "feminist," and therefore for the judge to read out attributes of Peter and Susan as characteristics of Mary. This would not make much sense.

others out on exams." However, once this is done, a direct path is established between "Mary in college" and "dishonest." Mary in college may subsequently be described as dishonest without activating the intermediate node pertaining to Mary's behavior. To state this possibility more generally:

Postulate 13. *After a judge has associated two concepts by connecting them through one or more intermediate nodes, a direct path is established between them. As a result, activation of one concept may subsequently lead the other to be activated independently of the spread of excitation through the intermediate nodes that first led to their association.*

In the present context, this postulate implies that although the substructures of schemata about individual persons may originally be formed on the basis of direct contact with these persons and their behavior, they may come over time to consist of general trait descriptions as well as concrete behavioral descriptions. Moreover, these trait descriptions may often be elicited independently of and even prior to the behavioral descriptions that originally led the traits to be associated with the person being described. There are several reasons why this may be true. For one thing, there may be higher residual excitation at general trait nodes than at behavioral nodes pertaining to a particular person, since these traits are often used to describe other persons and groups. Moreover, a stimulus person is apt to manifest several behaviors that are all associated with a general trait. Thus, a judge who has described this person several times over the course of their acquaintanceship may have associated the trait with him frequently, but in each case based upon a different observed behavior. Moreover, over a period of time, traits may be associated with a person both more frequently and more recently than many of the behaviors that originally mediated these associations. The association between the trait and the stimulus person may therefore become quite strong, even though the association of any particular trait-related behavior with this person is relatively weak. This reasoning implies that the strength of a trait's association with a stimulus person should increase with the frequency with which trait-related judgments of the person have been made in the past. This suggests the following hypotheses:

Hypothesis 5a. The frequency with which traits rather than behaviors are spontaneously used to describe individual persons will increase with the length of acquaintanceship with these persons.

Hypothesis 5b. The time required to generate spontaneous trait descriptions of individual persons will decrease with the length of acquaintanceship with these persons. However, the time required to generate spontaneous behavioral descriptions of others will not vary with the length of acquaintanceship.

Two other implications of this line of reasoning are worth noting. First, the possibility that trait concepts are more often used, and thus maintain a higher level of residual excitation than behavioral concepts, suggests that while both behaviors and traits may be associated with a person immediately after the behavioral information is received, the traits may continue to be reactivated easily and used to describe the person for some time, whereas the likelihood of reactivating the behaviors that led these traits to be assigned may decrease more rapidly as time goes on. Consequently, once traits are assigned to a stimulus person on the basis of their association with the behaviors describing him, these traits, rather than the behaviors, may come to be most easily recalled for use in describing the person. We will return to the implications of this possibility in the next chapter.

A second implication is related to the above. With reference to our earlier example, suppose that a trait description of Mary (e.g., "intelligent," "liberal," etc.) has been made as a result of the mediating association of Mary with either trait-related behavior ("gets As in calculus") or a more general schema ("feminist"). Furthermore, suppose that once this is done, information is received that leads one of these intermediate paths to be "broken." That is, the judge learns that Mary no longer gets As in calculus, or that she is actually not a feminist. Despite this information, the judge may still continue to infer that Mary has the traits that were originally assigned to her on the basis of these mediating links. (Note the consistency of this implication with evidence described in Chapter 2, concerning the persisting effects of information after debriefing; cf. Ross et al., 1975; Valins, 1974.)

Hypothesis 6. Once a person has been assigned a given trait on the basis of information about his behavior, this trait and its implications will be used as a basis for subsequent descriptions of and inferences about the person, independently of the original information, and even if the original information is invalidated.

Descriptions Based on Contradictory Evidence

A final issue associated with open-ended inferences is also made salient by the hypothetical structure in Fig. 3.4. That is, the trait inferences made about a person may be contradictory. For instance, "Mary in college" is linked both to "committed" (through the mediating node "feminist") and "frivolous" (through the node "sorority member"), and is also linked indirectly to both "kind" and "unkind." In some instances, the judge will stop processing (i.e., thinking about) the stimulus concept before both contradictory trait nodes are activated, and thus before the contradiction is called to his attention. If both nodes are activated, however, the judge might do one of two things. First, he might qualify his description to reflect the possibility that Mary is in fact inconsistent (i.e., "Mary in college sometimes seemed frivolous, but nevertheless was committed to being a feminist."). Or he may resort to a higher order process to integrate the implications of the two contradictory traits into a single judgment (e.g., "somewhat committed").

An obvious question is how a judge who accesses two contradictory traits recognizes that they are inconsistent. One possibility is suggested by Smith, Shoben, and Rips (1974), who postulate that judgments of the validity of statements of the form "As are Bs" are based on a comparison of the semantic features of the two concepts involved. A similar sort of feature-comparison process may be involved here. However, it seems equally likely that the recognition that two concepts are contradictory is based upon some higher order linguistic rules, acquired through learning (e.g., the rule that the categories A and not-A are mutually exclusive). A precise statement of this process will ultimately have to be incorporated within the general formulation we are proposing.

Directed Inferences of the Relation Between Two Concepts (Verification)

A second type of inference concerns the verification of a specified relation between two concepts. Such inferences, which are typically made in response to questions such as "Is Mary kind?" or "Are professors feminists?", are similar to those used to test implications of several memory models proposed elsewhere (Collins & Loftus, 1975; Glass & Holyoak, 1975; Smith et al., 1974). However, some additional considerations arise from the fact that the categories to which social inferences pertain are generally overlapping, and the inferences themselves are probabilistic (that is, the relation between the categories is typically inferred with a probability between 0 and 1). Following Smith et al. (1974), we will assume that directed inferences are frequently based upon a comparison of the "features" associated with the concepts involved. However, our conception of a "feature" is broader than theirs, and the precise comparison processes we will postulate are somewhat different. Two additional assumptions will be made. First, since a judge's information processing capacity is limited, the number of concepts he can consider in making a judgment is assumed not to exceed a certain maximum value, k. Second, the time a judge spends in searching memory for features before making an inference is assumed not to exceed some maximum time t. Given these assumptions, the following postulates seem reasonable:

Postulate 14. When a judge is asked to infer the relation between two concepts A and B (i.e., to infer the likelihood that A is B), *he*

will activate the nodes pertaining to each concept until either
(a) a period of time t has elapsed, or (b) the excitation from
each node has activated k attribute nodes directly or in-
directly related to it, whichever occurs first.

Postulate 15.   *Once the set of k (or fewer) attributes associated with A and B*
have been identified, the likelihood that the first concept is
inferred to be an instance of the second is a function of the
proportion of attributes in the set pertaining to the second
concept (B) that are also in the set pertaining to the first (A).
(In refinements of the postulate, it may be desirable to consider
a weighting of these attributes according to the strength of
their association with the concepts to which they are linked;
however, we will ignore this complication for the time being.)

In the above analysis, no distinctions have been made in the types of
"features" or "attributes" in the sets being compared. They are simply the first
k concepts activated by excitation spreading from the two stimulus concept
nodes. Thus, they may be other concepts in the superstructure, general traits,
physical attributes, or general or specific behaviors. Moreover, they may be
specific instances of these concepts. For example, suppose the judge whose
cognitive structure is described in Fig. 3.4 is asked to estimate the likelihood
that a professor is a feminist. "Mary now" may be one of the first k nodes
activated in the set connected to each schema node, and therefore its common
membership in each list may be one of the bases for evaluating the relation
between the two concepts. This allows for the possibility that inferences about
the relation between two categories may be based not only on the similarity of
the attributes characteristic of these categories, but also on the knowledge of
specific objects that are exemplars of both categories simultaneously. On the
other hand, we have assumed that (a) paths are more apt to be directed from
subcategory nodes to more general concept nodes than vice versa; and (b)
excitation is transmitted more rapidly along a path in the forward direction
than in the reverse direction. As a result, individual instances of categories are
less likely to be contained in the sets of concepts used in comparing them than
are more superordinate categories or attributes. This suggests an additional
hypothesis:

Hypothesis 7.   The inference that members of the one group belong to a
second group is more likely to be based upon general attributes that are
shared by members of these groups than upon knowledge of individual
members or subgroups that they have in common.

For example, the inference that businessmen are Republicans is more apt
to be based upon the conviction that both businessmen and Republicans are
conservative, or that both types of persons believe in free enterprise, than

upon knowledge that specific acquaintances or subgroups are both businessmen and Republicans.

Other implications of the above postulates are more subtle. For example, Postulate 16 allows for the possibility that the inference that A is B may differ from the inference that B is A. Note that inferences of the likelihood that one concept is an instance of a second are assumed to be a function of the proportion of activated concepts associated with the second that are common to those associated with the first. Specifically, the inference that A is B is a function of the ratio n_{AB}/n_B, where n_{AB} is the number of activated concepts that are common to both lists and n_B is the number of activated concepts associated with B. However, by the same token, the likelihood that B is A is a function of the ratio n_{AB}/n_A, where n_A is the number of activated concepts associated with A. Therefore, inferences that A is B will be greater than inferences that B is A to the extent that fewer concepts associated with B are activated than concepts associated with A, or $n_B < n_A$. This makes intuitive sense. For example, the number of attributes that are strongly associated with a concept may decrease as the concept becomes more abstract (e.g., fewer attributes are closely associated with "liberal" or "conservative" than are associated with "college student" or "Richard Nixon"). Thus, relatively fewer attributes of abstract categories are apt to be activated within a given time interval.[3] Consequently, judges should infer that instances of a concrete concept are more likely to be instances of an abstract one (e.g., that college students are liberal) than the reverse (that liberals are college students).

Priming Effects

Perhaps the most heuristically interesting implication of the above analysis is that directed inferences, like open-ended ones, are somewhat unstable. This is because the concepts used as a basis for these inferences may differ, depending upon the amount of residual excitation that has accumulated at the nodes pertaining to these concepts as a result of their prior activation (or the activation of related concepts). In other words, the inference that A is B may depend upon what other concepts related to A and B have recently been thought about prior to the time the inference is made.

For example, suppose a judge with the structure described in Fig. 3.4 is asked whether professors are kind. This judgment may be based upon a

---

[3]Since abstract categories contain more *members* than concrete categories, and individual instances of these categories are included in the sets of concepts being compiled, one might argue that a greater number of concepts will be sampled in the case of abstract categories than in the case of concrete ones. However, the paths connecting exemplars to general categories are typically directed from the exemplar to the category. Thus, excitation spreading from the general category to its exemplars takes more time to be transmitted, and therefore these exemplar nodes are less apt to be activated within any given time interval than are other types of concepts.

comparison of the first k features activated by excitation spreading from "professor" with the first k features activated by excitation spreading from "kind." However, the set of these concepts may not be the same if "Mary now" has recently been activated as would be if "George" had recently been activated or if neither particular instance of a professor had been activated. Alternatively, the inference that "Mary now" is a liberal may depend upon whether the judge's recent experiences have caused "feminist" or "professor" to be activated. Two general hypotheses seem reasonable on the basis of this analysis.

Hypothesis 8. A judge's inference of the likelihood that members of one category belong to a second will be greater if the judge has recently made judgments of persons whose attributes are associated with members of these categories than if he has made judgments of persons whose attributes are not associated with members of these categories. (Note: This should be true regardless of whether the persons themselves are members of the categories involved in the relation.)

Hypothesis 9. A judge's inference of the likelihood that a particular stimulus person has a given attribute will be increased by calling the judge's attention to social groups to which the person belongs and that are characterized by this attribute. (This should occur regardless of whether the stimulus person's membership in the group being "primed" is actually mentioned, or whether the judge is implicitly or explicitly asked to consider this membership.)

Finally, Postulate 13 implies that once a relation between two concepts has been verified, a direct link between the concepts is established, and therefore the relation will be verified more readily (and quickly) in the future. Thus, if a judge with the structure described in Fig. 3.4 confirms that Mary now is a liberal on the basis of the comparison processes described in Postulate 15, "liberal" will become directly associated with "Mary now." Consequently, "Mary now" will be inferred to be "liberal" in the future without the necessity of undergoing this comparison process. Moreover, since "liberal" is presumably associated with many other traits and behaviors in the judge's semantic structure (or implicit personality theory), "Mary now" will be judged more likely to have other characteristics that had previously been only remotely associated with her.

Response Time Differences

The preceding discussion has ignored possible differences in the time required to verify relations of the form "A is B," and the implications of these differences for cognitive functioning. There are at least two reasons why differences in verification time may occur. First, the k concepts used as a basis for comparing A and B may differ in the strength of their association with these concepts, and thus in the widths of the paths connecting them to the concept nodes. This suggests the following hypothesis:

Hypothesis 10. The time required to verify a relation between two categories of persons, or between a person and a group, is inversely related to the average strength of the relations between each category and the attributes most closely associated with each category.

Thus, for example, a judge's inference that businessmen are conservative should be made more quickly if the judge has a strong stereotype of one or both types or persons (and thus the attributes comprising the schema substructure are closely associated with the schema node) than if he does not.

Given that the judge has identified the two sets of attributes associated with the concepts being related, it may take additional time to compare them. In general, it seems reasonable to suppose that this comparison process will take less time when A and B have either many attributes in common or few in common (so that it is immediately clear whether or not they are related) than when they have a moderate number of common attributes (so that the relation is more ambiguous). For one thing, it may simply be easier to estimate the number of attributes the two sets have in common when nearly all or very few attributes of B are shared by A than when the overlap is more moderate. Also, the subjective "calculation" of the proportion of attributes of B that are shared by A may be easier when this proportion is very high or very low than when it is moderate. Smith et al. (1974) have found that the time required to verify a relation between two concepts is in fact less when the concepts are either semantically very similar or semantically very dissimilar than when their semantic features overlap to a moderate extent. The comparison processes they postulate to account for this are somewhat different from those assumed here. However, both the empirical evidence they report and the reasoning outlined above suggest the following hypothesis:

Hypothesis 11. The time required to infer the relation between two categories will be less when these categories have either many attributes in common or few in common than when they have a moderate number in common.

Note that according to the above analysis, the two factors postulated in Hypotheses 10 and 11 are independent, and therefore could combine additively to affect response times. This possibility can be empirically tested.

Inferences Based upon Several Attributes

The third type of inference is really just an extension of the first two. Here, the judge is asked to make an inference on the basis of a set of features rather than a single concept. For example, he may be asked to make inferences about a real or hypothetical person on the basis of information about several of this person's characteristics (traits, behaviors, role descriptions, etc.). These inferences may be either open-ended or directed. For example, judges may be asked what they think of intelligent feminists. Alternatively, they may be given a configuration of attributes describing a person and asked to predict whether the person would make a "successful graduate student."

The processes underlying these inferences may potentially be accounted for by Postulates 4–15. Excitation may emanate from many nodes simultaneously. The total excitation accumulating at any particular node is presumably the sum of the excitation transmitted to it along paths from other activated nodes. Thus, if the judge whose cognitive system is represented in Fig. 3.4 is asked to characterize an intelligent feminist, this description may activate "intelligent" and "feminist," and the combined excitation spreading from these nodes may serve to activate "Mary in college." Excitation may spread from this node to others (e.g., "Mary now" and attributes associated with it) that are used as a basis for the inference. This judge may thus infer that an intelligent feminist is likely to wind up as a kind university professor who dresses informally and makes one feel good when she is around. (Note the similarity between this example and the examples of script processing given in Chapter 2, concerning the prediction of graduate student performance.)

One implication of this conceptualization is that the greater the correspondence between stimulus attributes and attributes associated with a given schema node, the more quickly excitation will accumulate at the schema node, the more quickly the node will be activated, and the more likely it is that concepts related to this node will be used in making the inference. Note that schema nodes may be part of a vignette of the sort described in Chapter 2. Thus, the likelihood that a vignette (or the script in which it is contained) will be used to make inferences should increase with the correspondence between stimulus information and the schemata contained in this vignette.

The above examples pertain to open-ended inferences. In the case of directed inferences (i.e., judgments of the extent to which a person has a particular characteristic, or belongs to a specified category), three possibilities arise. Suppose a judge is asked whether a person described by stimulus information has a characteristic B. Once a particular schema in the superstructure has been activated by excitation from the nodes to which the information pertains, the judge may base his inference upon the similarity of features associated with this schema to those associated with B, in the manner implied by Postulates 14 and 15. For example, if the judge whose structure is described in Fig. 3.4 is asked whether an intelligent feminist is likely to be a professor, he may first activate "Mary in college," and then base his inference on a comparison between the attributes associated with this schema and those associated with "professor."

A second possibility is that the judge may simply make a direct comparison of the attributes associated with the target category ("professor") with those described in the stimulus information presented ("intelligent" and "feminist"), without activating a previously formed schema and the concepts in its substructure. The implications of these alternative possibilities differ in one important respect. The first comparison is not restricted to attributes described in the stimulus information, but includes additional attributes contained in the schema activated by this information. In the second case, however, only the attributes described in the stimulus information are used as a basis for comparison. The second case seems more likely to apply when situational factors predispose the judge to treat each piece of information separately, rather than thinking of a particular person described by the entire configuration. (Certain of these predisposing factors were noted in Chapter 2; others will be considered in detail in Chapter 8, where we discuss the applicability of algebraic formulations of information integration.)

A third, related possibility may arise when the stimulus attributes are not connected to a single node but are instead connected to nodes that are remote from one another in memory. For example, suppose the stimulus information described a person as "kind" and "brutal." These concepts are remotely associated in the judge's implicit personality theory, and are unlikely to be connected to the same schema node in the superstructure. Rather, different schemata are apt to be activated by this information, each pertaining to a different individual or group. In this instance, the judge may consider the implications of each piece of information separately, and may resort to a higher order process for integrating these implications (see Chapter 8).

3.3 THE ORGANIZATION AND USE OF SCRIPTS AND VIGNETTES

Our discussion of the organization of concepts in memory has focused upon schemata about persons and groups and the concepts associated with them. Although these schemata are fundamental ingredients of vignettes and scripts of the sort described in Chapter 2, the preceding discussion obviously does not capture all of the phenomena implied by a script-processing conceptualization. For one thing, a judge's representation of a person or object may depend considerably on the situational context in which this person or object is considered. To use an earlier example, the representation of "dog" elicited by the statement "the dog plays with the baby" may be quite different from the representation elicted by the statement "the dog frightens strangers." These differences are not simply a result of differences in the attributes directly associated with "plays with the baby" and "frightens strangers," but rather are unique to the "dog" schemata in the vignettes respectively activated by these two statements.[4] Similarly, the attributes a male uses to describe a female acquaintance may depend to some extent upon the particular situation in which he envisions her (e.g., giving a class lecture, or talking over a glass of wine). A mechanism must be provided for describing these situation-specific representations of persons and objects. Moreover, there must be a way to portray the organization of the schemata comprising a series of vignettes in scripts or sets of scripts.

Theoretically, the validity of Postulates 1–15 is independent of the particular manner in which information is organized in memory. Thus, to the extent that vignettes function as complex sets of concepts, these postulates have implications for script-based inference processes as well as those based on schemata per se. Efforts have been made to conceptualize the schematic representation of scripts and vignettes (Rumelhart & Ortony, 1977; Schank & Abelson, 1977). Rather than entering into a detailed discussion of this work, we will provide a simplified example of the possible representation of scripts and vignettes within the framework we have proposed in this chapter.

To do this, we will have to reconsider certain simplifying assumptions underlying our previous analysis. First, although it has been convenient to consider an actor's behavior (e.g., "helps") and the object of this behavior ("old ladies") as a single configural concept ("helps old ladies"), we will now need to treat them as separate concepts, as suggested by J. R. Anderson and Bower (1973). Second, we will need to take more seriously our earlier postulation that a general schema in the superstructure is divided into subschemata, each of which has its own substructure of attributes and concepts. Each of these subschemata may be a component of a different vignette.

Given these assumptions, vignettes and scripts may be represented in a manner similar to that suggested in previous sections of this chapter. As we noted in Chapter 2, the caption of a vignette may often be conveyed in a sentence of the form "A verbs B" (e.g., "a dog barks at strangers"). The component terms in this caption refer to three subschemata—one pertaining to A ("dog"), another to B ("stranger") and another to A's action ("barks"). Each subschema is related to a more general or abstract schema that is situationally independent.

The subschemata of objects and events in a vignette may be connected to those in other vignettes either directly or through the more general schema to

---

[4]That this is true can be seen intuitively by considering the description of the actor in each cell of a 2 × 2 design involving the type of actor ("the dog" vs. "the mother") and the type of behavior ("plays with the baby" vs. "frightens strangers"). Clearly, the effect of the behavioral description on characteristics attributed to the mother is qualitatively different from its effect on characteristics attributed to the dog.

which they are subordinate. For example, the subschema of "dog" in a "dog keeping away strangers" vignette may be connected to the subschema of "dog" in a "dog playing with children" vignette through their common relation to a more general schema of dog that is not situation-specific. A fragment of a judge's cognitive network containing these and other vignettes might be similar to that shown in Fig. 3.5. The triad of subschemata comprising each vignette is enclosed in dotted lines; each subschema is subscripted to indicate different instances of the more general schema to which it is subordinate. For simplicity, only schemata and subschemata are shown; the various attributes comprising their substructures are not indicated. Direct pathways connecting subschemata contained in different vignettes are also not indicated. These latter connections seem most likely to exist between temporally related vignettes describing a sequence of events. Here, it is reasonable to postulate a direct pathway connecting the "event" subschema (i.e., the verb concept) of one vignette with that of a second that temporally precedes or follows it. In such cases, a script may be viewed as a set of subschema triads that are connected by direct paths between the event subschemata contained in them.

The cognitive processes involved in accessing and using concepts in this network may be similar to those implied by Postulates 1–15. For example, suppose a judge with the cognitive structure described in Fig. 3.5 learns that a house has been robbed in his neighborhood. This may activate the node "$robs_5$," and "$house_5$" in the "stranger robs house" vignette, and thus should activate "$stranger_5$." Excitation from this node would then be transmitted to other nodes in the manner we postulated earlier, leading certain of these nodes to be activated. The order in which these nodes were activated should generally depend on the widths of the paths connecting them. Thus, the judge's flow of thought in the above example might be represented verbally as follows: "I see a house was robbed last night (initial stimulus). Probably some stranger did it. A fence would keep away strangers. But so would a dog. A dog would keep away cats as well. Children would like to have a dog to play with them. However, dogs mess up furniture. Besides, . . ."

The above example is of course incomplete. For one thing, it does not take into account the *directive* function of thought. Implicit in the above example is the cognizer's objective to prevent robberies and to evaluate alternative means of doing so. For example, once the "keeps away" schema node is accessed in reacting to the original stimulus information, it may be continually reactivated by the judge as he tries to make a decision about the best way to keep away strangers. (Such a decision may ultimately involve higher order processes of the sort mentioned in Chapter 2 and elaborated later in this book.)

Despite the general "directiveness" of thought, the cognizer's associations may detour his thoughts into marginally relevant vignettes. Hence, despite his

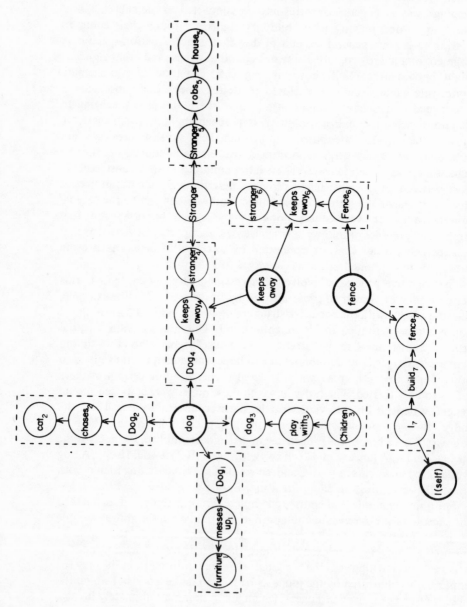

FIG. 3.5. Hypothetical portion of judge's cognitive network containing vignettes. Each set of nodes enclosed in dashed lines comprises a vignette.

central concern with preventing robberies, the judge in this example began to consider the pros and cons of owning dogs. Such a diversion would be most likely if the "dog" schema had been recently invoked, so that the various nodes involved possessed residual excitation and were easily activated. If these nodes had not been recently activated, the same train of thought would be unlikely, and might even appear nonsensical. Thus, if the judge were to state "I saw this article about a robbery, and it occurred to me that the kids might like to have a dog to play with," others might fail to see the "logic" involved. (Such "wild" leaps of thought are, in fact, frequently noticeable in conversation, particularly among children, who have not yet learned which of their associations are likely to be common to their audience.)

The dynamics of many inference processes involving vignettes and scripts of the sort described in Fig. 3.5 may be governed by Postulates 1–15. One obvious implication of these postulates, as suggested above, is that the nature of the attributes used to describe an object will depend upon which related vignette has been more recently activated. Thus, a judge with a cognitive system described in Fig. 3.5 may describe a dog differently if he accesses "dog$_4$" (in the vignette of a dog keeping away strangers) than if he accesses "dog$_3$" (in the vignette of a dog playing with children). The extent to which these subschemata are used as a basis for inferences may in turn depend upon how recently they have been activated in the past, and thus how much additional excitation is necessary to reactivate them. To this extent, many "priming" effects, as well as tendencies to rely upon concrete rather than abstract information in making inferences (p. 59), can be taken into account by the conceptualization we have proposed.

3.4 RELEVANT RESEARCH

Specific hypotheses derived from Postulates 1–15 have not been tested at this writing. However, the general implications of the proposed formulation are consistent with much contemporary research in social cognition. Two such implications are particularly worth noting at this time. First, the formulation implies that judges' inferences about a stimulus object may be influenced by systematically "priming" certain concepts that are directly or indirectly related to that object. Second, if a set of concepts or attributes have already been organized around a schema node pertaining to a person (or group), it should normally take less time to make inferences about the attributes of this person (or group), and these inferences should be made with greater probability, than if this a priori organization did not exist. Research bearing upon both matters is described below.

Priming Effects on Judgments

A Direct Test of Priming Effects on Impression Formation

The proposed formulation implies that if a concept has been activated in the course of making one judgment, some residual excitation should remain at the concept node, thereby increasing the likelihood that the node will be reactivated by other concepts that are connected to it. More simply, this implies that the likelihood of using a concept to encode one piece of information will increase to the extent that the concept has been previously activated for use in processing other information. Moreover, this priming effect should increase with the amount of residual excitation that exists at the concept node at the time the information is presented. Thus, it should increase with the number of times the concept has been previously activated, or primed, but should decrease with the time interval between the priming and the presentation of the information to be encoded.

These hypotheses were tested by Srull and Wyer (see Wyer & Srull, in press). Subjects initially performed a sentence construction task which was described as a test of how people perceive word relationships. This task was one of a series of four ostensibly unrelated experiments being conducted over the course of two experimental sessions. The task, patterned after a measure developed by Costin (1969) for a quite different purpose, consisted of a number of items, each of which required the subject to underline three words in a set of four that would make a complete sentence. Two possible sentences could be constructed from each item. However, in some cases (e.g., leg break arm his), all possible sentences conveyed hostility, whereas in other cases (e.g., paint box the pack) they did not. Responding to the first type of items was assumed to activate hostility-related concepts, and thus to prime these concepts for future use. Both the number and the proportion of these items in the questionnaire were varied over experimental conditions. Specifically, subjects completed either 30 or 60 items, either 20% (6 or 12 items) or 80% (24 or 48) of which were hostility related.

After completing the priming task, subjects were told that the remaining experiments were being conducted by someone else, and were either turned over immediately to another experimenter, told to return one hour later, or told to return 24 hours later. In all cases, the second experimenter began by administering part of an ostensibly unrelated study of impression formation.[5] Subjects in this phase first read a paragraph about a target person that described a series of events in the person's life. Some of the events (e.g.,

---

[5] Subjects' responses to a post-experimental questionnaire about which parts of the four tasks administered were related to the same hypothesis revealed that virtually no subjects realized that this task was formally connected to the one preceding it.

refusing to pay the rent until the landlord painted his apartment) could be interpreted as conveying either hostile acts or relatively neutral ones. Subjects were asked to form an impression of the person and then to rate him along a series of dimensions, some of which (e.g., hostile, kind, considerate, etc.) were directly related to hostility and others of which (boring, narrow-minded, interesting, intelligent, etc.) were evaluatively toned but unrelated to hostility. (Factor analyses confirmed this clustering.)

Ratings of the target persons along each set of dimensions are shown in Fig. 3.6 as a function of experimental manipulations. The priming effects are readily apparent. Moreover, the magnitude of the effect decreased over time as expected, but was a positive function of the number of times hostility was primed, independently of the number of filler items. The effect of priming generalized to judgments of the target along dimensions that were evaluative but not directly related to hostility, although these effects were less in magnitude. This generalization suggests that the target person, after having been judged as hostile, may also have been inferred to have other traits that were related to this characteristic in judges' semantic structure, or "implicit personality theory." While other formulations than the one proposed in this chapter can also account for these effects (see Wyer & Srull, in press), their consistency with this formulation is noteworthy.

A second test of priming effects in impression formation was conducted by Higgins, Rholes, and Jones (1977). In this study, subjects were initially exposed to one of two paired associated tasks. The response words used in each task were similar in their descriptive implications. However, the words were evaluatively positive (e.g., "self-confident," "bold," etc.) in one case and evaluatively negative ("conceited," "foolhardy," etc.) in the other. Then, ostensibly as part of a different study, subjects read a paragraph about a stimulus person whose behavior could be plausibly described by either set of test words. After reading the paragraph, subjects estimated how well they liked the person. Subjects evaluated the stimulus person more favorably when the priming words to which they had previously been exposed were evaluatively positive than when these words were evaluatively negative. Similar effects did not occur under control conditions in which the priming words used in the association task were also either favorable or unfavorable but were inappropriate for describing the stimulus person's behavior. These results, like Srull and Wyer's, suggest that judges interpreted the stimulus person's behavior as instances of concepts made salient to them in the priming task, and that the evaluative implications of these concepts then affected their later judgments of the person.

Evidence of Priming in Other Experimental Paradigms

Other evidence that the activation of a concept increases the judge's use of that or related concepts in subsequent inference making has been obtained in

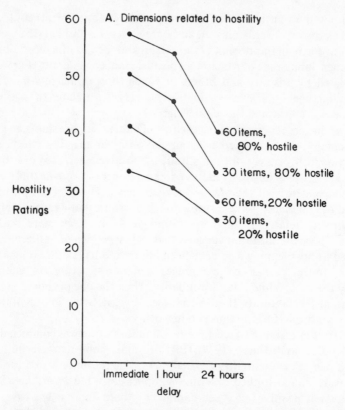

FIG. 3.6.   Mean ratings of target person along (a) dimensions related to hostility and

a variety of different situations. Much of this research is of specific relevance to issues raised in later chapters, and will be discussed in detail in the context of those issues. However, a brief summary of representative research will be provided here to convey the diversity of issues to which priming effects are relevant.

1. Kelley (1955) asked Catholic and non-Catholic subjects to report their religious beliefs after reading a biography of either the Pope or a nonreligious figure. Catholics who had read the Pope's biography subsequently conformed less to bogus group norms opposing Catholic dogma than did either Catholics who had read the nonreligious biography or non-Catholics who had read either biography. The Pope's biography contained no direct information pertaining to religious doctrine or practices. However, reading it may have activated a variety of related religious concepts among Catholic subjects (not

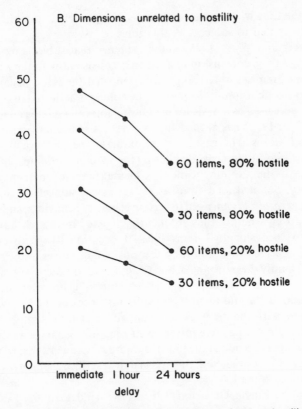

FIG. 3.6. (*cont.*) (b) evaluative dimensions unrelated to hostility as a function of number of priming items, percentage of priming items, and time interval between priming and stimulus presentation.

the least of which may have been the concept of themselves as Catholic) that were not activated by Catholics who had not read the biography, or by non-Catholics (who presumably did not have the concepts). These concepts may subsequently have influenced subjects' questionnaire responses.

2. Gouaux (1969) examined the effects of subjects' mood on their attraction to others. Some subjects first read statements expressing positive feelings ("I feel great!") while others read statements conveying negative feelings ("I wish I could go to sleep and never wake up"). Then all subjects evaluated a stimulus person on the basis of information about his attitudes. The first group of subjects reported greater attraction to the stimulus person than did the second. One explanation is that reading the positive statements activated certain evaluatively favorable concepts about people in general, while reading the negative statements activated concepts that were evaluatively unfavorable. These different concepts may have remained

activated at the time when subjects evaluated the particular stimulus person, and thus contributed to subjects' evaluations.

3. Henninger and Wyer (1976) found evidence that subjects report their beliefs in a syllogistic conclusion in a manner consistent with their beliefs in the syllogism's premises only if they have reported the latter beliefs before considering the conclusion. Presumably, the concepts activated in evaluating the premises were used as a basis for evaluating logically related conclusions.

4. Bem (1965, 1972) has argued that a person's self-judgments are based upon the implications of his past behavior. If this is true, one should be able to affect a person's self-judgments by altering the specific subsample of his past behavior that is salient to him at the time he makes these judgments. To test this possibility, Salancik and Conway (1975) asked subjects in one group whether they *occasionally* engaged in certain religious behaviors, and subjects in a second group whether they *frequently* engaged in these behaviors. In responding to "occasionally" items (i.e., "I occasionally go to church"), subjects were expected to search for a few positive instances of the behavior described, to identify these instances, and to agree with the items. In responding to "frequently" items ("I frequently go to church"), however, they were expected to search for and identify negative instances of the behavior, and thus to disagree with the items. As a result, subjects in the first group were expected to have more positive instances of religious behavior accessible to them than the second group at the time they were subsequently asked to judge their religiousness. As predicted, the first group described themselves as more religious than the second.

5. In a study by Lingle, Geva and Ostrom (1975) judges inferred a stimulus person's suitability for two occupations on the basis of four traits describing this person. In some cases, the two occupations required similar skills (e.g., store clerk vs. salesman), while in other cases, the two occupations were dissimilar (dentist vs. public accountant). Judges took less time to infer the stimulus person's suitability for the second occupation when it was similar to the first occupation they considered than when it was different. In the first case, asking judges to consider the first occupation apparently increased the accessibility of cognitions relevant to the second judgment, and thus increased the speed with which this judgment was made.

6. In an unpublished study by Carlston, discussed in Chapter 2, subjects made several inferences about high-school basketball teams after receiving their season's records and background information. Embedded in the background information were different explanatory scripts. These scripts were actually unrelated to the specific team being evaluated, but were intended to activate concepts useful in interpreting the team's performance. Scripts associated with the activated stimulus concepts were more often used to explain the team's performance than were scripts that had not been primed in this manner. Furthermore, the primed scripts continued to affect inferences

made from entirely different sets of stimulus information, provided the stimulus characteristics were sufficiently similar to those of schemata contained in the script.

Much of the above research, as well as other evidence of priming effects, will be noted in more detail in the chapters to follow.

The Role of Cognitive Schemata in Social Judgments

A spreading-excitation formulation implies that the greater the number of stimulus attributes that are contained in a given schema substructure, the more likely it is that this schemata will be activated, and therefore the more likely it is that subsequent inferences will be based upon this schema and the attributes related to it. A recent study by Cantor and Mischel (1977) bears upon this possibility. Judges first received trait information about stimulus persons that conveyed either (a) extraversion, (b) introversion, or (c) neither of these characteristics. In some conditions, the stimulus persons were explicitly described as representative of these personality types, while in other cases they were not. After receiving the information, judges read a list of traits including some from the original stimulus list and some new traits similarly varying in degree of implied extraversion. They were then asked both (a) to recall whether each trait was in the original stimulus list; and (b) to estimate the extent to which the stimulus person possessed the trait, regardless of whether it was in the original list. Stimulus persons were judged to have new traits associated with extraversion to a greater extent if they had previously been described by traits typical of an extravert than if they previously had been described by traits typical of an introvert. This was true regardless of whether the stimulus person had been explicitly characterized as extraverted or introverted. In addition, judges were more likely to recall traits that were not in the original stimulus set as having been in this set if they were consistent with the personality type conveyed by the stimulus configuration. This suggests that once a schema of a person is activated, judges may confuse the original information that led to its activation with other characteristics comprising the schema substructure, but not actually presented.

These data are consistent with our earlier suggestion that inferences based on several pieces of information may be mediated by the activation of a previously formed schema of a person or group. In this context, it is important to note that in control conditions, where judges were told that the stimulus person was either extraverted or introverted but the other traits in the description were not related to either personality type, the above differences in recognition did not occur. Thus, simply labelling the stimulus person as extraverted or introverted was neither necessary nor sufficient to activate a general schema of an extravert or introvert when the stimulus person's other characteristics did not fit this schema.

A second implication of the spreading-excitation formulation is that judgments of a person's attributes will be made more quickly if these attributes are closely associated with a previously formed schema node pertaining to that person. A study concerned with the effects of self-schemata on self-judgments (Markus, 1977) is relevant to this hypothesis. Judges were selected for this study on the basis of a pre-experiment questionnaire in which they described themselves as either highly independent, highly dependent, or neither. "Independent" was presumably contained in the self-schema substructures of judges in the first group, whereas "dependent" was contained in the self-schema substructures of judges in the second, and neither trait was strongly associated with the self-schemata of judges in the third. In the experiment, all three groups of judges were presented with individual adjectives that were semantically related to either "independent" or "dependent," and were asked to indicate whether each adjective did or did not describe them. The time required to report these judgments was recorded. Judges of course tended to assign traits to themselves that were consistent with their self-schema substructures. More interesting are the response time differences. Independent judges took less time to identify independent-related traits as characteristic of themselves than dependent-related ones, whereas dependent judges took more time to do so. Moreover, judges whose self-schemata contained neither "independent" nor "dependent" did not differ in their responses to the two types of adjectives. These data are therefore quite consistent with the spreading-excitation formulation we have proposed.

Effects of Thought on Polarization of Judgments. A final implication of the proposed formulation is perhaps the most interesting. Suppose that characteristics of a stimulus are generally similar to those that comprise a previously formed schema substructure. Then, presentation of the stimulus should lead the schema to be activated and used as a basis for judgment. Moreover, the longer the stimulus is thought about, the more attributes of the schema substructure should be activated, and therefore the more representative of this schema the stimulus should be judged to be. This suggests that judgments of the stimulus should become more polarized (i.e., the stimulus should be viewed as more similar to the prototypic schema) as one thinks about it for a longer period of time. On the other hand, this shift in judgment should not occur if a previously formed schema relevant to the judgment is unavailable.

Recent work by Tesser and his colleagues (Tesser, 1976; Tesser & Conlee, 1975; Tesser & Cowan, 1975, 1977) is of direct relevance to this hypothesis. In a typical situation, a judge is first asked to evaluate a series of test stimuli of a given type. Based on these judgments, a test stimulus is selected that has been evaluated either moderately favorably or moderately unfavorably. The judge is then either asked to think more carefully about this stimulus for a standard time period or is distracted from doing so. Finally the judge is asked to reevaluate the stimulus. If the initial rating of the stimulus is based upon the similarity of its attributes to those in a prototypic schema of a "good" or "bad" exemplar, then judgments of the stimulus should become more extreme under thought conditions but should not change appreciably under distraction conditions. This is typically the case. Moreover, the "polarization effect" increases in magnitude with the amount of time that the stimulus is continually processed under thought conditions (Tesser & Conlee, 1975).

If the above reasoning is correct, however, the effect should occur only if judges have a previously formed schema to use in judging the stimulus presented. Two studies by Tesser and Leone (1977) bear on this matter. In one study, judges were presented sets of stimulus adjectives and were told to rate either (a) a single person who possessed each set of attributes, or (b) a group of persons, each described by a different adjective in the set. It seems reasonable to assume that judges have previously formed schemata for judging individual persons but not for judging groups of unrelated persons. Consistent with this assumption, the polarization effect was significantly greater when individuals were judged than when groups were judged.

In a second study, male and female subjects were asked to consider either football plays or women's fashions. Males were assumed to have previously formed schemata for evaluating football plays but not women's fashions, whereas females were assumed to have previously formed schemata for evaluating fashions but not football plays. Consistent with predictions based on these assumptions, the polarization effect for football judgments was greater for males than for females, whereas the effect for fashion judgments was greater for females than for males.

A Note of Caution. While the phenomenon reported by Tesser is provocative, some caution should be taken in interpreting it and evaluating its generality. For one thing, there are other, somewhat more mundane interpretations of the results. For example, people who are asked to give a spontaneous reaction to a stimulus without much thought may not report a judgment as extreme as they feel may be justified due to apprehension over appearing foolish if future events should prove them wrong. However, if further thought does not alter their initial reaction, they may become more confident of the validity of their initial reaction and thus more inclined to report a judgment consistent with it. To this extent, the results obtained by Tesser and his colleagues may not indicate that thought increases the polarization of subjective judgments of a stimulus. Rather, they may reflect a "cautiousness" about reporting these judgments in the *absence* of thought.

In addition, none of the studies cited above provides direct evidence about the nature of the cognitive schemata that we assume to underlie the effects obtained. Nor is the theoretical nature of these schemata clearly stated. The formulation proposed in this chapter, or a refinement of it, may be helpful in clarifying these matters.

3.5 ALTERNATIVE FORMULATIONS

While the spreading-excitation formulation of memory has many interesting implications, alternative conceptualizations are also important to consider. Two such formulations may be worth noting briefly. One, also a network model, has been proposed by J. R. Anderson and Bower (1973). A second, quite different approach, which relaxes many of the formal structural assumptions required by a network formulation, has recently been suggested by Wyer and Srull (in press).

Anderson and Bower's Model of Associative Memory

While the network formulation proposed in this chapter has been applied primarily to the organization of previously acquired information and its effect upon inferences, Anderson and Bower focussed on the acquisition and storage of new information about persons and events. The formulation proposed in this chapter can also be applied to these phenomena as well as to the organization of previously acquired information and its effects on inferences. In fact, the proposed formulation can account for many of the same results predicted on the basis of Anderson and Bower's model, as we shall see. Nevertheless, the alternative approach and the assumptions underlying it are worth mention.

Statement of the Model

As Anderson and Bower note, a piece of new information about a person may often be conveyed in a propositional sentence (e.g., "the hippie is a teenager," "the hippie kissed the debutante," etc.). Such a sentence may be represented schematically in a tree structure consisting of two main branches, one pertaining to the subject of the sentence and the other to its predicate. The subject typically refers to a person (e.g., "the hippie") and the predicate typically refers to an attribute of this person such as his membership in a general category ("is a teenager") or a behavior he has manifested ("kissed the debutante"). The predicate may often be further broken down into a relation ("kissed") and an object ("the debutante"). Qualifications upon the event (i.e., when and where it occurred) can also be represented. However, for our present purposes we will restrict our attention to simple sentences, and will assume that each predicate functions as a single unit or concept.

An important implication of Anderson and Bower's formulation is that the manner in which information is organized may depend upon the order in

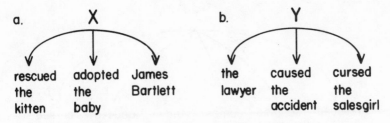

FIG. 3.7.   Theoretical network representations of information about (a) James Bartlett and (b) the lawyer.

which it is received. Consider an example taken from J. R. Anderson and Hastie (1974) that is particularly relevant to the representation of information about persons. Suppose a judge receives information that a person, James Bartlett, "rescued the kitten and adopted the baby." This information might be represented in memory in a manner analogous to that shown in Fig. 3.7a. In this diagram, the node X represents the concept about whom the information is presented, and the nodes "rescued the kitten" (a_1), "adopted the baby" (a_2), and "James Bartlett" represent properties of this concept. Note that a distinction is made between the name of the concept, "James Bartlett," and the concept itself. This is an important aspect of the formulation, as we shall see presently. Similarly, suppose the judge is also told that "the lawyer caused the accident and cursed the salesgirl." This information would be represented as shown in Fig. 3.7b, where in this case, "the lawyer," "caused the accident" (b_1), and "cursed the salesgirl" (b_2) are nodes representing properties of the concept Y.[6]

The effects of order of presentation on the organization of information became apparent when a judge is informed that James Bartlett is the lawyer either before or after receiving the behavioral information. If the information that James Bartlett is the lawyer is received beforehand, "James Bartlett" and "the lawyer" should be associated through a common node, X, representing both labels, and the behavior attributed to each will be related directly to this node as shown in Fig. 3.8a. However, if the judge is told that James Bartlett is the lawyer *after* receiving the behavioral information, the organization is likely to differ. Since there was no reason to assume that James Bartlett and the lawyer were the same person at the time the behavioral information was presented, two nodes, X and Y, would probably be formed, much as in the separate diagrams shown in Figs. 3.7a and 3.7b. The subsequent information that James Bartlett is the lawyer would then presumably lead either to an

---

[6]Anderson and Bower distinguish between a proper name, "James Bartlett," and a definite description, such as "the lawyer," since the latter is an instance of a more general category, lawyer, whereas "James Bartlett" is not. For our present purposes, however, this distinction is not important.

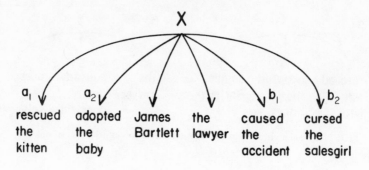

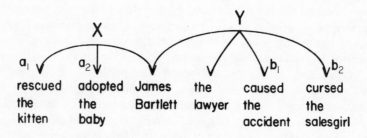

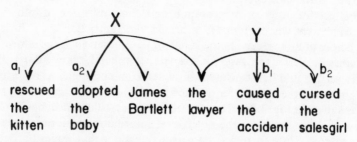

FIG. 3.8. Alternative cognitive representations of information about James Bartlett and the lawyer.

association between the name "James Bartlett" and the concept node Y, or to an association between the name "the lawyer" and the concept node X, producing one of the alternative structures described in Figs. 3.8b and 3.8c, respectively.

These structures have different implications for recall and inference processes under the two order conditions. For example, suppose a judge who is asked whether James Bartlett caused the accident responds by verifying the path connecting the two elements in memory. In the "Before" condition, this path consists of two links: "James Bartlett is X," "X caused the accident." In the "After" condition, however, the number of links depends upon the nature of the structure assumed. If the diagram in Fig. 3.8b is correct, the path would again consist of only two links: "James Bartlett is Y" and "Y caused the accident." However, if Fig. 3.8c is correct, four links would be involved: "James Bartlett is X"; "X is the lawyer"; "the lawyer is Y"; and "Y caused the accident." Alternatively, suppose the judge was asked to verify the statement "the lawyer rescued the kitten." Two links would again be required to establish this relation under Before conditions ("the lawyer is X"; "X rescued the kitten"). Under After conditions, four links would be required if Fig. 3.8b is correct ("the lawyer is Y"; "Y is James Bartlett"; "James Bartlett is X"; "X rescued the kitten") and two if Fig. 3.8c is correct ("the lawyer is X"; "X rescued the kitten").

Empirical Evidence

Anderson and Hastie (1974) tested the implications of the above analysis in a study that demonstrates the usefulness of reaction time procedures in diagnosing the organization of information about persons. Judges learned a set of propositions of the form "James Bartlett did A" and "the lawyer did B" either before or after they were told that James Bartlett was the lawyer. Then, in each condition, they were asked to verify both the original propositions ("James Bartlett did A," "the lawyer did B") and also new propositions that were derivable from the information ("James Bartlett did B" and "the lawyer did A"). The time required to make these verifications is shown in Table 3.1. Under Before conditions, the time required to verify derived propositions and original propositions was similar. This is consistent with the implications of the structure described in Fig. 3.8a. That is, predicates about James Bartlett and the lawyer under Before conditions emanate from a common concept node, and thus require the same number of links to verify. Under After conditions, however, the time to verify derived propositions about the lawyer ("the lawyer did A") was much greater than the time to verify original propositions about him and was also much greater than the time to verify the same propositions under Before conditions. These data are consistent with the structure shown in Fig. 3.8b, which predicts that four links are required to connect the concepts "the lawyer" and "did A," while only two are required to connect the concepts "the lawyer" and "did B."

Comparison of the times required to verify propositions about James Bartlett under After conditions raises an additional consideration. Fig. 3.8b suggests that two steps are required to verify both original propositions about James Bartlett ("James Bartlett is X"; "X did A") and derived propositions

("James Bartlett is Y"; "Y did B"). Based on the number of steps alone, the time required to verify the two types of propositions should not differ. In fact, however, derived propositions about James Bartlett were verified significantly more *rapidly* than original ones. This surprising finding is consistent with an additional assumption made by Anderson and Bower, namely, that in searching memory to establish relations like those in the present task, the more recently established paths are processed first. Thus, under After conditions, the path connecting "James Bartlett" to Y is more recently established than that connecting "James Bartlett" to X. As a result, the former path, and consequently concepts connected to Y (predicates of the form "did B"), will be searched before concepts connected to X (predicates of the form "did A"). This should increase the time required to verify propositions of the form "James Bartlett did A" in relation to the time required to verify derived propositions ("James Bartlett did B") under the After condition, and also in relation to the average time required to verify "James Bartlett did A" under Before conditions. Data in Table 3.1 are perfectly consistent with these hypotheses.

One further finding reported by Anderson and Hastie is of interest. Specifically, the differences described in Table 3.1 were greater during the initial phase of the recall and inference task than they were later on. Anderson and Hastie postulate that as a result of verifying derived statements of the form "the lawyer did A," the predicate "did A" becomes "copied" from node X to node Y. As a result, the sentence can subsequently be verified directly, in much the same manner as "the lawyer did B." This interpretation is of theoretical interest since it suggests that the representation of information about persons is affected not only by new information about these persons but also by inferences one makes about them on the basis of information already available. This is consistent with Postulate 13.

Errors in Recall. Although we have focused primarily on the use of reaction time data to diagnose differences in the organization of information, these differences should also affect the accuracy of recall. Specifically, as the complexity of the cognitive processes required to verify a proposition increases, the verification may not only take longer but is also more likely to be incorrect (i.e., the judge is more apt to conclude that a true proposition is false). In fact, error rate data collected by J. R. Anderson and Hastie (1974, shown in Table 3.1) confirm this speculation. Recall errors were by far the most frequent when reaction time was longest (i.e., when verifying original propositions of the form "James Bartlett did A" and new propositions of the form "the lawyer did A").

Comparison with a Spreading-Excitation Model. Given the structure postulated in Fig. 3.7b, a spreading-excitation formulation could of course

TABLE 3.1
Response Time and Errors in Recall as a Function of Order of Presenting Information and the Type of Proposition Being Inferred[a]

	Response Times		Errors in Recall	
	Before Conditions	After Conditions	Before Conditions	After Conditions
Original propositions				
James Bartlett did A	2.98	3.67	8.9%	26.0%
The lawyer did B	2.76	2.31	6.8%	2.6%
Derived propositions				
James Bartlett did B	3.11	3.23	10.4%	5.7%
The lawyer did A	2.75	3.99	12.0%	37.0%

[a]Adapted from J. R. Anderson & Hastie (1974).

also account for many of the results described above. For example, the concepts connected by newly constructed paths should have more residual excitation than those connected by paths that are used less recently, and thus the former relations should be verified more quickly. Nevertheless, ordered search strategies may ultimately have to be provided in developing a complete formulation of person memory. The importance of distinguishing between concepts and labels is also conveyed by this formulation, and should undoubtedly also be taken into account.

Implications for Social Inference: Effects of Stereotyping

While Anderson and Hastie studied the representation of verbal information about hypothetical persons, the conceptualization should also be applicable to the representation of information about actual persons. Note that each piece of information presented in the study (that is, each sentence) may be more generally conceptualized as the caption of a vignette describing someone's behavior in a particular situation. Sentences about particular instances (e.g., "James Bartlett") may be analogous to episodic vignettes, while statements about more general categories of objects (e.g., "lawyers") may be analogous to categorical vignettes. Then the general network model proposed by Anderson and Bower has implications for the representation and organization of episodic and categorical vignettes and scripts described in Chapter 2.

A related application of Anderson and Bower's model, and of the particular results obtained by Anderson and Hastie, concerns the determinants and effects of stereotyping. A stereotype may be conceptualized as a concept of a class of people with which certain attributes and behavioral features are associated. Its representation in memory may therefore be analogous to the structure shown in Fig. 3.6b, where the name of the concept node Y refers to a general class (e.g., "lawyer") rather than to a single representative of this class, and the nodes connected to it (b_1, b_2, etc.) refer to general behaviors and attributes associated with this class of persons. Suppose a judge with a stereotype of lawyers meets a particular person, James Bartlett, and attributes various personality and behavioral characteristics to him (a_1, a_2, etc.) on the basis of this interaction. His representation of this person may be analogous to that shown in Fig. 3.7a. Later on, however, the judge finds out that James is a lawyer. This should produce a structure similar in form to that shown in Fig. 3.8b. As a result, the judge should infer that James has certain of the behaviors and characteristics associated with lawyers (b_1, b_2, etc.) and also should infer that lawyers have certain of the specific behaviors associated with James (a_1, a_2, etc.) on the basis of his encounter with this individual. However, these latter inferences should take longer than the former ones, and so more "errors" should occur in making them. More generally, the characteristics of a particular acquaintance should be less apt to affect a judge's stereotype than are characteristics of the stereotype to affect inferences about the acquaintance. This conclusion is also consistent with that derived from the spreading-excitation model (see Hypothesis 4, p. 90).

More interesting, perhaps, is the implication that once a particular person is associated with a general category, it will take longer to recall characteristics or behaviors that were initially ascribed to him on the basis of personal encounters. Moreover, these characteristics and behaviors will be recalled less accurately. In other words, once the judge learns that James Bartlett is a lawyer, the judge will be less accurate in recalling characteristics that he attributed to James on the basis of their initial interactions, while at the same time he will attribute characteristics and behavior to James that he believes are typical of lawyers in general.

The above predictions have intuitive appeal. It is important to note, moreover, that the predictions apply even if the stereotype of lawyers is no more firmly entrenched in the judge's cognitive system than is the information about the relevant stimulus person. In other words, it is not a result of "distortion" of information to make it consistent with a stereotype to which one is necessarily committed. Rather, it is a consequence of the interrelatedness of the concepts in memory.

It should be noted, however, that the above predictions apply only to instances in which the stereotype is invoked after initial information about the target person has been received and stored. In some cases, a person may be identified as a member of a stereotyped class (i.e., as a male or female, or as a member of a particular ethnic group) either before or at the same time that other information about the person is accessed. In these cases, a structure similar to that shown in Fig. 3.8a would theoretically be formed, and the predictions would not necessarily hold.

Wyer and Srull's "Storage Bin" Model

Network models make quite explicit assumptions about the formal structure of long term memory and the interconnectedness of concepts contained in it. Such a model has the advantage of specificity, and moreover has many heuristic implications of the sort we have noted. However, many of the phenomena described in Chapter 2 concerning the representation of visual and verbal information, the use of schemata and scripts for making inferences, etc., are cumbersome to conceptualize in terms of such a model. A formulation developed by Wyer and Srull (in press) avoids certain of these difficulties. Although this formulation is still not fully developed, it seems capable of accounting for most of the phenomena to which network models are typically applied, and has some additional implications. Since details of the formulation have been presented elsewhere (Wyer & Srull, in press), we will not reiterate them here. However, a brief description of the approach may be worthwhile to convey a possible alternative to the spreading-excitation model we have postulated.

Wyer and Srull postulate two primary memory units. One, a *Work Space*, contains both (a) the output of various stages of processing (encoding and organization of information, integration, etc.) and (b) the input material that is operated upon. The second unit, which is analogous to long-term memory, is the *Permanent Storage Unit*. This unit consists of a series of content-addressable storage bins. These bins are of several types. *Semantic* bins contain attributes and behaviors and their "definitions" (clusters of characteristics that serve as bases for assigning them to stimulus elements). *Person* and *event* bins contain information about individual persons ("Mary Smith") or events ("last Friday night's party") or prototypic persons or events ("doctor," "getting an education," etc.). Each of these latter bins is tagged with a nominal representation of the object or event to which its contents refer. The bins themselves may contain several different types of information: a single trait or attribute, a judgment of the object or event to which the bin pertains, a schema, or configuration of attributes, or a script of the sort described in Chapter 2. Information of each type is treated as a single unit. A bin pertaining, for example, to a particular individual may contain several different schemata, each consisting of different attributes, each characterizing the person at a different point in the person's life or in a different social role.

Information is stored in the bins in the order it is received. Moreover, when information from a bin is required for use in interpreting new information or making a judgment, the bin is searched from the top down so that information at the top is most likely to be retrieved. When information drawn from a bin is no longer needed, it is returned to the top of the bin rather than to the position from which it was originally drawn. Thus, when several units of information are potentially applicable, the most recently used information will be at the top of the bin, and consequently will be the most likely to be retrieved and used.

Wyer and Srull postulate three general processes similar to those outlined in Chapter 1: encoding and organization, integration, and response selection. These processes are performed on either new information that enters the Work Space from external sources, on material retrieved from person and event bins in permanent storage, or both. Material in permanent storage (e.g., categorical schemata and scripts) is of course also used as a basis for interpreting or organizing new information. The material being processed, and also the results of this processing, are temporarily stored in the Work Space. However, only the result of processing, which may be either a judgment, a schema, or a script, is returned to permanent storage, being placed on top of the bin(s) to which it is relevant. While the original material remains available in the Work Space for a time after processing is completed, and thus may be able to be retrieved, the Work Space is ultimately cleared for other purposes. When this occurs, the original information is lost, and only the encodings of it transmitted to permanent storage can be retrieved for use in making judgments.

While the complete formulation proposed by Wyer and Srull is more complex, the above capsule description provides a feel for several of its more important implications. Three of these implications may be summarized as follows:

1. If information about a person or event has been retrieved from memory and re-encoded or reorganized, the revised schema will then be deposited on top of any previous information in the bin pertaining to that person or event. Thus, it is the re-encoded representation of the person or event, rather than the original encoding, that is most likely to be retrieved in the future for use in making additional judgments. Moreover, once a judgment is made of a person or event on the basis of certain information, the judgment is deposited in permanent storage on top of the information on which it was based. Therefore, the judgment itself, rather than the information that led to it, is more likely to be recalled and used in the future.

2. If judgments of a person or event are made a short time after new information about the object is presented, and therefore before this information is cleared from the Work Space, the judgments may be based in part upon the original material as well as on the subsequent encodings of it. Moreover, the material can be recalled accurately, in its pre-encoded and preorganized form. However, after a period of time has elapsed, and the

Work Space has been cleared, only the encoded material deposited in Permanent Storage is available. As a result, the encoding and organization of information is apt to have a greater effect on judgments over time, while implications of the original, pre-encoded information should have less effect. Similarly, the effect of encoding and organization of information on recall of this information is likely to increase over time. These predictions are equivalent to those proposed and tested by Carlston (1977), although derived from a somewhat different perspective. Carlston's results, discussed in the next chapter, thus provide support for these ideas.

3. Previously acquired concepts that have been recently used to encode or organize information for one purpose will be most likely to be retrieved from memory for use in processing additional, possibly completely unrelated information for a different purpose. On the other hand, concepts and schemata that have not been recently used may still be retrieved even after some time has elapsed provided that no subsequent information about the objects to which they pertain has been acquired, and the concepts therefore remain near the top of the bin in which they are contained.

The above formulation permits several of the phenomena described in this chapter and elsewhere in this book to be conceptualized. Priming effects of the sort we have described earlier are particularly easy to explain. The formulation can also account for evidence that once a script has been constructed for use in explaining or interpreting an event, this script will persist to affect subjects' judgments even after the information upon which it is based is rendered invalid (cf. Ross et al., 1975; Ross et al., 1977). Finally, it can account for the possibility noted in Chapter 2, that when unmentioned characteristics of a person or event have been inferred in order to interpret or explain the information one receives, these characteristics may erroneously be recalled as having actually been part of the original information.

An intriguing example of the latter phenomenon is provided in a study by Spiro (1977). In this study, subjects initially read one of two true stories about an engaged couple, with instructions that the information was being presented either as part of an experiment on memory or an experiment on "reactions to situations involving interpersonal relations." In each story, the man informs the woman that he does not want children. However, in one story the woman ostensibly shares the man's views, while in the other she expresses considerable upset at the man's position and enters into a bitter discussion of the matter as the story ends. It seems reasonable to suppose that subjects who read the first story with the objective of reacting to the interpersonal relations described are likely to interpret it with reference to a prototypic event schema of two persons who love one another, share similar views, get married, and live happily ever after. However, those who read the second story with the same set of objectives may interpret it with reference to a schema of a couple who initially love one another but find they cannot agree on matters of personal importance, wind up in personal conflict, and ultimately separate. In contrast, subjects who believe they are involved in a memory experiment may not invoke a prototypic schema at all in interpreting the information, and thus may store it with a minimum of encoding or interpretation.

After reading one of the two stories, subjects engaged in several minutes of routine activity unrelated to the experimental task. However, during this period, the experimenter "incidentally" remarked to some subjects that the couple eventually married and were still happily together, while telling others that the couple had eventually broken their engagement and had not seen each other since. Thus, in half the cases, the additional information was presumably consistent with the prototypic schema used to interpret the original material, whereas in the other cases it was inconsistent with this schema. According to the formulation proposed, the additional information should have little effect on memory-set subjects, whose sole objective is to remember the original material. However, subjects whose objective is to interpret and react to the interpersonal relations described are likely to attempt to incorporate the new information into their representation of the situation. To accomplish this when the outcome is not consistent with the prototypic schema they originally used to interpret the information, they may need to draw upon other prototypic event schemata applicable to the sort of interaction that might have taken place. This reconstructed representation will then be stored in memory rather than the original construction.

After performing a routine activity unrelated to task objectives, subjects were released. They returned either 2 days, 3 weeks, or 6 weeks later, at which time they were asked to recall the story they had read in the first session. In both conditions, they were explicitly told to include only ideas that were present in the story, and *not* to include any personal reactions or inferences they may have made. Thus, every precaution was taken to discourage subjects from adding material to their reproductions. In fact, subjects under memory-set conditions recalled the material with reasonable accuracy, and errors in their recall were not systematically affected by the additional information they received about the outcome of the couple's interaction. However, subjects whose original objective was to interpret the interpersonal relationship made frequent errors, the number of which increased over time. While the specific nature of these errors differed in detail, they were typically of the sort one would intuitively expect as a result of attempts to reconcile the ancillary material with the original information. For example, when subjects were first told that neither party wanted children but later were led to believe the couple had broken their engagement, several recalled the original information as stating that the couple had actually disagreed about having children; others recalled it as stating that one party ultimately changed his/her mind about the desirability of having children. In contrast, when subjects were told that the couple disagreed but wound up happily married, they tended to add details that minimized the implications of the disagreement, recalling that "the problem was resolved when they found that [the woman] could not have children anyway," or that while one person thought the matter was important, the other did not (for these and other concrete examples, see Spiro, 1977, pp. 144–145). These responses are all quite plausible explanations of the outcome of the couple's interaction that one might expect to invoke in an attempt to reconcile the unanticipated outcome with the initial information. What is striking is that these explanations were recalled as actually having existed in the information presented, despite explicit instructions not to include inferences or personal reactions. This is quite consistent with the general notion that if inferences about a person or event are made and are incorporated into the schematic representation placed in Permanent Storage, they are subsequently not distinguishable from aspects of the original information that are also contained in that representation. The increase in these effects over time is once again consistent with our notion that when the time interval is relatively short and the processing objectives have presumably not yet been accomplished, the original information as well as encoding are likely to be retained in the Work Space, and thus available for recall. When the anticipated delay in using the information is considerable, however, the Work Space may be cleared for other purposes, and so subjects must rely upon their reconstruction of this information in Permanent Storage when they are asked to recall it.

3.6 CONCLUDING REMARKS

The formulations of person memory proposed in this chapter are admittedly incomplete, and undoubtedly contain many ambiguities. Each, of course, is only an analogue of the actual cognitive processes that underlie memory storage and retrieval, and therefore must be evaluated on the basis of its integrative and heuristic value. The network model we have described in most detail has the advantage that the postulates of the model are stated with sufficient specificity that many empirically testable hypotheses can be derived from them. Several aspects of the formulation may be modified as conceptual deficiencies are identified and as empirical work calls into question the validity of certain specific assumptions underlying it.

However, our objective has not been to propose a definitive model. Rather, we have attempted to provide a vocabulary, a set of concepts, and a theoretical framework for thinking about the organization of information about persons and its potential role in social inference. We have suggested a way in which information about persons and events and groups of persons and events may be interrelated, and in which attributes of these persons and events are tied to people's implicit personality theories of how traits and behaviors are associated. Moreover, we have distinguished among three types of inferences, each of which has unique characteristics and which may invoke somewhat different underlying processes. To demonstrate the heuristic value of the model, we noted several general hypotheses suggested by implications of the model for social inference phenomena. These hypotheses concern the manner in which the activation of certain concepts can affect subsequent judgments, and the manner in which the organization of person information in memory can affect both the subsequent recall of this information and inferences based upon it. Several additional hypotheses may of course also be derived from the postulates we have proposed, certain of which will be pursued further in the next chapter.

The conceptualization of person memory proposed by Wyer and Srull, as we have described it here, is also necessarily sketchy, and omits several details that are necessary to understand the processes postulated by it and their implications. However, the description is sufficient to suggest a potentially useful alternative to a strict network model, in that it enables the consideration of complex configurations and their use in interpreting information about persons and events to be more easily conceptualized. Yet it is important to note that, with a few exceptions (noted by Wyer & Srull, in press), a network model is capable of accounting for many of the same phenomena predicted by the storage-bin conceptualization. The ultimate criterion for evaluating the two approaches may lie in their ability to stimulate useful and interesting avenues of research on social information processing. The present authors are as curious as anyone else about which formulation, if either, meets this criterion.

4

The Encoding of Information and Its Effects on Recall and Inference Making

Information is interpreted or encoded by identifying its referents as instances of concepts in memory. These concepts may be either vignettes, schemata, or trait or behavior categories at different levels of abstractness. Once an object is interpreted as an instance of a concept by comparing object and concept features, the object may be inferred to have attributes that are associated with the concept. The considerations raised in Chapter 3 develop two general points concerning these processes. First, when more than one concept can be used to encode information about an object or event, subsequent inferences about this element may depend to a considerable extent upon which encoding happens to be made. (For example, information that a man is standing in the middle of the street waving his hands may lead to quite different inferences about the man's attributes if he is encoded as a drunk than if he is encoded as a policeman. Alternatively, a person who is observed helping someone on an examination may be assigned different attributes if the behavior is interpreted as kind than if it is interpreted as dishonest.) Second, the manner in which a piece of information is encoded by a given person, and thus the effect it may have on subsequent judgments, may be substantially influenced by which concepts are most easily accessible to the person at the time the information is received, and thus by aspects of the person's immediate past experience that lead these concepts to be "primed."

While we have already described the general processes that theoretically underlie the determinants and effects of encoding, many specific facets of these processes remain to be considered. In this chapter, we attempt to focus in more detail upon the manner in which information is encoded, the factors that determine encoding, and the effects that encoding may have upon both information recall and judgments of stimuli to which the information is relevant.

Before embarking on this effort, however, two things should be noted. First, in this and later chapters of this volume we will often abandon the formal analysis and terminology associated with the models described in Chapter 3, resorting instead to more standard descriptions of these processes and the conditions in which they occur. This does not reflect an abandonment of the models themselves, which can be easily applied to the phenomena to be discussed. Rather, it reflects a consideration for readers who may have neither the interest nor the time to master completely the terminology and concepts embedded in these models, and thus may appreciate a description of these phenomena in more traditional language. However, the possibility of translating the concepts to be discussed into the terminology of these models should be kept in mind.

Second, while encoding processes may affect the recall and use of any kind of information, most of the social psychological research in this area, and hence most of the discussion to follow, focusses on the encoding of behavioral information. This discussion will have two main thrusts. First, we will consider the number and specificity of concepts used to encode information at the time it is first received. Then we will consider differences in the specfic concepts used to encode a person's behavior, and the effects of this encoding on subsequent inferences about the person.

4.1 THE UNITIZING OF INFORMATION

General Considerations

Encoding processes may be viewed as a way of managing the large amounts of information that people often have about others. There are undoubtedly limits to the amount of information a judge can receive and process at any one time. As the amount of information to which a judge is exposed increases, one of two things may occur. First, the judge may attend to and encode only selected aspects of the information that are either distinctive or are particularly relevant to judgments or decisions he expects to make. Second, he may attempt to characterize the implications of the information using more abstract concepts that are sufficiently few in number to fall within his processing limits. Thus, the amount of information presented and also the use to which the judge expects to put this information are potential influences on the way he will encode it.

For example, suppose a judge observes a boy helping a girl with her homework. If the judge has no other information to process at the time, he may encode the behavioral event in some detail, perhaps constructing an episodic vignette that captures specific aspects of the boy's physical appearance, his particular behaviors in giving help, and the situational context in which the behavior occurs. However, if the judge is attempting to process other information as well, he is less likely to encode the event in as much detail. Rather, he may simply store a symbolic description of it (i.e., the "caption" of the vignette, "the boy helped the girl with her homework") without more detailed schematic representations of each component.

In addition, a hierarchy of concepts at various levels of abstractness are potentially available for encoding a given behavior. The most concrete concepts may pertain to specific behaviors in particular situations (e.g., "helped Susan with her homework last night"). Concepts at increasingly higher levels of abstractness may pertain to general behaviors ("helps others"), general descriptions of these behaviors ("kind," "helpful"), and finally, at the highest level of abstractness, evaluative descriptions such as "good" or "bad." In general, the number of concepts required to encode a given set of behavioral information decreases as the abstractness of these concepts increases. Hence, the reasoning mentioned earlier suggests that the level of abstractness of concepts used to encode stimulus information will normally increase with the amount of this information. Several speculations made in earlier chapters are consistent with this hypothesis. For example, the hypothesis suggests that the schema substructures representing individual persons are likely to consist of relatively concrete behavior while the substructure of schemata representing entire categories of people (about which there is apt to be more information, accumulated over a long period of time) are more likely to consist of general traits. This prediction is consistent with Hypothesis 1, Chapter 3. The hypothesis also suggests that individuals about whom one has a lot of information (i.e., longstanding friends or enemies) will be represented more abstractly than people one has met less often, and therefore knows less about.[1]

The Encoding of Ongoing Behavior

The abstractness of concepts used to encode information is of particular importance in considering the processing of ongoing behavior. A judge who observes another's behavior over a period of time is obviously unlikely to encode every subtle movement this person makes. Rather, he is apt to divide the behavioral sequence into meaningful fragments or "frames" (vignettes, in Abelson's terms), in a process perhaps analogous to constructing a comic

---

[1]Other possibilities exist, however. For example, when much information about a person is available, the judge may construct a schema consisting of behaviors that he considers prototypical of the person and use it as a representation of him, ignoring other behaviors that have similar implications. This possibility is suggested indirectly by the work of Rosch (1973).

strip. Specifically, he may select "frames" that characterize transitions from one meaningful action to another. Thus, successive frames signify the beginning and end of an action, relevant details of which can be inferred indirectly. To give a trivial example, suppose a jduge is shown a picture of someone working at a desk, followed immediately by a picture of this person walking out the door of the room. The judge does not need additional information about the intervening events to infer that the person pushed back his chair, stood up, and walked away from the desk toward the door. The intervening behavior that one might use to "fill in" the undescribed interval between two frames could deviate in subtle ways from the actor's actual behavior, but these deviations are likely to be inconsequential for inferring what occurred. If, in fact, something out of the ordinary had occurred during this interval (e.g., the actor stumbling over a wastebasket and falling on his face), two or three more frames would have been required to convey the event's essential features. (For example, frames might be included showing the actor stumbling, hitting the floor, and picking himself up.) But even here, complete details of the event would be unnecessary.

It therefore seems reasonable to postulate that judges do not typically encode and store all of the details of ongoing behavior. Rather, they may only encode representative aspects that enable them to remember and interpret the events that occurred, and that permit them to reconstruct the "missing" behavioral details if later required to do so. This possibility has been investigated by Newtson and his colleagues (for a summary, see Newtson, 1976). In a typical study, judges observe a videotape of a person engaged in a series of routine acts similar to those occurring in everyday life. For example, one tape (Newtson, 1973) shows an actor completing a questionnaire. During the course of the tape, the actor gets up, gets a cigarette from his coat, looks for matches, lights the cigarette, throws the match toward the wastebasket, misses it, walks over and picks up the match, puts it in the basket, goes back to the questionnaire, stops and opens a book, flips through its pages, goes back to the questionnaire, and so on. Other tapes used have been similar in their general format (e.g., a man pacing and intermittently answering a telephone, a man removing stacks of books from a table and placing them on shelves). While viewing a tape, a judge is asked to press a button to indicate the points at which one meaningful act ends and another begins (i.e., breakpoints). The interval between successive breakpoints may be interpreted as a unit of behavior that is conceptually distinct from other units. The number of breakpoints is therefore an estimate of the number of meaningful acts into which the judge has analyzed the sequence of behavior he observed.

If our preceding analysis is correct, the breakpoints or "frames" identified through this procedure should contain most of the information necessary to reconstruct the action sequence, and thus should be those aspects of the sequence that the judge is most likely to encode and use to represent the sequence in memory. A study by Newtson and Engquist (1976) supports this hypothesis. After obtaining normative data on the location of breakpoints in each of a series of taped behavior sequences, the authors constructed new tapes in which frames located either near these breakpoints or between breakpoints (i.e., at *non*breakpoints) were omitted. Independent judges were then exposed to one of these edited tapes without being asked explicitly to identify breakpoints. After viewing the tape, they were shown missing frames taken both from this tape and from a different, related tape showing the same actor and general behavior. They were asked whether or not each frame came from the tape they had seen originally. Recognition of breakpoint frames was much more accurate than recognition of nonbreakpoint frames, suggesting that judges are more apt to encode and store information at breakpoints than information at nonbreakpoints, and that they therefore recall details of information at breakpoints more accurately.

These results confirm the existence of certain events in a behavioral sequence that people typically interpret as breakpoints, and indicate that information at these breakpoints is better remembered than information at nonbreakpoints. These events presumably represent changes in activity in the observed sequence, and are therefore events with high information value. However, this does not mean that individual or situational differences in these breakpoints correspond to differences in judges' recall or reconstruction of the events that occur in the sequence. To justify this conclusion, it would be necessary to show that the specific type and amount of material that judges recall can be predictably affected by inducing differences in the unitizing of a given sequence of behavior. Such a demonstration has yet to be reported.

Effects of Unitizing on Inferences

Under the standard instructional conditions constructed by Newtson, there is substantial interjudge agreement about the number and location of breakpoints. In general, however, these characteristics are apt to depend on the situational conditions in which the information is presented, and on the purpose for which the information is to be used. Other studies have been designed to investigate these possibilities and their implications. Unfortunately, the results of this research are not totally consistent, and have not demonstrated unequivocally that the units of information identified using Newtson's procedures are actually mediators of judgments rather than simply correlates of these judgments. This research must therefore be regarded as more provocative and heuristic than definitive.

Newtson predicted that the way in which a judge unitizes behavior will affect the kinds of attributions he will make on the basis of this behavior. Suppose, as Newtson assumed, that the number of units into which a behavioral sequence is analyzed affects the amount of information extracted from the sequence. The more information a judge extracts, the more confident he should be of the actor's attributes, and therefore the more likely he may be to use these attributes to explain the actor's future behavior. It follows that the more units a judge uses, the more he will exhibit these latter tendencies.

An experiment by Newtson (1973, Experiment 1) bears on the above hypothesis. Judges first watched a 5-minute videotape of an actor's behavior under instructions to break the sequence into either the largest or the smallest units that seemed "natural or meaningful." They then rated the actor along a variety of general trait dimensions (intelligence, honesty, sociability, etc.) and estimated their confidence that these ratings were correct. In addition, they predicted whether the actor's behavior in various other situations (e.g., failing to solve an arithmetic problem) was attributable to characteristics of the actor (e.g., low ability) or of the situation (task difficulty). Results supported the hypothesis described above. Despite no overall differences in their trait ratings, judges who analyzed the actor's behavior into small units expressed more confidence in these ratings. Small-unitizers were also more likely to attribute the actor's behavior in other situations to dispositional rather than situational factors.

There is, of course, some danger in interpreting these different judgments as a consequence of differences in unitizing rather than simply a correlate of these differences. The instruction to analyze the behavior into small units may have been interpreted by judges as an implicit "demand" to pay more attention to the actor, and may thus have led them to rate the actor differently for this reason and not because of small unitizing per se. To eliminate this problem, Newtson (1973, Experiment 2) led judges to analyze the actor's behavior into units of different sizes without explicit instructions do do so. A judge who observes unexpected behavior is likely to become more attentive to the behavior, and therefore may analyze it into smaller units than he would if the actor's behavior were routine. Based on this assumption, Newtson asked judges to view one of two tapes under instructions to analyze the behavior shown into natural and meaningful units, but without any explicit indication of what size these units should be. Each tape showed an actor engaged in a model-building task, consulting instructions, working on the model, rechecking the instructions, and so on. The two tapes were identical in all but one respect. In one (*deviant behavior*) tape, the actor stopped his routine model-building behavior after two minutes, removed his right shoe and sock, put them on the table, rolled up his left pant leg up to the knee, and then continued with the task. In the other (*normal behavior*) tape, the actor maintained his normal routine without interruption. After observing and unitizing one of the two tapes, judges completed rating scales similar to those obtained in the first study described above.

The unitizing data were consistent with the assumption that judges who observed the actor's deviant behavior would break his subsequent behavior into significantly smaller units than judges who did not observe him behave abnormally. However, there are unfortunately two reasons why differences in ratings made under these two conditions cannot be unequivocally attributed to this difference in unitizing per se. First, an increase in the attention paid to the actor's activities under deviant behavior conditions could affect ratings of the actor independently of the unitizing process. Second, ratings under deviant behavior conditions could be affected in part by the informational implications of the actor's bizarre activities, independently of the subsequent unitizing produced by these activities. These factors could help to explain why ratings made under normal and deviant behavior conditions did not parallel those obtained in the earlier study under large- and small-unitizing instructions, respectively. Specifically, in the first study, no differences occurred in trait ratings as a function of unitizing, whereas in the second study, these ratings were more extreme under deviant tape (small-unitizing) conditions. Moreover, although differences in confidence ratings and in explanations for hypothetical behaviors occurred in the first study, they did not occur in the second. Perhaps the actor's deviant behavior decreased judges' confidence in their inferences about the actor's personality, and therefore decreased their willingness to attribute his behavior in other situations to these characteristics. These effects may offset the increases in confidence and dispositional attributions typically produced by smaller unitizing per se.

Unitizing and Impression Formation

Although the analysis of person information into small units may indicate greater attention to details of this information, these details may not always be helpful in making inferences about the person. Suppose a judge observes a person's behavior with the intention of forming a general impression of his personality. The judge may feel that much of the more detailed behavioral information about a person is irrelevant to such an impression, and he may therefore be inclined to construct more general units that have clearer implications for the person's general traits. For example, an actor's behavior of getting up from a desk, walking over to his coat, taking out a cigarette, and lighting it may simply be encoded as "getting a cigarette." The details concerning how this was done are not of obvious relevance to the actor's general attributes. The perceptual units used may therefore be larger than they would be under conditions where the judge's objective is not to form an impression of the person.

Two lines of evidence bear on these matters. In a study reported by Newtson (1976), some judges observed a videotape of a target person with whom they expected to interact at a future time, while others viewed the same tape, but were explicitly told they would never meet the person. Presumably, the first group of judges were more motivated to form an impression of what the person would be like than the second group. Consistent with the reasoning outlined above, judges who anticipated interacting with the target person analyzed the behavior sequence into larger units than did judges who anticipated no interaction.

A more direct manipulation of judges' set to form an impression, used by Ebbesen, Cohen, and Lane (1975), had similar effects on unitizing. However, their study also raises questions about whether the larger units formed in the course of forming an impression are actually helpful in constructing this impression accurately. Judges viewed a tape of an actor under two conditions. Under *Memory Set* conditions, they were told to remember what the actor did in a way that would enable them to reproduce it later on. Under *Impression Set* conditions they were told to form a detailed impression of what the actor was like. The Memory Set judges broke the behavior into smaller units than Impression Set judges. This result is consistent with the expectation that people who try to form an impression will attend to larger units of behavior. After viewing the tape, half the subjects under each set condition were asked to recall details of the observed behavior, while the other half were asked to make trait ratings of these persons. In this study, Memory Set judges did in fact recall more details of the information than did Impression Set judges. However, later studies (Ebbesen, Cohen & Allen, 1977) have failed to replicate this result, except in cases where a substantial period of time (e.g., one week) has elapsed between the initial presentation of information and the recall task. Thus, the initial unitizing of this type of information does not seem to have a reliable effect upon its immediate recall.[2]

The detail in which judges encode ongoing behavior may nevertheless affect their subsequent use of this information in making judgments. Trait rating data collected by Ebbesen et al. (1977) suggest that this is the case. While mean trait ratings under the two set conditions were similar, they were more highly intercorrelated under Impression Set conditions than under Memory Set conditions. This difference is similar to that obtained by Newtson (1973) under large- and small-unitizing instructions, respectively. In addition, the pattern of intercorrelations among trait ratings by Impression Set judges was similar to the pattern of independent judges' estimates of trait co-occurrence (i.e., the likelihood that a person with each trait would have

---

[2]This conclusion may seem superficially inconsistent with the evidence obtained by Newtson and Engquist (1976) that information is better recalled at breakpoints than at nonbreakpoints; if Newston and Engquist are correct, then more information should be recalled when the behavior is analyzed into smaller units, since there are more breakpoints in this case. However, a distinction should be made between the recall of specific frames of a behavioral sequence and recall of meaningful behaviors of the actor. It is possible that regardless of the number of discrete frames into which ongoing behavior is analyzed, the judge may be able to reconstruct the behavior during nonbreakpoint intervals well enough to recognize details of the behavior.

each other trait). These estimates presumably reflect the typical judge's implicit personality theory of trait interrelations. In combination, these results provide an interesting and important insight into the different effects of the two instructional sets, and perhaps of differences in unitizing in general. It seems that Memory Set judges (small-unitizers) focus on details of the behavioral information as it is presented, without attempting to organize its implications into an integrated impression. Therefore, they may subsequently infer the actor's attributes directly from the particular aspects of the original behavior that they recall and consider relevant to the judgment. Since different behaviors may have implications for different attributes, the intercorrelations of trait ratings may be fairly low. In contrast, although Impression Set judges (large-unitizers) may be able to recall the behavioral information just as well as Memory Set judges when asked to do so, they may not use the behavioral information as a whole in making their trait ratings. Rather, they may organize their impression around a particular, salient behavior that has implications for one trait and may base other trait inferences upon their "implicit personality theories," ignoring the implications of other behaviors.

Processing Differences between Large- and Small-Unitizers

The above interpretation of set effects has at least two major implications. First, it appears that Memory Set judges (small-unitizers) do not form integrated impressions of the actor at the time information is received, and must therefore later search their memories for specific aspects of the actor's behavior that bear upon the traits being judged. If this is the case, these judges should take longer to generate their trait ratings than Impression Set judges (large-unitizers), who form their impression at the time the information is received. Supplementary response time data collected by Ebbesen et al. (1977) support this hypothesis.

Second, the implications of any particular behavior for an actor's traits may be fairly clear. Consequently, Memory Set judges, who presumably base their inferences directly on specific aspects of the actor's behavior, should make fairly similar trait inferences. However, Impression Set judges are likely to organize their impressions around different subsets of behaviors, depending on what is most salient to them, and the traits they infer on the basis of these subsets may differ. Hence, there should be greater variability among Impression Set judges' trait ratings than among Memory Set judges' ratings. This was also the case in the data gathered by Ebbesen et al.

Memory Set judges may typically use recalled behaviors to make inferences in either of two ways. First, they may simply search memory until they retrieve a behavior that is relevant to the trait judgment to be made, and then use the implications of this behavior to make the inference, without searching further. Second, they may scan the entire set of information they have stored about the actor, in order to identify *all* behaviors with implications for the trait judgment, and then base their judgment upon the composite implications of these behaviors. These possibilities have different implications. For example, if the first strategy is used, there should be no systematic relation between the total amount of information presented and the time required to make an inference. On the other hand, if the second strategy is used, any increase in the amount of information presented, and thus in the amount to be recalled, should increase the time required to make the judgment.

Research by Allen, Ebbesen, and Bessman (1977) suggests that which of the above strategies is used may depend on the type of trait to be inferred. Judges viewed one of several different segments of a single master tape portraying a series of behaviors. These segments varied in length, but were constructed so that the particular behaviors portrayed occurred the same proportion of times in sequences of each length. After viewing a segment under Memory Set conditions, judges inferred the likelihood that the actor had traits of two general types: concrete traits that were closely tied to the behaviors (e.g., clumsiness) and abstract traits that were further removed from particular behaviors (e.g., intelligence). They were also asked to verify certain details of the visual information presented. Response times were recorded in each case. The time required to verify details of the visual material increased with tape length, supporting the assumption that judges subjectively scanned the stored information in sequence to identify the detail being considered. The time required to infer abstract traits also increased linearly with tape length, suggesting that to make these inferences, judges also searched memory for all relevant behaviors manifested by the actor before arriving at a judgment. However, the time required to infer concrete traits was generally less than that required to infer abstract traits and was not linearly related to tape length, suggesting that in this case, judges based their inferences upon the first relevant behavior they encountered in their memory search and did not bother to seek further. In other words, a single instance of a behavior was considered sufficient for inferring a concrete trait but not for inferring an abstract trait.

Discussion

The results reported in this section provide a coherent picture of the effects that information unitization has on subsequent inferences. That is, judges who are either specifically instructed to analyze behavior into large units, or who do so with the intent of forming an integrated impression of the actor, are subsequently less apt to base their inferences of the person's traits on different aspects of his behavior, and more apt to base these judgments on their a priori assumptions about how traits are interrelated. Perhaps for this reason, they are less confident of their trait inferences, and are less apt to use the traits they infer to explain the actor's behavior in other situations, than are judges who analyze the actor's behavior into smaller units.

In one sense, the implications of these findings are somewhat ironic. That is, they suggest that explicit instructions to use an actor's behavior to form an impression of his personality may actually lead judges to pay *less* attention to the actor's behavior as a whole, and therefore to be less sensitive to differences in the implications of this behavior, than judges who do not have this objective when observing the actor. Interestingly, this difference may decrease with the time interval between the receipt of the original information and the judgments of the actor's traits. In a followup study, Cohen and Ebbesen (in press) replicated the differences in trait ratings described earlier when these ratings were made immediately after judges viewed the actor's behavior, but also obtained additional data seven days later. Memory Set judges' recall of the behavioral information at this later time was somewhat superior to that of Impression Set judges. However, the patterns of trait rating intercorrelations in the two instructional conditions were similar to one another and also to the pattern of normative trait co-occurrence estimates. Thus, once the actor's behavior became less salient, both groups appear to have based their inferences on the implications of their a priori implicit personality theories, rather than on the different aspects of the behavior they originally observed.

Despite the findings just reported, it would be incorrect to conclude that forming an impression on the basis of information about a person does not sometimes facilitate the organization and subsequent recall of this information. In videotapes of ongoing behavior, information is already organized into a meaningful sequence of events, and the formation of an impression does little to increase this inherent organization. However, when the information presented has no inherent interrelatedness, the organization of this information around an impression of a person may facilitate recall. This possibility is supported in a study by Hamilton and Katz (1975). Judges read a sequence of behavioral descriptions under instructions either to form an impression of a person who manifested these behaviors, or simply to try to remember as many of the behaviors as possible. Under these conditions, Impression Set judges recalled more behaviors than Memory Set judges.

In combination, the aforementioned studies suggest that when behavioral information is already well organized, the predisposition to form an impression of the actor may decrease attention to informational details, thereby diminishing recall of the information after a period of time. However, when the information is otherwise unrelated, such a predisposition may help the judge to organize it in a way that enables him to remember it better. This implies that the superiority of impression set recall to memory set recall (in the situation constructed by Hamilton and Katz) may increase with the heterogeneity of the behavioral descriptions, or alternatively, with the number of traits to which the behavior is relevant. For example, if the behaviors presented are all relevant to a single trait (e.g., honesty), a judge under Impression Set conditions may simply encode the composite as "honest," and may therefore be less likely to recall particular behaviors than a judge under Memory Set conditions, who is specifically asked to remember details. However, if each behavior presented has implications for a different trait, the organization of the behavior around an impression of a given person may facilitate recall relative to Memory Set conditions, as found by Hamilton and Katz.

A Note of Caution.   In our discussion, we have tended to equate an impression set with large-unitizing and a memory set with small-unitizing. This equivalence was suggested by the facts that: (a) differences in the instructional set produce differences in unitizing; and (b) differences in set and direct manipulations of unit size have similar effects on the intercorrelations among trait ratings. However, care must be taken in concluding that differences in unitizing are a determinant of differences in these inference patterns, rather than simply a correlate of them. There is no direct evidence that differences in the unitizing of information actually mediate inferences based on this information. Rather, differences in unitizing and differences in trait ratings may each be independent consequences of differences in instructional sets and in the stated purposes for which information is to be used. To clarify these matters, one must demonstrate that differences in unitization are necessary as well as sufficient conditions for differences in the patterns of trait ratings described above.

4.2 EFFECTS OF INITIAL ENCODING OF INFORMATION ON RECALL AND SUBSEQUENT JUDGMENTS

Two results obtained in Ebbesen's program of research are particularly provocative: First, the influence of a judge's semantic structure on his inferences about a stimulus person increases over time; and second, the fact that once a judge encodes the person in terms of traits implied by the semantic structure, his recall of the person's original behavior decreases more rapidly. These data suggest that once information about a person has been encoded in terms of previously formed concepts, these concepts and their semantic associates come to affect inferences about this person independently of the information initially presented. Moreover, the original information is subsequently less apt to be recalled. If these tendencies are general, they have many implications. For example, they suggest that once a person is identified as representative of a previously formed schema (or stereotype), he may be judged in terms of this schema rather than in terms of his actual behavior. At a more molecular level, once a particular person's behavior has been encoded, this encoding may affect subsequent judgments of the person independently of the behavior upon which it was initially based. Moreover, the magnitude of this effect may increase over time. These predictions are consistent with the model of memory proposed by Wyer and Srull (in press), described in Chapter 3. Some evidence bearing on these possibilities is described below.

The Autonomy of Abstract Encodings

A number of studies may be interpreted as evidence that higher level encodings of information become autonomous from the information itself, and may therefore affect later inferences even after the information is itself no longer retrieveable. For example, Yavuz and Bousfield (1959) found that subjects could identify the evaluative implications of foreign words even after they could no longer remember the definitions conveying those implications. Similarly, Carlston (1977) found that judges could accurately recall previous inferences they had made along several different trait dimensions, even when they could remember none of the stimulus episodes on which these inferences were based. Moreover, these inferences were recalled along several evaluatively inconsistent dimensions. This indicates that not only global evaluative impressions of a person but also encodings of his specific traits may persist when the original information about this person is no longer recalled.

Additional evidence suggesting that people's inferences may become autonomous of the information that initially precipitates them was obtained in a study by Lingle and Ostrom (1979). However, interpretation of their data is somewhat equivocal. In their study, subjects evaluated a stimulus person's suitability for an occupation on the basis of a set of personality traits. (These traits were displayed visually on a screen and were removed before the judgment was made). Then, three seconds after reporting this evaluation, they were asked to judge the person's suitability for a second occupation that was either similar or dissimilar to the first. The time required to make this second evaluation was recorded.

Subjects generally took less time to judge the candidate's suitability for the second occupation when it was similar to the first then when it was dissimilar. Subjects in the similar-occupation conditions may have based their second judgment on their first one, avoiding the time to review the original stimulus information that was required when dissimilar occupations were judged. A second possibility, suggested by the formulation outlined in Chapter 3, is that the first judgment primed features contained in the schema associated with the occupation being judged, thus increasing the speed of activating these same features when judging a second occupation with some of these features.

Lingle and Ostrom also varied the number of personality traits contained in the original stimulus information. If subjects base their second judgment on a review of the stimulus information, the time required to make these judgments should increase with the number of traits described. However, if they base their second judgment on the first judgment, then the size of the original stimulus set would be irrelevant, and should therefore have no effect. In fact, set size did not affect the time to make judgments of similar occupations, consistent with the latter hypothesis. However, set size also had no effect on the time to judge dissimilar occupations. This is intuitively surprising. That is, the first judgment would seem to be irrelevant to judgments of a dissimilar occupation, requiring subjects to review the original stimulus material. Perhaps once a judgment is made of one occupation, judgments of the second are based on a comparison of the features in the schemata associated with these two occupations rather than a comparison of the features of the second occupational schema with those in the original stimulus material. Thus, judgments would be similar if the two schemata are similar, and different if the two schemata differ, but the time required in each case would be independent of the amount of original information presented. However, there is an alternative interpretation. That is, perhaps subjects do in fact return to the original stimulus information to make the second judgement, but review only a few pieces of it, the number of which is fairly constant regardless of the number that was orginally presented. The relative merits of these two interpretations unfortunately cannot be distinguished.

Granting that the study nonetheless provides some tentative support for the autonomy hypothesis, two additional methodological notes should be added. First, in this study, the second judgments were made under real or implicit time pressure. It is conceivable that if subjects had been given an unlimited amount of time to make their judgments, they would have been more apt to re-examine the original information presented rather than relying upon their prior judgment. On the other hand, note that the second judgments were made within a very short period of time after the stimulus information had been presented, so the stimulus information was undoubtedly still quite salient at the time these judgments were made. It seems likely that with the passage of additional time, judges would be even *less* inclined to re-examine the original evidence than they were in the study reported. This speculation is in fact supported by Ebbesen's data and by other results to be presented later in this chapter.

The evidence as a whole therefore suggests that higher level encodings do become autonomous of the lower level encodings upon which they are based. If this is true, it implies that identical stimulus information may often lead to quite different judgments, depending upon the nature of the encodings that happen to mediate these judgments. This possibility will be examined in the next two sections.

Effects of Stereotypic Schemata
on Recall and Inference

The effects of cultural stereotypes on the recall and use of information have long been recognized (cf. Bartlett, 1932). However, a recent study by Cohen (1977) provides a nice demonstration of certain of these effects. In this study, two vocational roles, those of librarian and waitress, were examined. Preliminary data confirmed that judges typically had quite a different behavioral stereotypes of occupants of these two roles. For example, librarians were typically judged to have brown hair and glasses, to drink wine for dinner, to like salad and roast beef, to play the piano, and to like classical music; in contrast, waitresses were typified as blonde and without glasses, liking beer and hamburgers, playing the guitar, and liking pop music. Based on these normative data, videotapes were constructed of a woman coming home from work and interacting with her husband during the course of an informal birthday dinner he had prepared for her. Each tape contained cues consistent with each of the two stereotypes. Judges viewed one of these tapes after being told that the woman they would see worked either as a librarian in the city or as a waitress in a local coffee shop. Thus, the woman's vocational role was always consistent with half of the relevant cues in each tape and inconsistent with the other half. The judges were told to form an impression of the woman as if she were someone they had met in a real life situation. Then, after viewing the tape, they were asked to recall specfic information that was relevant to the two stereotypes (e.g., whether the woman had drunk beer or wine for dinner). This recall task was performed either immediately after watching the tape or several days later.

As expected, cues that were consistent with the actor's vocational role stereotype were recalled more accurately than those that were inconsistent with this stereotype. Moreover, errors of recall were typically in the direction of the stereotype. Finally, the number of stereotype-biased errors increased with the time between viewing the tape and the recall task. These data suggest that judges did indeed invoke a stereotypic schema in recalling the information and that their tendency to do so increased over time. In other words, the judges' encoding of the actor in a particular category had more effect on the actor's perceived characteristics as time went on, while the original information had less.

There are some interpretative ambiguities in this study. For one thing, since judges were informed of the actor's social role before they viewed the tape, it is unclear whether differences in recall reflect differences in the attention paid to various cues while watching the tape or differences in the reconstruction of this material after the fact. Perhaps if judges had not been informed of the actor's role until after they viewed the tape, they might have constructed a different representation of the persons than they did when they knew the actor's role at the outset. This is suggested by J. R. Anderson and Hastie's (1974) study, described in Chapter 3. However, if our generalization of the implications of this latter study is valid, it suggests that the effect of stereotyping may actually be greater in such "After" conditions than it was in the "Before" conditions constructed by Cohen.

Another problem in interpreting these data results from the forced choice procedure used to assess memory. On critical items, judges were asked whether the stimulus person had a characteristic representative of one stereotype or a characteristic representative of the other (e.g., whether the waitress drank beer or wine). Suppose that the proportion of cues the judge actually remembered was the same, regardless of whether they were consistent or inconsistent with the stereotype. Suppose further that in those cases where judges did *not* recall a cue, they typically *guessed* that the cue would be consistent with stereotype. Such guesses would be fortuitously correct when the cue was, in fact, consistent with the stereotype, and thus would increase the apparent accuracy of responses on the recognition task. This could produce the results obtained. In other words, the obtained difference in recognition accuracy may not indicate a difference in true recall accuracy, but rather may reflect the use of stereotypes in guessing under conditions where the judge has no recollection whatsoever of the actual stimulus event. Signal detection theory and methodology might be used to isolate these two contributors to recognition accuracy. Despite this problem, however, Cohen's provocative findings are consistent with the implications of other results to be reported below.

Effects of Encoding Specific Behaviors on Recall and Subsequent Judgments

General Considerations

We have hypothesized that the encoding of a person's behavior may be used as a basis for inferences about the person independently of his original behavior, and that the effect of this encoding may increase over time. These possibilities become particularly important when the behavior involved may be encoded in several ways, and each way may have different implications for the actor's other traits or behaviors. Consider our earlier example in which a person was observed helping another on an examination. Such behavior could be encoded either as "kind," "intelligent," or "dishonest." Moreover, suppose "kind" is typically associated with "likeable" in judges' semantic structures, "dishonest" with "dislikeable," and "intelligent" with neither "likeable" nor "dislikeable." Then, if judgments of the actor's likeableness are based upon the initial encoding of his behavior, and not upon the behavior itself, these judgments may be quite different, depending on which trait was originally used to encode the behavior. Specifically, an observer who has encoded the actor's behavior as kind, and who later bases his likeableness judgment entirely on this earlier encoding, would rate the actor as likeable, whereas an observer in similar circumstances who encoded the actor's behavior as dishonest would subsequently rate him as dislikeable, and an observer who had encoded the behavior as intelligent might give the actor a neutral evaluation.

The above considerations imply that evaluative judgments of an actor may be influenced directly by situational factors that predispose judges to encode behavior in different ways. The imposition of different kinds of interpolated judgment tasks accomplishes this quite easily. For example, judges might be asked to rate the actor on scales pertaining to kindness, honesty or intelligence before making an overall evaluation of him. On the other hand, similar effects should occur even if judges are not explicitly instructed to make direct inferences on these traits, but rather consider one or another traits implicitly while making some other judgment. For example, suppose three observers of the actor's behavior were asked, respectively, if they would like: (a) to have a date with the actor; (b) to study with him for an examination; or (c) to lend him money. In making these predictions, the observers are likely to encode the actor's behavior as "friendly," "intelligent," and "dishonest," respectively, and these encodings are apt to affect their subsequent judgments of the actor's likeableness in much the same way as the more direct questions.

This example raises the possibility that the concepts that a judge activates in interpreting information, and therefore the judgments he makes on the basis of this information, will depend on his perspective and objectives at the time the information is received. Suppose the actor's behavior in the situation described above was observed by: (a) the recipient of the actor's help on the examination; (b) another student who is also in need of help; and (c) a proctor. Alternatively, suppose the three judges are actually nonparticipants in the situation observed, but are asked to *imagine* themselves in these three roles. It seems likely that these either real or imagined perspectives would lead the concepts "kind," "intelligent," and "dishonest," respectively, to be activated and used to encode the actor's behavior. If the three judges were later asked how much they would like the actor, differences analogous to those described previously should occur.

A related implication of the preceding analysis (which is also implied by the priming effects postulated in Chapter 3) is that judgments of a person may depend upon the order in which they are made. Specific behaviors such as "helping someone out on exams" may be encoded at different times using both a favorable trait ("kind") and an unfavorable one ("dishonest"). But since evaluatively similar traits are more closely associated than evaluatively dissimilar ones (see Fig. 3.3), a kind person will generally be perceived as also honest, and a dishonest person will generally be viewed as also unkind. Thus, suppose one person who observes our actor is asked first to infer the actor's honesty and then his kindness, while a second observer is asked first to infer the actor's kindness and then his honesty. The first judgment by each observer will be based directly on the actor's behavior, while the second may be based in part upon the implications of the initial encoding. Therefore, the first judge is apt to label the actor as more "dishonest" than the second, who infers the actor's honesty after rating his kindness. Similarly, the second judge is more apt to infer the actor to be "kind" than is the first. (The implicit assumption that this may occur underlies the counterbalancing of judgment order in much social inference research.)

Once the actor's behavior is encoded it is unlikely that judgments will be based *exclusively* on the implications of that encoding. Rather, the judge's inference is likely to be a weighted function of the implications of this encoding and those of the original information. However, as Ebbesen's work suggests (see also Tulving, 1972), and as Wyer and Srull's memory model implies (see Chapter 3), the relative influence of this encoding may increase with the time interval between this encoding of the information and the final judgment.

Empirical Evidence

An extensive study by Carlston (1977) investigated the effects of judges' initial inferences about an actor on their subsequent judgments of him. This study demonstrated that such inferences affect the recall and interpretation of the original stimulus information as well as judgments of the actor's traits. The basic procedure used in this study was to present judges with information describing several of an actor's behaviors, then to interpolate a judgment task designed to affect the encoding of these behaviors, and finally to assess the judge's impressions of the actor along a number of additional trait dimensions. The type and implications of the interpolated judgments, and also the type of behavioral information presented, were varied in a manner described below.

Stimulus Materials.   The stimulus information in all conditions consisted of a set of six paragraphs, each describing a separate incident involving a fictitious student, John Sun. In combination, the incidents implied that John was either kind and dishonest or was unkind and honest. Since previous research had demonstrated that kindness and honesty were positively associated in people's implicit personality theories, judges were assumed not to expect these combinations of traits to coexist in a single person.

The incident sets varied not only in their trait implications but also in the nature of the incidents described. In *single-implication* sets, each incident was directly relevant to only one of the traits involved (kindness or honesty); specifically, the set included three incidents relating to one of the two traits, and three different incidents relating to the other. In *multiple-implication* sets, however, each incident in a set had implications for both traits simultaneously; that is, each described a behavior that either implied both kindness and dishonesty, or implied both unkindness and honesty. For example, two of the incidents in the single-implication condition conveying kindness and dishonesty described John as: (a) very polite and complimentary when a friend showed him her redecorated apartment (kind); and as (b) denying to an instructor that he had plagiarized a term paper (dishonest). In contrast, two of the incidents in the corresponding multiple-implication condition described John as: (a) saving a friend from embarrassment by going along with a story he had made up; and as (b) telling a poet friend that his poetry was very good, although John actually thought it was terrible. Alternatively, two of the six incidents in the single-implication condition conveying unkindness and honesty described John as: (a) taking his girl friend to a party where she didn't know anyone and abandoning her for the entire evening (unkind); and as (b) admitting to an instructor that he hadn't put much work into an exam and deserved to fail (honest). Two of the incidents in the corresponding multiple-implication conditions described him as: (a) telling his girl friend that he didn't like her new hair style; and (b) telling an instructor that his absentee roommate was not as sick as he had claimed to be. Thus, the stimulus sets taken as a whole always implied that John possessed evaluatively different traits. However, in some cases, these inconsistent implications are the result of different behaviors, while in others, the same implications could be drawn from any given behavior in isolation.

The manipulation described above was introduced to explore the possible mediating effects of interpolated judgments on the recall and interpretation of the original material. For example, a judge who describes an actor as kind may subsequently recall the behaviors on which this judgment was based more readily than behaviors irrelevant to the judgment, and this differential recall, as well as the interpolated judgment per se, might affect subsequent inferences about the actor. If this is so, however, the effect of these recall biases should be more pronounced in single-implication conditions than in multiple-implication conditions (where every behavior has the same implication). On the other hand, a judge who infers the actor to be kind may tend to bias his recall of the *implications* of the information presented to make them more evaluatively consistent with this trait. (For example, after judging John to be dishonest on the basis of information that he helped another on an exam, the judge may recall the behavior as "John cheats on exams," thus emphasizing dishonesty, and minimizing its implications for favorable qualities such as kindness.) If such distortions in the recall of the implications of original information affect subsequent judgments, however, their effects should be more pronounced in multiple-implication conditions than in single-implication conditions. These possibilities were investigated.

Judgment Conditions.   After judges received one of the four types of stimulus sets described above, they made ratings that directed their attention to one of the two evaluatively inconsistent aspects of John's character (either his kindness or his honesty). In some conditions, these ratings explicitly involved trait labelling, while in others, judges only implicitly assigned these labels. Specifically, judges run under *explicit rating* conditions rated John along scales bounded by the relevant trait terms (*kind* versus *unkind,* or *honest* versus *dishonest*). Thus, these judges were forced to translate their appeals of John's character into explicit trait terminology. In contrast, judges under *implicit rating* conditions rated John's suitability for a job that was described as requiring either kindness or honesty, but did not rate these traits per se.

After making their initial ratings, half of the subjects in each condition were given a five minute break (*short* delay), while the remainder were dismissed for a full week (*long* delay). In each case, when the subjects returned they rated John on a number of trait scales, including several related to kindness and honesty. Then they attempted to recall both the original stimulus information and their earlier interpolated judgments.

The nature of the interpolated judgments made was expected to affect subjects' impression of John, and hence their ratings of him along the final trait rating scales. Specifically, if judges use their ratings of John along the interpolated trait dimension as bases for their subsequent judgments of him along the final trait dimensions, these latter judgments should be more favorable when the interpolated trait judgment is favorable than when it is unfavorable. (For example, under conditions in which John was attributed kind and dishonest behaviors, subjects should evaluate him more favorably after an interpolated kindness judgment than after an interpolated honesty judgment.) However, if judges base their final ratings on a review of the original stimulus information they can recall, then the nature of their interpolated judgments should have no effect. Two sets of results are of particular interest in evaluating these possibilities and when they are most likely to occur. One concerns the effect of the type of behavioral information presented (i.e., whether it had single or multiple implications). The other concerns the combined effects of delay and the explicitness of the interpolated judgment.

Effects of Type of Information.   The effect of subjects' interpolated judgments depended in part upon whether each piece of behavioral information had implications for only one of the two traits or for both traits simultaneously. The nature of this contingency is shown in Fig. 4.1. Under single-implication conditions, final ratings were more favorable when the interpolated judgment had favorable implications than when it had unfavorable implications, as expected. Under multiple-implication conditions, however, more unfavorable ratings were made in the former conditions than in the latter.

The results obtained under single-implication conditions are consistent with the hypothesis that subjects recall their interpolated judgments and use them, in conjunction with their implicit personality theories, as bases for their

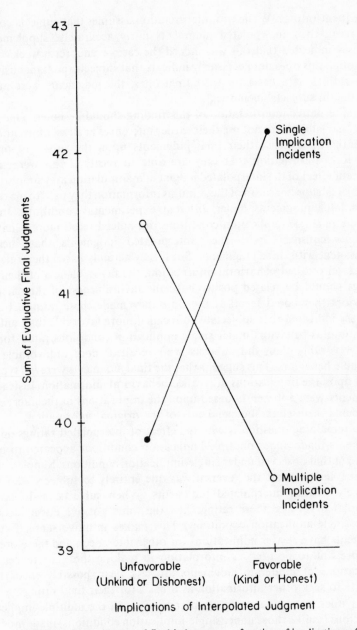

FIG. 4.1. Favorableness of final judgment as a function of implications of behavioral information for interpolated judgment and as a function of type of behavioral information.

subsequent ratings. While this interpretation assumes that subjects could in fact recall their interpolated judgments fairly accurately, supplementary analyses indicated that this was indeed the case, even after a week's delay. (Although this does not necessarily indicate that subjects spontaneously used these ratings as a basis for their final ones, the judgments were at least available in subjects' memories).

An alternative interpretation of this finding should be noted. One could argue that subjects do not use their earlier inferences at all as information per se. Rather, they base their final judgments upon the subset of original behavioral information that they are able to recall. If this were so, the apparent effect of the interpolated judgment manipulation may simply be due to subjects' superior recall of the stimulus information they used to make their interpolated judgments under different experimental conditions. In fact, subjects in single implication conditions did indeed recall more behavioral incidents consistent with their interpolated judgments than incidents inconsistent with these judgments. But if they actually based their final trait ratings on recalled behavioral information, the favorableness of their final ratings should be related positively to the favorableness of the particular behaviors they could recall at the time they made these ratings. Further analyses indicated that subjects who recalled more favorable than unfavorable stimulus behaviors under single implication conditions rated John no more favorably than did subjects who recalled more unfavorable than favorable behaviors. This suggests that the final judgments were *not* typically based upon the implications of recalled behavioral information. Instead, the judgments were apparently based upon the implications of the interpolated judgments themselves, independently of the original information.

The remaining question is why the effect of interpolated ratings on final judgments made under multiple-implication conditions appeared to be the reverse of that observed under single-implication conditions. Supplementary analyses showed that the reversal was due entirely to subjects who made relatively neutral interpolated judgments. When subjects made extreme interpolated ratings, these ratings had the same positive effect identified under single-implication conditions. This makes intuitive sense: Extreme judgments have clearer implications for other inferences, and therefore may be more apt to be used as information in making these inferences. The implications of moderate judgments are less clear, possibly encouraging subjects to seek other information as a basis for their final ratings.

This does not explain why so many judges in the multiple-implication conditions (unlike those under single-implication conditions) made moderate interpolated judgments. Conceivably the moderate judgments are a result of spontaneous encoding of the stimulus information *prior* to the interpolated judgment task. Each individual stimulus behavior was selected on the basis of normative data indicating that, when considered in *isolation*, it had extreme implications for both traits. However, when faced with a large amount of behavioral information, subjects may simply have focussed upon its implications for only one of the two traits and not both. Thus, suppose a judge who receives behavioral information implying both kindness and dishonesty spontaneously characterizes John as kind, and disregards the implications of the information for John's dishonesty. If he is then asked to make an interpolated judgment of John's kindness, he should of course rate John as very kind, and should ultimately use this extreme judgment in making his final judgment of John's honesty, in the manner suggested above. However, suppose he is asked instead to make an interpolated judgment of John's honesty. In this case, the subject may arrive at some compromise between the implications of the behavior presented and those of his spontaneous kindness judgment, thus rating John fairly neutrally. Subsequently, in making his final ratings, the judge may be more affected by his spontaneous (extreme) kindness judgment than by the neutral dishonesty judgment he actually reported. His final ratings would then appear evaluatively inconsistent with the stimulus information's implications for the interpolated judgment, as results in Fig. 4.1 suggest.

Effects of Delay and Type of Interpolated Judgment. Additional insight into the conditions in which interpolated judgments are used as bases for final ratings is provided by the combined effects of delay and type of interpolated judgment. The positive effect of interpolated judgments on final trait ratings was expected to increase with the time interval between the final judgment and the presentation of the behavioral information. This was in fact the case when interpolated judgments were explicit. However, time delay had the opposite effect when interpolated judgments were implicit. That is, these judgments had a positive influence on final ratings made only five minutes afterwards, but after a week this influence was no longer apparent. Perhaps the job appraisal involved in arriving at implicit judgments required more cognitive work than that required to make explicit judgments, causing implicit personality theories to be brought into play earlier. However, subjects who made implicit interpolated judgments reported relatively less confidence in their recall of these judgments; this may have diminished the effect of these judgments in long delay conditions. This interpretation is obviously speculative and requires further investigation.

Priming Effects on Encoding of Information and Inference Making

Despite certain ambiguities, Carlston's data provide strong general support for the hypothesis that after judges encode behavior in a certain way in order to make an initial judgment, they often use this encoding, rather than the original behavioral information, as a basis for their later judgments. Moreover, when the initial judgment involves explicit trait labels its effects may increase over time. Additional evidence in support of these conclusions has been obtained by Higgins, Rholes, and Jones (1977), in a study mentioned briefly in Chapter 3 in the context of "priming" effects. At that time, we noted that the likelihood that a judge uses a category to encode information increases to the extent that this or related categories have been activated in the recent past. To explore the implications of this possibility for impression formation, Higgins et al. first administered a color naming task to judges. As part of this task, each judge was required to remember 10 words, 4 of which were trait names. In two (*Applicable Priming*) conditions, the names could in each case be used to describe a set of stimulus behaviors that were presented later on. However, the descriptions were either all favorable (*adventurous, self-confident, independent,* and *persistent*) or all unfavorable (*reckless, conceited, aloof,* and *stubborn*). In two other (*Inapplicable Priming*) conditions, the four trait terms also had either favorable or unfavorable implications, but were inappropriate for describing the set of behaviors. After being exposed to one of these sets of trait terms as part of the "color naming task," judges ostensibly took part in an unrelated study of "reading comprehension." Here, they were asked to read the following paragraph about a stimulus person, Donald, whose behavior could be readily encoded using the trait terms in either of the Applicable Priming sets. (The two applicable trait terms, which were of course not contained in the paragraph read by judges , are given in brackets following each behavioral description):

> Donald spent a great deal of his time in search of what he liked to call excitement. He had ... risked injury, and even death, a number of times.... He was thinking, perhaps he would do some skydiving or maybe cross the Atlantic in a sailboat [*adventurous/reckless*]. By the way he acted, one could readily guess that Donald was well aware of his ability to do many things well [*self-confident/conceited*]. Other than business engagements, Donald's contacts with people were rather limited. He felt he didn't really need to rely on anyone [*independent/aloof*]. Once Donald made up his mind to do something, it was as good as done.... Only rarely did he change his mind, even when it might well have been better if he had [*persistent/stubborn*]. [Higgins et al., 1977, page 145]

After reading the above paragraph, half of the subjects under each priming condition were asked to characterize Donald's behavior in their own words, while the remaining judges were not. Then, all judges evaluated Donald. Finally, they attempted to recall exactly the content of the paragraph they had read. About two weeks later, all judges returned and again both evaluated Donald and attempted to recall the stimulus paragraph.

Results had several implications for both the effects of encoding and the reasons for their occurrence. First, of those judges who characterized

Donald's behavior in their own words under Applicable Priming conditions, 70% used trait terms that were mostly consistent in their evaluative implications with the priming words; however, only 25% of the judges used such terms under Inapplicable Priming conditions. These data suggest that judges did in fact encode behavior using primed concepts under conditions in which these concepts were appropriate for characterizing the behavior. When these primed concepts were not descriptively applicable, however, their evaluative implications had no effect on characterizations of Donald.

If applicable priming affects the encoding of Donald's behavior, and if the evaluative implications of these encodings are the basis for judges' subsequent evaluations, Donald should be evaluated more favorably when applicable priming terms are favorable than when they are unfavorable. However, the favorableness of inapplicable priming words should have no effect on Donald's evaluations. Moreover, if the effects of encoding increase over time relative to the effects of the original stimulus information, these differences should be greater several days after the stimulus material was presented than they were at first. Data shown in Table 4.1 support these predictions. It is also worth noting that priming effects were not contingent upon whether or not judges made overt characterizations of Donald's behavior before evaluating him. This suggests that the encoding that apparently mediated judges' evaluations occurred automatically during the course of reading the stimulus material (under a "reading comprehension" set) and did not depend on whether judges were required to make these encodings overtly.

Note. It is important to distinguish between the increase in priming effects over time reported by Higgins et al. and the decreased effects of priming over time reported by Srull and Wyer in the study described in Chapter 3. In the latter study, the time interval between the priming task and the presentation of the stimulus material was manipulated. A decreased effect over time in this case may occur for reasons implied by the spreading excitation model of memory described in Chapter 3. In contrast, in the study

TABLE 4.1

Mean Desirability Rating of Target Person as a Function of Applicability of Priming, Evaluative Implications of Priming Words, and Time Interval between Stimulus Information and Final Judgment[a]

	Applicable Priming		Inapplicable Priming	
	Favorable	*Unfavorable*	*Favorable*	*Unfavorable*
Immediate judgment	.80	.30	.30	.30
Final judgment	.95	–.75	.20	–.20

[a]Adapted from Higgins et al. (1977).

by Higgins et al. this interval was held constant, and the time interval between the initial encoding of the information presented and the subsequent judgment was varied. Once the encoding has been made, the effect may decrease less rapidly over time than the effect of the original information presented, for reasons noted earlier in this chapter and also suggested by the formulation developed by Wyer and Srull (in press). Thus, both sets of results are consistent with the general formulation outlined in this volume.

4.3 ILLUSORY CORRELATIONS: EFFECTS OF ENCODING OF INFORMATION ON INFERENCES OF RELATIONS AMONG CONCEPTS

The effects of encoding described above have implications for an intriguing phenomenon first uncovered by Chapman (1967) and more recently applied by Hamilton and Gifford (1976) to social inference. This research suggests that concepts that are used infrequently to describe persons or events are judged to co-occur more often than is objectively the case. Thus, suppose one group of persons, A, contains more members than a second group, B. Furthermore, suppose trait X is more frequently used to characterize people than trait Y. Finally, suppose that the relative proportions of people with X and Y are objectively the same in both groups. Nevertheless, judges may infer B and Y (the two infrequently used concepts) to co-occur with a greater probability than A and Y. Consequently, if X and Y have different evaluative implications, this overestimation of the co-occurrence of B and Y may lead B to be evaluated differently than A, and to be assigned other characteristics associated with Y with relatively higher probability.

Support for this possibility was obtained in two studies by Hamilton and Gifford (1976). In each study, stimulus materials were constructed consisting of statements about members of two groups, A and B. These statements described either desirable or undesirable behaviors manifested by individual members of the two groups. The numbers of statements pertaining to A and B, and describing desirable and undesirable behaviors, were varied systematically in each study in the manner described in Table 4.2a. That is, statements about members of A occurred more often than statements about members of B. The *proportion* of times that each type of behavior was assigned to members of each group was the same within each experiment. However, undesirable behaviors were less common than desirable ones in Experiment 1, but were more common than desirable ones in Experiment 2.

In each experiment, judges were instructed that the study was concerned with "how people process and retain information that is presented to them visually." They were then exposed to a random sequence of the 39 (or 36) statements on slides and asked to read each statement carefully as it was

TABLE 4.2
Actual and Predicted Frequencies of Co-occurrences of Behaviors Manifested by Majority-
and Minority-Group Members[a]

		Experiment 1		Experiment 2	
		Group A	Group B	Group A	Group B
A.	Actual numbers of stimulus sentences				
	Desirable behaviors	18(67%)	9(33%)	8(67%)	4(33%)
	Undesirable behaviors	8(67%)	4(33%)	16(67%)	8(33%)
B.	Numbers of behaviors attributed by subjects				
	Desirable behaviors	17.5(65%)	9.5(35%)	5.9(49%)	6.1(51%)
	Undesirable behaviors	5.8(48%)	6.2(52%)	15.7(65%)	8.3(35%)
C.	Actual and estimated frequencies of uncommon behaviors of members of A and B				
	Actual	8(31%)	4(31%)	8(33%)	4(33%)
	Estimated	8.9(34%)	5.7(44%)	8.2(34%)	6.6(55%)

[a]Adapted from Hamilton & Gifford (1976).

presented. After exposure to these statements, three sets of judgments were made in counterbalanced order. First, judges were presented with each of the behaviors described in the stimulus statements and were asked to infer whether the behavior had described a member of A or a member of B. Second, they made direct estimates of how many of the statements about members of each group described desirable (or undesirable) behavior. Third, they rated both group A and group B along a series of trait dimensions with evaluative implications (e.g., popular, sociable, intelligent, lazy, irritable, etc.).

Data pertaining to the first two sets of ratings are shown in Tables 4.2b and 4.2c as a function of the desirability of the behavior and of the group to which the behavior was assigned. The results of each experiment have similar implications. The relative proportions of "common" behaviors (desirable in Experiment 1, and undesirable in Experiment 2) attributed to members of A and B were similar to the actual proportions of times they occurred in the stimulus information (see Table 4.2b). However, the relative proportion of "uncommon" behaviors attributed to the minority group (B) was much greater (51%) than was objectively the case (33%). Moreover, judges' own estimates of the frequency with which uncommon behaviors were associated with majority-group members were similar to the actual frequency of their association, while their estimates of the frequency with which uncommon behaviors were assigned to minority-group members was substantially greater than the actual frequency (see Table 4.2c).

If judges' evaluations of group members are mediated by their attributions of desirable and undesirable behaviors to these members, the biases described above should affect the favorableness of traits assigned to these members. Results supported this hypothesis. Specifically, although the actual proportions of desirable and undesirable behaviors assigned to members of A and B were the same, judges evaluated A more favorably than B along trait dimensions in Experiment 1, but less favorably than B along these same dimensions in Experiment 2.

Although illusory correlation phenomena appear reliable, the reasons for their occurrence remain unclear. There are at least two possible explanations. First, low frequency (uncommon) characteristics may be interpreted by the judge as "novel" or "distinctive." If these characteristics are encoded as instances of the same category ("novel" or "distinctive"), a direct association between them may be established that affects subsequent inferences about the likelihood of the relation's occurring. Second, an uncommon *relation* between two categories may be more attention-getting, and therefore its frequency of occurrence may be over-predicted for this reason (Tversky & Kahneman, 1973). The implications of these two interpretations are not necessarily the same. For example, two classes of elements may be fairly large but virtually nonoverlapping, while two other classes may be small but have many more members in common than the first two (larger) classes. In such instances, it is unclear whether overestimates of the co-occurrence of the two classes would be greater in the first case or in the second. In Hamilton and Gifford's study, the frequency of occurrence of the *relation* to be inferred and the frequency of occurrence of *category* instances involved in the relation were confounded. Hence, the relative validity of the two interpretations cannot be evaluated.

Despite this ambiguity, the findings reported by Hamilton and Gifford are provocative for both practical and theoretical reasons. For example, the authors point out the implications of their findings for stereotyping. Suppose unfavorable behaviors are less commonly exhibited by persons in general than are desirable behaviors. If this is the case, then even though majority and minority group members manifest behaviors of each type with objectively equal probability, judges will typically overestimate the proportion of undesirable behaviors manifested by members of the minority group, and consequently will evaluate members of this group unfavorably. This impact stems in part from the fact that higher level encodings seem to become autonomous of the stimulus information on which they are based, producing independent effects on subsequent inferences. Moreover, these effects may increase with time. These conclusions have far-reaching implications for social inference processes, since they suggest that judgments may be influenced not only by the implications of information per se, but also by situational or contextual factors that predispose judges to encode the information in different ways. These contextual factors may actually be related to informational characteristics only indirectly, and yet they may have substantial effects on inferences. These possibilities extend our notions of priming effects, and also open up new avenues of investigation dealing with the determinants and consequences of people's directed thought processes.

The considerations raised earlier in this chapter suggest still other implications. For example, suppose that a given person is a member of both a large, well-known group and a small, uncommon group. Moreover, suppose that a given behavior may be encoded using either a very common trait label or a very uncommon one. If the implications of Hamilton and Gifford's results are valid, the person should be inferred to manifest the behavior with higher probability if the person and his behavior are interpreted as instances of infrequently used concepts (groups or traits) than if they are interpreted as instances of frequently used concepts. Priming effects similar to those constructed by Higgins et al. (1977) could be used to test this hypothesis.

III

IDENTIFYING THE IMPLICATIONS OF INFORMATION FOR JUDGMENTS

Once information is encoded or interpreted, its use in making inferences may often depend upon assumptions the judge makes about its implications. For instance, the inference that a person who helps another out on an examination is kind is based in part on the assumption that persons who help others out typically have this attribute. In considering even this mundane example, however, three questions arise. One concerns the factors that affect subjects' likelihood of making a given assumption, or that affect their belief that the assumption they make is valid. It is certainly not *always* the case that a person who helps another out on an exam is kind. Whether this assumption is made, and the belief held that it is valid, may depend on characteristics of the information presented and its situational context.

Second, although information may be available for use in making judgments, its implications may not be recognized. The extent to which the implications of a given piece of information are considered may depend in part upon the nature of other available information. For example, in some instances certain aspects of the information available may distract the judge from attending to other relevant aspects. In other cases, when information is either unclear or potentially disturbing, it may stimulate the judge to seek additional knowledge, either present in the judgmental situation or stored in memory, that will help him to evaluate its implications. Information may also provide a standard for interpreting the implications of other pieces of information. Thus, for example, information that another person works 18 hours a day may be used as a basis for evaluating the implications of one's own work day for one's own industriousness.

A third set of questions concern the precise cognitive processes surrounding the use of assumptions about the implications of information to arrive at judgments. As we will argue, these processes may often be syllogistic. (In the above example, the inference that the target person is kind may be based upon reasoning that the target person helped someone on an exam and that if a person helps someone out under these circumstances, he is kind.)

The three chapters in this section are concerned with these matters. In Chapter 5, we consider certain characteristics of the information presented about a person or event that affect one's evaluation of its implications. In Chapter 6, we will direct our attention to the indirect effects of information upon the identification of other relevant information, and the perceived implications of this information. Finally, in Chapter 7, we will present a general formulation of the process of construing the implications of information for a judgment. This formulation, which is based in part upon the syllogistic formulation of inference processes proposed by McGuire (1960) and Wyer (1975c), provides a conceptual link between certain of the issues raised in the previous section of this volume and those of concern here.

5   Characteristics of Information that Affect Its Perceived Implications

The assumptions a judge makes about the implications of received information may be influenced in part by the particular subset of his past experience that he happens to retrieve and use as a basis for interpreting this information. (For a detailed analysis of these possibilities, see Chapters 2 and 4.) These assumptions may also be affected by the context in which the information is presented or, finally, by general characteristics of the information itself. These characteristics have been studied primarily in the area of impression formation, where liking for a person is inferred on the basis of personality adjectives describing him. The extent to which the results of this research generalize to conditions involving other types of information and other types of judgments has not been clearly established. However, certain generalizations seem reasonable. For instance, conceptual similarities exist between certain factors known to affect the contribution of adjective descriptions to liking judgments and factors postulated to affect attributions based upon behavioral information. These similarities will be examined in this chapter.

Several informational characteristics that affect the contribution of personality adjectives to liking judgments have been discussed in detail elsewhere (Wyer, 1974b, Chapter 8). We will concentrate here upon a subset of variables that appear to be of greatest potential relevance to a general understanding of factors that affect the perceived implications of information for judgments. These variables include information ambiguity, inconsistency, order of presentation, novelty and redundancy. We will argue that these factors influence judgments primarily insofar as they affect different assumptions that judges are apt to make about the implications of the information they characterize. Much of our discussion in the pages to follow will focus upon the nature of these assumptions and their effects. In discussing each factor, we will first define it as precisely as possible and describe briefly some of the existing research bearing on its effects, drawing mainly from the impression formation literature. Then, we will consider the relevance of the informational factor to an understanding of other types of inferences. We will devote the greatest attention to the effects of novelty and redundancy, and will propose a conceptualization based upon these effects that enables many aspects of social attribution theory (Bem, 1972; Jones & Davis, 1965; Kelley, 1967, 1971; Weiner et al., 1971) to be integrated.

5.1. ORDER OF PRESENTATION

Of the several informational characteristics that may affect judgments, the most widely studied has been the order in which information is presented. The effects of order were explored extensively in the context of research on communication and persuasion conducted by Hovland and his colleagues (Hovland, 1957), and have more recently been investigated within both the impression formation paradigm (Anderson, 1968b; Anderson & Norman, 1964; Hendrick & Costantini, 1970; Wyer, 1973b) and in the area of social attribution (for a summary, see Jones & Goethals, 1971). The question is simple: when is the first information presented most influential (a *primacy* effect) and when does the final information have greatest influence (a *recency* effect)? However, the answer is complex. A variety of factors may contribute to order effects, including: (a) differences in the attention paid to information at different points in a sequence; (b) forgetting; (c) discounting of information that is inconsistent with previously acquired information; and (d) interpretation of later information in a way that makes it consistent in meaning with earlier information. As Jones and Goethals (1971) point out, the relative contributions of these factors may depend very much upon the type of information involved, the instructional and situational conditions in which it is presented, and the type of judgment to be made.

Research performed in the impression formation paradigm (for a review, see Wyer, 1974b) tends to suggest that when judges estimate their liking for hypothetical persons described by a list of personality adjectives, primacy effects occur. These effects seem primarily attributable to decrements in the attention paid to adjectives at the end of the stimulus series (Hendrick & Costantini, 1970). However, as Jones and Goethals note, the frequent failure to detect the contribution of other factors in this research may be due to the nature of the stimulus materials generally used, and also to the artificiality of the judgmental task. Order effects produced by discounting and reinterpretation appear more evident when adjectives are presented in sentences rather than listed (Wyer, 1973b). Moreover, in other stimulus domains (e.g., attitude statements), the tendency to interpret information as semantically consistent with previous information from the same source has been clearly demonstrated (Wyer & Schwartz, 1969).

Jones and Goethals (1971) report compelling evidence that order effects also depend upon situational factors that affect subjects' interpretation of presented information. Judges watched a video tape of a student engaged in a series of brief conversations. The sequence was arranged so that the actor was either initially "accepting and benevolent" in the early conversations but "rejecting and pessimistic" in the later ones, or was initially rejecting but subsequently accepting. Each stimulus sequence was witnessed under one of two instructional conditions. In one case, judges were told that the behavioral vignettes were presented in the order they actually took place over the course of the semester. In the other condition, judges were told that the vignettes were presented in random order. In the latter "random" condition, primacy effects occurred, similar to those detected in much of the impression formation research. That is, judges rated the actor as more accepting when the "accepting" vignettes occurred at the beginning of the videotape than when they occurred at the end. In the "natural order" condition, however, no clear primacy or recency effects occurred. Anecdotal evidence obtained from judges' written descriptions of the stimulus persons is illuminating. In the random condition, few subjects developed integrated impressions (or "scripts") of the person that would account for his behavior; many, when asked to describe their overall impression of the person, either reiterated the observed behaviors, ignored half of the information, or described the target person as "confused" or "insecure." In contrast, judges under the natural order condition typically developed hypotheses to account for the student's inconsistency, explaining his shift in outlook in terms of external events that occurred during the semester. This difference has important implications for the cognitive processes underlying person perception under different instructional conditions (a topic we will return to in Chapter 8). More generally, it suggests that the nature of order effects depends heavily upon judges' assumptions about why the information occurs in the order it does, and therefore the scripts they form in an attempt to interpret this information (see Chapter 2).

A series of studies by Jones, Rock, Shaver, Goethals, and Ward (1968) provides additional evidence that order effects reflect the scripts judges form in trying to interpret ordered information. In these studies, judges evaluated an actor's ability and motivation from information about his performance on a series of tasks. In some conditions, the actor solved more problems at the start of the series than at the end, while in others, he solved more problems at the end than at the beginning. Judgments of the actor's intelligence were greater when he had been more successful on the initial tasks, a primacy effect. Additional results eliminate the possibility that this effect reflects decreases in the attention paid to later trials. For example, in some conditions subjects estimated the probability of their success before each trial, a procedure that presumably increased the attention paid to all trials in the sequence. This might be expected to decrease any primacy effects resulting from attention decrement (cf. Anderson, 1968b, Hendrick and Costantini, 1970). In fact, however, this procedure *increased* rather than decreased the magnitude of the primacy effect, in contrast to impression formation studies using adjectives as stimulus information.

This leaves a script interpretation as the most plausible explanation for these results. As outlined in Chapter 2, judges may have used the actor's initial performance to construct a script of the actor that had implications for his ability, and then interpreted subsequent changes in performance in a manner consistent with this script (e.g., as due to changes in the actor's effort or changes in task difficulty). Note that this interpretation assumes that judges formed a script during the sequence of trials before the performance changes occurred. If the script were not constructed until after the changes had occurred, it would presumably incorporate those changes, resulting in different effects. Thus, in the Carlston study described earlier (page 39), where judges were given season records for basketball teams, recency effects were obtained in most conditions. That is, judges who viewed an improving win-loss record rated the team's ability higher than those who viewed a declining win-loss record. Since the judges viewed the entire record at the same time, they probably formed scripts that were consistent with the observed changes in performance (e.g., "team ability declined due to injuries to key personnel") rather than simply with the early performance trials, as in the Jones, et al. study. This suggests that various factors affecting the timing of script construction—such as information rate and volume, attention, motivation, and so on—may have consequences for the kinds of judgments made from ordered information.

In conclusion, no single explanation of order effects applies in all situational conditions and to all types of judgments. Factors such as attention decrement may account for the primacy effects obtained when the order of presentation of information is itself not very meaningful. However, other factors may be critical when the order itself conveys information about the actor's characteristics or the conditions in which his behavior is manifested. Thus, unlike the effects of other informational characteristics we consider in this chapter, the effects of order of presentation are unlikely to generalize over different stimulus and judgmental conditions.

5.2. AMBIGUITY AND UNCERTAINTY

Definition and Measurement

Information is ambiguous to the extent that the judge is uncertain about its implications for the inference he is trying to make. As we noted in Chapter 1, this inference may often be based upon an underlying distribution of the judge's beliefs that the object belongs to each of several alternative cognitive categories he considers relevant to the inference (Wyer, 1973a). If this is so, the ambiguity of a piece of information may be conceptually defined in terms of the dispersion of this distribution. For example, suppose an object described by A is believed to belong to each of five cognitive categories with the probabilities shown in Fig. 5.1a, and an object described by B is believed to belong to these categories with the probabilities shown in Fig. 5.1b. Then, A would be more ambiguous than B. If the cognitive categories correspond to values along an ordinal or interval scale, the ambiguity of A and B might be estimated by the standard deviation of these distributions. In other cases, it may be more appropriate to use an information index of uncertainty,[1] which does not require assumptions about the ordinal nature of these categories. (In this regard, while the distributions shown in Fig. 5.1 are approximately normal, they need not be in general.)

A distinction should be made between a judge's uncertainty about the membership of an object in various cognitive categories relevant to his judgment, and his uncertainty about its membership in the *response* categories available to him for communicating this judgment. Suppose that, as in Fig. 5.1, the cognitive categories relevant to a judgment correspond to categories along each of two rating scales. The subjective distribution of beliefs about the object's membership in the set of cognitive categories may therefore be projected onto the scales as shown. The judge's uncertainty about the information's implications for the object's membership in the response categories comprising scale 1 is greater than his uncertainty about its implications for the object's membership in the categories comprising scale 2, since his beliefs are distributed over more response categories in the former case. (Alternatively, the ambiguity of the information is greater when the first scale is used.) Thus, information ambiguity depends not only upon its perceived implications for membership in various cognitive categories but

---

[1]This index, proposed by Wyer (1973a), is expressed in the equation

Ambiguity = $-\Sigma p_i \log_2 p_i$

where p_i is the subjective probability, or belief, that the object being judged belongs to category i.

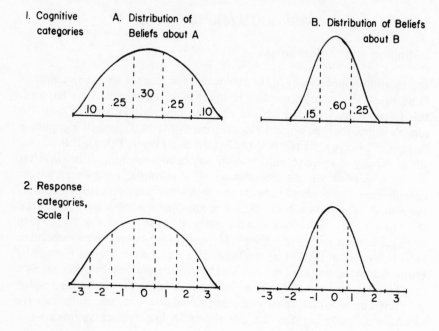

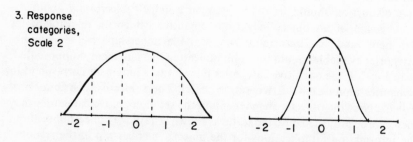

FIG. 5.1.   Distribution of beliefs about objects A and B over a set of cognitive categories, and over two sets of response scale categories related to these cognitive categories.

also upon the judge's assumptions about the relation of these categories to the response categories he is required to use. It also depends upon the particular type of judgment to be made. For example, information that a person does not cheat on examinations may have clear implications for his membership in a particular category pertaining to honesty, but may have unclear implications for his membership in categories pertaining to friendliness.

Some evidence that bears on the validity of this conceptualization has been obtained. Wyer (1973a) presented one group of subjects with sets of 1 or 2 adjectives and instructed them to distribute 100 hypothetical persons described by the adjectives in each set along a response scale of likeableness. Subjects in a second group rated a *single* person described by each adjective set, and then, after making this rating, reported their uncertainty about the validity of this rating along a second scale. The mean uncertainty expressed by subjects in this second group was correlated .74 over adjective sets with the mean value of an information index of uncertainty based upon the distributions generated by subjects in the first group (see Footnote 1), and .69 with the standard deviation of these distributions. Hinkle (1976) obtained similar results using different stimulus sets.

As we have defined it, the ambiguity of a particular piece of information may be affected by factors other than simply the nature of the information itself (e.g., the source of the information, its context, the type of judgment to be made, etc.). Thus, a variety of situational, informational and individual difference factors may affect the use of information because of their mediating effects upon the judge's perception of the information's ambiguity. Moreover, given an independently defined measure of ambiguity, these possibilities can be investigated empirically. We will elaborate upon these possibilities presently.

Effects of Ambiguity

It seems reasonable to suppose that ambiguous information will affect judgments less than unambiguous information. This hypothesis received support in a study of impression formation performed by Hinkle (1976). Based upon distributions generated by pilot subjects, Hinkle first estimated the ambiguity of personality adjectives with respect to their implications for liking. A second group of subjects then reported their liking for persons described by pairs of these adjectives varying systematically both in ambiguity and in evaluative implications. As expected, ambiguous adjectives had relatively less influence on liking judgments than unambiguous adjectives. In addition, the influence of each adjective was greater when the adjective accompanying it was ambiguous than when it was not. This suggests that when judges are confronted with ambiguous information, they not only pay less attention to this information, but pay more attention to other information available. Hinkle showed that accurate quantitative predictions of judges' inferences can be made by assuming the relative weight of each adjective to be an inverse function of its ambiguity, as defined on the basis of data collected for each subject separately.

A second finding reported by Hinkle is of considerable theoretical and empirical interest. Groups of four adjectives, A_1, A_2, B_1, and B_2, were selected such that each adjective led to the same liking judgment when it was used in isolation to describe a person. However, two of the adjectives, A_1 and A_2, were high in ambiguity, while the other two, B_1 and B_2, were low. Hinkle found that using the two ambiguous adjectives in combination to describe a person had greater effect upon liking for him than did using the two unambiguous adjectives in combination. Upon first consideration, these findings seems counterintuitive. However, note that the *reduction* in ambiguity is likely to be greater when two adjectives with initially ambiguous implications are combined than when two relatively unambiguous adjectives are combined. (If the latter two adjectives were each completely unambiguous when considered in isolation, a further reduction in ambiguity by combining them would be impossible.) In the above example, the ambiguity of A_1 and A_2 in combination would therefore be less, relative to that of each adjective considered separately, than would the ambiguity of B_1 and B_2 in combination. If the extremity of judgments based upon information is an inverse function of the ambiguity of this information, judgments based upon the two A adjectives would then be more extreme (relative to the judgment based on each separately) than would the judgment based upon the B adjectives, as Hinkle's results suggest. A more formal analysis of this phenomenon is provided in Chapter 8 in terms of its implications for algebraic inference processes.

Implications for Other Effects of Information and Other Types of Judgments

The above conceptualization gains importance in light of evidence that many other informational characteristics are related to ambiguity. For example, adjectives with extreme implications are less ambiguous than those with relatively neutral implications. Moreover, controlling for extremity, adjectives with unfavorable implications are less ambiguous than those with favorable implications (Wyer, 1974b). Therefore, adjectives with either extreme or unfavorable implications should have relatively more influence when they are combined with other information, while the influence of the accompanying information should be relatively less.[2] This often turns out empirically to be true (Birnbaum, 1974; Wyer & Hinkle, 1976; Wyer & Watson, 1969, Experiment 1).

---

[2]A distinction should be drawn between the influence of a piece of information on a judgment and the extremity of the judgment itself. A piece of information may have extreme implications for judgments along a particular scale, but still may have little influence upon these judgments when it is combined with other information. However, one indication of the importance of a piece of information is the extent to which the information accompanying it produces differences in judgments. For example, if a variation in the information accompanying A affects judgments less than does a similar variation in the information accompanying B, the relative influence of A upon these judgments is greater than the relative influence of B. For an elaboration of this logic, see Chapter 8.

The combined effects of extremity and negativity may also be understood from this perspective. First, compare the effect of an adjective that elicits a rating of –5 when presented in isolation to the effect of an adjective that elicits a rating of –2. The first adjective has both more extreme and more unfavorable implications than the second. It should therefore be much less ambiguous than the second adjective, and should consequently have greater influence when it is combined with other information. However, now compare the effect of an adjective that elicits a rating of +5 in isolation to the effect of one that elicits a rating of +2. Here, although the implications of the first adjective are more extreme, they are less unfavorable. As a result, the two adjectives may not differ appreciably in ambiguity, and consequently may have about equal influence. In general, this reasoning predicts that unfavorable adjectives will become more influential as their implications become more extreme, while favorable adjectives will not. This seems empirically to be the case (Anderson, 1965).

A variety of situational factors may also affect the contribution of information to judgments through their mediating effects upon its ambiguity. For example, information from unreliable sources may be more ambiguous and therefore less influential. This prediction has been frequently supported (Birnbaum, Wong, & Wong, 1976; Rosenbaum & Levin, 1969; Wyer, 1974b) and is hardly surprising. However, the implications of Hinkle's research are again of interest in this context. Suppose that when each of four pieces of information is presented in isolation, pieces A_1 and A_2 from an uncredible source lead to the same judgments as do pieces B_1 and B_2, respectively, from a credible source. Then, A_1 and A_2 in combination should lead to a more extreme judgment than B_1 and B_2 in combination, despite the fact that its source is relatively less credible.

While the research described above was restricted to the effects of one type of information (personality adjectives) on one type of judgment (liking for a person), the results obtained seem likely to generalize to other types of information and inferences. For example, consider the effect of an actor's behavior on inferences about the actor. The ambiguity of this information may be affected by other aspects of the situation in which the behavior occurs. Specifically, an actor's decision to deliver a speech advocating capital punishment may have more ambiguous implications for the actor's personal opinion if the actor is offered $25 to deliver the speech than if he is offered very little or nothing. Alternatively, an actor's success on a task may have more ambiguous implications for his ability if the task is easy than if it is difficult. Thus, in each case, the information should have relatively less effect on judgments in the first condition described than in the second.

These predictions, which are consistent with theory and research reported elsewhere (e.g., Bem 1965; Calder, Ross, & Insko, 1973; Weiner et al., 1971), are hardly suprising. However, the use of an independently defined index of ambiguity would help to evaluate alternative interpretations of these effects. The interpretation we have proposed is only one of several possibilities. For example, consider the different judgments of the actor's opinion under high-pay and low-pay conditions. Although this difference could result from the effects of pay on the perceived implications of the actor's behavior, it could also result from the direct implications of the pay itself. (For example, judges may assume that people who are offered high pay to defend a position are less apt to favor this position than persons who are offered little pay, irrespective of their actual decision to defend or not defend the position.) In this latter event, the effect of pay would not necessarily be mediated by its effect on the ambiguity of the behavioral information. Use of an independently defined index of ambiguity could help to separate these two alternative interpretations. Suppose that, instead of making a single estimate of the actor's position on capital punishment under the two pay conditions, judges estimated the probability that the actor's position corresponded to each of the available response scale categories. If the effect of pay is mediated by its effect on the interpretation of the actor's behavior, the distributions of probabilities under the two pay conditions might be similar to those shown in Fig. 5.2a. However, if the effect of pay is independent of the effect of the actor's behavior, the distributions might be more similar to those shown in Fig. 5.2b. Thus, a

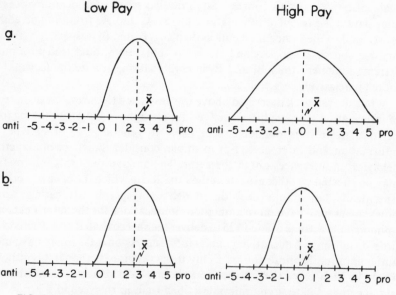

FIG. 5.2. Hypothetical distribution of beliefs about an actor's position on capital punishment under high and low pay conditions, (a) if pay affects the interpretation of the actor's behavior; and (b) if pay affects judgments independently of the actor's behavior.

consideration of ambiguity not only enables the effects of several different informational factors to be conceptually and empirically interrelated, but also helps to evaluate alternative hypotheses concerning the effects of information under different conditions.

5.3. INCONSISTENCY

Judgments based upon several pieces of information are apt to be affected by the extent to which this information is inconsistent. However, the precise role of information inconsistency remains unclear. This is partly because the nature of the construct itself is unclear. There are two distinct, although often confounded, types of inconsistency. One, *semantic* inconsistency, refers to the extent to which pieces of information can simultaneously be valid. For example, Wyer (1970a) defined two personality trait adjectives as inconsistent if a single person was less likely to be described by these adjectives in combination than would be expected by chance. Thus, if the probability of a person being described by A (P_A) is .5 and by B (P_B) is .8, A and B would be inconsistent if the probability of being described by both A and B in combination were less than .4 (the product of P_A and P_B). A second type (*implicational* inconsistency) is defined in terms of differences in the implications of the information presented for the judgment to be made (cf. Anderson & Jacobson, 1965). To illustrate the difference between semantic and implicational inconsistency, consider the adjectives *bold, rash* and *cautious*. It is hard to imagine a person who is both bold and cautious simultaneously, while a bold person is very apt to be rash. On the other hand, both *bold* and *cautious* are considered to be favorable attributes, and thus to have similar implications for how well a person possessing them would be liked, whereas *rash* is usually considered to be unfavorable, and thus to have different implications for liking than the other two adjectives. Thus, *bold* and *cautious* are semantically inconsistent, but consistent in their implications for liking, while *bold* and *rash* are semantically consistent, but inconsistent in their implications for liking.

Semantic and implicational inconsistency would seem likely to have different effects on the manner in which information is used to make judgments. However, such a difference has not been clearly demonstrated. Wyer (1970a) manipulated the semantic inconsistency of two adjectives, holding constant the evaluative implications of the adjectives involved, and found that judges discount the adjective with the most ambiguous evaluative implications when inconsistency is moderate, but discount the entire set of adjectives when the inconsistency is extreme (for an elaboration of this interpretation, see Wyer, 1974b). In an earlier study, Anderson and Jacobson (1965) found evidence that implicationally inconsistent adjectives are discounted. Specifically, when stimulus persons were described by either one unfavorable and two favorable adjectives or by one favorable and two unfavorable adjectives, the "odd" adjective appeared to receive less weight. In this study, however, the magnitude of discounting was not significantly greater when certain adjectives in the set were nearly antonyms (e.g., *honest* and *deceitful*) than when they were not (*honest* and *reckless*). This finding seems contrary to Wyer's evidence that semantic inconsistency does have an effect over and above that of implicational inconsistency. However, no direct measure of semantic inconsistency was obtained by Anderson and Jacobson, and this factor may not actually have been effectively manipulated. That is, persons described by evaluatively inconsistent characteristics in this study may not have been believed less likely to have these characteristics in combination than were persons described by the antonyms. Another possibility is that under the conditions constructed by Anderson and Jacobson, judges did not attempt to form integrated impressions of the persons described by each set of adjectives, and so semantic inconsistencies among the adjectives had little effect. There is some evidence (Wyer, 1973b) that when the information is presented in a form similar to that encountered in everyday life (i.e., in sentences, such as "John is honest and deceitful," rather than simply listed) the discounting produced by inconsistency is increased.

The need to clarify the effects of each type of inconsistency becomes apparent when considering other types of information and other types of judgments. For example, suppose a judge is asked to estimate a person's belief in war (as a means of resolving conflict) on the basis of information that the person has volunteered to deliver a pro-war speech. Suppose further that this information is accompanied by evidence from another source that either (a) the person has refused to advocate this position; (b) the person is a registered conscientious objector; or (c) the person's friends are opposed to war. In each case, one of the two pieces of information implies that the person is likely to believe in the use of war, while the other implies that he is apt to oppose war. However, the semantic inconsistency of the two pieces of information (conceptualized in terms of the likelihood that both pieces are true) is apt to differ in the three cases. While it seems unlikely that judges would process each set of information similarly in arriving at a judgment, the existence of processing differences has not been demonstrated.

5.4. NOVELTY AND REDUNDANCY

The effects of information novelty and redundancy are of particular interest since they have implications for several theoretical and empirical issues outside the area of "impression formation" research. For example, these factors are implicitly considered in theoretical formulations of the effects of behavioral information. A detailed discussion of these matters is therefore warranted. In this section, we first define novelty and redundancy, point out the relation between them, discuss procedures for assessing them, and summarize the research bearing on their effects on judgments made in impression formation tasks. Then, we will consider the implications of this discussion for inference phenomena outside the impression formation area, focusing in particular upon social attribution processes, and will show how theory and research in this area may be conceptualized and interrelated in terms of novelty and redundancy.

Definition and Measurement

Although the effects of information novelty and redundancy have typically been investigated separately (cf. Dustin & Baldwin, 1966; Feldman, 1966; Schmidt, 1969; Wyer, 1968, 1970a), the two characteristics are conceptually similar. A piece of information about an object is *novel* if it is applied infrequently to objects of the type to which it pertains. For example, the information that a person is "brutal" would be more novel than information that he is "stupid" because people are less frequently described as "brutal" than as "stupid." More formally, the novelty of a piece of information A is a function of the quantity $1 - P_A$, where P_A is the a priori belief that an object of the sort described will have the characteristic implied by the information.

 Redundancy has typically been used to describe the relation between two or more specific pieces of information. That is, one piece, B, is redundant with another, A, to the extent that the implications of B can be inferred from A with high probability. Thus, the description of a person as "trustworthy" would be redundant with a description of him as "honest," if a person described as "honest" is considered likely to have the characteristics implied by "trustworthy." More generally, the redundancy of B with A is a function of the quantity $P_{B/A} - P_B$, where P_B is the a priori belief that an object has the characteristic implied by B, and $P_{B/A}$ is the conditional belief that the object has this characteristic, given that it is described by A.[3]

---

[3]An alternative index of the redundancy of A and B would the be the extent to which beliefs that an object would be described by both (P_{AB}) is greater than the product of the beliefs that an object would be described by each considered separately, or the extent to which $P_{AB} > P_A P_B$. Considered from this perspective, redundancy and inconsistency can be conceptualized as opposite ends of a single dimension pertaining to the quantity $P_{AB} - P_A P_B$, where positive values imply redundancy and negative values imply inconsistency (see previous discussion of this construct). A more formal treatment of this possibility is provided elsewhere (Wyer, 1970a, 1974b).

The conceptual similarity between novelty and redundancy is obvious from the preceding analysis. That is, the only difference between the two constructs lies in the fact that redundancy is typically used to describe a relation between two or more specific sets of information, whereas novelty is used to describe a relation between one piece of information and one's a priori expectancies. Thus, a piece of information about an object is novel if it is not "redundant" with the judge's preconceptions about the object. Alternatively, a piece of information is redundant with a second piece if it is low in novelty within the population of objects described by the second.

Measurement. The probabilistic definitions proposed above suggest the possibility of developing quantitative measures of novelty and redundancy. One procedure was used by Wyer (1968, 1970a) in the domain of personality adjectives. To collect relevant data, subjects indicated which adjectives in a list of 240 they would use to describe each of several stimulus persons. The sample of people considered was assumed to be representative of those that subjects knew or had read about. The proportion of times that each adjective i was used to describe a person, pooled over subjects and stimulus persons, was assumed to reflect the likelihood that i would be used to describe persons in the general population, and therefore to be an index of P_i. Moreover, the conditional probability that each adjective (j) was applied to a stimulus person, given that each other adjective (i) was used to describe him, was used as an index of $P_{j/i}$. Thus, it was possible to determine both the novelty of each adjective and its redundancy with every other adjective. The use of this procedure assumes that the proportion of judges who actually use an adjective to describe a person selected at random from the general population is an estimate of each individual judge's belief that the adjective would describe such a person. Data reported in other situations (Wyer & Goldberg, 1970) suggest that this assumption is not too unreasonable. Similar procedures could be used to obtain estimates of the novelty or redundancy of information of other types.

Theoretical and Empirical Effects

The effects of novelty and redundancy may be conceptualized by applying a model of information integration similar to that proposed by Fishbein (1963). That is, suppose for simplicity that a judgment about an object, J_O, is an additive function of the implications of two attributes, A and B, each weighted by the belief that O possesses that attribute; that is,

$$J_O = P_A V_A + P_B V_B$$

(5-1)

where V_A and V_B are the implications of A and B for the judgment, respectively, and P_A and P_B are the beliefs that the object possesses these attributes. If no explicit information is presented about the object, the values of P_A and P_B are likely to be less than one. However, suppose reliable information is presented that the object has attribute A. Then, P_A should increase to unity, and P_B should become equal to $P_{B/A}$ (the belief that the object has B given that he has A). As a result,

$$J_{O,A} = V_A + P_{B/A}V_B \tag{5-2}$$

The effect of the information about A is the difference between $J_{O,A}$ and J_O, or

$$\Delta J_O = J_{O,A} - J_O = (1-P_A) V_A + (P_{B/A} - P_B) V_B \tag{5-3}$$

Note that if A and B are independent, $P_B = P_{B/A}$, and the effect of adjective A is simply the quantity $(1-P_A)V_A$; in other words, the effect is equal in magnitude to the implications of A, multiplied by its novelty as defined previously.

Now suppose additional information is presented that the object definitely possesses B as well as A. Then $P_B = 1$, and the judgment of O, $(J_{O,AB})$, would be

$$J_{O,AB} = V_A + V_B \tag{5-4}$$

The incremental effect of B, given that the object is already known to possess A, is

$$\Delta J_O = J_{O,AB} - J_{O,A} = (1-P_{B/A}) V_B \tag{5-5}$$

That is, to the extent that B is redundant with A (so that $P_{B/A}$ approaches unity), the effect of adding the information about B is lessened.

There is evidence to support the implications of this analysis. According to Equation 5-3, for example, information should have greater effect when it is novel (when P_A is small) than when it is not (P_A is large); moreover, the magnitude of this difference should increase with the extremity of the implications of this information. Wyer (1970a) found evidence supporting this hypothesis in impression formation research. According to Equation 5-5, the effect of adding a piece of information B to a second piece, A, will be less when its redundancy with A, $(P_{B/A})$, is high than when it is low, but the magnitude of this difference will be greater when the implications of B are extreme. Evidence supporting this prediction has also been obtained (Wyer, 1968).

5.5. IMPLICATIONS OF NOVELTY AND REDUNDANCY EFFECTS FOR SOCIAL ATTRIBUTION: A CONCEPTUAL INTEGRATION

The role of information novelty and redundancy in judgmental processes is of particular interest in light of the relation of these variables to concepts developed in other areas of theory and research. This relation is most apparent in the literature on social attribution. A general concern in this area has been with the extent to which information about an actor's behavior is likely to be used to infer characteristics of the actor, of the object toward whom the behavior is directed, or of the situation in which the behavior occurs. Four general theoretical formulations, by Kelley (1967), by Jones and Davis (1965), by Bem (1965, 1972), and by Weiner et al. (1971), bear upon this concern. Let us first conceptualize inferences based upon behavioral information in terms suggested by the above analyses, and then consider the implications of this conceptualization for these formulations.

General Conceptualization

Traits are typically attributed to a person on the basis of certain behaviors he is believed to manifest. This does not always mean that the person has actually been observed to manifest behavior relevant to these traits in a specific situation. Rather, the trait attributions may be made because the person is assumed a priori to manifest the behavior toward others in general or in situations in general, based upon the judge's previous experience with persons of the sort being evaluated. To the extent that a given actor is assumed a priori to perform trait-relevant behavior in a variety of situations involving a variety of other persons, information that he has done so in any specific situation is less novel (or more redundant with previous information acquired), and therefore this information will have less effect upon judgments of the actor.

The above analysis is somewhat oversimplified. The a priori expectancy that a given actor (P) will manifest a behavior toward another (O) in a given situation, and therefore the redundancy of information that he has actually done so, has three possibly independent components. One concerns the likelihood that P would also manifest the behavior toward O in situations other than that to which the information refers. A second pertains to the likelihood that P would manifest the behavior toward a variety of persons other than O in the situation in question. The third concerns the likelihood that P's behavior would also be manifested by persons other than P under comparable circumstances. However, these three components do not all have the same implications for a judgment of the actor's traits. For example, if the actor is expected to manifest the behavior toward many other persons in many situations, he may indeed be assumed to have a high degree of the trait to which the behavior is relevant. However, if the actor's behavior is expected to be manifested by many other persons as well, the actor may not be attributed any more of the trait than that possessed by persons in general; that is, he may be inferred to be average or neutral with respect to this trait.

The combined effects of the above considerations may be formalized in a manner suggested by our previous analysis of redundancy and novelty effects. Specifically, suppose a given actor P behaves in some way toward a specific object O under a particular situational condition X. Suppose further that evidence that this behavior generalizes over situations, objects and actors has implications for one of P's attributes. We will refer to these implications as $V_{\bar{X},P}$, $V_{\bar{O},P}$, and $V_{\bar{P},P}$, respectively, where the first letter in each subscript indicates the element (P, O, or X) over which the behavior generalizes, and the second refers to the element being judged. Then, as suggested by our more general analysis (see Equation 5-1),

$$J_P = P_{\bar{X}}V_{\bar{X},P} + P_{\bar{O}}V_{\bar{O},P} + P_{\bar{P}}V_{\bar{P},P} \tag{5-6}$$

where $P_{\bar{X}}$, $P_{\bar{O}}$ and $P_{\bar{P}}$ are the judge's beliefs that P's behavior generalizes over situations, objects and actors, respectively. Similar equations can also be written to describe judgments of O, (J_O), and X, (J_X); that is,

$$J_O = P_{\bar{X}}V_{\bar{X},O} + P_{\bar{O}}V_{\bar{O},O} + P_{\bar{P}}V_{\bar{P},O} \tag{5-7}$$

and

$$J_X = P_{\bar{X}}V_{\bar{X},X} + P_{\bar{O}}V_{\bar{O},X} + P_{\bar{P}}V_{\bar{P},X} \tag{5.8}$$

The above equations imply that the effects of an actor's behavior on judgments of the actor himself, the object, and the situation are interrelated through the mediating effects of this information upon $P_{\bar{X}}$, $P_{\bar{O}}$, and $P_{\bar{P}}$. However, these effects also depend upon the judge's perceptions of the implications of the behavior's generalizing over situations, objects and actors for the particular judgment to be made ($V_{\bar{X},P}$, etc.). The direction of these implications may often be predicted a priori. For example, suppose information is presented that P helps O across the street, and that judgments are to be made of attributes of P, O, and the situation that might account for, or be *correspondent* with, this behavior. For purposes of our example, assume that these attributes are P's kindness, O's age, and the situational pressure on P to manifest the behavior. The greater the generalizeability of P's behavior toward O over situations, the more likely it is that either P is kind or O is old, but the less likely it is that there is pressure on P to manifest the behavior in this particular situation; to this extent, $V_{\bar{X},P}$ and $V_{\bar{X},O}$ are apt to be

TABLE 5.1

Assumed Direction of Implications of the Generalizeability of an Actor's Behavior on Judgments of the Actor, the Object, and Characteristics of the Situation[a]

	Implications for		
	Judgments of Actor (J_P)	Judgments of Object (J_O)	Judgments of Situation (J_X)
High generalizeability over situations (high $P_{\bar{X}}$)	positive ($V_{\bar{X},P} = +$)	positive ($V_{\bar{X},O} = +$)	negative ($V_{\bar{X},X} = -$)
High generalizeability over objects (high $P_{\bar{O}}$)	positive ($V_{\bar{O},P} = +$)	negative ($V_{\bar{O},O} = -$)	positive ($V_{\bar{O},X} = +$)
High generalizeability over actors (high $P_{\bar{P}}$)	negative ($V_{\bar{P},P} = -$)	positive ($V_{\bar{P},O} = +$)	positive ($V_{\bar{P},X} = +$)

[a]Characteristics being judged are assumed to be correspondent with the behavior manifested. If a characteristic is not correspondent, the directions of the implications described in the table should be reversed.

positive, while $V_{\bar{X},X}$ is apt to be relatively negative.[4] Second, the greater the generalizeability of P's helping behavior to persons other than O, the more probable it is that either P is kind or that situational pressures are exerted on him to provide help (e.g., his scoutmaster is watching him); however, the less likely it is that O is exceptionally old, or in particular need of aid for other reasons. In other words, $V_{\bar{O},P}$, $V_{\bar{O},O}$, and $V_{\bar{O},X}$ are apt to be positive, negative, and positive, respectively. Finally, the greater the generalizeability of P's helping behavior to other actors, the more likely it is that O is old or that there are situational pressures to manifest the behavior, but the less likely it is that P is necessarily any more kind than the average person; that is, $V_{\bar{P},P}$ is negative, while $V_{\bar{P},O}$ and $V_{\bar{P},X}$ are positive.

The directional implications described above are summarized in Table 5.1. Note that the implications of two of the three types of generalizeability for each judgment are positive, while the implications of the third are negative. When differences in the magnitudes of these implications are unknown in

---

[4]It may be less correct to say that the generalizeability of P's behavior over situations has negative implications for the existence of situational pressure than to say that the failure for P's behavior to generalize over situations has positive implications for the existence of this pressure. In either event, however, an increase in the belief that a behavior generalizes over situations should decrease the inferred pressure on P to manifest the behavior, or J_X. For purposes of our present discussion, it will be easier to assume that $V_{\bar{X},X}$ is negative, and equal in magnitude to the positive implications of the behavior's *not* generalizing over situations. Similar considerations surround the interpretation of "negative" implications of generalizeability over actors for judgments of P, and generalizeability over objects for judgments of O.

advance, it is difficult to predict the influence of information that simultaneously affects more than one type of perceived generalizeability.

If a judge learns that an actor P has behaved in a particular way towards O in situation X, this information may cause him to revise his beliefs about the behavior's generalizeability over situations, objects, and actors ($P_{\bar{X}}$, $P_{\bar{O}}$, and $P_{\bar{P}}$). These revisions will presumably affect any judgments he makes about these elements. Thus, suppose a judge learns that P offers help to O. This behavior should increase the judge's beliefs concerning all three types of generalizeability. If it increased each belief to unity, his judgment of P, based upon Equation 5-6, would simply be

$$J_P = V_{\bar{X},P} + V_{\bar{O},P} + V_{\bar{P},P}$$

The change in judgments produced by the behavioral information would be the difference between this quantity and the judgment predicted on the basis of a priori beliefs in the generalizeability of the behavior, or

$$\Delta J_P = (1-P_{\bar{X},i})V_{\bar{X},P} + (1-P_{\bar{O},i})V_{\bar{O},P} + (1-P_{\bar{P},i})V_{\bar{P},P}$$

where the subscript i refers to the initial (prebehavior) values of the beliefs involved. Note that the coefficient of each component (i.e., $1-P_{X,i}$) is conceptually equivalent to the index of novelty described earlier in this section. That is, the more novel the behavior with respect to a given element (P, O, or X), the greater effect it should have on judgments. In general, of course, it is unlikely that information about an actor's behavior in a particular situation will increase beliefs in its generalizeability to unity. A more general statement of its effect would be the following, where f refers to the final (postbehavior) value of the beliefs involved:

$$\begin{aligned}\Delta J_P &= (P_{\bar{X},f} - P_{\bar{X},i})V_{\bar{X},P} + (P_{\bar{O},f} - P_{\bar{O},i})V_{\bar{O},P} + (P_{\bar{P},f} - P_{\bar{P},i})V_{\bar{P},P} \\ &= \Delta P_{\bar{X}}V_{\bar{X},P} + \Delta P_{\bar{O}}V_{\bar{O},P} + \Delta P_{\bar{P}}V_{\bar{P},P}\end{aligned} \qquad (5\text{-}9)$$

Analogous equations can be derived for the effects of the behavioral information upon judgments of O and X:

$$\Delta J_O = \Delta P_{\bar{X}}V_{\bar{X},O} + \Delta P_{\bar{O}}V_{\bar{O},O} + \Delta P_{\bar{P}}V_{\bar{P},O} \qquad (5\text{-}10)$$

$$\Delta J_X = \Delta P_{\bar{X}}V_{\bar{X},X} + \Delta P_{\bar{O}}V_{\bar{O},X} + \Delta P_{\bar{P}}V_{\bar{P},X} \qquad (5\text{-}11)$$

According to these equations, the change in judgments produced by an actor's behavior in a particular situation is a function of the extent to which knowledge of this behavior changes beliefs in its generalizeability over situations, objects, and actors. To illustrate the applicability of these equations, suppose a judge is asked to infer a male person's (P's) kindness on the basis of information that the person has offered help to either (a) a beautiful young woman, or (b) an ugly old man. The a priori beliefs that P would offer help to a beautiful woman in a variety of situations ($P_{\bar{X}}$), and that people other than P would offer help to her in this situation ($P_{\bar{P}}$), are both apt to be high, and information that P actually did offer aid will do little to alter these beliefs. The a priori belief that P would offer help to people other than O in this situation may be more moderate, but may also not be appreciably affected by information that he offered to help a beautiful woman. Thus, $\Delta P_{\bar{X}}$, $\Delta P_{\bar{O}}$ and $\Delta P_{\bar{P}}$ are all apt to be low.

In contrast, the a priori belief that P would help an ugly old man in a variety of situations is apt to be low initially, but may increase following information that P actually helped him in this particular situation. The belief that P's behavior would also be manifested towards persons other than O is also apt to increase (if P offers help to an ugly old man in the situation, he is apt to offer help to anyone). Finally, the belief that other people would help O may also increase to some extent following information that P has done so. Hypothetical values of $P_{\bar{X}}$, $P_{\bar{O}}$, and $P_{\bar{P}}$, and changes in these beliefs, are shown in Table 5.2 for both the beautiful girl and the ugly old man examples. If the implications of P's behavior generalizing over situations and objects for judgments of P's kindness are both positive (e.g., +3) and the implications of his behavior generalizing to other actors is negative (-3), the predicted judgments, and changes in these judgments, may be computed on the basis of Equations 5-6 and 5-11. These values, which are also shown in the table, indicate that P's behavior should affect judgments of his kindness to a greater extent when O is an old man than when O is a beautiful woman. Note that this analysis also has implications for differences in the effects of behavioral information on judgments of O and of the situational pressure on P to manifest the behavior, since these are presumably also mediated by changes in $P_{\bar{X}}$, $P_{\bar{O}}$ and $P_{\bar{P}}$. While the discerning reader may take exception to the arbitrary values assigned to these probabilities, or with the values assigned to different types of generalizeability, the example nevertheless demonstrates that differences in the effects of behavioral information on judgments can be conceptualized in terms of its effects on the components of Equations 5-6, 5-7, and 5-8.

Despite the ostensible concern of attribution theory and research with the change in judgments produced by behavioral information, research in this area has typically compared only the final (post-behavior) judgments under different situational and informational conditions. These judgments reflect the combined effects of both the behavior manifested and a priori beliefs in its generalizeability over persons and objects under the conditions being compared. Equations 5-6, 5-7, and 5-8 are of considerable value in evaluating the implications of this research, and also in tying together various theoretical formulations upon which it is based. To see this, let us apply the proposed

TABLE 5.2

Predicted Change in Judgments of P's Kindness (J_P) and Assumptions Underlying It, Following Information that P has Helped (a) a Beautiful Woman and (b) an Ugly Old Man

	P_X	$V_{X,P}$	$P_X V_{X,P}$	P_O	$V_{O,P}$	$P_O V_{O,P}$	P_P	$V_{P,P}$	$P_P V_{P,P}$	J_P
A. Beautiful woman										
Prebehavior	.8	+3	+2.4	.5	+3	+1.5	.8	-3	-2.4	+1.5
Postbehavior	.8	+3	+2.4	.5	+3	+1.5	.8	-3	-2.4	+1.5
Change	0	0	0	0	0	0	0	0	0	0
B. Ugly old man										
Prebehavior	.3	+3	+0.9	.5	+3	+1.5	.3	-3	-0.9	+1.5
Postbehavior	.8	+3	+2.4	.8	+3	+2.4	.4	-3	-1.2	+3.6
Change	.5	0	+1.5	.3	0	+0.9	.1	0	-0.3	+2.1

formulation to issues addressed by four major theoretical formulations of social attribution: Kelley's (1967) model of attribution processes, Jones and Davis' (1965) correspondent inference theory, Bem's (1965, 1972) theory of self-perception, and Weiner's formulation of outcome attribution (Weiner et al., 1971).

Kelley's Attribution Theory

Theoretical Considerations.

Kelley (1967) postulates that the attributions a judge makes on the basis of a person's (P's) behavior toward another person or object O are mediated by his assumptions about three factors: *consistency* (the extent to which the actor would manifest the behavior toward O in other situations), *distinctiveness* (the extent to which P is apt to manifest the same behavior toward objects or entities other than O under comparable situational conditions), and *consensus* (the extent to which persons other than P are apt to manifest the same behavior toward O under comparable conditions). These characteristics correspond directly to the three probabilities in Equations 5-6, 5-7, and 5-8. That is, consistency and consensus are positive functions of $P_{\bar{x}}$ (situation-generalizeability) and $P_{\bar{P}}$ (actor-generalizeability), respectively, while distinctiveness is a negative function of $P_{\hat{O}}$ (object-generalizeability).[5]

Kelley (see also Orvis, Cunningham & Kelley, 1975) postulates that an actor's (P's) behavior is apt to be attributed to P's own characteristics when, in addition to this behavioral information, there is evidence of high consistency (high $P_{\bar{x}}$), low distinctiveness (high $P_{\hat{O}}$), and low consensus (low $P_{\bar{P}}$). It is apt to be attributed to a characteristic of the object, O, when there is evidence of high consistency (high $P_{\bar{x}}$), high distinctiveness (low $P_{\hat{O}}$), and high consensus (high $P_{\bar{P}}$). Finally, it is apt to be attributed to situational factors when there is evidence of low consistency (low $P_{\bar{x}}$). In later work (Orvis, Cunningham & Kelley, 1975), high distinctiveness (low $P_{\hat{O}}$) and low consensus (low $P_{\bar{x}}$) were also assumed to contribute positively to situational attributions; however, the justification for these latter assumptions is unclear, for reasons we will note presently.

Kelley was primarily concerned with *causal* attributions (inferences of the extent to which an actor's behavior is due to characteristics of one element or

---

[5]Kelley's terminology is somewhat confusing since high consensus and high consistency imply high generalizeability of behavior over actors and situations, respectively, whereas high distinctiveness implies *low* generalizeability over objects. The reader who is not already familiar with this terminology may have difficulty keeping these relations in mind. In principle, clarity would be increased by restricting our discussion to a consideration of the effects of different types of generalizeability, without recourse to Kelley's terminology. However, Kelley's terms are used so extensively in this area of research that their retention seems nearly mandatory.

another), rather than with trait attributions (inferences of the magnitude of an element's characteristics). He therefore did not explicitly consider the distinction we have made between beliefs in the generalizeability of behavior ($P_{\bar{x}}$, etc.) and the perceived implications of generalizeability for the particular trait to be inferred ($V_{\bar{x},P}$, etc.). However, the combinations of conditions that Kelley assumes will maximize attributions of P's behavior to characteristics of P and O are identical to those predicted on the basis of Equations 5-6 and 5-7. On the other hand, the conditions that Orvis et al. assume will lead to situational attributions are not those implied by Equation 5-8. Specifically, this equation implies that behavioral information should have greatest effect on judgments of situational factors when there is evidence of low distinctiveness and high consensus as well as low consistency (that is, when the behavior would typically be manifested by other actors and toward other objects in the same situation, but not manifested in other situations). To make the two formulations consistent, the implications of behavior in a situation having high object-generalizeability and high actor-generalizeability ($V_{\bar{O},x}$ and $V_{\bar{P},x}$) would have to be negative rather than positive.

A more basic distinction between Kelley's conceptualization and the one suggested here concerns the manner in which information bearing upon the three types of generalizeability combines to affect judgments. Kelley (1971) postulates the existence of causal schemata, or configurations of information, that judges use as a basis for their attributions. For example, the configuration of high situation-generalizeability, high actor-generalizeability, and low object-generalizeability (high consistency, high consensus, and high distinctiveness) is assumed to function as a prototypic description of behavior that is due to an attribute of the object; the combination of high situation-generalizeability, high object generalizeability and low actor-generalizeability characterizes behavior that is due to an attribute of the actor, and so on. From the present perspective, however, each type of generalizeability information may be considered separately, and may contribute independently to judgments of all three elements (the actor, the object and the situation) in a manner predictable from the magnitude of its effects upon the component beliefs comprising Equations 5-6, 5-7, and 5-8.

Empirical Evidence

Two studies bear directly upon these matters. In the first study (McArthur, 1972), judges received information about a particular actor's behavior toward another person or object in a particular situation (e.g., "John laughs at the comedian,"), accompanied by information assumed to reflect either high or low consensus ("Almost everybody who hears the comedian laughs at him," versus "Hardly anyone who hears the comedian laughs at him,"), either high or low distinctiveness ("John does not laugh at almost any other comedian," vs. "John laughs at almost every other comedian,"), and either high or low consistency ("In the past, John has almost always laughed at the same comedian," vs, "In the past, John has almost never laughed at the comedian,"). Based upon this information, judges were asked to decide whether the behavior was caused either by something about the actor ("John"), by something about the object ("the comedian"), by something about the particular circumstances (the situation), or by some combination of all three.

McArthur's data do not provide direct tests of Equations 5-6, 5-7, and 5-8, which pertain to judgments of the magnitude of correspondent attributes possessed by the three elements (P, O, and X). However, since judges had no prior experience to draw upon in judging the hypothetical actor (or the hypothetical situation), their attribute judgments would presumably have been equivalent to their causal judgments. For example, the judgment that John's laughter was due to John's characteristics is equivalent to an inference that John has a "good sense of humor," while the judgment that John's laughter was due to the comedian is equivalent to an inference that the comedian was "funny." Moreover, the relative proportion of judges who attributed the actor's behavior to each element (P, O or X) should reflect the relative magnitude of judges' inferences that the element has an attribute correspondent with this behavior. Given these assumptions, the data reported have several implications for the proposed formulation. Three general conclusions seem justified.

1. Attributions to the actor were related negatively to both consensus and distinctiveness, but were related positively to consistency. Alternatively, these attributions increased as actor-generalizeability ($P_{\bar{P}}$) decreased and as both object-generalizeability ($P_{\bar{O}}$) and situation-generalizeability ($P_{\bar{X}}$) increased.

2. Attributions to the object were related positively to consistency, distinctiveness and consensus. That is, they increased as object-generalizeability ($P_{\bar{O}}$) decreased and as both actor-generalizeability ($P_{\bar{P}}$) and situation-generalizeability ($P_{\bar{X}}$) increased.

3. Attributions to the situation were related positively to distinctiveness and negatively to consistency, while the overall effect of consensus was not reliable. That is, they increased as both object-generalizeability ($P_{\bar{O}}$) and situation-generalizeability ($P_{\bar{X}}$) decreased, but were not reliably affected by actor-generalizeability ($P_{\bar{P}}$).

The first two sets of findings are consistent in direction with implications of Equations 5-6 and 5-7. However, the third set is not consistent with Equation 5-8. Moreover, in contradiction to implications of all three equations, the effects of the three types of generalizeability information were highly interactive. While these latter results could be disturbing to the formulation we have proposed, they may be an artifact of confounded implications in the information McArthur used to manipulate distinctiveness and consensus. The information assumed to convey high or low distinctiveness (e.g., "John does not laugh at almost any other comedian," versus "John laughs at almost any other comedian,") does not specify the situational conditions in which the behavior occurs, and could just as easily imply that John laughs (or does not laugh) at comedians in a variety of situations in addition to that in which his behavior toward O occurred. To this extent, judges may have interpreted the distinctiveness information as having direct implications for consistency as well. Similarly, consensus information (e.g., "Almost anyone who hears this comedian laughs at him,") was not explicitly tied to the immediate situation, and thus it may also have been assumed to pertain to other situations. (Items used in the other stimulus replications constructed by McArthur have a similar property.) The interactive effects of the different types of information could therefore be partially due to nonindependence of their *direct* implications for the generalizeability manipulations. This nonindependence could also account for the discrepancy from predictions based upon Equation 5-8. That is, if the information intended to convey high object-generalizeability was interpreted by judges as also implying high situation-generalizeability, it could produce a decrease in situational attributions of sufficient magnitude to override the increase expected on the basis of the information's implications for distinctiveness per se. The failure to detect a positive effect of consensus information on situational attributions may be the result of a similar confounding.

The interactions detected by McArthur might also be interpreted as indirect support for Kelley's hypothesis that people respond to generalizeability information configurally rather than in terms of its individual components. This possibility was investigated more directly by Orvis et al. (1975). These authors argued that when complete information about the conditions surrounding a behavioral event is unavailable, judges use prototypic schemata to infer unknown aspects of these conditions. Three schemata similar to the configurations described earlier were hypothesized. Specifically, one configuration, characterized by high consistency, low distinctiveness, and low consensus (high P_X, high P_O, and low P_P), was assumed to describe behavior that was due primarily to the actor's attributes. A second, characterized by high consistency, high distinctiveness, and high consensus (high P_X, low P_O, and high P_P), was assumed to describe behavior that was due to the object's attributes. The third, characterized by low consistency, high distinctiveness, and low consensus (low P_X, low P_O, and low P_P) was assumed to describe behavior attributable to a situational factor. Thus, if judges learn that an actor's (P's) behavior toward O in a given situation generalized to other objects but not to other actors, they should apply the first of these prototypic schemata and infer the behavior to generalize over situations as well. Or, since high consensus information is unique to the second schema, judges who learn that an actor's behavior generalizes to other actors should complete the schema by inferring that the behavior generalizes to other situations but not to other objects.

To test these hypotheses, Orvis et al. used the same stimulus materials constructed by McArthur but varied the availability of consensus, distinctiveness, and consistency information. After reading a description of a particular event (e.g., "John laughed at the comedian,"), some subjects received only consensus information, others only distinctiveness information, others only consistency information, and others two of the three types of information. Then, in each case, judges inferred the extent to which the behavior would generalize over the elements about which no information was presented. For example, if they were told only that "almost everyone who hears the comedian laughs at him" (high $P_{\bar{P}}$), they inferred how many other comedians John laughs at ($P_{\bar{O}}$) and also how many times John has laughed at the same comedian in the past ($P_{\bar{X}}$).

The authors concluded that their results supported a configural, or schematic, interpretation of the manner in which judges used the information available to them. However, a reorganization of the data calls this conclusion into question. Table 5.3 shows the mean inference of each characteristic, averaged over the two studies reported by Orvis et al., as a function of information about the other two characteristics presented either separately or in combination. These data suggest the following:

1. Inferences of situation-generalizeability ($P_{\bar{X}}$) are a positive function of both object-generalizeability ($P_{\bar{O}}$) and actor-generalizeability ($P_{\bar{P}}$). (Or, in Kelley's terms, inferences of consistency are a positive function of consensus and a negative function of distinctiveness.)

2. Inferences of object-generalizeability ($P_{\bar{O}}$) increase with situation-generalizeability ($P_{\bar{X}}$) and decrease with actor-generalizeability ($P_{\bar{P}}$). (Alternatively, inferences of distinctiveness are a negative function of consistency and a positive function of consensus.)

3. Inferences of actor-generalizeability ($P_{\bar{P}}$) increase with situation-generalizeability ($P_{\bar{X}}$) and decrease with object-generalizeability ($P_{\bar{O}}$). (That is, inferences of consensus are a positive function of both consistency and distinctiveness.)

If judges responded to information configurally in the manner postulated by Orvis et al., the effects of different types of information in combination would not necessarily be predictable from the effects of each type presented separately. Morever, the effects of a given type of information should normally depend upon the type of information accompanying it. Results do not strongly support this hypothesis. Situation-generalizeability did have

TABLE 5.3
Inferences of Each Type of Generalizeability as a Function of Available Information
Bearing Upon Generalizeability of Other Types[a]

A. Inferences of $P_{\bar{x}}$ (high $P_{\bar{x}}$ = high consistency)	Low $P_{\bar{o}}$ (high distinctiveness)	No information	High $P_{\bar{o}}$ (low distinctiveness)
High $P_{\bar{p}}$ (high consensus)	0.87	1.63	2.32
No information	0.17	—	2.04
Low $P_{\bar{p}}$ (low consensus)	0.45	0.72	1.78

B. Inferences of $P_{\bar{o}}$ (high $P_{\bar{o}}$ = low distinctiveness)	Low $P_{\bar{x}}$ (low consistency)	No information	High $P_{\bar{x}}$ (high consistency)
High $P_{\bar{p}}$ (high consensus)	1.57	–0.28	0.47
No information	–0.92	—	0.78
Low $P_{\bar{p}}$ (low consensus)	–0.36	1.54	1.63

C. Inferences of $P_{\bar{p}}$ (high $P_{\bar{p}}$ = high consensus)	Low $P_{\bar{x}}$ (low consistency)	No information	High $P_{\bar{x}}$ (high consistency)
High $P_{\bar{o}}$ (low distinctiveness)	–0.73	–0.22	–0.18
No information	–0.05	—	0.18
Low $P_{\bar{o}}$ (high distinctiveness)	0.37	1.40	1.20

[a]Adapted from Orvis et al. (1975).

little influence upon inferences of actor-generalizeability unless information about object-generalizeability was available. With this one exception, however, the effect of each type of information was not appreciably different when it was accompanied by information of another type than when it was not.

These data, then, do not clearly support the configural hypothesis proposed by Kelley (1971). Rather, information about certain types of generalizeability typically had independent effects upon inferences of other types. The nature of these effects is nevertheless important. Specifically, information designed to increase beliefs that an actor's behavior generalizes to other actors also increases beliefs that the behavior generalizes over situations, while decreasing beliefs that it generalizes to other objects. Information intended to increase beliefs that an actor's behavior generalizes to other objects also increases beliefs that it generalizes over situations, but decreases beliefs that it generalizes over actors. Finally, information that an actor's behavior generalizes over situations increases beliefs that it also generalizes both to other actors and to other objects. To the extent that attributions to P, O, and X are mediated by these different beliefs, the above interrelations might contribute to the interactive effects of generalizeability information reported by McArthur.

Unfortunately, however, conclusions based upon the study of Orvis et al. should be treated with some caution. By using McArthur's stimulus materials, the authors introduced confounds similar to those we noted earlier, that may have artifactually increased the apparent interdependence of different types of generalizeability information. To permit firm conclusions to be drawn, information would need to be presented in a way that would not have direct implications for more than one type of generalizeability. (For example, to induce low differentiation, one might present the information "John would laugh at almost any other comedian under the same circumstances," thus eliminating any direct implications the information might have for John's behavior in other situations.)

Indirect Inferences of Generalizeability— Correspondent Inference Theory

In the preceding discussion we were concerned with the effects of information bearing directly upon the generalizeability of behavior over actors, objects, and situations. In many instances, however, this information is unavailable; rather, a judge is called upon to make an inference on the basis of information about a single behavioral event that takes place in a particular situation. In these circumstances, the judge must infer generalizeability indirectly, on the basis of both his previous experience and his interpretation of other cues available in the situation.

Equations 5-6, 5-7, and 5-8 help provide insight into the nature of these effects. For example, suppose a judge observes P help someone across the street, and is asked to infer P's kindness. Presumably, the implications of the behavior's generalizeability over situations and objects ($V_{\bar{x}}$ and $V_{\bar{o}}$) are positive, while the implications of its generalizeability to other actors ($V_{\bar{p}}$) are negative (see Footnote 4). According to Equation 5-6, the judgment of P should be a function of these implications, each weighted by the judge's belief that P's behavior does in fact generalize in the manner indicated. In the absence of any other information about P, O, or the situation, each of these beliefs is apt to increase as a result of observing P's behavior in the particular situation. Since the implications of two of the three factors are positive, the result may be a net increase in inferences that P is kind. For similar reasons, the observed event may produce a net increase in inferences that O is friendly (Equation 5-7) and that situational constraints exist to induce P to manifest this behavior (Equation 5-8).

However, suppose that in addition to being told of P's behavior, the judge is informed that P is a priest. Since priests are typically assumed to manifest altruistic behavior in a variety of situations, this information should increase the judge's beliefs that P's behavior will generalize both to other objects ($P\acute{o}$) and other situations ($P\bar{x}$). From Equation 5-7, it is clear that these effects should produce an increase in $J\bar{P}$, or in estimates of P's kindness. However, their influence upon judgments of O's friendliness, and of the situational pressures on P to manifest this behavior, is less apparent. One might intuitively expect O to be judged less friendly if the actor is described as a priest than if he is not, since in the former case, the actor's social role provides an alternative explanation for his behavior. However, since $V_{\bar{x},o}$ is positive and $V_{\acute{o},o}$ is negative, Equation 5-7 implies that for this to be the case, either $\Delta P\bar{x} < \Delta P\acute{o}$ or $|V_{\bar{x},o}| < |V_{\acute{o},o}|$. Analogous considerations arise in analyzing the effect of information on inferences of situational constraints (Jx).

Equations 5-6, 5-7, and 5-8 are of particular interest when applied to attribution processes of the sort to which correspondent inference theory pertains (Jones & Davis, 1965; for a recent extension, see Jones & McGillis, 1976). A central thesis of this formulation is that behavior is more likely to be attributed to a characteristic of the actor (P) if there are few external pressures or incentives to manifest the behavior. Thus, a person who speaks out on a topic will be attributed a stronger personal belief in his stated position when there are no apparent pressures on him to take this position than when he is ostensibly coerced into doing so. Alternatively, since people are often expected to agree publicly with the views of their audience, a person who advocates a position his audience favors is apt to be attributed a weaker belief in this position than is someone who advocates a position his audience opposes (cf. Mills & Jellison, 1967).

Equations 5-6, 5-7, and 5-8 can be used to describe and extend upon these predictions. To illustrate this, let us consider a well-known study by Jones, Davis, and Gergen (1961). Judges listened to a person being interviewed for a job that ostensibly required either inner-directed qualities or other-directed qualities. In the interview, the applicant's responses suggested that he either did or did not possess the qualities required by the job for which he was applying. After listening to the interview, judges rated the applicant with respect to the traits to which his behavior pertained. When the applicant's behavior implied attributes congruent with job requirements, judges rated him as possessing only moderate amounts of these traits, little different from those attributed to the average person. However, when his behavior was incongruent with job requirements, judges rated the applicant as having extreme amounts of the traits correspondent with this behavior. In other words, the applicant's behavior was less apt to be used as an indication of his underlying attributes when there were external reasons for his behavior (i.e., desire to get the job). These findings are quite consistent with implications of correspondent inference theory. In terms of Equation 5-6, this result would be due to the fact that P's behavior was believed more likely to generalize over situations (i.e., $P_{\bar{x}}$ was higher) when this behavior was inconsistent with job requirements than when it was not. If this explanation of the results of Jones et al. is correct, the applicant's behavior under different conditions should also affect judgments of situational characteristics. That is, since the implications of the behavior's generalizeability over situations ($V_{\bar{x},x}$) for judgments of situational constraints is apt to be negative, judges should infer that there is less pressure on P to manifest job-appropriate behavior when P's actual behavior is inconsistent with job requirements than when it is congruent with these requirements (see Equation 5-8). While this prediction is intuitively appealing, it was not tested directly by Jones et al.

The preceding analysis does not do justice to many facets of correspondent inference theory, which takes into account factors such as the similarity between the consequences of a chosen behavior and the consequences of alternative behaviors, the social desirability of this behavior, etc. However, it seems reasonable to suppose that these factors may also affect attributions through their mediating influence on assumptions about the generalizeability of the actor's behavior over persons, objects and situations. To this extent, the proposed formulation may incorporate the effects of these factors as well.

Self-Perception Theory

While correspondent inference theory has been applied largely to judges' inferences about other persons in situations where the judges are not themselves involved, Bem's (1965, 1972) self-perception formulation pertains to inferences a judge makes about himself or others in situations in which he personally is the actor. Bem argues that often when a person is asked to judge himself, this judgment is not ready-made in memory, and he may thus construct it from information that happens to be salient to him at the time. Often, this information will consist of behavior the judge has recently performed. In these instances, the judge is apt to analyze the implications of his behavior for the judgment much as he would evaluate the implications of another person's behavior in the same situation. Thus, for example, a judge who has witnessed someone else volunteer to speak in support of a particular concept may infer that this person favors the concept. Analogously, a judge who himself has volunteered to speak in support of the concept may subsequently infer from this behavior that he personally favors the concept.

If people do in fact use their own behavior as information upon which to base their self-judgments, it seems reasonable that the use of this information will be mediated by assumptions similar to those embodied in Equations 5-6, 5-7, and 5-8. That is, Equation 5-6 implies that a judge will interpret his behavior as an indication of a correspondent attribute (in the above example, as an indication of his belief in the position he has advocated) to the extent he assumes that the behavior he has manifested would generalize over situations and (if relevant) objects but is unlikely to generalize to other actors. A judge's assumptions about the generalizeability of his behavior may be based in large part upon his recall of past behavior he has manifested in various situations, and his past observations of others' behavior under comparable conditions. However, the behavior manifested in many experimental tests of self-perception theory is quite novel, and moreover is manifested under unfamiliar circumstances. (How frequently, for example, is one asked to advocate a position with which he does not agree, either for pay or voluntarily?) In these cases, the judge has little past experience to draw upon in evaluating the generalizeability of his behavior, and must therefore rely upon other information provided in the situation, much as an outside observer would. Therefore, situational factors that decrease the actor's belief that his behavior would generalize over situations ($P_{\bar{X}}$) should decrease his perception that he has an attribute correspondent with this behavior. For example, if an actor advocates a position for pay, he may assume that he is engaging in this activity for the pay, and would not do so under conditions in which he is not paid. As a result, $P_{\bar{X}}$ should be relatively low, and J_P (the actor's self-judgment of his belief in the position advocated) should be less than it would be if the actor had advocated the position in the absence of an incentive. This prediction is of course supported by the results of several studies (e.g., Brehm & Cohen, 1962; Calder, Ross, & Insko, 1973; for a review, see Zajonc, 1968). Note, however, that Equation 5-6 suggests an alternative interpretation of this finding. For example, the offer of pay to advocate the position may affect not only the actor's belief that his behavior would generalize to other situations ($P_{\bar{X}}$), but also his belief that others would manifest this behavior in the same situation ($P_{\bar{P}}$). That is, the judge may assume that nearly anyone would advocate the position for pay, but that few persons would do so without pay. Since $V_{\bar{P},P}$ is negative (Table 5.1), the weaker belief in the position advocated under high pay conditions than under low pay conditions could be a result of a difference in this assumption as well as in $P_{\bar{X}}$. The research performed to date has not distinguished between these two interpretations.

The preceding analysis, considered in isolation, does not add appreciably to an understanding of attribution phenomena identified by self-perception theory. However, it enables the effects of behavior on self-judgments, and differences in these effects over experimental conditions, to be interpreted in terms of specific mediating assumptions that underlie these judgments.[6] Moreover, it helps to explain the simultaneous effects of behavior on both (a) judgments of different elements (P, O, and X) and (b) different judgments of the same element. Specifically, Equation 5-6 implies that the effect of differences in $P_{\bar{X}}$ produced by a given experimental manipulation will be a multiplicative function of $V_{\bar{X},P}$ (the implications of the behavior's generalizing over situations for the judgment of P). These implications clearly depend upon the attribute being judged and its correspondence with this behavior. For example, the behavior "helping a person across the street" is apt to have more implications for judgments of the actor's kindness than for judgments of his intelligence. Alternatively, the delivery of a speech advocating mercy killing is apt to have more implications for the actor's belief in mercy killing than for his belief in capital punishment. However, if the relative magnitudes of these implications are known, the relative effects of P's behavior on these attributions should be predictable from Equation 5-6.

Weiner's Model of Outcome Attribution

Our preceding discussion focussed on the effects of an actor's behavior on perceptions of the actor, other persons, or situational factors. A similar approach may be taken in conceptualizing the effects of behavioral consequences on attributions. Suppose a judge observes an actor (P) perform an achievement task, and then is told that the actor has either succeeded or failed. This information could have implications for several characteristics of both the actor and the situation (for example, the actor's ability, the effort he has expended, the difficulty of the task, and luck). Weiner et al. (1971) report a series of studies concerned with these matters. The results of these studies suggest that, in general, judge's inferences of unstable characteristics (effort or luck) are affected most by outcomes of the actor's present performance when these outcomes deviate from expectations based upon the actor's past performance. Independently of this tendency, inferences of the actor's ability, effort, and luck are greater when the actor has succeeded whereas inferences of task difficulty are greater when the actor has failed.

The conditions that affect the relative magnitudes of these attributions can be conceptualized in terms of Equations 5-6, 5-7, and 5-8 if the components are assumed to refer to the generalizeability of the actor's *outcome* in the

---

[6]For example, the contingencies of role-playing effects on actors' perceptions (a) that they are personally responsible for the action; and (b) that the act may have negative consequences for themselves or others (Collins & Hoyt, 1972) may be conceptualized in terms of the effects of these factors on an actor's assumptions concerning the generalizeability of his behavior to other situations or to other actors.

situation rather than of his behavior per se. To illustrate, suppose P succeeds on a particular task. The generalizeability of this outcome over tasks has positive implications for P's ability, while its generalizeability over actors has negative implications (that is, the more people other than P who would also succeed on the task, the less likely it is that P has more than average ability). To this extent, supplementary information that affects a judge's beliefs in the generalizeability of P's success should influence the degree to which this outcome affects judgments of P's ability. However, these same beliefs should also mediate judgments of both the actor's effort and of situational factors such as task difficulty. To apply the proposed formulation rigorously to these inference phenomena, one would need a prior understanding of the implications of generalizeability information for each type of judgment. Once this was obtained, however, the present approach would enable judgments of the various attributes identified by Weiner et al. to be interrelated in terms of a common set of mediating assumptions about the generalizeability of P's outcomes over actors and situations. Moreover, it enables differences in the effects of outcome information on various judgments to be conceptualized in terms of differences in its effects upon these assumptions. While a rigorous development of such a conceptualization is beyond the scope of the present discussion, the general approach we have outlined may be worth considering in future work in this area.

5.6. CONCLUDING REMARKS

In this chapter, we have considered the role of several characteristics of verbal information in social inference that may affect perceptions of its implications. We have particularly concentrated on the effects of novelty and redundancy, and used a conceptualization of these effects as a vehicle for integrating much of the theory and research on the effects of behavioral information on inferences about the actor, the object of his behavior, and characteristics of the situation in which the behavior takes place. In many instances, our analysis of these effects may have seemed complex and cumbersome. However, the formulation has the advantage of providing an explicit statement of the functional relations among the factors that potentially underlie the effects of behavior on judgments. Moreover, it enables situational and individual differences in judgments to be conceptualized in terms of differences in a common set of mediating assumptions that may underlie judges' inferences. Further research is required to test the implications of this formulation more rigorously. However, its potential heuristic and conceptual value makes efforts along these lines desirable.

6

Indirect Effects of Information on Judgments

In the preceding chapter, we focussed on the direct implications of information for judgments of a person or object (e.g., the implications of an actor's behavior for inferences about the actor, or the person toward whom this behavior was directed). However, as we noted in the introduction to this section, certain information available in a situation has an *indirect* effect on judgments as well. That is, it may affect the influence of other information presented.

At least four types of indirect effects can be identified, the first of which has already been discussed.

1. *Priming effects.* As we noted in Chapters 3 and 4, some pieces of information may prime concepts (scripts, vignettes or schemata) that are then used to encode or interpret other available information. For example, the description of a person as "aggressive" may be interpreted differently when the person is also described as "hardworking" than when he is also described as "hostile," and therefore the judgment based upon this description may differ.[1] On the other hand, these differences in interpretation may occur even if the priming concepts are applied to a different person from the one described as "aggressive," or are made salient in a previous situation (Higgins, Rholes & Jones, 1977; Wyer & Srull, in press).

2. *Directive influences.* In some instances, a given piece of information may stimulate the judge to attend more carefully to other information presented.

---

[1] For an elaboration of this possibility and a discussion of research bearing on it, see Wyer, 1974b, pp. 236–51, and also Chapter 8 of this volume.

This may be particularly true if the first piece of information is incongruous or is otherwise difficult to interpret.

3. *Distracting effects.* If the addition of information exceeds the judge's information processing capacity, it may interfere with, or distract the judge from processing, other available information that is relevant to the judgment being made.

4. *Comparative effects.* The characteristics of one object or event may provide a standard, or frame of reference, for judging other objects and events. For example, judgments of a particular person's intelligence may be based not only on information about his own performance on a given task, but also on information about another person's performance on this or a similar task; that is, the second person's performance may provide a comparative standard for judging the ability of the first.

The indirect effects of information are of particular interest in connection with two quite different issues. The first, which primarily involves a consideration of the directive influence of information, concerns the effect of a judge's internal emotional state (i.e., his feelings, mood, or general arousal level) on the judgments he makes. The second, which emphasizes the comparative function of information, concerns the effect of information about one person on judgments of others. In this chapter, we will focus our attention on these two issues. While this focus may seem somewhat restrictive at first glance, it will allow us to consider a wide range of phenomena from a common perspective.

6.1 THE ROLE OF INTERNAL EMOTIONAL REACTIONS IN JUDGMENTAL PROCESSES

General Considerations

The effects of judges' subjective emotional reactions on their inferences have been considered in numerous areas of research and theory, including cognitive inconsistency (Festinger, 1957; Osgood & Tannenbaum, 1955), interpersonal attraction (Byrne, 1969; Clore, 1975), communication and persuasion (Leventhal, 1970), social comparison (Schachter & Singer, 1962), and attribution (Miller & Ross, 1975; Shaver, 1975). Assumptions concerning the precise nature of these "internal emotional reactions" vary with the theorist and the substantive issue of concern, and are often not clearly specified. For example, it is often unclear whether the critical feature of these reactions is an autonomic state of arousal or drive, or is a cognitive state of comfort or discomfort that may or may not be accompanied by physiological arousal. As we shall see, the few attempts to distinguish between the cognitive and physiological components of subjective emotional reactions suggest that the cognitive states of pleasantness or unpleasantness, not the accompanying physiological arousal, have the primary influence on judgments.

A person's emotional state may be a previously conditioned subjective response to either an external stimulus object or an internal representation of an object recalled from memory. In addition, the emotional state may be created by cognitive conflict such as that resulting from the need to solve a difficult problem, to make a decision, or to resolve an inconsistency between cognitions with different implications. However the emotional reaction is elicited, it could affect judgments in many of the ways enumerated at the beginning of this chapter. First, it could have informational value; for example, one's liking for a person may be based partly on one's subjective feeling of pleasantness when the person is around. Second, the emotional reactions could "prime" different sets of previously formed cognitions that have implications for the judgment to be made. Third, the reaction could interfere with the processing of other available information. For example, the fear-arousing nature of a communication may affect judgments based upon its informational content because the fear or arousal generated serves as internal "noise" that prevents the judge from thinking up counterarguments. This possibility has been considered in detail elsewhere (McGuire, 1968b; Wyer, 1974b) and need not be reiterated here. Finally, a judge's emotional state could have a directive influence. When the reason for his emotional state is unclear to him, the judge may pay more attention to other available information that might help him to explain his reaction (Schachter & Singer, 1962). Moreover, if the reaction is unpleasant, the judge may seek ways of eliminating it.

The alternative effects described above are not mutually exclusive; they could all contribute simultaneously to judgments. Their relative contributions in any given case may depend on the nature of the situation and the type of the judgment to be made. In the pages that follow, we will focus primarily upon the directive influence of emotional reactions, although other effects will also be considered. This influence will be examined with reference to four bodies of literature, concerning (a) the effect of counterattitudinal behavior on self-judgments; (b) the effects of an event's consequences on judgments of participants in the event; (c) the effect of internal affective reactions on interpersonal attraction; and (d) the effects of nonverbal behavior on judgments of the actor. While these areas of research are not typically considered in combination, common conceptual threads underlie this work, as we will see.

Subjective Reactions to Cognitive Inconsistency

We noted earlier that arousal or discomfort may often be created by awareness of an inconsistency among one's cognitions (beliefs, attitudes or opinions). The assumption that cognitive inconsistency is phenomenologically aversive, and stimulates efforts to eliminate the inconsistency, underlies many theories of cognitive organization and opinion change (cf. Festinger, 1957; Osgood & Tannenbaum, 1955; Heider, 1958). However, the precise nature and role of these subjective, inconsistency-produced reactions have only recently been identified in an important series of studies by Zanna, Cooper, Higgins and their colleagues (for a review, see Zanna & Cooper, 1976).[2] These authors assume that when a person engages in behavior that he considers improper or inconsistent with his own beliefs (i.e., 'dissonant"), he will experience discomfort that he will then seek to explain. If the person correctly interprets his reaction as a consequence of his belief that he behaved counterattitudinally, he may attempt to eliminate the discomfort by convincing himself that his behavior was not inappropriate after all (e.g., that his beliefs are consistent with the implications of his behavior). However, to the extent that the judge interprets the discomfort as due to some other factor, he will not change his judgments concerning the behavior or its implications. The research conducted by Zanna et al. was designed both to explore the implications of this line of reasoning, and also to pinpoint more precisely the nature of the subjective reactions assumed to stimulate this judgmental behavior.

In an initial test of this hypothesis (Zanna & Cooper, 1974), judges were administered a drug (in fact, a placebo) that they were led to believe would affect their short term memory. Some subjects were told that the drug would have no side effects, others were told it would create tension, and still others were told it would have a relaxing, tranquilizing effect. Then, while waiting for the drug to take effect, subjects participated in an ostensibly unrelated study of attitudes that involved writing an essay advocating a position with which they were known initially to disagree. Half of the subjects in each drug condition were given a choice of whether or not to participate in this attitude study (*high choice* conditions) while the others were not given any opportunity to refuse (*low choice* conditions). Then, subjects reported their attitude toward the position they had advocated. Subjects in low choice conditions were expected to attribute their counterattitudinal behavior to external pressure and not be bothered by it. High choice subjects were expected to experience discomfort as a result of their behavior. However, those who were told that the drug they had taken created tenseness were expected to attribute their discomfort to the drug. In contrast, those who were told the pill had no side effects were expected to attribute their discomfort to the inconsistency between their opinion and the position they advocated in their essay. These subjects should therefore try to eliminate this discomfort by

---

[2]Although earlier studies (Cottrell & Wack, 1967; Waterman & Katkin, 1967; Zimbardo, Cohen, Weisenberg, Dworkin & Firestone, 1966) attempted to identify the drive inducing properties of cognitive dissonance, the results of these studies are equivocal, for reasons pointed out elsewhere (Wyer, 1974b, p. 400–402).

TABLE 6.1
Mean Attitude Toward Position Advocated as a Function of Choice and
Alleged Side Effects of the Drug[a]

Decision Freedom	Potential Side Effects of the Drug		
	Arousal	None	Relaxation
High choice	$3.40_a{}^b$	9.10_b	13.40_c
Low choice	3.50_a	4.50_a	4.70_a

[a]Reprinted from Zanna & Cooper (1974).
[b]Cell means with different subscripts are different from each other at the 1% level by the Newman–Keuls procedure.

changing their opinion to one more consistent with that implied by their behavior. Finally, subjects who experienced discomfort under conditions where the drug was ostensibly a relaxant were expected to infer that they were particularly upset, since they experienced discomfort despite the tranquilizing effect of the pill. These subjects were therefore predicted to manifest the greatest change in attitude toward the position advocated. Results, shown in Table 6.1, were entirely consistent with these hypotheses.

Individual Preferences in Attributions of Discomfort

The study described above provides compelling evidence that a judge will seek explanations for an internal emotional state and, if the state is aversive, will eliminate it through change in the cognitions that he believes gave rise to it. However, important questions remain. For one thing, the study does not explain why judges attribute their discomfort to the drug alone when two explanations for it are viable. Even when the drug ostensibly produces tension, the judge's counterattitudinal behavior remains a second *possible* source of his discomfort. Hence, some attempt to eliminate this inconsistency might be expected here as well. In fact, such an attempt does not occur. There are at least two reasons why this is so. First, attitude change may be inherently unpleasant, since it implies wishy-washiness and thus reflects negatively on the person who reports changing his attitude (cf. McGuire & Millman, 1965). Second, a change in one's self-judgment is apt to have implications for many other cognitions, and therefore may require changes in these cognitions as well. These changes may involve the expenditure of considerable cognitive energy, and may therefore be resisted (for an elaboration of this hypothesis, see Chapter 7). Both possibilities imply that people are less apt to attribute their discomfort to their counterattitudinal behavior when alternative explanations for it are viable.

This hypothesis was supported indirectly in a study by Zanna, Higgins & Taves (1976). Some subjects were told that a drug they had been administered (again, a placebo) produced tenseness, others were told it produced no side effects, and still others were told nothing whatsoever about the drug. Subjects then wrote a counterattitudinal essay under high choice conditions, and finally, reported their beliefs in the position advocated. Subjects changed their attitudes significantly less when they were told that the drug would create tension than when they were told that it had no side effects, replicating the findings of Zanna and Cooper. However, subjects who were given no information about the pill's side effects responded like those who were told it would create tension; that is, they showed no change at all in their attitude toward the advocated position. Thus, given no information to the contrary, these subjects appeared to attribute their discomfort to the drug and not to their inconsistent behavior, thus avoiding the need to change their attitude.

This reasoning implies that the tendency to attribute discomfort to factors other than attitude-inconsistent behavior should increase with the difficulty of eliminating the discomfort through attitude change. Evidence for this was obtained by Gonzales and Cooper (cited in Zanna & Cooper, 1976). Here, subjects again wrote a counterattitudinal essay under either high or low choice conditions similar to those described above. Subjects who were moderately opposed to the position they advocated changed their opinions more (in the direction of the position) under high choice than under low choice conditions. However, subjects who were strongly opposed to the advocated position presumably found it more difficult to alter their opinions and changed them very little under either choice conditon. Although this is not too surprising in and of itself, responses to a subsequent measure are illuminating. Specifically, in response to a question about the discomfort produced by a new lighting system in the experimental rooms, strongly committed subjects judged the lights to produce considerable discomfort, whereas moderately committed ones indicated no such reaction. Moreover, discomfort ratings by strongly committed subjects were significantly greater under choice than under low choice conditions. This suggests that the strongly committed subjects experienced discomfort from behaving in a way inconsistent with their beliefs; however, rather than attributing their discomfort to their inconsistency, they blamed it on the lights. Furthermore, they misattributed more blame when the discomfort they experienced was presumably greater (under high choice conditions). Apparently, these subjects were either unwilling or unable to change their opinions in order to eliminate discomfort, and so sought an alternative explanation for it.

Some qualifications may need to be placed on this conclusion, however. In a study by Pittman (1975), subjects were asked to prepare and deliver a counterattitudinal speech under conditions in which they either did or did not anticipate receiving electric shocks as part of a second experiment to be conducted. Subjects changed their attitudes toward the advocated position less when they anticipated shock than when they did not, suggesting that they attributed the discomfort produced by their counterattitudinal behavior to the shock when this alternative explanation was available. In a second set of conditions, however, a confederate posing as another subject expressed concern about the impending speech, indicating that she was "nervous and worried" about it. In this condition, subjects changed their attitudes *more* toward the position advocated when they anticipated shock than when they did not. Apparently in this case subjects did not attribute their discomfort about delivering the speech to their worry about the shock, but rather attributed their worry about the shock to their concern about their counterattitudinal behavior. This suggests that when subjects receive external cues that their counterattitudinal behavior *does* underlie their discomfort, they will attribute this discomfort to their behavior, and therefore will change their attitudes in an attempt to reduce this discomfort. Moreover, with the misleading cues, they may even misattribute discomfort from other sources to their behavior.

The Nature of "Discomfort" Produced by Attitude-Inconsistent Behavior

Additional questions exist concerning the nature of the internal reaction that mediates attitude change following counterattitudinal behavior. This reaction has at least two components: autonomic arousal and the cognitive experience of discomfort that accompanies this autonomic state. Although the two components are related, this relation could be either of two types. On one hand, the awareness that one has engaged in counterattitudinal behavior may create undifferentiated cognitive discomfort, and this in turn may lead to autonomic arousal. However, this arousal may not itself be a critical mediator of opinion change; rather, the cognitive unpleasantness that produces this arousal is the critical mediator. On the other hand, awareness of counterattitudinal behavior may directly produce arousal that is experienced as aversive, and the cognitions associated with this unpleasant autonomic state may then stimulate one to seek explanations for this state and ways to reduce it. To the latter extent, cognitive discomfort and autonomic arousal would both be necessary preconditions for the opinion change that ultimately occurs.

Two studies bear on these alternative possibilities, each using variants of the pill manipulation devised by Zanna and Cooper (1974). In the first experiment (Zanna, et al., 1976), subjects were administered a placebo that they were told would either make them tense, have no effect, or induce an experience of "pleasant excitement." After writing a counterattitudinal essay under high choice conditions, subjects in the "tense" side-effect condition changed their opinions less than those who were told the drug would have no side effects. This is consistent with earlier findings. However, subjects in the "pleasant excitement" side-effect condition actually changed their opinions nonsignificantly *more* than did those in the no side-effect condition. This suggests that the allegedly arousing nature of the drug is not in itself sufficient to induce judges to attribute their discomfort to the drug rather than to the inconsistency between their behavior and their initial opinion. In a second study, Higgins, Rhodewalt and Zanna (in press) again used the placebo procedure, but this time manipulated the pleasantness and arousing nature of the ostensible side effects independently. That is, subjects were essentially told that the pill would make them feel either (a) pleasantly stimulated, (b) unpleasantly stimulated, (c) pleasantly sedated, or (d) unpleasantly sedated. Analyses of the effects of counterattitudinal behavior under these conditions showed that opinion change was greater when the side effects were described as pleasant than when they were described as unpleasant, while the description of the pill as either arousing or sedating had no effect. This suggests that the opinion change induced by attitude-inconsistent behavior occurs because the behavior produces cognitive discomfort and that the presence of autonomic arousal per se is not necssary.

Effects of Behavioral Consequences on Judgments of Self and Others

While we have devoted ample attention in this volume to the effects of behavior on judgments, we have dealt very little with the effects of the consequences of this behavior. In fact, abundant research has been done on the effects of behavioral consequences information on judgments of the actor, the person toward whom the act is directed, and other aspects of the behavioral situation. There have been two major thrusts of this research. One is concerned with the effects of achievement task outcomes (e.g., success or failure) on judgments of both the actor and the task. A second has investigated the effects of the severity of an action's consequences on judgments of either the perpetrator or the victim. These concerns appear quite different from those discussed in the preceding section. However, research and theory bearing on them also have implications for the directive function of internal emotional reactions.

Effects of Success and Failure

Much of the research on the effects of success and failure on judgments has been stimulated by the work of Weiner and his colleagues (Weiner et al. 1971). This work has been of partiuclar interest because the judgments examined are potentially mediators of subsequent achievement activity. For example, a person who fails may be inspired to work harder in the future if he attributes his failure to lack of effort than if he attributes it to lack of ability (Dweck, 1975).

A major issue in this area concerns the relative effects of informational and motivational factors on causal attributions. This issue is particularly relevant in the case of self-judgments. The analysis outlined in Chapter 5 suggests that if performance on a particular task appears to generalize over tasks and situations but not over actors, it is likely to be attributed to characteristics of the actor rather than to situational factors. An actor is thus more likely to attribute the outcome of his performance to his own characteristics (e.g., his ability) if he perceives it to differ from that typically obtained by other persons than if he perceives it to be similar to that normally attained by others (or in other words, if his outcome has low actor-generalizeability; see Chapter 5). Moreover, he is more apt to attribute his outcome to this own personal characteristics if this outcome is similar to those he has attained in previous achievement situations than if it is inconsistent with his past outcomes (i.e., if his outcome has high situation-generalizeability). Thus, for example, if the actor perceives himself as typically successful in achievement activity, he is apt to attribute his success on a given task to his ability but to attribute his failure to external situational factors.

On the other hand, considerations in the previous section suggest that if a judge receives an outcome that produces an unpleasant cognitive state, he may search for an explanation that will minimize this unpleasantness. Success, which is socially desirable, is generally unlikely to produce discomfort, so the actor is likely to attribute his successful performance to himself (e.g., his ability) without bothering to seek alternative explanations. However, failure may induce discomfort, and may therefore lead the actor to seek explanations for this outcome that minimize this discomfort. Such explanations will be those that do not have negative implications for his self-esteem. It follows that people will typically attribute their success to their own ability regardless of whether alternative explanations exist, but will attribute their failure to a lack of ability only if no other explanations for this outcome are viable.

It is surprisingly difficult to separate the effects of expectancies, as outlined above, from the effects of self-esteem considerations (cf. Miller & Ross, 1975). People are in fact more likely to attribute their success to their ability than their failure (Feather & Simon, 1971). This could indicate that people tend to avoid attributing outcomes to factors that reflect negatively on themselves and therefore produce discomfort. However, it would also be predicted on the basis of considerations outlined in Chapter 5. That is, if people typically expect to suceed rather than fail, they may perceive their failure on a given task as unlikely to generalize to other achievement situations, and may consequently be more apt to attribute their outcome to external or unstable factors (e.g., luck).

However, there is also quite strong support for the role of self-esteem maintenance. A study by Arkin, Gleason and Johnston (1976) is particularly noteworthy. Subjects were asked to administer therapy to another to eliminate a mild phobic reaction. Although the therapy administered was actually the same in all cases, subjects were led to believe that the treatment they used was the only one available to them (low choice conditions) or was one of several alternatives from which they could choose (high choice conditions). Moreover, they were told that the treatment to be used was typically either successful or unsuccessful. After receiving this information, subjects themselves administered the treatment, and ostensibly either succeeded or failed. They then estimated the extent to which this outcome was attributable to their manner of administering the treatment (i.e., their ability).

Information that the outcome of the therapy was the same when administered by the subject as it was when administered by others should have suggested to the subject that this outcome was due to inherent properties of the therapy rather than to attributes of the administrator. Hence, if the subject attended to these cues, he should attribute himself relatively less responsibility for the outcome when given this information, particularly when he had no choice over the treatment used. However, results shown in Table 6.2 indicate that in fact, subjects accepted less responsibility under these conditions only when the therapy failed. When the actor succeeded, he attributed this outcome to his ability regardless of either choice or the outcome typically obtained by others. In contrast, he attributed failure to himself only if there was no viable alternative explanation (i.e., only if he had choice over which treatment to use and others had typically succeeded using the treatment). The fact that information about others' performance did not

TABLE 6.2
Mean Attribution of Responsibility by the Actor to Himself[a]

	Positive Actual Outcome		Negative Actual Outcome	
	Positive Expected Outcome	Negative Expected Outcome	Positive Expected Outcome	Negative Expected Outcome
High perceived choice	6.63	6.13	7.13	4.25
Low perceived choice	6.38	6.75	4.13	4.63

[a]Adapted from Arkin, Gleason, & Johnston (1976, p. 156).

produce parallel results under success and failure conditions is difficult to explain on the basis of informational considerations alone. It seems more reasonable to conclude that judges who succeeded explained their performance in terms of their own ability without seeking other possible explanations. However, those who failed, for whom such an explanation would be unpleasant, sought additional information, and accepted this explanation only if no alternative was plausible. This general conclusion is quite consistent with that drawn on the basis of research on counterattitudinal advocacy; only the source of discomfort, and the alternative means of eliminating it, are different.

Attributions of Responsibility for Other Types of Outcomes: The "Just World" Hypothesis

Other research has focussed on judgments made of people on the basis of consequences over which they have no direct control. Much of this work has been stimulated by Lerner and Simmons' (1966) hypothesis that people believe in a just world; that is, people believe that good things will happen to good people, and bad things will befall bad people. As a result, judges may predict an event's consequences for a person from information about that person's general attributes; they may also evaluate the person differently on the basis of consequences that have befallen him. This may reflect the application of implicational molecules of the sort postulated by Abelson and described in Chapter 2; i.e., [A is bad; bad things will befall A] or [A is good; good things will befall A]. Equity considerations may also be involved (cf., Walster, Berscheid & Walster, 1973); that is, people may be attributed "inputs" (favorable or unfavorable qualities) that are commensurate with their outcomes. However, there are other possible explanations. Lerner and Simmons postulate that people wish to believe that the world is generally just in order to maintain their conviction that they will personally get what they deserve and will not become the faultless victims of misfortune. Thus, information that a person has had a misfortune may create discomfort, since it raises the possibility that the judge could fall victim to a similar fate. This discomfort may stimulate the judge to seek a justification for the event that does not threaten his belief in a just world. One is that the victim is not a desirable person, and therefore deserves the fate that has befallen him. Hence, the victim of misfortune may be disparaged, and he may be disparaged more as the judge feels more threatened.

While substantial research has been performed to test various aspects of this hypothesis (cf. Miller, 1977a, b; for a review, see Lerner, Miller & Holmes, 1976), the initial test of this hypothesis by Lerner and Simmons (1966) remains of particular interest. Groups of judges witnessed a female subject (the "victim") ostensibly receive a series of painful shocks for making errors in performing a learning task. In one (*continued shock*) condition, judges were told after observing the shocks that the task would continue for several more trials, thus giving the impression that the victim would receive still more shocks in the future. In a second (*no continuation*) condition, they were told that the experiment was over, and thus that no more shocks would be administered. In a third (*continued reward*) condition, they were told that the experiment would continue, but that they could vote on whether the victim would continue to receive negative reinforcement (shocks for wrong answers) on the next series of trials, or whether she would instead receive positive reinforcement (monetary rewards for correct responses). In this latter condition, observers were told (truthfully) that the vote had been to change to positive reinforcement conditions.

Following exposure to one of the above conditions, observers evaluated the victim along several evaluative semantic differential scales. These ratings were negative in all conditions, relative to subjects' self-ratings along the same scales. However, subjects rated the victim most unfavorably when they were told that she would continue to receive shocks ($M = -25.8$), followed by conditions in which the experiment was ostensibly over ($M = -12.9$), and finally by conditions in which they believed the victim would subsequently be rewarded ($M = -5.1$). Assuming that the net aversiveness of the victim's outcome is a function of the difference between (a) the expected number of shocks administered during the course of the experiment and (b) the expected number of positive reinforcements (if any) administered, these results suggest that the greater the net aversiveness of the victim's outcome, the more she was derogated.

The above results are consistent with the interpretation that when people realize that someone has been victimized, this induces discomfort which they try to eliminate by convincing themselves that the victim actually deserved this treatment. The results obtained in two other conditions run by Lerner and Simmons strengthen this interpretation. In one, observers again voted on whether the victim should receive positive or negative reinforcements on the second set of trials, but his time the results of the vote were not announced. In fact, all but one observer voted to administer positive reinforcement. Nevertheless, the victim was rated just as unfavorably in this condition ($M = -25.5$) as when the judge believed she would definitively continue to be shocked on the future trials. In other words, the observer's own vote to reward the victim was insufficient to decrease his unfavorable evaluation of the victim unless it was clear that the victim would not actually be abused further. This finding is of particular importance since it suggests that the adversity of the victim's outcome is the critical factor underlying derogation of the victim, independently of the judge's personal responsibility for this outcome.

In still another condition, observers were led to believe that the victim protested that she did not wish to participate further, but then agreed to continue after being told the observer could not receive laboratory credit unless she did. This "martyrdom" condition is likely to engender the greatest discomfort, since the victim is ostensibly suffering for the observer's benefit. Consistent with this assumption, the victim was derogated more in this condition ($M = -34.0$) than in any other.

An Alternative Interpretation.   Lerner and Simmons' results are quite consistent with the general hypothesis that a judge who experiences discomfort may seek ways to minimize it, and that one way of doing this is by altering his perception of himself or another (e.g., the victim). However, alternative interpretations of their findings should be noted. For instance, the observers' evaluations of the victim may be based upon scripts they construct of how the victim is likely to behave toward them in a hypothetical interaction. It seems likely that the more adversely the victim has been treated, the worse mood she will be in, and the more likely she is to complain about her unfair treatment to the observer. Recognition of this possibility may lead the observer to expect a generally unpleasant interaction with the victim, and also to anticipate feeling embarrassed about having passively watched the victim suffer. This anticipated discomfort may be particularly acute in the "martyr" condition, where the victim has suffered for the observer's benefit. If observers use this script as a basis for their judgments, these judgments are likely to vary over the five conditions in precisely the way reported by Lerner and Simmons. While this interpretation seems quite plausible, the consistency of Lerner and Simmons' results with other considerations raised in this paper is nonetheless noteworthy.

The Role of Arousal and Affect in Judgments of Interpersonal Attraction

A judge's estimate of his liking for another person is often assumed to be mediated by, if not based upon, his subjective affective reaction to this person (cf. Byrne, 1969). For example, a judge who is asked how well he likes another individual may base this inference on the feelings he recalls having in the presence of the other. Alternatively, the mention of the other's name, or information about him, may elicit conditioned emotional responses in the judge, and these responses may provide the basis for the judge's overt expression of liking.

The hypothesis that one's internal affective state has direct informational effects upon judgments of attraction seems quite plausible. However, an unequivocal test of this hypothesis has been elusive. A provocative study by Clore and Gormly (1974) is representative. Here, physiological measures of judges' arousal were obtained while they received information that another person's attitudes were similar or dissimilar to their own. If judges use their internal emotional reactions to infer their attraction to a person, this similarity information should affect their attraction only to the extent that the information elicits these mediating reactions. Consistent with this hypothesis, Clore and Gormly found that the relation between attitude similarity and judgments of attraction increased as a function of the judge's arousal level. Unfortunately, other interpreations of these data are plausible. For one thing, the arousal levels in this study were based on overall measures obtained throughout the administration of the feedback information. Hence differences in arousal could have reflected differences in subjects' general involvement in the experiment rather than their reaction to the similarity information per se. If so, the results obtained could simply indicate that subjects who were more interested in the experiment (i.e., more aroused) were more sensitive to the similarity information than those who were bored.

A second strategy for investigating the informational properties of judges' subjective reactions is to manipulate experimentally their perceptions of their emotional reactions to the stimulus information. This procedure was used in a well-known series of studies by Valins (1966, 1974) described briefly in Chapter 2. Male subjects received false feedback about their heartrate as they observed photographs of nude females. As expected, evaluations of photos were more favorable when the heartrate feedback accompanying their presentation was rapid than when it was normal. Moreover, these effects persisted even after subjects were told that the heartrate information was false, and was therefore unrelated to their true reactions. Possibly the heartrate information led judges to direct their attention to attractive details of the stimulus photos in an attempt to explain their ostensible reactions, and this in turn led to a persisting increase in their liking for these photos. In other words, while judges' ratings were affected by their apparent emotional reactions, these effects were more directive than informational. Whether *true* emotional reactions have a similar function remains unclear. Judges may be more influenced by their emotional reactions when these reactions are made salient in an artificial experimental situation than they would be in other situations. In this regard, the directive influence of heartrate information on judgments may not be limited to subjects' *own* emotional reactions. Kerber and Coles (1977) found that judges' reports of their attraction to stimuli were influenced just as strongly by false heartrate information about another person's reactions to the stimuli as by information about their own apparent reactions. Thus, external indications of anyone's emotional reactions may lead judges to attend more carefully to stimuli regardless of whose reactions they are.

A third strategy is to manipulate judges' actual emotional reactions independently of reactions elicited by a stimulus person and to see if the emotional reactions influence judgments of the stimulus. However, it is difficult to ascertain that such manipulations affect emotional reactions per se and not the availability of other information. For example, several attempts have been made to demonstrate the effect of a judge's mood on his liking for others. In one study (Gouaux, 1969), some judges were initially asked to make self-referent statements that conveyed either good feelings (e.g., "I feel enthusiastic and confident," "I feel great,"), while others were asked to make statements describing negative feelings ("I feel tired and depressed," "I want to go to sleep and never wake up,"). Judges in the first condition subsequently reported more attraction to a particular stimulus person than did those in the second. One interpretation of this effect is that making the first set of statements put judges in a better mood than did making the second set, and that feelings associated with these moods combined with feelings about the stimulus person to affect judgments of his characteristics. This interpretation is strengthened by evidence that the manipulation did in fact affect judges' self-reported moods. However, it seems equally likely that the manipulation primed different sets of previously formed cognitions about the likeableness of persons in general (see Chapter 3). These cognitions could have contributed to judgments of the stimulus person regardless of the emotional reactions that accompanied them.

A somewhat different manipulation of mood was attempted by Griffitt and Veitch (1971). Subjects in this study received information about the similarity of their attitudes to those of a stimulus person while in either large or small groups, and in a room at either high or normal room temperature. Subjects then rated their attraction to the stimulus person. Judges reported less attraction to the person when the room was crowded than when it was uncrowded, and less attraction when the room was hot than when it was at normal temperature. These effects did not significantly depend on the stimulus person's similarity in attitude to the judge. The data therefore suggest that environmental factors that induce unpleasant feelings in judges decrease their attraction to others. However, it is again unclear whether these effects occurred because subjects used their feelings per se as a basis for judging their attraction to the stimulus person. It is quite conceivable that the conditions that produced these feelings again elicited different previously formed cognitions about persons in general (e.g., "Having people around can certainly be irritating and uncomfortable," "People should know better than to run experiments in rooms as hot as this one," etc.), and that judges used these cognitions as bases for evaluating the stimulus person in particular.

In fact, Bleda, Bell and Byrne (1973) obtained indirect evidence that the pleasantness of one's mood per se is *not* the determining factor in attraction judgments. Judges in this study watched either humorous or serious television commercials before receiving information about a stimulus person. In some instances, the serious commercials had a depressing effect on subjects' reported moods, but simultaneously elicited feelings of social concern. Here, the unpleasant commercials *increased* expectations of liking for the stimulus person relative to conditions in which humorous commercials were shown. Thus, in this experiment, judges' attraction to the stimulus person was clearly not mediated by their emotional reactions per se, but rather was based upon the cognitions accompanying these reactions.

In summary, the research on interpersonal attraction has not yet clearly demonstrated that emotional reactions have direct *informational* effects on judgments. Rather, their effects may be of two types. First, the reactions, or the conditions that produce them, may elicit previously formed cognitions about persons in general that affect judgments of the particular person being rated. Second, these reactions may exert a directive influence, in that they lead judges to attend more carefully to certain characteristics of the stimulus person in order to explain their feelings. This latter possibility is explored in more detail below.

The Effects of Nonverbal Behavior on Perceived Intimacy and Attraction

Theoretical Considerations

The possibility that feelings of discomfort induce people to seek explanations for these feelings has interesting implications for the effects of more subtle nonverbal behavioral information on interpersonal attraction. Suppose a judge experiences either a pleasant or an unpleasant emotional reaction while interacting with another person, and seeks information that helps him to explain this reaction. In some instances, the events that produce this reaction may be obvious (e.g., compliments or criticisms, agreements or disagreements, etc.). However, in other cases, these cues may be rather subtle, and the judge may not be immediately aware of them. For example, a judge may find himself engaged in conversation with someone who stands closer to him than is usual or who gazes at him with more or less intensity than would normally be the case. This behavior may make the judge feel vaguely uneasy without his being aware of precisely what is causing his uneasiness. He may therefore fail to attribute his uneasiness to the characteristics that actually annoy him, but instead may attribute them to more general characteristics of the other. Consequently, he may decrease his liking for the person.

A more formal conceptualization of these processes is suggested by Patterson's (1976) formulation of the effects of nonverbal communication. Patterson's model is presented in terms of "arousal," but it is equally applicable if the internal state is assumed to be cognitive rather than physiological. Patterson also focusses on intimacy, while our extension is applicable to both positive and negative relations among persons. Thus, our analysis is not entirely consistent with Patterson's, but nevertheless is based largely on ideas comprising his formulation.

Patterson notes that a given interaction is characterized by a certain level of intensity, which is conveyed by the involved parties' individual and interpersonal behavior. Certain of these reactions may be nonverbal, such as the amount of eye contact, the spatial distance between the parties, etc. For each participant in an interaction, a certain level of intensity is optimal, or maximally desirable (Argyle & Dean, 1965). Thus, situational and behavioral characteristics that convey either greater or less than optimal intensity may increase a participant's discomfort and consequently may decrease his attraction to the other.

The factors that contribute to a particular level of intensity may be compensating (cf. Argyle & Dean, 1965). For example, suppose perceived intensity increases both with the amount of eye contact and with spatial proximity. Then, to maintain a given level of intensity, an increase in spatial proximity would be accompanied by decreased eye contact, and vice versa. It is reasonable to suppose that each person in a given interaction will behave in a way that establishes the level of intensity at which he feels most comfortable. If one party changes his behavior in order to optimize his personal comfort in the interaction, this will produce a corresponding change in the other's level of comfort. If this latter change is positive, the other is apt to attribute favorable characteristics to the actor, and increase liking for him. However, if the change is negative, the other may attribute unfavorable characteristics to the actor, and decrease liking for him.

This analysis helps to conceptualize a variety of effects of nonverbal behavior on interpersonal attraction. For example, suppose a judge interacts with another whose spatial proximity to him is varied. Holding all other factors constant, there should be a curvilinear relation between the judge's proximity to the other and his liking for the other. That is, as proximity decreases, liking should first increase to a maximum and then decrease. However, suppose further that perceived intensity is also a positive function of the frequency of eye contact. Then, the spatial proximity corresponding to the judge's optimal level of intensity should be less when the other maintains eye contact with him than when he does not.

To see more generally the interactive effects of intensity-related variables on attraction, suppose two characteristics, X and Y, are positively related to perceived intensity. The theoretical effect of one variable, X, on the comfort a judge experiences in his interaction with another is shown in Fig. 6.1 at each of three levels of the second variable, Y. Note that the level of X corresponding to an optimal level of intensity decreases as the intensity implied by Y increases. Thus, the effects of differences in intensity produced by one variable depend on the value of the second. For example, suppose X and Y are spatial proximity and eye contact, respectively. Then, the figure indicates that when two persons are close together, an increase in eye contact will decrease the comfort they experience in the interaction, and therefore

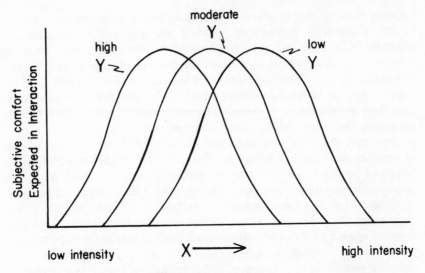

FIG. 6.1. Subjective comfort experienced in an interaction as a function of two variables, X and Y, that are related positively to perceived interaction intensity.

their attraction to one another. When they are far apart, however, an increase in eye contact will have the opposite effect. At intermediate distances, either high or low eye contact may produce less attraction than moderate eye contact. The effects of combinations of other intensity-related variables may be analyzed similarly.

It is important to note that although the intensity of a given interaction may be perceived as optimal by a participant, this does not mean that he is necessarily attracted to the other person. It only implies that he will be relatively more attracted to the other than he would be if the interaction were either more or less intense. Thus, a given party to the interaction may actually dislike the other, but may dislike him less when the intensity of the interaction is optimal than when it is not. Similarly, although two people may interact at a level of intensity that is optimal for both, this does not necessarily mean that they are equally attracted to one another. Nor, for that matter, does it mean that the degree of comfort experienced by the two parties to the interaction is the same. Rather, it means only that each person's comfort, and his attraction to the other, are *relatively* greater than they would be if the intensity of the interaction were less optimal.

Preference Differences in Interaction Intensity. The intensity that a judge considers optimal in a given interaction is apt to depend upon both individual and situational factors. For example, a person may consider a higher level of intensity to be optimal in interactions with members of the opposite sex than in interactions with members of the same sex. Alternatively, females may generally prefer more intense interactions than males, regardless of the sex of the person with whom they interact. Moreover, situational factors may determine the subjective intensity of an interaction. For example, a given distance may be perceived as more intense if the two parties are in an open field than if they are in an elevator, or more intense if there are few other persons in the vicinity than if there are many.

The effects of specific individual and situational differences on perceptions of intensity, and the levels people consider to be optimal, are matters for empirical investigation. However, the effects of such differences are neatly conceptualized within the framework proposed. For example, suppose that one judge (B) prefers a more intense interaction with a target person (X) than does a second judge (A). Hypothetical relations between the subjective intensity of each judge's interaction with X and the comfort he experiences in the interaction are illustrated in Fig. 6.2. Thus, suppose that perceived intimacy is a positive function of either spatial proximity or eye contact. Then, Fig. 6.2 implies that a stimulus person whose spatial proximity to the target corresponds to point X_1 will be liked more by judge A than by judge B, whereas a person who is spatially closer (i.e., at point X_2) will be liked more by B than by A. Alternatively, a person who maintains high eye contact may be liked more by B than by A, while a person who maintains little eye contact will be liked more by A than by B.

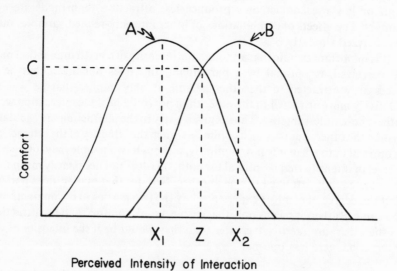

FIG. 6.2.   Subjective comfort of interaction as a function of perceived intensity for two persons, A and B, who prefer different levels of intensity (X_1 and X_2, respectively).

When two parties to an interaction differ in the level of intimacy they perceive as optimal, it is impossible for both to be perfectly comfortable. In these conditions, behavior in the interaction may stabilize at a point where both parties are equally comfortable (or uncomfortable). Thus, if judges A and B in Figure 6.2 were to interact, and the intimacy–attraction curves corresponding to them were similar to those shown, the point at which both persons would be equally comfortable would occur at the intersection of the two curves, or at point Z. The intensity of the relation would therefore be predicted to stabilize at this level. Note that the magnitude of the discomfort experienced by both parties, and therefore the parties' attraction to one another, will be a function of the difference in the a priori levels of intensity considered optimal by the two participants. That is, if the two levels considered optimal by A and B were farther apart than those shown in Fig. 6.2, the two curves would be less overlapping, and the comfort corresponding to the point of intersection of the two curves, C, would be less. Their attraction to one another would therefore be less. This has some implications. For example, suppose situational conditions arise that increase B's preference for a high level of intimacy, so that his comfort-intensity curve is displaced to the right relative to its position in Fig. 6.2. In this event, the point at which B's intimacy gradient intersects with A's will also move to the right, and therefore the interaction will become more intense. Ironically, however, the level of comfort corresponding to this point of intersection (C), and thus the two parties' attraction to one another, will be lessened. In other words, an increase in B's preference for an intimate interaction with A might actually lead to an increase in the intimacy of their interaction, but might at the same time decrease A's and B's attraction to one another.

Empirical Evidence

While little research bears directly on the validity of this formulation, certain studies are suggestive. Ellsworth and Carlsmith (1968) exposed judges to an interview situation in which the interviewer (a) made either favorable or unfavorable remarks about people in the judge's birth-order category (first born or later born), and (b) manifested either frequent or infrequent eye contact with the judge. It seems reasonable to suppose that the interviewer's unfavorable statements decreased judges' desired intimacy levels, while his favorable comments increased it. Therefore, the optimal intimacy levels of judges under these conditions may correspond conceptually to those of judges A and B in Fig. 6.2. If the level of intimacy implied by low and high eye contact in the situation corresponds conceptually to levels X_1 and X_2, respectively, this would predict that increasing eye contact would increase liking for the positively-commenting interviewer, but would decrease liking for the disparaging interviewer. Results support this prediction.

Results of a later study (Ellsworth & Ross, 1975) are less easily predicted a priori by the formulation, but are nonetheless interesting to interpret in these terms. Subjects were encouraged to engage in a personally revealing discussion with another person of the same sex, who either maintained or avoided eye contact with the speaker.[3] Female subjects' liking for another female was a positive function of eye contact, whereas male judges' liking for another male was not appreciably affected. This would be consistent with the proposed formulation if females prefer higher levels of intimacy with other females than males prefer with other males. Females' liking–intimacy-level curves would then be positioned in a manner more closely corresponding to that of Judge B in Fig. 6.2. Unfortunately, Ellsworth and Ross did not run opposite sex pairs, so it is unclear whether the difference is actually attributable to the sex of the subject, to the sex of the other, or to the combination.

The preceding analyses are of course not restricted in applicability to eye contact and physical proximity. Changes in body position and posture may contribute to subjects' perceptions of intimacy, and may be subject to similar considerations (cf. Mehrabian, 1969). Hence our analyses and discussion of research should be considered only representative and not exhaustive.

Conclusions

Research on counterattitudinal advocacy, interpersonal attraction, and the effect of outcome information is generally consistent in its implication that judges' internal emotional states are important contributors to social inferences. These effects may be primarily directive rather than informational. That is, cognitive discomfort may lead the judge to seek information that helps to explain its occurrence. It may also stimulate the judge to change inferences about himself or others in a manner that decreases this unpleasant cognitive state. While these possibilities have long been recognized by research on cognitive consistency (Festinger, 1957; Heider, 1958; Osgood & Tannenbaum, 1955), two conclusions are worth noting. First, the critical mediator of these effects appears to be cognitive rather than physiological, as evidenced by research on counterattitudinal advocacy. Second, emotional states may be induced in many ways, not only by cognitive inconsistency, and may therefore mediate judgments in a variety of situations to which consistency theories are not directly applicable. Thus, the role of internal emotional states is of methodological as well as theoretical importance in research on social inference. For one thing, it suggests that experimental

---

[3]Two other conditions were run in the study, in which eye contact was contingent upon whether the speaker's statements were personally revealing. However, data under these conditions were not appreciably different from those in which gaze was noncontingent.

conditions that elicit internal reactions in judges may lead them to make different use of available information, and thus to make different inferences than under conditions that do not elicit these reactions. This possibility warrants further investigation.

6.2 EFFECTS OF INFORMATION ABOUT OTHER PERSONS ON JUDGMENTS OF A TARGET PERSON

Quite different considerations surround judges' use of information about one person to make inferences about a second. Here, the indirect effects of information result from its use as a basis for comparison in evaluating the implications of other relevant information. On one hand, a judge may assume that people who interact in a given situation are likely to have attributes in common (i.e., that "birds of a feather flock together"); thus, information about one person's characteristics may have a direct, positive effect on judgments of the other. On the other hand, a judge may use one person as a standard relative to which a second, target person is compared. In this case, information about the first person may have an indirect, *contrast* effect upon judgments of the target. For example, the more intelligently one person behaves, the less intelligent the second may appear by comparison, and therefore the less intelligent the latter will be judged. Finally, one person's characteristics may be used to interpret the implications of other information presented. For example, whether an actor's public statements are interpreted as an indication of his personal beliefs may depend upon whether his audience is seen as favoring or opposing the position advocated (cf. Mills & Jellison, 1967). Since the last, interpretative effect is discussed elsewhere in this volume (see Chapters 5 and 8), we will devote our present attention to the first two effects described above.

The direct (positive) and indirect (contrast) effects of information about one person on judgments of a second may in fact be highly related. A formulation that provides insight into the possible nature of this relation is described below. This formulation is admittedly oversimplified, but it helps to conceptualize factors that may underlie the postulated effects and the conditions under which they are likely to occur.

A Simple Model of Social Comparison

For simplicity, assume that characteristics of two persons, P and O, may be assigned values along to dimensions of judgment, A and B. If the scales used to measure A and B are interval, and if values along the two dimensions are related monotonically, the difference between ratings of P and O along one dimension may be represented as a linear function of the difference between their ratings along the second. That is,

$$J_{P,A} - J_{O,A} = w_{A,B} (J_{P,B} - J_{O,B}) \tag{6-1}$$

where $J_{i,j}$ is the judgment of person i along dimension j and $w_{A,B}$ is a constant that embodies both the scale constant for transforming units of B to units of A and the correlation between the values along these two scales.[4] (The value of $w_{A,B}$ may be either positive or negative, depending upon whether the correlation is positive or negative; for simplicity, however, we will typically assume a positive value.) Rewriting this equation slightly,

$$J_{P,A} = J_{O,A} + w_{A,B} (J_{P,B} - J_{O,B}) \tag{6-2}$$

Equation 6-2 implies that the judgment of a target person (P) along dimension A is:

1. a *positive* function of the value assigned to a second stimulus person, O, along this same dimension, A;
2. a *positive* function of the value assigned to P along the other dimension, B, weighted by the strength of the relation between B and A; and
3. a *negative* function of the value assigned to O along the other dimension, B, weighted by the strength of the relation between B and A.

As presented above, Equations 6-1 and 6-2 are simply mathematical descriptions of the relations among judgments along two scales, and as such have no necessary implications for social inference processes. However, these equations may also describe the relations among judges' actual perceptions of values along different related dimensions. Thus, Equation 6-2 may describe the manner in which information represented on the right side of the equation combines to affect estimates of the value on the left (that is, judgments of target person P along dimension A). Suppose a judge receives information bearing upon $J_{O,A}$, $J_{P,B}$, $J_{O,B}$, and $w_{A,B}$ and is asked to infer the value of the target person along A ($J_{P,A}$). Then, if Equation 6-2 is valid, the stimulus information should combine to affect these judgments in a manner similar to that described above. Moreover, since Equation 6-2 specifies a precise functional relation among the informational variables, its validity as a description of inference processes can be tested using functional measurement methodology (Anderson, 1970).

---

[4]Geometrically, the correlation of values along A and B may be represented as the cosine of the angle between vectors pertaining to A and B in multidimensional space, and thus as a constant that determines the magnitude of the projection of B onto A.

To the extent that Equation 6-2 is a description of judges' actual inference processes, the equation suggests the conditions in which information about one person will have positive rather than negative effects on judgments of another. That is, judges of a target person (P) along a given dimension (A) will be affected positively by information about a stimulus person (O) along the same dimension, but will be affected negatively by information about the stimulus person along a different but related dimension (B). For example, judgments of P along a 0–10 scale of intelligence may be affected positively by information about O's intelligence ratings along this scale, but may be affected negatively by information about O's performance on an ability task that presumably requires intelligence.

These predictions are based upon the assumption that the various components on the right side of Equation 6-2 vary independently, so that the value of one component does not affect values of the others. For example, the predicted negative effect of information about O's characteristic B ($J_{O,B}$) on judgments of P along dimension A ($J_{P,A}$) assumes that this information does not also affect judgments of P along B ($J_{P,B}$). However, if values of all three components are not explicitly stated and are not known (a priori) by the judge, the assumption of their independence is unlikely to be valid. The equation is nevertheless useful in conceptualizing the nature of dependencies that a judge may assume to exist under different conditions, and the effects of these assumptions on his inferences.

In considering these dependencies, it is important to note that values along the dimensions involved may in many cases be communicated using labels that are not clearly defined (e.g., numbers along a rating scale). In these cases, the judge may believe scale values along the two dimensions to be related, but may be unsure of the appropriate criterion for transforming values along one dimension into values along the second. He is therefore forced to make certain implicit assumptions about this criterion in order to report his judgment. The nature of these assumptions and their implications will be considered for three separate cases involving a judge who is asked to rate a target person (P) along a dimension A, based upon either (1) information about a stimulus person (O) along this same dimension; (2) information about O along a different but related dimension; or (3) information about *both* P and O along a different but related dimension.

Case 1: Effects of Information about Another (O) Along the Dimension of Judgment (A)

Suppose first that no information is available about either P or O along dimension B, and that information is provided about O along dimension A (i.e., about $J_{O,A}$). In the absence of information to the contrary, the judge may assume that P and O are both representative of the same general population, and thus likely to be similar along B (i.e., $J_{P,B} = J_{O,B}$). Alternatively, he may assume a constant difference between P and O along this dimension ($J_{P,B} -J_{O,B} = c$).

In the latter event, Equation 6.2 reduces to:

$$J_{P,A} = J_{O,A} + w_{A,B} \, c = J_{O,A} + k \qquad (6-3)$$

where k is a constant for any given combination of dimensions A and B. In other words, information about O along A should have a positive effect on judgments of P along this dimension.

As a concrete example, assume that dimension A pertains to intelligence and dimension B to performance on an intellectual ability test, and that the response scales used to report values along these dimensions are as shown in Fig. 6.3. Suppose a judge is asked to rate P's intelligence based upon information that the rating of another person (O) along A is either 0 (Fig. 6.3a) or 2 (Fig. 6.3b). Given no other information, and no a priori indication of the relation between values along the intelligence scale and values along the performance scale (B), the judge may assume that P and O are both about "average," and that their performance on the intellectual ability test would fall near the scale midpoint. He may therefore subjectively position the intelligence response scale (A) so that O's rating along this scale corresponds to this "average" value along B. P's rating along A would then also correspond to this value. As a result, the judge's rating of P's intelligence should increase as a function of the value assigned to O along this scale. However, this would be due primarily to the effect of the information about O on the judge's perception of the correspondence between values along the intelligence scale (A) and values along the related performance scale (B).

Case 2: Effect of Information about Another Along a Different Dimension (B)

Now suppose that the judge is asked to rate the target person (P) along A, on the basis of information about O along a *different* but related dimension, B. If no other information is available, the judge may again assume (as in Case 1) that the two persons are either similar along B or that they differ by a constant amount (= c). Thus, while the information about O along B may influence ratings of P along the B dimension, the difference between P's and O's ratings along B may be unaffected. Then, Equation 6-3 implies that information about O along B should affect judgments of P along A ($J_{P,A}$) only to the extent that it affects the value implicitly assigned to O along this same dimension ($J_{O,A}$). If the judge assumes O to be "average," and interprets O's value along B as corresponding to an "average" value along A, then information about O along B should not affect judgments of P along A.

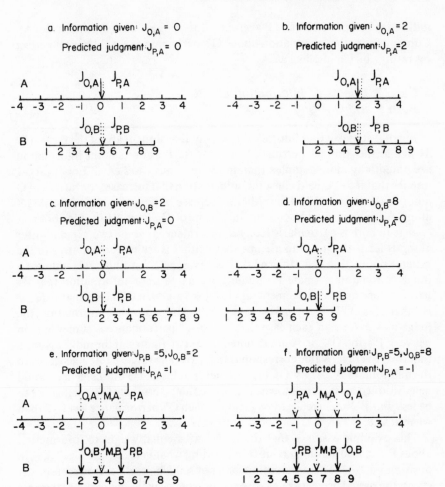

FIG. 6.3.   Hypothetical judgments of P along dimension A ($J_{P,A}$) as a function of different combinations of information about O along A ($J_{O,A}$) and information about P and O along B ($J_{P, B}$ and $J_{O,B}$). Solid arrows denote information available, and dotted arrows denote judgments to be inferred.

This can again be illustrated with reference to a concrete example and Fig. 6.3c and d. In this case, assume that the judge is asked to rate P's intelligence along A given information that O's performance on an ability task receives a rating along B of either 2 or 8. Given no other information, the judge may again assume that P and O are both about "average," and therefore that P's performance would be about the same as O's. Thus, his predictions of P's performance rating should increase with O's rating along this scale. However, regardless of whether O's performance rating is 2 (Fig. 6.3c) or 8 (Fig. 6.3d), a judge may assign both O and P average values along the intelligence scale (A). Consequently, the information about O's performance would have no effect on ratings of P's intelligence.

Case 3: Effects of Information about Both P and O Along B

Finally, suppose that information is available along B about the target (P) as well as the stimulus person (O). In this case, the effects of the information are potentially more complex than in the previous cases cited. Equation 6-1 implies that if $J_{P,B}$ is held constant, information that increases the ratings of O along B ($J_{O,B}$) could produce either a decrease in the judgment of the target along A ($J_{P,A}$), an increase in the judgment of O along A ($J_{O,A}$), or both. A change in both is particularly likely if the evidence that the two persons differ along B leads the judge to assume that neither is truly representative of the general population (i.e., that neither is "average"). To illustrate, suppose a judge is asked to estimate P's intelligence based upon information that P's performance on an achievement task ($J_{P,B}$) is 5 and that O's performance ($J_{O,B}$) is either 2 (as in Fig. 6.3e) or 8 (as in Fig. 6.3f). Given no other information, the judge may assume in each case that "average" performance is somewhere in between P's and O's, or $J_{M,B}$ as denoted in the two figures. If the judge assumes that this "average" value corresponds to an average value of intelligence, or to the midpoint of A ($J_{M,A}$ = O), his judgments of P's and O's intelligence should be positioned along A as shown. That is, he should estimate O's intelligence to be less, but P's intelligence to be greater, when O's performance level is 2 than when it is 8.

This example assumes that the judge gives equal weight to information about P and information about O in deciding what value is "average" (i.e., in positioning $J_{M,B}$). This assumption may not hold in practice. However, in any event, the model predicts a negative relation between the change in judgments of one person along A ($J_{O,A}$) and the change in judgments of a second person along this dimension ($J_{P,A}$).

General Implications

While the preceding analysis may seem to be much ado about relatively little, it has some interesting implications. First, information about one person along a given dimension should have a positive effect on judgments of a second target person along the same dimension. However, it may sometimes have a contrast effect on judgments of the target along a different dimension from the one to which the information is directly relevant. Whether this contrast effect actually occurs depends upon whether the target's value along the stimulus dimension is also known a priori by the judge, or for other reasons is assumed to be independent of the value assigned to the stimulus person along this dimension.

This analysis leads to several hypotheses concerning the conditions in which contrast effects are likely to occur. The effects of information about others on self-judgments are of particular interest. For example, a person is more likely to have specific information about himself along dimensions pertaining to concrete, observable characteristics than he is to know the value he should be assigned along an abstract dimension. This is particularly likely if these latter values are along an unfamiliar, numerical scale such as those often used in psychological experiments. Therefore, information about a stimulus person (O) along a general attribute scale (A) is apt to have positive effects upon a person's (P's) self-judgment along this same scale (Case 1). On the other hand, information about a stimulus person along a related abstract attribute dimension (B) may have little effect upon P's self-judgment along A (Case 2); finally, information about a more concrete characteristic of O that is related to the attribute measured along A is likely to have a negative, or contrast, effect on P's self-judgment along A (Case 3). Thus, a judge's rating of his own intelligence along a 7-category scale may be increased by presenting information that someone else (O) has a value of "6" along this scale; however, it may be unaffected by information that O has a rating of "6" along a 7-category scale of competence (an abstract dimension related to intelligence), and (assuming that P knows his own IQ score) may be affected negatively by information that O has an IQ of 155. Alternatively, the favorableness of P's self-rated opinion of women's liberation might be decreased by giving him information that O has an unfavorable opinion of women's liberation, (Case 2) but might be increased by giving him information that O has advocated abolition of women's voting privileges (Case 3).

This framework is also useful in conceptualizing the different effects that information about another person may have on a target person's self-judgments and an observer's judgments of the target. Suppose that the response dimension A pertains to a general attribute and that a stimulus dimension B pertains to a characteristic related to this attribute. If the characteristic to which B pertains is concrete, the target may have a clearer a priori perception of his position along this dimension than will an observer. If this is so, information about someone along B is apt to produce a greater contrast effect on the target's self-judgment along A than on an observer's judgment of him along this dimension. On the other hand, if this stimulus dimension (B) is more abstract, neither the target nor the observer may have an a priori basis for assigning values along this dimension. In this case, the effect of the information on the target's self-judgments and observer's judgments to him may be similar.

Empirical Evidence. While a vigorous test of Equation 6-2 as a description of social judgment has not been performed at this writing, the results of several studies seem consistent with the implications of this conceptualization. For example, Wyer, Henninger, and Wolfson (1975) gave feedback to female subjects about their own and another's performance on an achievement task and then asked them to judge both their own competence and the other's competence. This situation is analogous to Case 3. According to our analysis, subjects should use O's performance as a comparative standard in judging their own competence, and should decrease their judgments of their own competence as O's performance level increases. In fact, this is what happened.

In contrast, studies of attitude and opinion change (cf. Wyer, 1975c;Wyer, Henninger, & Hinkle, 1977) have shown information about another person's attitude to contribute positively to subjects' judgments of their own attitude. In these experiments, only information about the other's *general* attitude was presented, rather than specific beliefs upon which this attitude was presumably based. Moreover, the information about the other was along essentially the same dimension used by subjects to rate themselves. The situation is therefore similar to Case 1, and so a positive effect of the other's opinion on subjects' self judgments would indeed be expected. There have been no empirical investigations of the effect of information about another person's specific beliefs upon subjects' reports of their own attitude along a dimension related to these beliefs. Theoretically, this effect should depend upon whether subjects themselves have clearly defined a priori beliefs in the issue to which the information pertains. If they have such beliefs, the information should produce a contrast effect on their reported attitudes (see Case 3).

Effects of Perceived Similarity

A related application of the proposed formulation concerns the extent to which the perceived similarity of two people affects the use of information about one person on judgments of the other. Suppose again that A and B are two positively related dimensions of judgment, and that a judge receives information about the value of stimulus person (O) along dimension A. According to Equation 6-2, the difference between this value and the value assigned to the target person (P) along A depends upon the perceived similarity of P and O along other relevant dimensions (i.e., the similarity of $J_{P,B}$ to $J_{O,B}$). However, this analysis is obviously oversimplified. For one thing, P and O are unlikely to be perceived as equally similar along all dimensions relevant to the judgment being made. Rather, the perception of these persons' overall similarity to one another may be a composite function of their similarity along several different dimensions. (It is sometimes useful to conceptualize the overall similarity of two persons in terms of their proximity in multidimensional space; cf. Nygren & Jones, 1977). Moreover, it seems reasonable to suppose that perceived similarity is not a stable characteristic. Rather, it depends upon the particular attribute dimensions that are accessed by the judge at the time he makes his inference. Which dimensions happen to be considered at any time may vary with the situational context in which the judgment is made, or with other factors that "prime" certain dimensions rather than others (for a detailed analysis of priming effects, see Chapter 3 and 4). For example, differences between two persons along a dimension of "teacher vs. student" may be considered more when the two are interacting in the teacher's office then when they are drinking beer at a pub, while the fact that one is male and the other female may be less salient in the former situation than in the latter. If this is true, and if Equation 6-2 is valid, the effect of information about one person on judgments of another should depend upon the particular dimensions that happen to be accessed and used in comparing the two persons under the situational conditions in which the judgment is made.

Indirect evidence of this possibility is provided by Kelley's (1955) study of the effects of reference group salience. In this study, Catholic subjects were asked to read a biographical sketch of either the Pope or a nonreligious historical figure. Then they responded to a series of religion opinion items that in each case were accompanied by bogus group norms purporting to represent the opinions held by college students in general. Some of these items pertained to matters of Catholic dogma, and the norms presented were contrary to the implications of this dogma. It is reasonable to suppose that without reading the Pope's biography, Catholic subjects considered themselves to be similar to other students. However, reading the biography of the Pope may have made salient the dimension "Catholic vs. non-Catholic" and therefore a distinction between themselves and "students in general" that was not otherwise considered. To this extent, their judgments of items pertaining to Catholic dogma should have deviated more from the normative values attributed to students in general. Results were consistent with this hypothesis: Catholic subjects who read the Pope's biography conformed less to normative judgments of items that opposed Catholic dogma than did Catholics who had read the other, irrelevant biographies.

Conclusions

Our analysis of how information about one person can affect judgments of a second may seem overly complex. However, it helps to identify the factors that may need to be taken into account in understanding the nature of these effects and when they occur. Equation 6-2 provides a precise and empirically testable statement of the combined effects of these various factors. More generally this equation enables the effects of information about one person on judgments of a second to be diagnosed in terms of the mediating assumptions that may underlie these effects.

It should be noted that many of the effects predicted are for *ratings* of attributes along the category scales used to report these judgments, rather than for true subjective judgments of the attributes involved. A distinction should of course be made between the effects of information on subjective judgments and its effects on the language used to report these judgments. While a detailed discussion of response language effects on judgments is beyond the scope of this discussion, the reader is referred to Upshaw (1969, 1978) and Wyer (1974b) for more general analyses of these effects.

6.3 CONCLUDING REMARKS

In this chapter, we have considered two types of indirect effects of some information on one's perception of the implications of other available information. First, we have shown how a judge's internal emotional state, or the cognitive discomfort produced by this state, may lead the judge to seek information that helps him to interpret characteristics of the situation and of persons involved in it in a way that will eliminate or minimize this discomfort. In addition, we have discussed the manner in which the perceived implications of information about oneself may be influenced by information about others. A complete understanding of judgmental processes will ultimately need to take into account both direct and indirect effects of information, and to isolate the relative contributions.

7

The Role of Syllogistic Reasoning in Inferences Based Upon New and Old Information*

To recapitulate, someone who is asked to judge a person, object, or event presumably searches for information that is relevant to this judgment. This information may be either stored in memory or available in the immediate situation in which the judgment is made. Once this information is identified, the judge construes its implications for the judgment to be made, and then reports this judgment in a language the recipient will understand.

Several issues raised by this rather simplistic description have been addressed in earlier chapters in this volume. One set of questions concerns which information is most likely to be selected and brought to bear on a judgment at any given time, and the factors that stimulate an active seeking of judgment-relevant information. These issues were discussed both in Chapters 2 through 4 and, from a different perspective, Chapter 6. A second set of questions, concerning the manner in which the implications of information are evaluated, was considered in detail in Chapter 5. While the present chapter will also bear on these matters, it will primarily focus upon a third question that has not yet been considered fully, that is, the precise nature of the inference process that underlies the use of information to arrive at the judgments one reports.

In Chapter 2 we argued that people often use the information they have available to access a script or schema of a prototypic person or situation, and then use the contents of this script to either infer characteristics of the person to whom the information is relevant or to predict the nature of events involving the person. However, certain aspects of this process were left understated in our analyses. For example, in using a script or schema to make inferences about a particular person or event, the judge must somehow

---

*This chapter was co-authored by Jon Hartwick.

extrapolate from the prototypic cognitive representation to the particular person or event he is judging. Moreover, his ultimate judgment may be modified by the strength of his belief that this representation is in fact applicable, and that the information that led it to be accessed is valid. For example, a person who is asked to evaluate the honesty of an acquaintance may recall being told that the acquaintance cheated on an exam, and may identify the implications of this behavior for the person's honesty based upon criteria similar to those noted in Chapter 5. However, he may also consider the possibility that the information about the person's behavior is invalid, and take into account the implications of this possibility as well.

In this regard, an important point needs to be made about the equations proposed in Chapter 5 for describing the relations among the perceived implications of behavioral information. These equations were for predictive purposes, and were not intended to describe the actual psychological processes involved in making an inference on the basis of behavioral information. Moreover, certain factors were not considered at all, such as the perceived validity of the information presented. A more complete psychological account of these inference processes is necessary. While the processes postulated in presenting our memory model (Chapter 3) may ultimately be able to account for certain of these inferences, a more phenomenologically oriented description of these processes, which has heuristic value in its own right, may be in order at this time.

It seems reasonable to suppose that the process of arriving at judgments based on information we receive or retrieve from memory is often syllogistic in nature. Many decisions we make, and many conclusions we draw on the basis of information we receive, involve such reasoning. For example, we may decide to go to a particular restaurant because we are told that (a) a friend likes the restaurant, and we believe that (b) if this friend likes a restaurant, it is usually a very good place to eat. Or, we may conclude that marijuana should be legalized because we learn that (a) marijuana is psychologically and physically harmless, and we believe that (b) if something is harmless, it should be freely accessible. Or, we may infer that a person is likely to be honest on the basis of (a) information that the person has returned a lost wallet in a given situation, and (b) the belief that people who return lost property under these conditions are typically honest. (The factors postulated in Chapter 5 to influence the perceived implications of behavioral information would presumably affect this latter belief.) Syllogistic reasoning may even be involved, at least implicitly, in script processing. For example, the professor who accesses a previously formed script of a prior graduate student while evaluating the credentials of a new applicant may base his evaluation on (a) his belief that the new candidate is actually like the graduate student to whom the script pertains, and (b) his belief that if the new candidate is like the former student, he would actually wind up the same way.

In this chapter, we will consider in more detail the nature of these syllogistic processes and will propose a descriptive model that enables specific predictions to be drawn concerning their use. We will then consider certain implications of the formulation and the assumptions underlying it, touching bases with theory and research considered in earlier chapters when relevant.

7.1. A MODEL OF SYLLOGISTIC INFERENCE

Statement of the Model

We begin this discussion with an example that provides an intuitive feel for the inference processes to be considered in this chapter and for the assumptions underlying the model we propose for describing these processes. Suppose a judge is asked to estimate the validity of an assertion about a person or event with which he is familiar. To make this estimate, the judge presumably activates a search for information that bears on this assertion. The information may be obtained either from the immediate judgmental situation or from memory. If the person has recently stated his belief[1] in the same or a similar assertion, he may simply retrieve and report his prior judgment without looking further. When a prior judgment has not been made, however, or if this judgment is not readily accessible, the person may search for another previously acquired belief or piece of factual information that has relevant implications. This information may then be considered in terms of the implications it would have both if it were true and if it were false. Thus, for example, suppose a person is asked his belief that an acquaintance, Mary, is liberal. If he has not recently thought about this possibility and cannot recall a previously formed belief about Mary's liberalness, he may search memory for other information (i.e., other propositions, and beliefs in these propositions) that may be relevant. When such information (e.g., the proposition that Mary favors equal rights legislation) is encountered and recognized as relevant, the person may construe its implications (i.e., the likelihood that if Mary favors equal rights legislation, she is liberal), based on other information he may have available and considerations such as those raised in Chapter 5. If the person believes there is some likelihood that the proposition is false (i.e., that Mary does *not* favor equal rights legislation), then he may identify the implications this would have as well (the likelihood that if Mary does not favor equal rights, she is liberal). The person's overall judgment that the target statement is true would then be the sum of these two

---

[1] In this context, a *belief* is defined as a subjective estimate of the likelihood of a relation among persons, objects or events, or of the likelihood that a statement about them is true. Note that the former beliefs are similar to those denoted directed inferences in Chapter 3.

sets of implications, each weighted by his belief that the information is and is not true, respectively.

The foregoing analysis implicitly assumes that when a person is asked to report his belief in a proposition, he does not engage in an exhaustive search for all possible information bearing on it. Rather, he searches only until he encounters a single piece of information or a single concept (another proposition, a script, etc.) that he considers relevant. He then bases his judgment primarily upon this information or concept. Additional considerations may enter into the judgment in the course of estimating the likelihood that the target proposition is true if the information identified is not true. However, these considerations may also not be exhaustive. Rather, they may be based on an intuitive impression of what would happen if the information were not true, without considering any specific factors.

It is of course an oversimplification to say that a person who is asked to evaluate a proposition will *always* use only the first relevant piece of information he retrieves as a basis for his evaluation. When a judgment is important, or when ample time is provided for making it, several pieces may be retrieved. In such instances, the judge may estimate the implications of each piece separately, and then arrive at an overall judgment that represents some composite of these implications (for a discussion of these combinatorial processes, see Chapters 8 and 9). Even in these instances, however, the judge is unlikely to consider all of the information that is potentially available to him. Rather, he may identify only a sample of this information that is most easily accessible to him, and may take it and its implications as representative of the population (cf. Tversky & Kahneman, 1973). This conceptualization, if valid, obviously implies that the beliefs one reports may depend greatly on which of several alternative subsets of information he happens to stumble upon in his search. This conclusion is consistent with that drawn in Chapter 4. Later sections of the present chapter are devoted to a further consideration of this possibility.

The above description of cognitive processes may be formalized by applying the syllogistic model of social cognition proposed initially by McGuire (1960) and more recently by Wyer (1974a, 1975c; Wyer & Hartwick, in press). The target proposition in the above example ("Mary is liberal") can be considered the conclusion of two syllogisms, the premises of which are based on the proposition retrieved from memory. The premises of one syllogism pertain to the implications of the retrieved proposition's being true (specifically, "Mary supports equal rights legislation; if Mary supports equal rights legislation, she is liberal") and the premises of the other pertain to the implications of the proposition's being false ("Mary does not support equal rights legislation; if Mary does *not* support equal rights legislation, she is liberal"). Note that the two sets of premises are mutually exclusive; both sets cannot simultaneously be valid. One's belief in the target proposition may therefore be a function of the sum of his beliefs in the two sets of premises. If A and B are used to denote the proposition retrieved from memory and the target proposition (the conclusion), respectively, and if beliefs are reported in units of probability, this sum may be represented by the equation:

$$P_B = P_A P_{B/A} + P_{A'} P_{B/A'} \qquad\qquad (7\text{-}1)$$

where P_B is the belief in the conclusion B, P_A and $P_{A'} (= 1 - P_A)$ are beliefs that A is and is not true, respectively, and $P_{B/A}$ and $P_{B/A'}$ are conditional beliefs that B is true if A is not true, respectively.

The above equation theoretically provides an exact quantitative description of the relation between a person's belief in a conclusion and his belief in other propositions that are brought to bear upon it. To this extent, it is theoretically capable of predicting the magnitude of change in one belief (i.e., P_B, in Equation 7-1) produced by a given change in other related beliefs (e.g., P_A). Moreover, if the equation is generally valid, the quantitative discrepancy between a person's actual belief in B and the implications of his beliefs in the premises may indicate a temporary inconsistency among these beliefs. Alternatively, it may indicate the extent to which beliefs other than those associated with the proposition A have been used as a basis for inferring the likelihood of B.

Equation 7-1 and its derivatives have in fact been used effectively to investigate a variety of theoretical and empirical questions concerning social inference and cognitive organization, including belief and opinion change (Wyer, 1970b, 1975a; Wyer & Polsky, 1972), impression formation (Wyer, 1973a,b), the relation between interpersonal similarity and interpersonal attraction (Wyer, 1972), the elimination of inconsistencies among beliefs (Henninger & Wyer, 1976; Rosen & Wyer, 1972; Wyer, 1974b), and the manner in which the implications of previously formed beliefs combine with the implications of new information to affect inferences (Wyer, 1976a). Certain of these applications will be noted later in this chapter. Before embarking on this discussion, however, it may be worthwhile to present two rigorous tests of the validity of the formulation in describing the processes to which it theoretically pertains.

Empirical Evidence

Three general criteria have been used to evaluate the validity of Equation 7-1 as a description of how people use their beliefs in syllogistically-related propositions to make inferences. One is whether information that bears directly on the validity of the component propositions combines functionally to affect beliefs in the conclusion as implied by Equation 7-1. A second criterion is whether the equation provides a *quantitatively* accurate description of these inference processes. The third criterion is whether beliefs that are not related in the manner implied by Equation 7-1 are in fact perceived by subjects to be inconsistent. The studies below bear on these issues.

Validity in Describing Syllogistic Inference

The value of the formulation lies in its ability to characterize the organization of beliefs about familiar issues and events of concern to subjects, and to describe the use of previously acquired beliefs as informational bases for subsequent ones. However, in evaluating the validity of the model as a description of syllogistic inference, it was advantageous to use materials pertaining to issues about which people lacked preconceptions, thus enabling beliefs in premises to be manipulated independently. Specifically, subjects were presented sets of information about the frequency with which persons had a hypothetical gene (identified by a letter of the alphabet), the frequency with which persons with the gene had a given attribute (also denoted by letter), and the frequency with which persons without the gene had this attribute. These frequencies, which were described using the adverbs *usually, sometimes,* and *rarely,* were expected to convey high, moderate, and low probabilities of the relations described, respectively. Each set of statements was of the form:

Persons *usually* (*sometimes, rarely*) have gene A.
Persons with A *usually* (*sometimes, rarely*) have attribute B.
Persons without A *usually* (*sometimes, rarely*) have attribute B.

In all, 27 sets of three statements were constructed to convey all possible combinations of P_A (the likelihood that a person has A), $P_{B/A}$ (the likelihood that a person has B if he has A) and $P_{B/A'}$ (the likelihood that a person has B if he does not have A). Subjects read each set of statements and then estimated the likelihood that a particular person (described by first name) had attribute B (P_B), followed by each of the three component probabilities to which the information directly pertained. Here, as in most other studies to be reported in this chapter, judgments were made along a scale from 0 (not at all likely) to 10 (extremely likely) and were divided by 10 prior to analyses to convert them to units of probability.

Two mathematical criteria may be used to evaluate the validity of Equation 7-1 in describing inferences. First, if the equation is a valid description of the manner in which information bearing upon beliefs in the premises combines to affect beliefs in the conclusion, the informational manipulations of P_A and $P_{B/A}$ should have multiplicative effects upon beliefs in B; specifically, estimates of P_B should increase with $P_{B/A}$, but the magnitude of this increase should be greater when P_A is high then when it is low. Beliefs in B should also increase with $P_{B/A'}$; however, in this case, the effect should be greater when P_A is low ($P_{A'}$ is high) than when it is high. Data in Fig. 1b and 1c support these predictions.[2] Statistical analyses corroborated the above interpretation (for details, see Wyer, 1975b).[3]

A second criterion for evaluating the validity of Equation 7-1 is quantitative. If a judge's estimates of the four equation components are in units of probability, his actual estimate of P_B should be numerically equal to the value of the expression on the right side of the equation. To explore this possibility, predicted values of P_B were calculated for each subject separately for each of the 27 sets of stimulus statements, assuming that $P_{A'} = 1 - P_A$.[4] Obtained values, averaged over subjects, are plotted in Fig. 7.2 as a function of mean predicted values. If the model were perfectly accurate, each of the 27 points would fall on the 45-degree line shown. In fact, the standard error of the difference between mean obtained and mean predicted values (σ_e)[5] was .047, or less than half a scale unit.

Relations Among Previously Formed Beliefs. If judges typically use the syllogistic processes described by Equation 7-1 to make inferences from new information, and these inferences are then stored in memory, this equation

---

[2]Note that when the value of one conditional belief (e.g., $P_{B/A}$) is zero, this does not necessarily mean that P_B is zero, since the other conditional belief may contribute to judgments. Thus, the curves in Figs. 1b and 1c are expected to cross at a point at which the conditional belief is nonzero.

[3]If P_A combines multiplicatively with $P_{B/A}$ and $P_{B/A'}$, the two interactions described in Figs. 7.1b and 7.1c should each be concentrated in a single degree of freedom corresponding to the linear × linear component, and the residual, after eliminating this component, should be zero (for an elaboration of the basis for this prediction, see Anderson, 1970). In fact the bilinear component was significant ($p < .05$) in each case and accounted for over 96% of the total sums of squares associated with the interaction, whereas the residual was nonsignificant in each case ($p > .20$) and accounted for less than 4% of the total sums of squares.

[4]In fact, subjects' estimates of P_A and $P_{A'}$ typically sum to a value slightly greater than 1 (i.e., 1.1); however, this discrepancy, which decreases when subjects report these beliefs a second time (Rosen and Wyer, 1972), is not sufficiently great to offset the practical advantage of generating predictions of P_B on the basis of three rather than four other beliefs.

[5]Specifically,

$$\sigma_e = \sqrt{\frac{\Sigma(O_i - E_i)^2}{n}}$$

where O_i and E_i are the observed and predicted values of P_B for the ith stimulus. Note that E_i is the exact value of the expression on the right side of Equation 7-1, based upon subjects' actual numerical judgments of P_A, $P_{B/A}$ and $P_{B/A'}$, and does not involve the introduction of best-fitting slope and intercept parameters estimated through curve-fitting procedures.

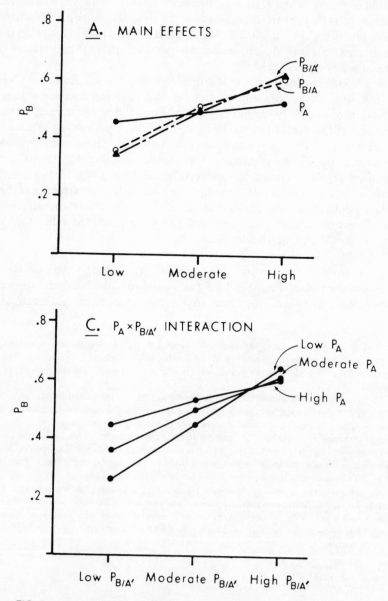

FIG. 7.1.   Main effects and interactions pertaining to P_B as a function of P_A, $P_{B/A}$, and $P_{B/A'}$ (reprinted from Wyer, 1975b, p. 97).

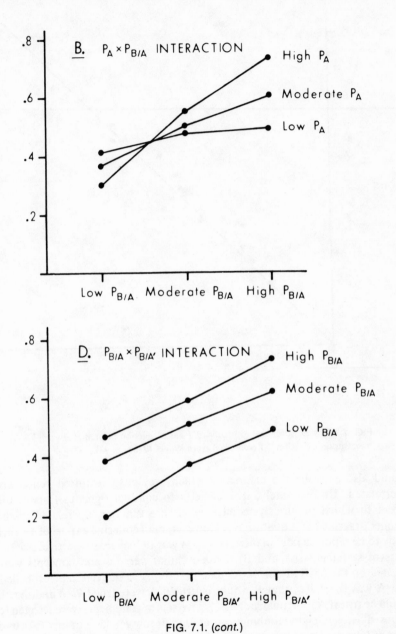

FIG. 7.1. (cont.)

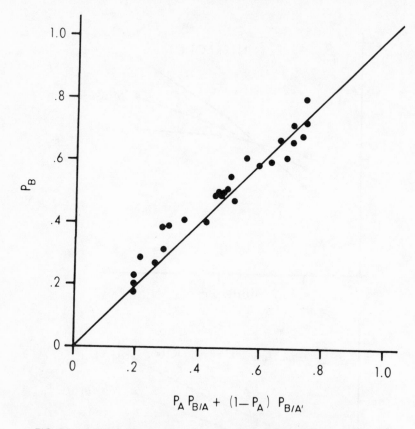

FIG. 7.2.   Mean obtained estimates of P_B as a function of predicted values based upon Equation 7-1 (reprinted from Wyer, 1975b, p. 98).

should also describe the manner in which previously acquired beliefs are interrelated. Unfortunately, it is difficult to conduct rigorous tests of the extent to which previously formed beliefs are functionally related in the manner described by Equation 7-1. However, data collected as part of a larger study to be reported later in this chapter (Wyer, 1976a) are suggestive. Briefly, pairs of statements (A and B) about familiar persons and concepts were selected on the basis of normative data pertaining to subjects' a priori beliefs that A was true (P_A), that B would be true if A were true ($P_{B/A}$) and that B would be true if A were not true ($P_{B/A'}$). Two sets of statements were selected to represent each of eight combinations of high or low P_A, high or low $P_{B/A}$, and high or low $P_{B/A'}$. For example, under conditions where a priori beliefs in all three premises were high, one pair of statements was "a newborn baby cries" (A) and "a newborn baby is loved by its parents" (B). In selecting statement

TABLE 7.1

Mean Beliefs in B (P_B) as a Function of Beliefs in A
(P_A), in B Given A ($P_{B/A}$), and in B Given not-A ($P_{B/A'}$)

	High P_A	Low P_A
1. $P_A \times P_{B/A}$		
High $P_{B/A}$	.75	.52
Low $P_{B/A}$	.28	.42
2. $P_A \times P_{B/A'}$		
High $P_{B/A'}$	.60	.61
Low $P_{B/A'}$	.42	.33

pairs, no consideration was given to judges' unconditional beliefs that B was true (P_B). However, these estimates were subsequently tabulated and are shown in Table 7.1. Their relations to a priori beliefs in premises are those implied by the model. While these data are not definitive, they are consistent with the assumption that subjects use previously acquired beliefs as well as beliefs formed on the basis of abstract information to make inferences in the manner implied by Equation 7-1. We will consider this possiblity in more detail later in this chapter.

Validity as an Index of Belief Inconsistency

The third consideration in evaluating the extent to which Equation 7-1 provides a psychologically valid description of cognitive functioning is whether beliefs that are not related in the manner implied by this equation are regarded as inconsistent. If this were not the case, the assumption that the equation describes the manner in which persons actively arrive at conclusions they believe follow from salient "premises" would be suspect.

If the equation is valid, perceptions of the inconsistency (Inc) of a set of syllogistically related beliefs should be a function of the absolute difference between predicted and obtained values of P_B, that is:

$$Inc = |P_B - [P_A P_{B/A} + (1 - P_A)P_{B/A'}]| \tag{7-2}$$

To test this hypothesis, 36 sets of four statements each were constructed. The form of each set of statements was the same, specifically:

1. A person belongs to group A.
2. If a person belongs to A, he has attribute B.
3. If a person does *not* belong to A, he has attribute B.
4. A person has attribute B.

Each statement in a given set was followed by an 11-point scale from 0 (not at all likely) to 10 (extremely likely), and a value along each scale was circled to represent a hypothetical subject's belief in the statement. The values assigned to the four statements in each set, divided by 10, were assumed to correspond directly to P_A, $P_{B/A}$, $P_{B/A'}$, and P_B, respectively. The values of these four beliefs were manipulated systematically. In each case, judges were asked to assume that a hypothetical subject had reported the four beliefs in the set, and then to estimate their inconsistency.

The theoretical inconsistency of the beliefs in each set, as defined by Equation 7.2, is shown in Fig. 7.3 as a function of the manipulated values of the four beliefs comprising this equation. As can be seen, the theoretical pattern of effects of $P_{B/A}$ and $P_{B/A'}$ differs substantially at each combination of levels of P_A and P_B. The mean obtained judgments of inconsistency, shown in Fig. 7.4, exhibit similar patterns. The major discrepancy appears to occur when the two conditional beliefs are both .5 and $P_B = P_A$; here, perceived inconsistency appears to be affected by the difference between the two unconditional beliefs, over and above the value predicted by Equation 7-2. Statistical analyses, reported in more detail elsewhere (Henninger & Wyer, 1976, Experiment 1), bear out this interpretation.[6] The correlation between mean predicted and mean obtained values of inconsistency was .935. Moreover, the proportion of variance accounted for by each of the 15 main effects and interactions involving P_A, P_B, $P_{B/A}$, and $P_{B/A'}$ was very similar to that theoretically predicted on the basis of Equation 7-2.

The studies reported in this section provide some support for the validity of the proposed model as a description of syllogistic inference. Moreover, they support the assumption that beliefs are regarded as inconsistent when they are *not* related in the manner implied by this equation.

A Similation of Belief Change Processes

People should not only infer their belief in a conclusion B from their belief in A and its implications, but also should change their belief in the conclusion if, for some reason, their belief in A is altered. This change can also be described quantitatively. That is, suppose new information is presented that produces a change in beliefs in a premise A. If A is salient to the person at the time he subsequently reports his belief in B, the change in the latter belief would be predictable from the equation:

---

[6]Variation in subjects' judgments of inconsistency should theoretically be concentrated in only 8 of the 35 degrees of freedom associated with various combinations of values of the four beliefs comprising Equation 7-2. In fact, these 8 degrees of freedom accounted for 93.4% of the total predictable sums of squares, with the remaining 27 degrees of freedom accounting for only 6.6%.

$$\Delta P_B = \Delta[P_A P_{B/A} + (1 - P_A)P_{B/A'}]$$ (7-3)

where $P_{A'}$ is assumed = $1 - P_A$. If the information affects only P_A, leaving its implications (reflected in the conditional beliefs $P_{B/A}$ and $P_{B/A'}$) unchanged, the equation simplifies:

$$\Delta P_B = \Delta P_A(P_{B/A} - P_{B/A'})$$ (7-4)

The magnitude of change in P_B produced by a given change in P_A is therefore a direct function of the difference between the two conditional beliefs that B is true if A is and is not true. This difference is conceptually equivalent to the perceived relevance of one's belief in A to his belief in B.

A direct test of the above conceptualization may be worth noting briefly. The study (Wyer, 1970b) was analogous to a traditional study of belief change, and involved inferences about the sort of events that might occur in everyday life. However, the persons and events involved were fictitious. Thus beliefs were based primarily upon information provided in the experiment.

Specifically, nine hypothetical situations were constructed, each around a different set of propositions A and B (e.g., "There will be a riot at State University," and "University President Smythe will be fired,"). The information about each situation was presented in two paragraphs. The first paragraph established subjects' "initial beliefs"; that is, it conveyed a low value of P_A (in our example, a low likelihood of there being a riot at State University) and implied one of nine possible combinations of $P_{B/A}$ (high, moderate, or low) and $P_{B/A'}$ (high, moderate, or low). However, the conclusion to be inferred (B) was not mentioned. Information in the second paragraph increased the likelihood that A was true while leaving the two conditional beliefs relatively unchanged. After reading each paragraph, subjects reported their belief that B was true (P_B), followed by their beliefs corresponding to other components of Equation 7-1 (P_A, $P_{B/A}$, and $P_{B/A'}$). Figure 7.5 shows mean obtained values of P_B after reading each paragraph, and also the change in P_B after reading the second paragraph, plotted as a function of mean predicted values. These data again show a close quantitative fit of the model; the standard error of the difference between mean and obtained predicted values of P_B was .035, and of ΔP_B was .051 (about half of a scale unit).

Evaluation

In combination, the studies described above provide support for the assumption that people do process information syllogistically in drawing conclusions from new information they receive, and that Equation 7-1

234

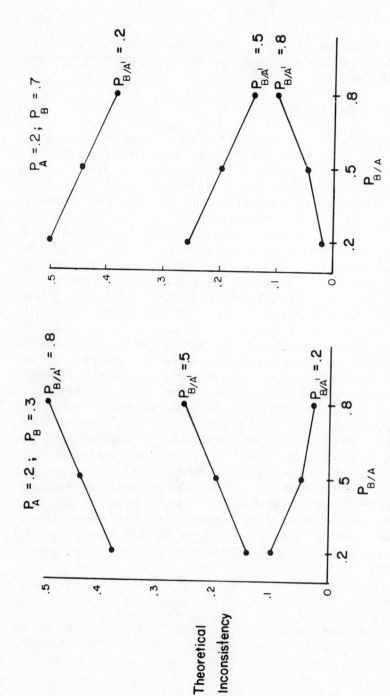

FIG. 7.3. Theoretical inconsistency, based upon Equation 7-2, as a function of manipulated values of $P_{B/A}$ and $P_{B/A'}$ at each combination of P_A and P_B (reprinted from Henninger & Wyer, 1976, p. 682).

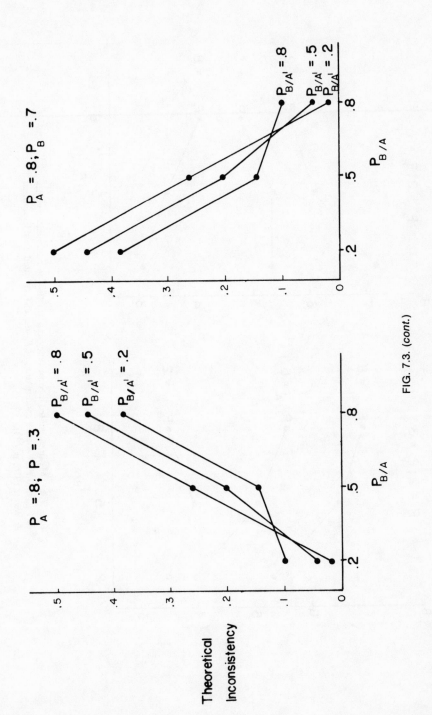

FIG. 7.3. (cont.)

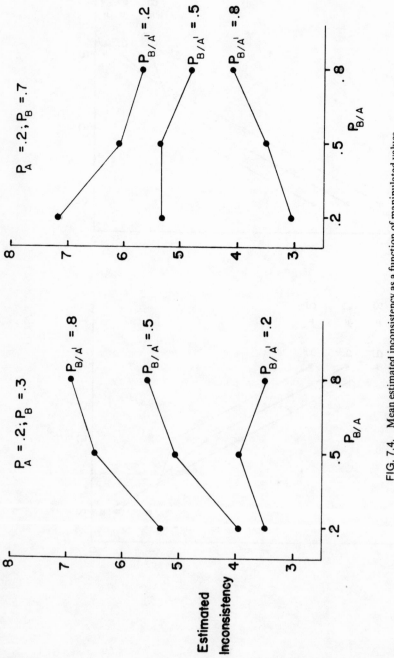

FIG. 7.4. Mean estimated inconsistency as a function of manipulated values of $P_{B/A}$ and $P_{B/A'}$ at each combination of P_A and P_B (reprinted from Henninger & Wyer, 1976, p. 683).

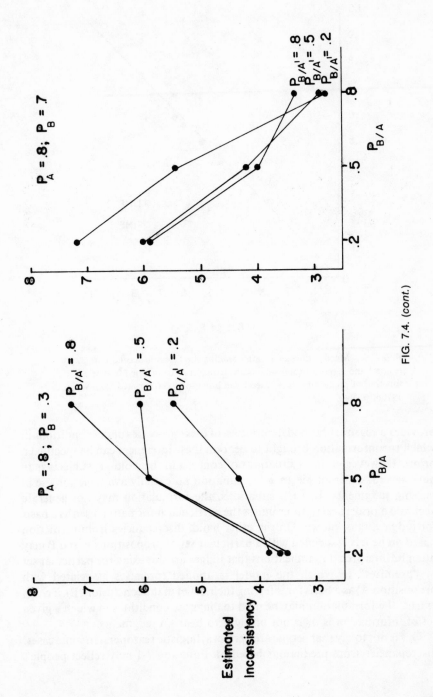

FIG. 7.4. (cont.)

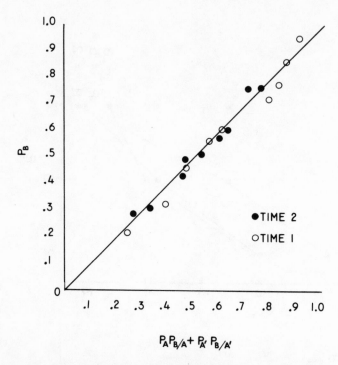

FIG. 7.5.   Mean ratings of P_B after reading the first and second paragraph (times 1 and 2, respectively), and mean change in P_B from time 1 to time 2, as a function of predicted values based upon Equation 7-3 (reprinted from Wyer, 1970b, p. 564).

provides a reasonably good description of these processes under conditions in which the information brought to bear on these inferences can be specified a priori. However, in most situations of concern in this volume, subjects may have several different pieces of information potentially available for use in making judgments. In such situations, the formulation may not generate accurate a priori descriptions unless the particular information used as a basis for judgments is known. On the other hand, discrepancies from prediction based on beliefs associated with a particular set of propositions A and B may often be interpreted as indications that judges are not using the particular set of "premises" to which the model is applied (premises associated with proposition A) as a basis for inferring their belief in the conclusion (B). To this extent, the formulation may be used to diagnose conditions in which a given set of information is or is not brought to bear on judgments.

This is not to say that people are perfect syllogistic reasoners. In some cases, discrepancies from predictions based on Equation 7-1 may reflect people's

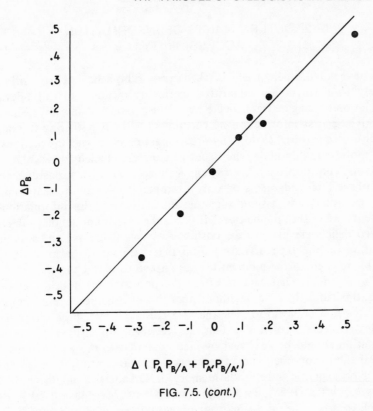

FIG. 7.5. (cont.)

failure to process information in the manner implied by this equation. Indeed, discrepancies from predictions have often been noted which seem concentrated in the component containing the negative conditional ($P_{B/A'}$); see Wyer (1970b, 1975b, 1976a). While these discrepancies are practically very small in magnitude, they do suggest that people do not reason in precisely the fashion we have hypothesized. Moreover, people may often invoke nonlogical rules in drawing conclusions (Chapman & Chapman, 1959; Woodworth & Sells, 1935). It may ultimately be possible for several of these rules to be incorporated into the formulation proposed here. We consider this possibility, and data bearing upon it, in the appendix to this chapter.

The aforementioned considerations once again call attention to the need to specify factors that affect when a particular piece of information is likely to be retrieved and used as a basis for inferences under conditions in which syllogistic reasoning is apt to occur. The next section of this chapter is devoted to this matter. Then, in the later sections, we will turn to some applications of the formulation to social inference processes of the sort of general concern in this volume.

7.2. DETERMINANTS OF INFORMATION ACCESSIBILITY

As we have noted, a person who is asked to report his belief in a proposition is unlikely to perform an exhaustive search of memory for all relevant information bearing on this belief. Rather, the person may in many instances use only the first information he encounters without bothering to search further unless required to do so by situational pressures (e.g., instructions to think more carefully about the issues of concern, challenges by others to defend one's position, etc.). Tversky and Kahneman (1973) also postulate that people base their judgments on only a sample of information that is most easily accessible, and assume that the implications of this information is representative of the "population." If this is the case, it implies that subjects' reported beliefs are likely to be unstable, varying over time and situation depending on the type of information that happens to be most readily available to them at the moment they are asked to report them.

To understand what factors affect the accessibility of belief-relevant information, and thus the likelihood that this information is used to infer one's beliefs, it is useful to view the idea conveyed by a proposition as a complex concept. To this extent, its retrieval for use in processing information should be governed by factors similar to those governing the retrieval and use of other types of concepts of the sort typically investigated in research on semantic and episodic memory (J. R. Anderson and Bower, 1973; Collins & Loftus, 1975). Two major factors have been postulated in this research to affect the accessibility of previously acquired information and concepts related to it. The first, suggested by theoretical considerations raised in earlier chapters of this volume, is the recency with which the information has been used in the past. The second is the amount of processing required to interpret or encode the information at the time it is first received (cf. Craik & Lockhart, 1972). Let us consider these factors in the context of the issues of concern in this chapter.

Effects of Recency

The theoretical and empirical effects of recency have been described in detail in Chapters 3 and 4. That is, if a concept has been recently accessed and used in making a judgment, the likelihood that it will be reactivated and used as a basis for judgments in the same or a different situation is increased. Thus, as Carlston (1977) and Lingle and Ostrom (1979) found, people who have made a judgment of a target person on the basis of stimulus information are more likely to use this judgment as a basis for subsequent ones than to use the original stimulus information. This general phenomenon has both specific and general implications for the processing of information of the type considered in this chapter.

The "Socratic Effect": A Reinterpretation

Direct evidence that subjects use their recently reported beliefs in some propositions as bases for inferring the validity of subsequently conceived propositions comes from recent research on the "Socratic effect." This effect refers to the tendency for syllogistically related cognitions, once made salient, to become more internally consistent over time (cf. Henninger & Wyer, 1976; McGuire, 1960; Rosen & Wyer, 1972; Wyer, 1974c). In these studies, subjects are typically asked to report their beliefs in several sets of propositions of the sort to which Equation 7-1 is relevant. The propositions comprising each set, which concern contemporary social issues and concepts familiar to subjects, are typically distributed randomly throughout the questionnaire. Thus, in some cases, propositions occupying the position of conclusion B in Equation 7-1 follow the propositions serving as premises (propositions of the form "A," "if A, then B," etc.), whereas in other cases, they occur before these premises. Suppose subjects who are asked to report their beliefs in B search memory for other salient concepts or beliefs that have implications for it. If a subject has recently reported his belief in A, he should typically recall this belief and use it as a basis for his judgment of B. As a result, he should infer his belief in the conclusion in the manner implied by Equation 7-1, and the set of beliefs associated with A and B should appear consistent (as defined by Equation 7-2). However, suppose a subject evaluates the conclusion *before* the premises. Then, the subject may often retrieve concepts *other than A* to use as a basis for his judgment. Moreover, in subsequently evaluating A, he is unlikely to use B (a proposition implied *by* A), but rather will retrieve beliefs that, if true, have implications *for* A. As a consequence, the sets of beliefs reported in the latter condition are more likely to be inconsistent.

Data reported by Henninger (1975; see also Henninger & Wyer, 1976, Experiment 2) support this line of reasoning. In this study, the order in which syllogistically-related beliefs were reported in the belief questionnaire was systematically varied, and the inconsistency of these beliefs, as defined by Equation 7-2, was investigated as a function of this order. As expected, the mean inconsistency of beliefs was lower when the proposition corresponding to premise A preceded the conclusion B than when this order was reversed.

The above analysis suggests a reinterpretation of the Socratic effect, as inferred from an increase in the consistency of syllogistically-related beliefs over repeated administrations of the questionnaire. This effect has often been attributed to a tendency for subjects to reorganize related beliefs once inconsistencies among them are made salient as a result of reporting them in close temporal proximity (McGuire, 1960; Rosen & Wyer, 1972; Wyer, 1974b). However, the differences in consistency observed in these studies may also have resulted from differences in the salience of premise A at the time subjects reported their beliefs in the conclusion B. When beliefs are reported in the first session of the experiment, their inconsistency should depend on whether beliefs in the conclusion are reported before or after beliefs in the premises, as noted above. However, when subjects report their beliefs during the second session, the premises, having been considered in the first session, are more likely to be recalled and used to evaluate the conclusion regardless of the order in which they occur in the questionnaire. Beliefs should therefore appear generally consistent in the second session. This is in fact the case (Henninger & Wyer, 1976).

This reasoning implies that a decrease in inconsistency over sessions should be apparent primarily when conclusions are judged after premises in the first session. When premises are considered before the conclusion, inconsistency should be low initially and may not decrease further over time. Henninger's results support this prediction.

Not all premises may need to be explicitly called to subjects' attention in order for A to be retrieved for use in evaluating B. In a second study (Henninger & Wyer, 1976, Experiment 3), the number and type of related beliefs reported in the first session of the experiment were varied. Subjects who reported their beliefs in A alone during the first session exhibited less inconsistency among the beliefs they reported in the second ($M = .141$) than did subjects who did not initially report their beliefs in A ($M = .169$). In contrast, whether or not beliefs in the conclusion were reported during the first session did not affect inconsistency in the second ($M = .151$ vs. $M = .159$). These results in combination support our general assumption that subjects use premises as bases for inferring the validity of conclusions, but do not use conclusions as a basis for inferring the validity of syllogistically related premises.

Although not formally applying Equation 7-1, studies in other paradigms have similar implications. An experiment by Salancik and Calder (1974) is particularly provocative. Subjects reported the frequency with which they engaged in a series of behaviors related to religiousness (going to church, praying, etc.) either before or after they reported their personal religiousness and the favorableness of being religious. In addition, they reported various demographic characteristics associated with religion (the religiousness of their upbringing, the religiousness of friends, etc.). When subjects are asked to report their religious beliefs, they may search memory for aspects of their background and experience that have implications for these judgments. If they have previously reported the frequency of engaging in certain religious behaviors, these particular behaviors and the cognitions associated with them are likely to be retrieved and their implications used as a basis for judging their religiousness. However, if they are not asked to report these behaviors, the likelihood of retrieving them spontaneously is lessened. The reported frequencies of religious behaviors should therefore be more highly correlated with self-judgments of religiousness when these behaviors are reported before self-judgments are made than when they are reported afterwards. This was in fact the case. When attitude measures were completed after behavioral measures, attitudes were correlated over .90 with behavioral indices, and less than .14 with demographic characteristics. However, when attitudes were reported before responding to the behavioral items, they were correlated only .75 with the behavioral measure, and over .47 with demographic variables. This suggests that these subjects not only tended to sample a different (although overlapping) subset of their past behavior to use as a basis for their judgments, but also tended to use nonbehavioral information to a greater extent under these conditions.

Effects of Belief Accessibility on Changes in Related Beliefs

The foregoing studies suggest that subjects' beliefs in a given proposition may be systematically altered by varying the particular cognitions they are asked to report beforehand. These systematic differences are often hard to detect using the procedures employed in the Socratic-effect research described earlier unless individual differences in the beliefs in premises are taken into account. However, an unpublished study by Wyer and Henninger (1978) is suggestive. In this experiment, sets of syllogistically-related propositions were constructed so that in all cases, the premise A had positive implications for the conclusion B (i.e., B was believed more likely to be true if A was true than if A was not true). In such instances, making A more accessible to the subject by asking him to report his belief in it is likely to increase beliefs in B that he reports later on. Results bear out this possibility. That is, beliefs in conclusions were significantly stronger in the second session of the experiment (when beliefs in all premises and their implications had previously been reported) than in the first (when beliefs in premises were often reported after beliefs in conclusions).

More provocative demonstrations of these effects, using different procedures, have been reported by Salancik and his colleagues. In one (Salancik & Conway, 1975), subjects were initially asked whether they agreed or disagreed with a series of items concerning the frequency with which they engaged in religious behavior. However, in some conditions, items describing pro-religious behavior contained the word "occasionally" (e.g., "I occasionally attend a church or synagogue"), whereas in other conditions, these same items contained the word "frequently" ("I frequently attend a church or synagogue"). (In the case of antireligious behaviors, these adverbs were reversed in the two conditions.) Salancik and Conway reasoned that in responding to items containing "occasionally," subjects would search for positive instances of the behavior described, would typically find one, and would therefore agree with the items. In deciding how to respond to items containing "frequently," however, they would search for negative instances of the behavior, would again typically find one, and would therefore disagree with the item. As a result, after completing the questionnaire subjects should have more pro-religious behaviors salient to them in the first condition than in the second, and should therefore subsequently infer themselves to be more religious in the first case. Results supported this hypothesis. Unfortunately, several attempts to replicate and build on these specific findings in Wyer's laboratory have been unsuccessful, for reasons that are not entirely clear. However, the study is nevertheless noteworthy in the context of the considerations under discussion.

A second study by Salancik (1974), using a different procedure, is equally intriguing. Here, students were asked to complete a series of open-ended statements about their classroom behavior near the end of a course. In one condition, each sentence was completed following the phrase "in order to" (i.e., "I raise my hand in class in order to . . . "), while in the other condition, it was completed following the phrase "because I" ("I raise my hand in class because I . . . "). Salancik reasoned that responding to the first set of statements would predispose students to think of extrinsic reasons for their behavior (i.e., " . . . in order to get a good grade"), while responding to the second set would predispose them to think of intrinsic reasons (i.e., " . . . because I want to understand what is going on"). Upon completing the questionnaire, students were asked how much they had enjoyed the course. These ratings were subsequently correlated with final course grades (an extrinsic factor). As expected, this correlation was much higher in the first condition (where extrinsic considerations were presumably made more accessible to subjects at the time they reported their enjoyment of the course) than in the second (where intrinsic factors were made more accessible).

Implications for Belief and Opinion Change

The considerations outlined above have more general implications for a conceptualization of belief-change and opinion-change processes. Specifically, it suggests that the influence of belief-change techniques may often be interpreted in terms of the effectiveness of these techniques in making accessible previously acquired information and concepts that have implications for those beliefs. Two bodies of literature of particular relevance to these considerations are worth noting briefly.

Role-Playing Effects on Self-Judgments. We have postulated that subjects typically do not perform an exhaustive search of memory in making a judgment, but rather tend to use the judgment-relevant information that is most easily accessible. This assumption also underlies the self-perception formulation proposed by Bem (1972). Specifically, suppose a person has recently engaged in a behavior that has implications for his self-judgment. If the person is subsequently asked to make this judgment, he is likely to retrieve and use the behavior as a basis for his inference, rather than previously acquired information that may be equally relevant.

A compelling demonstration of this possibility is provided in a study by Bem and McConnell (1970). Subjects who had initially reported their beliefs in a proposition one week earlier were asked to write an essay advocating a position contrary to these beliefs. Some subjects were given a choice as to whether or not they would write the essay, while others were not. Then, after writing the essay, some subjects in each choice condition reported their beliefs a second time, while others were asked to recall the position they had reported a week before. Subjects under free choice conditions should perceive their behavior to have positive implications for their beliefs in the position advocated, while subjects under forced choice conditions should regard their behavior as an unreliable index of their beliefs, and therefore should search further for belief-relevant information. Consistent with this hypothesis, subjects reported their beliefs to be more in favor of the position advocated under free choice than under forced choice conditions. More intriguing, however, is the finding that subjects also recalled their *prebehavior* beliefs as more consistent with the position they advocated under free choice than under forced choice conditions. Indeed, the average error in recalling their prebehavior belief was virtually identical in both magnitude and direction to the apparent change in beliefs manifested by the first group of subjects. This indicates that people who have recently manifested a belief-relevant behavior not only may use this behavior as information about their present beliefs, but also may use it as information about what their beliefs must have been before manifesting the behavior, without seeking further for information that is perhaps equally or more relevant to their judgments.

As noted above, however, the behavior may have less effect if subjects are stimulated to retrieve other previously acquired information in addition to this behavior. Snyder and Ebbesen (1972) found that when subjects were asked to collect their thoughts on the issue to which their essay pertained before writing the essay (thus making previously formed beliefs and belief-relevant information salient to them), the effect of writing the essay on their post-behavior beliefs was attenuated. This indicates that people do use information in addition to their behavior as bases for inferring their beliefs when this information is easily accessible.

Communication and Persuasion. The preceding examples concern the effects of recent behavioral information on beliefs and attitudes. However, similar considerations arise in the case of information from other sources. In many instances, a persuasive message may contain unfamiliar factual information that has implications for beliefs in the target proposition. However, in some cases, a communication may simply consist of assertions that the recipient already believes to be true with high probability, but that, if true, have positive implications for the position to be advocated. (For example, a communication supporting the proposition that abortion should be freely available may assert that a person should have freedom of choice over whether she has children, thus reminding the recipient of his previously formed belief that this is true. In contrast, a communication opposing abortion may assert that taking a life is immoral, thus directing the recipient's attention to his previously formed belief in this proposition.) Thus, when the recipient is asked later to report his opinion, he is more apt to retrieve this subset of "primed" cognitions than others and to use them as a basis for his judgment, leading him to report a belief that is consistent with the position being advocated in the message.

The basic assumption underlying this analysis is that the belief-relevant cognitions stimulated by a communication, rather than the content of the communication itself, provide the material upon which recipients' subsequent judgments are based. This point was compellingly made by Greenwald (1968), who notes that surprisingly little evidence exists for a relation between the influence of a persuasive communication and the recall of its specific contents. Greenwald argues that reading or listening to a communication may stimulate a variety of thoughts associated with the issue being discussed. These thoughts may of course consist simply of encodings or interpretations of the communication content. However, they may also consist of previously acquired information supporting the assertions contained in it, or counter-arguments against these assertions. These cognitions rather than the communication content per se may then provide the basis for subjects' subsequent inferences of the validity of the position being advocated.

To the extent that the communication presented is opposed to the recipient's initial position, it is likely to stimulate counterarguing. Under such conditions, factors that prevent these cognitions from being generated should decrease the likelihood that they will subsequently be accessed and used as a basis for beliefs in the target person, and therefore should increase the effectiveness of the communication. Research on the effects of distraction (for a summary and theoretical analysis, see Wyer, 1974a) are consistent with this line of reasoning. For example, Festinger and Maccoby (1964) presented a communication attacking fraternities to subjects, accompanied by either a film of the speaker or a humorous silent film. The beliefs of fraternity members, who would normally be inclined to generate counterarguments against the communication, were more strongly influenced under distraction than under no distraction. In contrast, nonmembers of fraternities, who were unlikely to generate counterarguments in any condition, were equally influenced regardless of distraction.

Summary

Much of the research reported in this section did not directly apply the syllogistic formulation we have proposed, and thus does not provide direct evidence for its utility in describing the phenomena investigated. However, these phenomena can clearly be conceptualized in terms of this formulation. To this extent, the formulation potentially provides a means of investigating more precisely the processes of belief and opinion change suggested by the work of Salancik, Greenwald, and others, as well as the Socratic effect research to which the formulation is directly applicable.

Effect of Amount of Processing

The likelihood of retrieving information for use in making a judgment may depend not only on the recency with which the information has been used in the past, but also on the amount of cognitive activity involved in interpreting this information and its implications. Craik and Lockhart (1972; see also Craik, 1977) hypothesize that information is better recalled when it is processed more "deeply" or extensively. If this is true, the recall of belief-relevant material may be partly a function of the amount of cognitive work involved in processing it, either at the time it is first presented or later on.

This possibility has important implications in the context of the syllogistic inference formulation proposed here. The likelihood of retrieving any particular proposition A for use in evaluating a second, B, may be a function of the amount of cognitive work involved in responding to A at the time it was initially considered. The amount of cognitive work may be affected by several factors, three of which will be discussed here: the plausibility of A, the clarity of A's implications for other, related propositions, and the inconsistency between beliefs in A and beliefs in other propositions to which A is relevant.

Plausibility and Clarity of Implications

A person who is called upon to evaluate a proposition presumably searches memory for information that has implications for its validity. However, the search is apt to be less extensive if the proposition is highly plausible, or intuitively likely to be true, than if it is less so. Indeed, one reason why propositions *are* plausible is simply that abundant information implying their validity is stored in memory, and that some of this information is quickly and easily retrievable for use in evaluating them. In addition, relatively implausible propositions (e.g., "Edward Kennedy is a close friend of Richard Nixon") may be more unfamiliar, or deviant from expectancies, than plausible ones (e.g., "men often suffer heart attacks while shovelling snow"), and therefore may be more interesting and thought provoking. In either event, the evaluation of relatively implausible propositions may stimulate more cognitive activity than the evaluation of plausible ones, and thus the former propositions may be more readily recalled.

The likelihood that one proposition is brought to bear on a second may also depend on the strength and clarity of its implications for the second proposition. In some instances, these implications may not occur to a subject unless he is asked directly to consider them. For example, few people probably think of the possibility that discarded cigarettes and matches cause forest fires when they are asked to evaluate the likelihood that cigarette smoking will cause a lumber shortage. However, if a person is explicitly asked to consider the implications of this possibility for the target proposition, the likelihood that these implications are subsequently retrieved and brought to bear upon the target may depend in part upon their strength. This dependency could be of two types. First, it may take more cognitive work to evaluate the implications of one proposition for another when these implications are weak or unclear. On the other hand, when the implications of one proposition (A) for the validity of a second (B) are strong, calling them to a person's attention may stimulate him to revise his beliefs in B to take these implications into account. The net effect of these two types of cognitive activity is difficult to predict a priori.

Preliminary data collected by Wyer and Henninger (1978) bear on certain of these considerations. Subjects reported their beliefs in a set of randomly ordered, syllogistically related propositions of the sort to which Equation 7-1 theoretically pertains. Both the plausibility of the proposition denoted A in each set (operationalized in terms of the strength of the belief in A), and the strength or clarity of A's implications for the conclusion B (i.e., inferred from the magnitude of the normative belief that B is true if A is true) were manipulated. (In all cases, however, A had positive implications for B; that is, B was believed more likely to be true if A was true than if it was not true.) An example of the use of pairs of propositions (A and B) representing each combination of these variables may be helpful:

1. High plausibility, clear implications—(A) Vast oil resources lie under the frozen earth of Antarctica. (B) The settlement of Antarctica will be vastly accelerated in the next few years.
2. High plausibility, unclear implications—(A) Men frequently suffer heart attacks while shoveling snow. (B) Exercise is bad for the heart.
3. Low plausibility, clear implications—(A) The all-volunteer Army is accepting an increasing number of mentally retarded recruits. (B) The overall level of intelligence of Army personnel will decline in the coming years.
4. Low plausibility, unclear implications—(A) Edward Kennedy is a good friend of Richard Nixon. (B) Edward Kennedy made illegal contributions to Nixon's presidential campaign fund.

TABLE 7.2

Probability of Recalling Propositions as a Function of A's Plausibility, A's Implications for B, and Judgment-Recall Order

	Recall Before Questionnaire		Recall After Questionnaire	
	High Plausibility	Low Plausibility	High Plausibility	Low Plausibility
Recall of A				
Strong implications for B	.18	.21	.36	.45
Weak implications for B	.06	.36	.33	.53
Recall of B				
Strong implications for B	.08	.20	.22	.45
Weak implications for B	.10	.32	.28	.40

After completing the questionnaire, subjects returned for a second session a week later and were asked to recall as many of the propositions in the questionnaire as possible. This was done either before or after completing the belief questionnaire a second time. The probabilities of recalling A and B are tabulated in Table 7.2 as a function of experimental variables. Both propositions were recalled significantly better when A's plausibility was low than when it was high. This suggests that when A was relatively implausible, not only A but also propositions related to A were thought about more extensively.[7]

Two contingencies in the results are noteworthy, however. First, the effect of A's plausibility on recall of the conclusion B was strong regardless of the clarity of A's implications for B. However, its effect on the recall of A itself was significantly greater when A's implications for B were unclear ($M = .20$ vs. $M = .45$ under low- and high-plausibility conditions) than when they were more readily apparent ($M = .26$ vs. $M = .33$). This suggests that when A has

---

[7]The higher recall of B when A's plausibility was low than when it was high might be attributed to the fact that B was also less plausible in the former conditions. Recall differences could thus be a direct effect of plausibility. However, beliefs in B were only slightly lower when A was low in plausibility ($M = .34$) than when it was high ($M = .37$); this difference is not of sufficient magnitude to account for the substantial difference in recall obtained in Table 1. Moreover, although beliefs in B were lower on the average ($M = .36$) than beliefs in A ($M = .50$), B was recalled slightly less well ($M = .26$) than A ($M = .32$). This also argues against the interpretation that recall differences are due simply to a general tendency for statements to be recalled better when beliefs in them are low.

unclear implications for B, its implausibility stimulates thought about both A and B. However, when A has clear implications for B, its implausibility leads subjects to think primarily about B.

The second contingency concerns the effect of recalling beliefs before or after reporting them in the second session. These conditions differ in two ways. First, beliefs were reported twice in the first condition before recalling statements but only once in the second condition. Second, items were recalled immediately after reporting beliefs in them in the first case, but after a week delay in the second. If differences in recall are due primarily to the second factor, they may provide insight into the extent to which the effects of plausibility and implication strength are due to processing differences at the time items were first considered or to differences in processing during the time interval between experimental sessions. The effect of plausibility on the recall of unconditional propositions (A and B) was substantial when beliefs were recalled immediately after completing the questionnaire, regardless of implication strength. However, this effect was maintained over time when A's implications for B were unclear, but decreased over time when these implications were relatively obvious. This suggests that when A's implications for B were clear, neither A nor B was thought about subsequently, and so the effects of plausibility decreased over time. When A's implications for B were less clear, however, subjects may have engaged in further processing of belief items, with the result that the initial effect of A's plausibility is retained.

Conditional Recall Probabilities.   The extent to which one proposition has been thought about in relation to another may be reflected by the extent to which the recall of one proposition in a set is facilitated by recall of the second. The above interpretation implies that this facilitation is greater when A's plausibility is low, or when A's implications are unclear, than under other conditions. This is in fact the case. The overall probability of recalling A given that B was and was not recalled, and also the probability of recalling B given that A was and was not recalled, are shown in Table 7.3 as a function of A's plausibility, its implications for B, and delay interval. Recalling one item facilitated recall of the other when A's implications for B were unclear, regardless of the time interval between completing the questionnaire and recall. In addition, a week's delay increased the facilitating effect when A was implausible but had clear implications for B. In contrast, when A was both plausible and had clear implications for B, recalling one proposition had a negligible effect on recall of the other.

In combination, the above results suggest a reasonably clear picture. Responding to relatively implausible propositions stimulates subjects to think more about both the validity of these propositions and their implications for other ones. Consequently, both these statements and other, related statements are remembered better later on. However, the active

TABLE 7.3
Conditional Probabilities of Recall of A and B, Given Recall or Nonrecall of the Other Proposition

	Given That A Was Recalled	Given That A Was Not Recalled	Difference	Given That B Was Recalled	Given That B Was Not Recalled	Difference
Beliefs recalled a week after completing the questionnaire in Session 1:						
High plausibility, clear implications	.133	.061	.072	.333	.176	.157
High plausibility, unclear implications	.800	.053	.747	.500	.014	.486
Low plausibility, clear implications	.706	.063	.643	.750	.078	.672
Low plausibility, unclear implications	.690	.118	.572	.769	.166	.603
Beliefs recalled immediately after completing questionnaire in Session 2:						
High plausibility, clear implications	.448	.174	.274	.720	.258	.462
High plausibility, unclear implications	.630	.112	.518	.739	.175	.564
Low plausibility, clear implications	.611	.318	.293	.611	.318	.293
Low plausibility, unclear implications	.581	.147	.434	.782	.373	.409

processing of implausible statements appears to dissipate quickly after completing the questionnaire when their implications for other items in the questionnaire are clear; thus, the effect of a statement's plausibility on its recall and the recall of related propositions persists over time only if its implications are sufficiently ambiguous that additional processing is required to evaluate them.

Effects on Reported Beliefs.   We have argued that if beliefs in a set of syllogistically related propositions have been reported at one point in time, the subsequent recall of premise A for use in evaluating the conclusion B may be more likely if A is implausible than if A is plausible. Moreover, this tendency may be greatest when implications of A for B are unclear. The effects of these factors on beliefs in the conclusion are difficult to predict. This is because the conditions that lead A to be retrieved more readily (that is, low P_A and low $P_{B/A}$) and to be used more *frequently* as a basis for beliefs in B are also those in which the magnitude of change in B produced by taking A into account is less.

However, correlational analyses provide indirect evidence of the effects predicted on the basis of differences in recall probability. Since the premises used in Wyer and Henninger's study all had positive implications for beliefs in B, subjects should typically increase these beliefs more when they have thought more about A's implications for B's validity. Moreover, this cognitive activity should also lead to better recall of B. Therefore, to the extent that thinking about A's implications for B mediates changes in beliefs in B, there should be a positive correlation between the recall of the proposition B before reporting beliefs in it during the second session and increases in beliefs in this proposition. When A's plausibility was low, this correlation was significantly positive, and was somewhat greater when A's implications for B were unclear ($r = .403$) than when they were clear ($r = .302$). However, when A's plausibility was high, these correlations were negligible ($r = -.064$ and $r = .021$, respectively). These data suggest that when A's plausibility was at a level that stimulated subjects to think about its implications, they did in fact increase their beliefs in B more to the extent that they thought about it more (as evidenced by the greater recall of this proposition). However, when A's plausibility was high, and thus subjects tended less to think about its implications, the cognitive activity that led them to recall B did not systematically affect their beliefs in this proposition.

Some Caution Concerning Generalizeability.   The data described above seem sufficient to conclude that the cognitive activity required to evaluate implausible propositions makes these propositions more easily accessible and thus makes them more likely to be invoked in the future as a basis for other beliefs for which they have implications. It is important to note, however, that these effects may occur only if the subject has the possible implications of these propositions called to his attention (e.g., by being asked to evaluate them). If subjects in the first session had not been explicitly asked to evaluate conditional propositions (i.e., "if A, then B"), but had only been asked to report their beliefs in unconditionals ("A," "B"), they might not have recognized the possible relation of A and B when A's implications were unclear, and thus the effects of A's plausibility on recall of B might not have been detected.

Effects of Inconsistency

McGuire (1960) postulated that when someone becomes aware of inconsistencies among his cognitions, he will engage in cognitive activity to eliminate them. If this is the case, and if recall is a function of amount of processing, there should be a positive relation between the initial inconsistency of cognitions and the recall of propositions to which these cognitions pertain. Moreover, if the reduction of inconsistencies, like the recall of propositions, is a reflection of the expenditure of cognitive energy, there should be a positive relation between the recall of propositions and the decrease in inconsistency of beliefs associated with them.

This possibility was also investigated in the study described above. The correlation between the inconsistency of beliefs associated with A and B and the recall of propositions to which the beliefs pertained was a negative function of A's plausibility but a positive function of implication strength. Thus, the correlation was more positive when A was implausible but had clear implications for B (mean $r = .343$) than when one or the other of these conditions was not met (mean $r = -.110$). This suggests that the cognitive activity resulting from awareness of belief inconsistency increases when A is relatively implausible but has clear implications for B.

In addition, decreases in inconsistency over experimental sessions were correlated consistently positively with recall of beliefs when A's implications for B were clear (mean correlation = .222) but not when they were unclear ($M = -.027$). This suggests that the implications of A for B must be clear in order for the cognitive activity mediating both recall and inconsistency reduction to be manifested.

General Effects of Thought on Reported Beliefs

We have argued that, in many instances, a person who is called upon to evaluate a proposition may use only the first relevant information he retrieves as a basis for his judgment rather than searching for other previously acquired information that may also be relevant. However, this is obviously not always the case. Certainly on matters of considerable personal importance (getting married, taking on a new job, etc.), people may often weigh the implications of several pieces of previously acquired or new information simultaneously. Moreover, there may be situational demands to think carefully about a judgment or about the object being judged. Presumably, as people think more about an object, they bring more previously acquired information to bear on it, and so their judgments may change relative to conditions in which less information is retrieved.

The effect of thought about an object on judgments of the object depends upon the implications of the additional information retrieved as a result of this thought. If these implications are similar to those of the first information considered, they may increase one's confidence in one's initial opinion, leading to a more extreme judgment than would result from considering less information. On the other hand, if the implications of the additional information differ from those of the original information, they may weaken the initial opinion, resulting in a less polarized judgment. A related consideration is, of course, the extent to which additional relevant information is actually available to be retrieved. If a person has little prior information to bring to bear on a judgment, additional thought should have little effect.

Research by Tesser described in more detail in Chapter 3 is worth reconsidering in this context (for a summary, see Tesser, 1978). In this research, subjects typically re-evaluate a target stimulus, either after being told to think about it or after being distracted from doing so. Evaluations typically increase in extremity under "thought" conditions relative to "distraction" conditions. As suggested in Chapter 3, in judging a stimulus subjects may often invoke a previously formed configuration (or schema) of attributes belonging to a prototypic object of the type being judged (e.g., a good or bad person, a good or bad football play, etc.) which, if present, has positive or negative implications for the judgment to be made. A person who uses a prototypic schema to evaluate a target stimulus may identify more schema-related attributes in the target to the extent that he thinks more about it. If these attributes have similar evaluative implications, the evaluation of the target should therefore increase with the number of attributes identified (Anderson, 1965; Fishbein & Hunter, 1964), and thus with the amount of thought that underlies their identification. As a concrete example, suppose a judge is asked to evaluate a target person on the basis of information that he is both intelligent and friendly. In doing so, the judge may evaluate the target favorably, based upon some composite of the evaluative implications of these two adjectives alone (i.e, the assumptions that if a person is intelligent, he is likeable, and that if he is friendly, he is likeable). However, if the judge is then asked to think more about the target person, he may access a prototypic schema of the type of person who has the two attributes. This schema may also contain their attributes typically associated with intelligence and friendliness. These associated traits are likely to be evaluatively similar to the two stimulus traits (cf. Rosenberg & Sedlak, 1972). If the judge is now asked to re-evaluate the target person, and considers the implications of these associated traits as well as the original ones, his judgments of the stimulus person may become more favorable than they were initially. For similar reasons, thinking about a target person described by two negative traits may elicit a prototypic schema of a person with other unfavorable qualities as well, and thus may produce a more extremely unfavorable evaluation than would occur on the basis of the information presented alone.

Tesser's findings are consistent with this interpretation, and suggest that they occur only under conditions in which subjects do in fact have a previously formed prototypic schema for use in making judgments (see Tesser & Leone, 1977, described in Chapter 3). However, this interpretation should be treated with some caution, for reasons noted earlier. That is, the results obtained in Tesser's studies could easily reflect a tendency for judges to be initially cautious in *reporting* extreme subjective judgments in the absence of thought, rather than an increase in the extremity of their actual judgments following an increase in thought.

In addition, it is unclear why thought should always increase polarization of an opinion rather than decreasing it. In terms of the formulation proposed in this chapter (Equation 7-1), whether the previously acquired information identified through thought increases or decreases the extremity of an opinion (i.e., one's belief in B) depends upon whether its implications are positive ($P_{B/A} > P_{B/A'}$) or negative ($P_{B/A} < P_{B/A'}$), as well as upon the belief in the validity of the information itself (P_A). McGuire (1960) postulates that thought typically increases the consistency of related cognitions, as evidenced by the Socratic effect discussed earlier. However, whether this increased consistency is attained through an increase or decrease in beliefs in a conclusion depends upon whether the implications of beliefs in the premises being thought about are more or less extreme than the initial belief in the conclusion. The effects obtained by Tesser may therefore not generalize to stimulus domains and experimental conditions in which thought is likely to lead information to be accessed that has *less* extreme implications than that upon which initial judgments were based.

Summary and Conclusions

The results reported in this section are generally consistent with the hypothesis that if information is processed extensively at one point in time, either in order to respond to it or as a result of instructions to think about it, this information may be more likely to be recalled in the future and brought to bear on judgments to which it is relevant. Additional research is necessary to tie down several interpretative and empirical ambiguities associated with the results obtained to date, and to demonstrate more directly the mediating link between the particular information recalled as a result of extensive processing and the judgments that are theoretically affected by it. However, the research conducted thus far provides some useful leads in coming to grips with these phenomena.

7.3. THE INTEGRATION OF BELIEF-RELEVANT INFORMATION

In our discussion this far, we have generally concentrated on the effect on judgments of either previously acquired information retrieved from memory, or of new information about hypothetical events to which previously formed beliefs are irrelevant. In many judgment situations, a person must consider the implications of *both* new and previously acquired information, and must combine these implications in order to arrive at judgments to which the information directly or indirectly pertains.

The nature of these integration processes must ultimately be understood in order to arrive at a complete understanding of syllogistic inference. While research on these questions is limited, the formulation proposed in this chapter can be used to conceptualize the nature of the effects described. Let us therefore turn briefly to these questions and preliminary data bearing upon them.

Suppose a person receives a persuasive communication containing assertions that, if true, have implications for a conclusion B. Based on beliefs he has acquired in the past, the person may not agree completely with these assertions. The person must therefore combine the implications of his previously formed beliefs with those of the information presented to arrive at judgments of the validity of (a) the assertions themselves, and (b) the conclusion upon which they bear.

The processes whereby this is accomplished are not entirely clear. The nature of this ambiguity can be conveyed with a rather mundane example. Suppose a person receives information that (a) newborn babies rarely cry, that (b) if newborn babies cry, they are usually loved by their parents, and that (c) if newborn babies do not cry, they are rarely loved by their parents. Then the person is asked the likelihood that a particular baby, John, would be loved by his parents. If the person attends only to the information presented, he may reason that although John is unlikely to cry (P_A is low), babies who do not cry are not apt to be loved by their parents ($P_{B/A}$ is low), concluding from this that John is unlikely to be loved by his parents. However, suppose the person believes that in reality, newborn babies are very likely to cry, but are typically loved by their parents regardless of whether they cry or not. This set of a priori beliefs implies that John *is* apt to be loved by his parents. Thus, if these a priori beliefs affect the person's inferences, his belief in the conclusion should be greater than the value implied by the information given. However, there may be two reasons for this. First, the person may simply ignore the implications of the new information and rely solely on his previously formed beliefs. Second, he may use the new information, but interpret its implications as more consistent with his previously formed beliefs than is actually the case.

An extension of Equation 7-1 may be used to investigate these possibilities. Assume that a person's belief in a proposition i is a composite (e.g., sum or average) of the implications of the information presented and the implications of his a priori belief in the proposition; that is,

$$P_i = w_{i,I}P_{i,I} + w_{i,O}P_{i,O} \tag{7-5}$$

where the subscripts I and O refer to the implications of the information presented and the person's "original" or a priori beliefs, respectively, and $w_{i,I}$ and $w_{i,O}$ are weights that reflect the relative influence of I and O, respectively. Substituting these expressions into Equation 7-1,

$$P_B = (w_{A,I}P_{A,I} + w_{A,O}P_{A,O}) (w_{B/A,I}P_{B/A,I} + w_{B/A,O}P_{B/A,O}) +$$
$$(1 - w_{A,I}P_{A,I} - w_{A,O}P_{A,O}) (w_{B/A',I}P_{B/A',I} + w_{B/A',O}P_{B/A',O}) \tag{7-6}$$

This equation has several implications. First, a person's a priori beliefs in each premise and in the implications of the presented information should have additive effects upon his estimates of the likelihood that this premise is true. However, if these estimates then combine to affect beliefs in B in the manner implied by Equation 7-6, eight two-way interactions should occur, one pertaining to each of the eight products obtained by expanding the expression comprising the right side of this equation. Specifically:

1. Differences in the belief that B is true if A is true ($P_{B/A}$) should have greater effect on beliefs in B (P_B) when the belief in A (P_A) is high than when it is low. If a priori beliefs in the premises and the implications of the information presented are varied independently, and if Equation 7-6 is valid, interactions should occur involving (a) $P_{A,O}$ and $P_{B/A,O}$; (b) $P_{A,O}$ and $P_{B/A,I}$; (c) $P_{A,I}$ and $P_{B/A,O}$; and (d) $P_{A,I}$ and $P_{B/A,I}$; each of which should have the general pattern described above.

2. Differences in beliefs that B is true if A is not true ($P_{B/A'}$) should have more effect on beliefs in B when the belief in A is low than when it is high. Therefore, if the above conceptualization is correct, interactions showing this general pattern should occur involving (a) $P_{A,O}$ and $P_{B/A',O}$; (b) $P_{A,O}$ and $P_{B/A',I}$; (c) $P_{A,I}$ and $P_{B/A',O}$; and (d) $P_{A,I}$ and $P_{B/A',I}$.

The relative magnitudes of these interactions depend on the relative weights attached to a priori beliefs and on the implications of the new information presented. If people completely ignored the implications of the new information presented ($w_{i,I}$ = O for all i), the six interactions involving informationally manipulated values of P_A, $P_{B/A}$, and $P_{B/A'}$ would be nonsignificant. Alternatively, if people based their evaluation of the conclusion only on the implications of the information presented, and ignored their a priori beliefs ($w_{i,O}$ = O for all i), the six interactions involving a priori beliefs would be negligible. In general, both sets of weights are apt to be nonzero, but their relative magnitudes are likely to vary with such factors as the familiarity with the objects and events involved, the quality of the information presented, and the credibility of its source.

To apply the proposed formulation to these matters (Wyer, 1976a), subjects were explicitly instructed to ignore their previously formed beliefs in drawing conclusions about familiar objects and events. While these conditions were somewhat artificial, the data obtained were expected to indicate the extent to which persons can, in fact, ignore their a priori beliefs in processing information that is relevant to these beliefs. Two stimulus replications, each consisting of eight different A–B pairs, were selected on the basis of normative data in such a way that the pairs varied systematically with respect to subjects' a priori beliefs that A was true (high $P_{A,O}$ vs. low $P_{A,O}$), that B was true if A was true (high $P_{B/A,O}$ vs. low $P_{B/A,O}$) and that B was true if A was not true (high $P_{B/A',O}$ vs. low $P_{B/A',O}$). Although beliefs in B were not considered in selecting these statement pairs, these beliefs, tabulated after the fact in the manner described in Table 7.1 (page 231), indicate that in the absence of other information, they are related to beliefs in premises in the manner implied by Equation 7-1.

For each A–B pair, sets of stimulus statements were then constructed that represented each of eight combinations of informationally manipulated values of these beliefs ($P_{A,I}$, $P_{B/A,I}$, and $P_{B/A',I}$). The latter manipulations were performed by inserting the adverbs *usually* or *rarely* into the statements presented. For example, the set used to represent low $P_{A,O}$, low $P_{B/A,O}$, and high $P_{B/A',O}$ was presented in the form:

Surgeons *usually* (*rarely*) perform their operations carelessly.
Surgeons who perform their operations carelessly are *usually* (*rarely*) competent.
Surgeons who do not perform their operations carelessly are *usually* (*rarely*) competent.

Judges received each set of statements with instructions to assume that the statements were definitely true and then, on the basis of these statements, to estimate the likelihood that a conclusion, B, was true (in the above example, the likelihood that "X, a surgeon, is competent"). After making this judgment

(P_B), subjects reported their likelihood that each premise was true (i.e., beliefs corresponding to P_A, $P_{B/A}$, and $P_{B/A'}$).

Subjects' reported judgments of each premise were affected by both their a priori beliefs in the premise and by the implications of the new information presented. Moreover, these effects were independent, suggesting that Equation 7-5 provides a valid description of the manner in which the two sources of information combine to affect subjective judgments. More generally, these results suggest that subjects interpreted the new information differently, depending upon their a priori beliefs; for example, their interpretation of the frequencies implied by the adverbs *usually* and *rarely* may have depended upon their a priori beliefs that the relation described was likely or unlikely to hold.

Although only interactions involving informationally manipulated values were significant in analyses of beliefs in the conclusion (P_B), seven of the eight predicted interactions were of the nature expected on the basis of Equation 7-6 (see Tables 7.4 and 7.5). Since the incremental effects of a priori beliefs on judgments of premises were relatively small, the indirect effects on estimates of P_B should theoretically be even smaller, and may therefore not have been of sufficient magnitude to detect statistically. It is important to note that in the absence of new information, subjects' beliefs in B were strongly related to their a priori beliefs in premises in the manner predicted (see Table 7.1). It therefore seems reasonable to conclude that previously formed beliefs in premises affect beliefs in conclusion in the manner implied by the proposed formulation when no information bearing on the premises is presented, and

TABLE 7.4

Mean Estimates of P_B as a Function of A Priori and Informationally Manipulated Values of P_A and $P_{B/A}$[a]

	Informationally Manipulated Value of $P_{B/A}$			A Priori Value of $P_{B/A}$		
	High	Low	Difference (D)	High	Low	Difference (D)
Informationally manipulated value of P_A						
High	.764	.295	.469	.549	.511	.038
Low	.549	.491	.059	.526	.514	.012
A priori value of P_A						
High	.667	.388	.279	.551	.505	.046
Low	.646	.396	.250	.524	.520	.004

[a]Reprinted from Wyer (1976a, p. 313).

TABLE 7.5

Mean Estimates of P_B as a Function of A Priori and Informationally Manipulated Values of P_A and $P_{B/A}$[a]

	Informationally Manipulated Value of $P_{B/A'}$			A Priori Value of $P_{B/A'}$		
	High	Low	Difference (D)	High	Low	Difference (D)
Informationally manipulated value of P_A						
High	.564	.496	.068	.539	.521	.018
Low	.754	.286	.468	.526	.497	.046
A priori value of P_A						
High	.661	.394	.267	.554	.501	.053
Low	.656	.387	.269	.526	.517	.009

[a]Reprinted from Wyer (1976a, p. 313).

that these effects are still apparent when new information is provided, even when people are instructed to ignore their a priori beliefs when processing this information. These preliminary data demonstrate the potential heuristic value of the proposed formulation in diagnosing syllogistic inference processes, and suggest a framework for subsequent research in which the relative weights of a priori beliefs and new information are systematically manipulated. For example, when subjects are simply asked to read a persuasive communication bearing upon the premises of a syllogism, without being explicitly told to assume that it is true, the relative influence of subjects' a priori beliefs in the premises ($w_{i,o}$) should be greater than that observed in the study described above. However, the processes underlying judges' conclusions may be the same whether based on the communication or on their a priori beliefs.

7.4. IMPLICATIONS FOR SOCIAL EVALUATION PROCESSES

The issues raised in this chapter, and the framework we have proposed for conceptualizing them, are relevant to social inference processes in a variety of domains. However, some special considerations arise in applying these notions to social perception and interpersonal attraction.

When a person is asked to estimate his liking for another, he may search memory for attributes of the person that have implications for this judgment. As we have noted, the attributes retrieved may often be the ones that have been most recently applied to the person in the past, or have most recently been used to encode the person's behavior. The process of using these attributes to infer liking may be syllogistic. That is, having accessed the characteristic honest, a subject may base his judgment that a target person is likeable on his beliefs that (a) the person is honest and that if he is honest, he is likeable; and (b) the person is not honest, but that even if he is not honest, he is likeable. Thus, suppose a judge who is asked to evaluate a target person O retrieves attribute X and uses this as a basis for his judgment of the person. The above inference process should theoretically be described by the equation

$$P_L = P_X P_{L/X} + P_{X'} P_{L/X'} \tag{7-7}$$

where P_L is the belief that he would like the person, P_X and $P_{X'} (= 1 - P_X)$ are beliefs that the person does and does not have X, and $P_{L/X}$ and $P_{L/X'}$ are beliefs that a person would be liked if he did and did not possess X, respectively.

In applying this equation, however, some additional considerations arise. First, many attributes of a person have implications for liking, and these implications, considered in isolation, may not all be the same. Thus, if a judge who is asked to evaluate someone considers a single trait possessed by the person, his evaluation will be consistent with the implications of that trait (as defined by Equation 7-7) but may be inconsistent with the implications of other traits the person possesses. On the other hand, the piece of "information" a judge retrieves about a person may not always consist of a single trait. Rather, it may be a "schema," or cluster of traits and personal characteristics (see Chapter 3). If this is true, predictions of liking based on the implications of a particular trait may be inaccurate unless the trait is itself the name of a prototypic schema (e.g., an "honest person") that is used as a unit as a basis for judgments.

Three studies, each with a somewhat different focus, have applied the proposed formulation (or extensions of it) to social evaluation phenonema. Since these studies bear indirectly on certain of the general questions raised above, each may be worth reviewing briefly.

Liking for Hypothetical Persons

If a subject reads a paragraph describing a person's behavior in a given situation (e.g., that he has returned a lost wallet), he is likely to encode the behavior in terms of a general trait to which the behavior is directly relevant (e.g., "honest"). If the subject is then asked if he would like the person, he may retrieve the trait and use it as a basis for his prediction. If this is the case, these predictions should be described by Equation 7-7. Suppose, however, that after making the judgment, the subject is asked to infer other traits the target person might possess. The subject may also generate inferences of these traits on the basis of the original information presented. However, since these traits were not considered at the time liking for the person was judged, the latter judgment should be more inconsistent with the implications of these traits than with those of the trait most directly implied by the stimulus information.

These general predictions were supported in a study by Wyer (1973c). The procedure was analogous to that used in the simulated study of belief and opinion change described previously (Wyer, 1970b). Subjects read sets of two paragraphs describing a hypothetical person's behavior. One paragraph in each pair described a behavior that implied a high degree of a given attribute X (i.e., a high value of P_X), while the second described a different behavior that implied a low degree of the attribute (a low value of P_X). (For example, in one case, where the attribute was "honest," the target person was described in one paragraph as finding and returning a lost wallet containing a large sum of money, and in the other paragraph as stealing an examination from a professor's office.) After reading each paragraph, judges first reported their beliefs that they would like the person if they were actually to meet him (P_L), followed by their beliefs that he had the specific attribute to which the behavior in the paragraph pertained (P_X) and their beliefs that he had each of two standard attributes, *intelligent* and *sarcastic*. Finally, they estimated the various conditional beliefs that the person would be liked if he did and did not have X, if he was and was not intelligent, and if he was and was not sarcastic. Mean obtained beliefs that the target person would be liked, and changes in these beliefs after reading the second paragraph in each pair, are plotted in Fig. 7.6 as a function of predicted values based upon beliefs about the attribute to which the information most directly pertained (X). The quantitative accuracy was somewhat less than in previous studies in which judgments of hypothetical situations were investigated (cf. Wyer, 1970b). This could indicate that not all subjects actually encoded the behavior with the trait assumed, or that some subjects, rather than considering the implications of the trait alone, constructed a configural representation of a person who would engage in the behavior and used this as a basis for their inference rather than the trait per se. However, consistent with the general conceptualization described above, predictions based upon trait X were more accurate than predictions based on the standard traits (intelligent and sarcastic) that were not directly implied by the information presented and were inferred after liking was estimated.

Inferences about Real Persons:
Effects of Similarity on Attraction

The processes postulated to underlie the effects described above should also apply when subjects are asked to infer their liking for real persons on the basis of limited information. This possibility was explored in a situation analogous to that to which cognitive balance theory (Heider, 1958) and similarity-attraction theory (Byrne, 1969) are applicable. Each subject initially described himself to another with respect to a characteristic expected to be relevant to liking (e.g., recreational interests, socioeconomic background, attitude toward communism, etc.). Then he reported his initial beliefs that he would like the other, that the other would like him, that the other was similar to him with respect to the characteristic he had personally described, and conditional beliefs that he would like the other (or the other would like him) if they were or were not similar with respect to this characteristic. After making these ratings and performing an interpolated task, each subject received bogus feedback to the effect that the other perceived them to be either very similar or very dissimilar with respect to the target characteristic, thus increasing or decreasing the subject's own belief in their similarity. New ratings of the other person and predictions of the other's reactions to the subject were then obtained.

Beliefs in liking were predicted from beliefs about similarity on the basis of the equation

$$P_L = P_{Sim}P_{L/Sim} + (1-P_{Sim}) P_{L/Sim'} \tag{7-8}$$

where P_L is either the subject's belief that he would like the other (O) or his belief that the other would like him, P_{Sim} is the subject's belief that he and O are similar with respect to the characteristic to which feedback pertained, and $P_{L/Sim}$ and $P_{L/Sim'}$ are conditional beliefs associated with the implications of the similarity to the judgment.

Before receiving feedback information, when subjects' predictions of their liking for one another were apt to be based upon criteria other than similarity with respect to the particular characteristic to which this information was relevant, these predictions were unsystematically related to beliefs about their similarity in this respect. However, following feedback, subjects' liking estimates were affected by this information and its implications in a manner implied by the above equation. Although predictions were reasonably accurate, two markedly deviant points occurred in predicting changes in subjects' beliefs that they would like the other under high similarity conditions. In both cases, actual liking was not as high as that predicted by the above equation, suggesting that the positive feedback under these conditions was not taken into account by subjects in estimating their liking for the other, despite their beliefs in its importance. It is unclear why this was so.

Predictions of Judgments along Category Scales

In most research on social evaluation processes, subjects are asked to estimate the *amount* of their liking for a person along a category scale, rather than reporting the probability that they would like such a person. However, as argued in Chapter 1, the basic reasoning processes involved may be similar. That is, a person who is asked to report his liking for another along a category

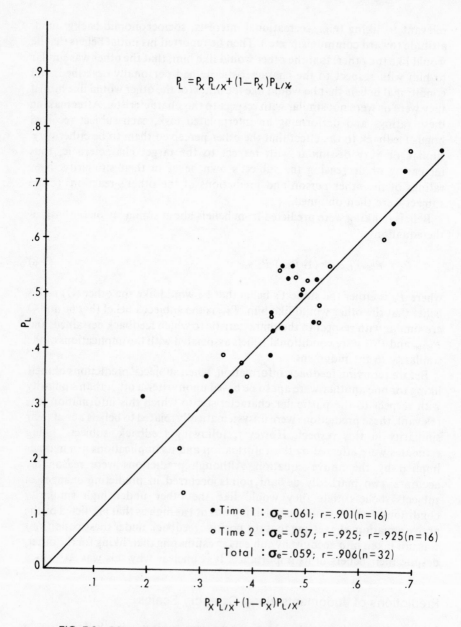

$$P_L = P_X P_{L/X} + (1 - P_X)P_{L/\bar{X}}$$

Time 1 : $\sigma_e = .061$; $r = .901(n=16)$

Time 2 : $\sigma_e = .057$; $r = .925$; $r = .925(n=16)$

Total : $\sigma_e = .059$; $r = .906(n=32)$

FIG. 7.6. Mean obtained estimates of P_L after reading the first and second paragraphs about each stimulus person (times 1 and 2, respectively), and mean changes in these estimates from time 1 to time 2, as a function of mean predicted values based upon Equation 7-7 (reprinted from Wyer, 1973c, pages 242 and 246).

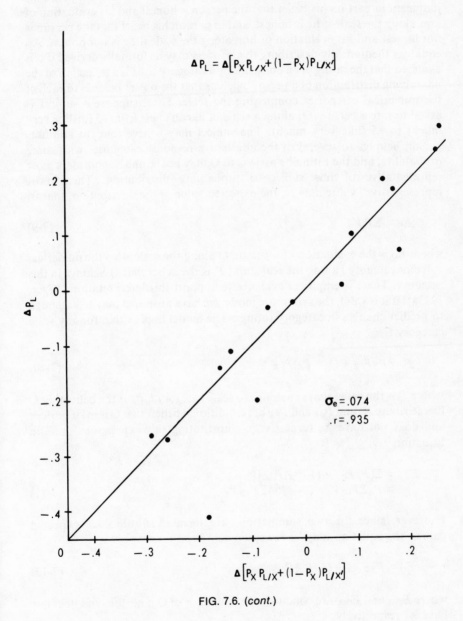

FIG. 7.6. (cont.)

scale and who retrieves information about the person's honesty may base his judgment in part on his belief that the person is honest and his evaluation of him along the scale if he is honest, and in part on his belief that the person is not honest and his evaluation of him along the scale if he is not honest. An equation theoretically describing this process may be formally derived if it is assumed that the rating of an object along a category scale is a reflection of the underlying distribution of a person's beliefs that the object belongs to each of the numerical categories comprising the scale. Thus, suppose a subject is asked to rate a person (O) along a scale of likeableness from –5 (dislike very much) to +5 (like very much). The subject may believe that the stimulus person belongs to several of the alternative response categories with some probability, and the rating he assigns to O may be the one he considers most representative of this subjective probability distribution. This "most representative" value may be the expected value of the distribution, that is,

$$E_O = \Sigma P_i V_i \tag{7-9}$$

where E_O is the evaluation of a person O along the scale, V_i is the numerical value of category i along the scale, and P_i is the belief that O belongs in this category. There is empirical evidence to support this interpretation (Wyer, 1973a). If it is valid, the syllogistic model we have proposed may be extended to predict changes in category ratings. The model implies that for any scale category i,

$$P_i = P_X P_{i/X} + (1 - P_X) P_{i/X'} \tag{7-10}$$

where P_i is the belief that O belongs to scale category i, P_X is the belief that O has attribute X, and $P_{i/X}$ and $P_{i/X'}$ are conditional beliefs that O is in i if he does and does not have X, respectively. Substituting this expression for P_i in Equation 7-9,

$$\begin{aligned} E_O &= \Sigma[P_X P_{i/X} + (1-P_X)P_{i/X'}]V_i \\ &= P_X \Sigma P_{i/X} V_i + (1 - P_X) \Sigma P_{i/X'} V_i \end{aligned} \tag{7-11}$$

However, since the two summations are themselves subjective expected values, the equation may be rewritten

$$E_O = P_X E_{O/X} + (1-P_X)E_{O/X'} \tag{7-12}$$

where $E_{O/X}$ and $E_{O/X'}$ are conditional evaluations of O if he does and does not have X, respectively.

The validity of Equation 7-12 was tested empirically (Wyer, 1973a) using a procedure identical to that described in the first experiment reported in this section. That is, subjects received pairs of paragraphs describing the behavior of a hypothetical person. The behavior described in each pair pertained to a particular trait (X). However, in this study, rather than reporting the beliefs that the stimulus person would be liked, subjects rated the person along an evaluative scale from −10 (dislike very much) to +10 (like very much), and also reported their conditional evaluations of a person who did and did not possess X ($E_{O/X}$ and $E_{O/\bar{X}}$) along a similar scale. Mean obtained evaluations of the stimulus person after reading each paragraph, and changes in these evaluations, are shown in Fig. 7.7 as a function of mean predicted values. While it was not possible in this study to provide a rigorous test of the functional relations between components of the predictor equation and ratings of O, the quantitative accuracy of the model in predicting both evaluations and changes in evaluations is impressive. (As in other studies reported in this chapter, this accuracy was obtained without the use of ad hoc curve-fitting parameters.[8])

7.5. CONCLUDING REMARKS

In this chapter, we have attempted to provide a general conceptualization of the role of syllogistic reasoning in social inference, and of the conditions in which previously acquired information is accessed for use in this reasoning. While the research applying the specific formulation proposed here has already been extensive, much more work is required to circumscribe the conditions in which the processes implied by this formulation are invalid, as well as to pinpoint more precisely the amount and type of information that are involved in these processes. However, if the formation is valid, it provides a means of diagnosing the conditions in which particular pieces of information are used as a basis for forming beliefs about one's social environment, and a framework for exploring more rigorously some of the questions raised in this volume. (For further discussion, see Appendix A).

APPENDIX A

Nonlogical Factors that Contribute to Inferences

The research summarized in Chapter 7 provides good support for both the possible role of syllogistic reasoning in social inference and the utility of Equation 7-1 and its derivatives as a description of this reasoning. However, it is intuitively evident that judges sometimes draw conclusions that do *not*

---

[8]On the basis of jacknifing procedures developed by Mosteller and Tukey (1968), neither the estimated slope nor the estimated intercept of the best-fitting linear function relation obtained to predicted values of E_O (1.03 and .32, respectively) differed significantly from its theoretical value (1 and 0, respectively).

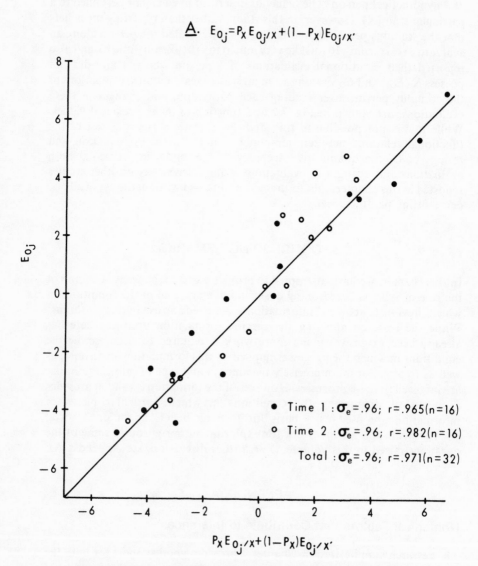

FIG. 7.7. Mean obtained evaluations of the stimulus person after reading each paragraph (at times 1 and 2) and mean change in evaluations from time 1 to time 2, as a function of mean predicted values based on Equation 7-7 (reprinted from Wyer, 1973a, p. 453).

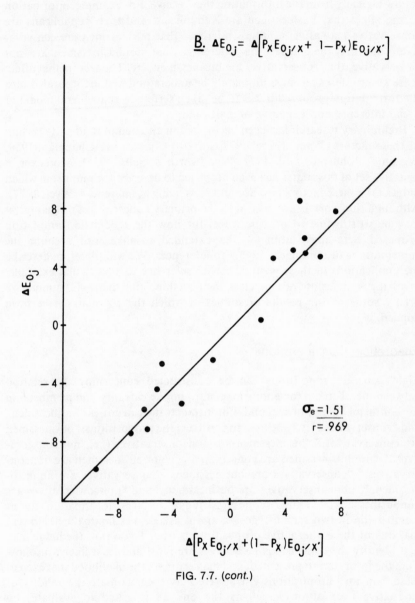

B. $\Delta E_{0j} = \Delta\left[P_X E_{0j/X} + (1-P_X)E_{0j/X'}\right]$

$\sigma_e = 1.51$

$r = .969$

FIG. 7.7. (cont.)

follow logically from the information they receive. For example, information to the effect that businessmen are Republicans and that Republicans are conservative may affect a judge's inference that businessmen are conservatives, but may also affect his inferences that nonbusinessmen are not conservative, that conservatives are businessmen, etc. The factors that affect these latter inferences must ultimately be understood and incorporated into the formulation proposed if it is to be taken seriously as a general model of social inference and cognitive organization.

Preliminary research has been performed in an attempt to identify certain of these factors (Wyer, 1975c, 1977; see also Chapman & Chapman, 1959; Wason & Johnson-Laird, 1972; Woodworth & Sells, 1935). Moreover, a tentative set of postulates has been proposed to describe the manner in which judges take these factors into account in arriving at inferences (Wyer, 1977). Although this work is not central to the primary concerns in this chapter, it may be worthwhile to provide a feel for how the syllogistic formulation proposed here may ultimately be extended to take into account the contributions of nonlogical factors to inferences. We will therefore describe the implications of these postulates with reference to a particular example, involving conclusions about class membership, and then will summarize briefly some of the results of studies in which the postulates have been applied.

Theoretical Considerations

Eight general propositions can be constructed concerning the relation between membership (or nonmembership) in one category and membership (or nonmembership) in a second. For instance, the categories "businessmen" and "conservatives" may be used to construct the propositions: "businessmen are conservatives," "businessmen are nonconservatives' (i.e., not conservatives)," "nonbusinessmen are conservatives," "nonbusinessmen are nonconservatives," "conservatives are businessmen," "conservatives are nonbusinessmen," "nonconservatives are businessmen," and "nonconservatives are nonbusinessmen." Thus, suppose a judge receives information about membership in two such categories, and is asked to estimate the likelihood that one of these alternative propositions is true. To do this, the judge may first identify the conclusions he believes are most and least likely to follow from the information presented, and may estimate the likelihood that each of these "anchor" propositions is true. He may then estimate the validity of alternative propositions (such as the one he is asked to evaluate) by comparing them to one of these "anchors." Thus, if the conclusion believed most likely to follow in our example is "businessmen are conservatives," judgments of the validity of this proposition and its contradictory ("businessmen are not conservatives") would function as positive and negative anchors, relative to which the validity of the target proposition is compared.[9]

The question is what criteria the judge uses in making these comparisons. First, note that of the eight alternatives conclusions to be drawn, four ("businessmen are conservatives," "conservatives are businessmen," "nonbusinessmen are nonconservatives" and "nonconservatives are nonbusinessmen") are symmetric, in that the subject and the other either both pertain to membership in the categories or they both pertain to nonmembership. The other four ("businessmen are nonconservatives," etc.) are asymmetric. Wyer (1977) postulated that judges compare the proposition to be evaluated (the target proposition) to the anchor proposition that has the same degree of symmetry. Thus, the target proposition "conservatives are businessmen" would be compared to the positive anchor "businessmen are conservatives," whereas the target "nonbusinessmen are conservatives" would be compared to the negative anchor ("businessmen are nonconservatives"). While this postulate seems somewhat arbitrary, it is based in part upon evidence that statements containing similar elements are judged to be similar in validity (Chapman & Chapman, 1959; Woodworth & Sells, 1935) and in part upon the observation that the implications of certain propositions within each set of four have related logical implications (e.g., if all businessmen are conservatives, it would necessarily mean that all nonconservatives were not businessmen).

Once the appropriate anchor is identified, the judge may base his inference of the target proposition's similarity to the anchor on three criteria. One, similarity in *logical implications*, refers to whether the test and anchor propositions are logically related in the manner just described. A second, similarity in *content*, refers to whether the target and anchor contain identical elements ("businessmen," "conservatives," "nonbusinessmen," or "nonconservatives"). The third, similarity in *form*, refers to whether the subject and the object of the target proposition pertain to the same categories as the subject and object of the anchor, respectively. Thus, in our example, the proposition "businessmen are conservative" is identical to the positive anchor proposition, and therefore is similar to it in all three ways. However, each of the remaining three propositions is similar to the anchor in one and only one way; specifically, one proposition ("conservatives are businessmen") is similar to it in content, a second ("nonconservatives are nonbusinessmen") is similar to it in logical implications, and the third ("nonbusinessmen are

---

[9]The designation of such statements as contradictories does not imply that they cannot both be true if the implicit quantifier of X is not univeral (i.e., if "X are Y" and "X are Y'" are interpreted to mean that some X are Y and that some are not Y, respectively). However, if one of the two statements is the most likely to follow from the information given, the other is necessarily the least likely to follow.

nonconservatives") is similar to it in form. Analogously, one of the four propositions hypothetically compared to the negative anchor ("businessmen are nonconservatives") is similar to this anchor in all three ways, while the others ("nonconservatives are businessmen," "conservatives are nonbusinessmen," and "nonbusinessmen are conservatives") are similar to it in only one way (content, logical implications, or form, respectively).

It is assumed that the judge will view the stimulus information as differentially implying target propositions in the two sets. Specifically, he is likely to see propositions that he compares to the positive anchor as more likely to follow from the stimulus information than propositions that he compares to the negative. Within each set of four, he will of course evaluate the target proposition that is identical to the anchor as identical to it in validity. His judgments of the remaining three propositions in each set depend on the relative importance of content similarity, similarity in logical implications, and form similarity. These relative contributions are matters for empirical investigation. However, if judgments of all eight alternative target propositions are obtained, these contributions can be identified using standard analysis of variance procedures (Wyer, 1977). Suppose (as resarch in fact suggests) that content similarity contributes most, followed by similarity in logical implications and then form similarity. Then, if a judge is told that businessmen are conservatives, he will believe that a statement to this effect is most likely to be true followed in order by "conservatives are businessmen," "nonconservatives are nonbusinessmen," and then "nonbusinessmen are nonconservatives." Moreover, he will believe that "businessmen are nonconservatives" to be least likely to be true, followed in order by "nonconservatives are businessmen," "conservatives are nonbusinessmen," and "nonbusinessmen are conservatives." Finally, he should judge each of the first four propositions as more likely to be true than any of the second four.

Empirical Evidence

The evidence for the applicability of the analyses outlined above has been encouraging. In an initial study (Wyer, 1977, Experiment 1), judges were told to assume that each of several individual stimulus propositions about the relation between two categories was true, and then to estimate the validity of each of the eight alternative target propositions. In each case, the statement identical to the stimulus proposition and its contradictory were assumed to function as positive and negative anchors, respectively. As predicted, the four target propositions that were hypothetically compared to the positive anchor were almost invariably judged more likely to be true than the four propositions that were hypothetically compared to the negative anchor. Moreover, content similarity contributed most to judgments, followed by similarity in logical implications, and then form similarity. The relative contributions of these factors appeared to generalize across diverse stimulus domains involving abstract categories ("members of A" and "members of B"), familiar categories in subset relations to one another ("collies" and "dogs"), and overlapping categories ("businessmen" and "conservatives," or "women's liberationists" and "apathetic persons"). Since these stimulus propositions varied in their a priori validity, this generalizability is particularly noteworthy. That is, although judges' previously formed beliefs in the validity of stimulus and target propositions may well have affected their judgments (see p. 259), these effects were apparently independent of the effects of the factors postulated here.

If the results of the above study are generalizable, the informational factors that affect judges' beliefs in a conclusion of the form "X are Y" should have systematic and predictable effects on their beliefs about other conclusions involving X and Y. This suggests a way of expanding the syllogistic formulation proposed earlier in this chapter in a way that will account for the effects of information that bears on a syllogism's premises on conclusions that do not necessarily follow from these premises. This possibility was explored in a second study (Wyer, 1977, Experiment 2). Specifically, judges read information bearing on premises of the form:

X are (*usually*) (*rarely*) W.
If X are W, they are (*usually*) (*sometimes*) (*rarely*) Y.
If X are *not* W, thery are (*usually*) (*sometimes*) (*rarely*) Y.

Eighteen different sets of statements, representing different combinations of the adverbs shown in parentheses, were presented in each of four content domains similar to those used in Experiment 1. In each case, judges were asked to assume that the stimulus propositions were true, and then to indicate probabilities of traits for the syllogistically related conclusion ("X are Y") and each of the other seven possible conclusions pertaining to X and Y.

The experimental procedures described above were assumed to manipulate beliefs corresponding to P_A, $P_{B/A}$, and $P_{B/A'}$ in Equation 7-1. The manipulations of (a) P_A and $P_{B/A}$ and (b) P_A and $P_{B/A'}$ had the expected multiplicative effects on inferences that the syllogistically related conclusion B (i.e., "X are Y") was true, consistent with the implications of this equation. More important, these manipulations also affected inferences of the likelihood of alternative conclusions in a manner generally similar to that predicted on the basis of the results of Experiment 1. That is, the manipulations generally affected judgments of propositions that were identical to the assumed anchors ("X are Y" and "X are Y'") most strongly, followed in order by judgments of propositions that are similar in content to the anchors ("Y are X" and "Y' are X"), judgments of propositions that were similar to the anchors in logical implications ("Y' are X'" and "Y are X'") and judgments of propositions that were similar in form to the anchors ("X' are Y'" and "X' are Y"). These effects generalized over content domains. While a few interesting deviations from predictions occurred (for details, see Wyer, 1977), the degree of generalizeability that existed was sufficiently encouraging to suggest that the role of nonlogical factors may ultimately be incorporated into the formulation proposed.

IV

Integration Processes

In our discussion of script processing in Chapter 2, we noted that a judge may sometimes fail to access a script, vignette, or schema to use in making inferences on the basis of the information presented to him. This may be a consequence of factors such as the novelty or the inconsistency of the information available. Or, the conditions in which the information is presented may prevent the information from being processed configurally. In addition, the evidence one brings to bear on a judgment may often have several alternative implications, depending upon the interpretation placed on it and the assumptions underlying its use. Under such conditions, the judge may often resort to a higher order rule for combining the separate implications of the information into a single judgment that he considers most appropriate.

Several possible rules might be employed. In some instances, when the implications of information are inconsistent, the judge may attempt to arrive at a compromise, or average of these implications. In other cases, where the implications of various pieces of information are similar, they may serve to strengthen one another, and thus have a "summative" effect. In still other cases, an "algebraic" process may not be invoked at all. For example, a person who believes that graduate students are invariably intelligent, hardworking, and underpaid may conclude that professors do not exploit graduate students if he is told that they do not exploit intelligent people. Moreover, this may be true regardless of whether he believes that professors exploit hardworking and underpaid people, since someone who is not intelligent cannot be a graduate student regardless of what other attributes he may have. This reasoning is similar to that implied by set-theoretic considerations.

The final two chapters of this volume are devoted to these matters. In Chapter 8, we will consider algebraic inference processes and the conditions under which they may occur. In Chapter 9, we will concentrate on a more specific but quite important type of inference, namely, the evaluation of generalizations about the relations among different classes of persons and objects, based upon different types and amounts of information about the relations among specific instances of these classes. The importance of considering this matter is apparent from our discussion in Chapter 5, where we noted that judgments of people's attributes are often mediated by implicit assumptions about the generalizeability of their behavior to other persons, objects, and situations. Here, we will consider the processes of making generalizations in more detail, and will identify contingencies involving the type of behaviors and objects involved and the type of information presented. presented.

The focus of our discussion in the next two chapters may seem restricted, in that it does not directly consider other types of rules, such as those derived from cognitive balance theory (Heider, 1958; for refinements and elaborations, see Cartwright & Harary, 1956; Feather, 1967; Insko & Schopler, 1967; Abelson & Rosenberg, 1958), which are neither strictly algebraic nor syllogistic. However, there is actually very little evidence that balance principles have much validity as general descriptions of cognitive functioning, despite the continued interest in applying them (Wyer, 1974b). Certain implications of these rules, and contingencies in their validity, are in fact noted in the context of other discussions in this volume. The reader who is interested in a more detailed analysis of balance theory and research is referred to Chapters 5 and 10 of Wyer (1974b).

8
Algebraic Inference Processes

A judge who has several different pieces of information about an object may sometimes respond to this information configurally, as a single unit. That is, the various pieces of information in combination may stimulate access to previously formed schemata or vignettes that are then used in making the inference. Processes involved in such configural responding are discussed at length in Chapters 2 and 3. However, a judge may have difficulty responding to information configurally under certain conditions, and thus may need to consider the implications of each piece separately in order to make a judgment. If that judgment is numerical (i.e., a rating of some object characteristic on a response scale), it is conceivable that the judge will invoke some sort of arithmetic or algebraic rule to combine these separate implications into a single value.

Formal models have been postulated to describe algebraic inference processes, and most research on algebraic inference processes has been conducted within the framework of one or more of these models. Indeed, because of their conceptual simplicity and quantitative precision, no other general formulations of social inference have received as wide attention. Such models appear applicable to a wide range of inference phenomena (cf. Anderson, 1971a, 1974a). Several specific forms of these models have been developed, each based upon a somewhat different set of assumptions (for a summary of various models, see Wyer, 1974b, Chapter 9). Of these, the most successful, and thus by far the most influential, has been the weighted average formulation developed by Norman Anderson (1965, 1968a, 1971a). Unfortunately, it is not completely clear whether this success indicates that the model provides a generally valid description of judges' cognitive functioning in a variety of situations, or whether the model's accuracy is peculiar to the idiosyncratic judgmental situations typically constructed to test its validity. This latter possibility will be elaborated presently.

In this regard, it is important to distinguish between algebraic *models* of information integration and the psychological *processes* they are intended to describe. As we will see, applications of such models (in the situations of concern in this volume) have traditionally been aimed only at describing the relation between stimulus input characteristics and reported judgments, and have seldom attempted to investigate more directly the mediating processes that produce this relation and the conditions under which these processes may occur. In this chapter, we will first consider the assumptions underlying formal algebraic models of social inference, with particular emphasis upon the weighted averaging formulation proposed by Anderson (1965, 1971a). In this discussion, we will focus primarily on implications of this model for the psychological processes it purports to describe. In the course of this analysis, we will attempt to identify conditions in which algebraic inference processes are most likely to occur, and in which algebraic descriptions of these processes are therefore most likely to apply. Then, based upon those considerations, we will review and evaluate the implications of representative research bearing upon the role of algebraic processes in making different types of social inferences. Finally, we will outline another essentially algebraic formulation, Gollob's *Subject–Verb–Object* approach to social cognition, which avoids many of the deficiencies of more traditional models.

8.1. THEORETICAL CONSIDERATIONS

Basic Algebraic Models

Suppose a judge is given several different pieces of information and is asked to make a judgment on the basis of this information. Under certain circumstances, the judge may first construe the implications of each piece of information separately for the inference to be made. Then, he may subjectively sum these implications to arrive at an overall judgment (perhaps weighting the implications by their relevance or importance for the judgment). Alternatively, the judge may average these various implications to arrive at his inference.

A consideration of these alternative possibilities has led to the postulation of two general types of algebraic models. One, a *summative* model, is described by the equation:

$$J = \sum_{i=0}^{M} w_i V_i \tag{8.1}$$

where V_i is the scale value of the implications of the ith piece of information brought to bear upon the judgment J, and w_i is the absolute weight attached to these implications. (The nature of these scale values and weights is considered in detail below.) The second, a weighted averaging model of the sort proposed by Anderson (1965), postulates that the judgment is a weighted average of these implications; that is,

$$J = \frac{\sum_{i=0}^{N} w_i V_i}{\sum_{i=1}^{N} w_i} \qquad (8.2)$$

Both models provide for the possible effects of the judge's previous experience as well as of new information acquired in the judgmental situation. This is done by assigning a weight (w_O) and scale value (V_O) to the implications of the judge's "initial impression," obtained before specific information is received about the object.

While Equations 8-1 and 8-2 look mathematically similar, their implications differ in several important respects. Consider two sets of information, A and B, such that pieces in each set vary systematically in their implications for a judgment J. Suppose that only one piece of information, say A, is presented. Then, according to a summative model, (Equation 8-1),

$$J = w_O V_O + w_A V_A$$

and according to an averaging model (Equation 8-2),

$$J = \frac{w_0 V_0 + w_A V_A}{w_0 + w_A} = \frac{w_0}{w_0 + w_A} V_0 + \frac{w_A}{w_0 + w_A} V_A$$

Now suppose B is added. Then, according to Equation 8-1,

$$J = w_O V_O + w_A V_A + w_B V_B$$

and according to Equation 8-2,

$$J = \frac{w_0 V_0 + w_A V_A + w_B V_B}{w_0 + w_A + w_B}$$

$$= \frac{w_0}{w_0 + w_A + w_B} V_0 + \frac{w_A}{w_0 + w_A + w_B} V_A + \frac{w_B}{w_0 + w_A + w_B} V_B$$

Suppose the absolute weights and scale values of the information (V_A, V_B, w_A, and w_B) are all independent. Then, Equation 8-1 predicts that the effect of differences in the implications of A (V_A) will not depend upon the weight attached to B (w_B), and thus will not even depend upon whether or not B is present. However, the averaging model implies that the effect of A information will be less when the weight of B (w_B) is high than when it is low, and will be less when B information is present (i.e., $w_B > O$) than when it is not ($w_B = O$). Diagnostic tests of the validity of the two models as descriptions of information integration processes are typically based upon these different implications.

An important feature of the averaging model described by Equation 8-2 is worth mentioning. The model can obviously account for instances in which judgments based upon two pieces of information, A and B, in combination fall somewhere in between the judgment based upon A alone and the judgment based upon B alone. However, suppose that $w_O = w_A = w_B = 1$, that $V_O = 0$, and that $V_A = V_B = 8$. Then, applying Equation 8-2, the judgments based upon A alone and upon B alone would be equal to $(0 + 8)/2$, or 4, but the judgment based upon both A and B in combination would be equal to $(0 + 8 + 8)/3$, or 5.3. Thus, Equation 8-2 implies that the judgment based upon two (or more) pieces of information can sometimes be *greater* than the judgment based upon either piece considered separately, despite the essential "averaging" property of the model.

Assumptions and Implications Underlying the Application of Algebraic Models

As we have noted, algebraic models of the form of Equations 8-1 and 8-2 have often been successful in describing the functional relation between characteristics of different pieces of information and judgments based upon this information. Nevertheless, some caution must be taken in concluding from this success that the psychological processes underlying these judgments are indeed algebraic, or that model parameters (e.g., weights and scale values) have any correspondence to characteristics of the information presented as the judge himself perceives it. In light of the extensive research applying these models, surprisingly little effort has been devoted to directly validating the various implicit assumptions underlying their application.

For one thing, values of model parameters are seldom estimated directly (for exceptions, see Hinkle, 1976; Wyer, 1969a). Rather, they are inferred after the fact by applying either functional measurement methodology (Anderson, 1970) or, in some cases, more complicated curve-fitting procedures (cf. Chandler, 1967). Moreover, the use of these post hoc parameter estimation procedures often requires certain (somewhat arbitrary) simplifying assumptions concerning the invariance of various model parameters over sets of information. Note that if the weight and scale value of a piece of information were allowed to vary with its context, these parameters would need to be defined and measured separately for each set in which the piece is contained. In such an event, there would be no way to invalidate the model without independent estimates of these parameters; that is, one could account post hoc for any judgment based upon any set of information, simply by postulating values of w_i and V_i for each piece that are unique to the set.

In testing algebraic models, therefore, the question has not been so much whether such models can in principle account for judgments, but rather whether certain simplifying assumptions underlying their test are justified. One such assumption, which underlies most applications of these models, is that the scale value assigned to each piece of information is invariant over stimulus configurations; that is, the implications of each piece of information are assumed not to depend upon its context. The validity of this assumption remains surprisingly controversial, at least in the domains to which algebraic models are typically applied (Kaplan, 1974; Ostrom, 1977; Wyer, 1974a), although it is clearly invalidated by research in other paradigms such as those described in Chapter 4. A second assumption in earlier research was that the absolute weight of each piece of information (w_i) is constant and independent of its scale value (V_i). As we shall see, recent evidence has often shown this latter assumption to be invalid.

The application of Equations 8-1 and 8-2 requires still other assumptions about the psychological referents of model parameters, and about the manner in which judges process the information they receive in arriving at their inferences. These latter assumptions seem intuitively more likely to hold in some kinds of inference situations than in others. A consideration of these assumptions may therefore help to circumscribe conceptually the conditions in which formal algebraic models are likely to provide valid descriptions of judges' actual cognitive functioning. We shall discuss certain of these assumptions in some detail. In this discussion, we will focus primarily upon the weighted averaging model proposed by Anderson (Equation 8-2), since this model has been most widely and successfully applied. However, many of the issues raised are equally applicable to other algebraic formulations.

Implications for the Judgmental Processes

Anderson (1971a) identifies two fundamental components of the judgmental process: *valuation* and *integration*. Valuation involves the determination of the various weights and scales assigned to the information presented about an object. Integration refers to the manner in which these weights and scale values are combined to arrive at a subjective judgment of the object. A third, *response* process may also be involved (that is, the process of transforming the subjective judgment of the object into the response language available for reporting this judgment). While the nature of this process is often of considerable importance (cf. Parducci, 1965; Upshaw, 1969; Wyer, 1974b, Chapter 3), we will restrict our attention here to valuation and integration.

The postulation of these subprocesses assumes that they are conceptually if not operationally separable. In general, valuation is assumed to occur independently of, and prior to, integration. Anderson (1971a) notes that in some instances, in which stimuli "interact," this assumption may not be strictly valid; however, he contends that "the assumption that the stimuli do not interact seems to be justified in an important group of situations [p. 173]." A question arises, however, as to the number and general characteristics of these situations. It may be noted that the postulation of conceptually distinct valuation and integration processes differs in implications from much of our earlier discussion of the manner in which information is encoded and stored in memory. For example, when information is interpreted in relation to a schematic or configural representation of the judgment object, the postulation of separate valuation and integration processes is not very meaningful.

One question surrounding the distinction between valuation and integration centers around the interpretation of w_i, or the weight attached to each component piece of information. In applying models such as Equations 8-1 and 8-2, the magnitude of the weight attached to each piece of information is usually inferred after the fact from the influence of this information upon judgments (cf. Anderson 1967, 1970). In such instances, the psychological referent of these weights is sometimes unclear. There may sometimes be an a priori basis for considering a piece of information to be more or less relevant or important (e.g., its ambiguity, the credibility of its source, etc.). In these cases, the importance of a piece of information may indeed be estimated during an initial valuation phase of the inference process. In other cases, however, it seems likely that the apparent weight attached to a piece of information, as inferred from its relative influence upon judgments, is actually a derivative of the integration process and has no independent referent. For example, Warr (1974) has hypothesized that when judges are asked to make an inference on the basis of several pieces of information, they first identify the piece with the most extreme implications and make a tentative judgment on the basis of these implications. They then modify this judgment to some degree, depending upon the implications of the remaining pieces. As a result of this process, the information with the most extreme implications appears to have the greatest weight. However, this differential weighting does not occur as a result of a prior valuation process; rather, it is a by-product of the manner in which information is processed during the integration phase.

In some instances, a given piece of information may have a variety of possible implications, and its effect may be some function of the particular subset of implications that the judge happens to consider when he makes his inference. When several pieces of information are presented in combination, the relative weights attached to them may reflect the relative numbers of implications of each piece that are "sampled" by the judge at the time the information is presented. Since a judge's information-processing capacity is limited (Miller, 1956), it seems likely that the number of sampled implications of a given piece of information, and therefore the magnitude of its influence, will decrease as the total amount of available information (i.e., the number of other pieces presented) becomes greater. Such a decrease would be consistent with an averaging model, although the underlying *integration process* is not averaging at all. Moreover, differences in the relative weight attached to different pieces of information may reflect the fact that some pieces are more novel, attention-getting, or relevant than others, so that a relatively greater number of their implications may be sampled.

The Psychological Referents of Weights and Scale Value Differences in Unitizing of Information

To the extent that Equations 8-1 and 8-2 describe the judges' actual inference processes, they imply that presented information is encoded by breaking it up into discrete pieces or units, and assigning each a subjective weight and scale value. In many applications of these models, the information presented consists of a list of personality adjectives, and each adjective is arbitrarily assumed to serve as a unit of information. Whether this assumption is valid is rarely established.

Anderson (1970) notes that if certain conditions are met, the level at which informational units are specified is of little practical importance. For example, suppose a piece of information i as specified in Equation 8-2 is psychologically composed of several subelements of information at a more molecular level. However, suppose that the scale value of i is itself a weighted average of the scale values of the subelements, that is,

$$V_i = \frac{\Sigma w_{ij} V_{ij}}{\Sigma w_{ij}} \quad \text{and} \quad w_i = \Sigma w_{ij}.$$

Then $w_i V_i = \Sigma w_{ij} V_{ij}$. If this were the case, the theoretical value of J in Equation 8-2 would be identical, regardless of whether the equation is written in terms of the weights and scale values at the molar level (i) or at the more molecular one (j).

While this analysis seems plausible, its general validity is somewhat questionable. As we suggested in Chapter 4, the same sequence of behavioral information may lead to different judgments, depending upon situational and instructional conditions that affect the units (fine or gross) used by judges to encode it. It is reasonable to suppose that judgments based upon other types of information will also depend upon the size of the units into which it is analyzed, and that the size and nature of these units may depend upon a variety of situational and informational factors. For example, judges may make less fine discriminations among different pieces of information as the total amount of available information increases, due again to their limited information-processing capacity. As a result, the size of the units into which information is analyzed may increase with the amount of information presented, and thus the psychological referents of the parameters comprising Equations 8-1 and 8-2 may change.

Other evidence for the importance of considering informational units in integration processes has recently been obtained in an unpublished study by Carlston and his students. Subjects received information implying that a stimulus person possessed two different personality traits. In some (single implication) conditions, however, the two traits were implied by different behavioral episodes while in the other (multiple implication) conditions, the two traits were both implied by each of the episodes. The implications of the information presented in each condition were the same, as determined by pretest ratings, and the same total quantity of information was presented in each condition. Nevertheless, subject's judgments of the stimulus person differed in the two conditions. Subjects who read single implication episodes tended to assimilate both trait implications, making relatively extreme ratings along both trait dimensions. In contrast, subjects who read multiple implication episodes tended to focus on only one or the other implied trait, making relatively extreme ratings along the direction pertaining to this trait but relatively neutral ratings along the other direction. Thus, these subjects tended to derive only a single implication (presumably the one most salient to them) from a single episode. This tendency emphasizes the need to determine the psychological units into which information is partitioned in understanding the number and type of implications actually taken into account by judges, and thus the contributions of this information to their judgments.

The general validity of Anderson's argument may be questioned on still other grounds. For example, in some instances, a judge may treat two or more pieces of information as a single configural cue, with implications that affect judgments independently of, and *in addition to,* those of the component pieces considered separately. Examples of this were noted in earlier chapters. For instance, suppose a judge is told that (a) P has argued in favor of euthanasia to O, and (b) O is opposed to euthanasia. The judge may treat P's advocacy of the position and O's opposition to it as separate informational cues, each of which has implications for a judgment, and may assign a "scale value" to each. In addition, he may treat the two pieces in combination as a single unit of information, "P disagrees publically with O," and assign this unit its own "scale value."[1] Similar situations may arise when other types of information are presented. For example, if the two adjectives "warm" and "unfriendly" are used in combination to describe a person, they may convey the impression that the person is also "inconsistent." This inferred attribute may contribute to judgments of liking for the person independently of the implications of "warm" and "unfriendly" considered in isolation.

Nonequivalence of Scale Values and Reported Judgments. An additional consideration that makes it important to attend more closely to the psychological referents of weights and scale values is that, in theory, the scale values assigned to information and the judgment based upon it are not isomorphically related. Thus, it is sometimes hard to know whether two pieces of information lead to different judgments because of a difference in their scale values or because of differences in other model parameters. For example, suppose one wishes to determine the relative scale values of two pieces of information, A and B, and to do so, obtains judgments based upon each piece in isolation. Based upon Equation 8-2, these judgments would be represented theoretically as follows:

$$J_A = \frac{w_0 V_0}{w_0 + w_A} + \frac{w_A V_A}{w_0 + w_A}$$

and

$$J_B = \frac{w_0 V_0}{w_0 + w_B} + \frac{w_B V_B}{w_0 + w_B}$$

Suppose that in fact, J_A is greater than J_B. This could mean that the scale value of A (V_A) is greater than the scale value of B (V_B). However, it could also mean that the weight of A (w_A) is greater than the weight of B (w_B). This latter possibility is not unlikely. As we have already noted, factors such as ambiguity and novelty are apt to affect the influence of information, and it is reasonable to suppose that differences in these characteristics are reflected by differences in the weights assigned to the different pieces of information involved. However, without knowing a priori how A and B differ with respect

---

[1]The relative magnitudes of these three scale values may vary considerably with the type of judgment to be made. For instance, P's disagreement with O may be considered irrelevant to judgments of P's attitude toward euthanasia, but may have negative implications for judgments of his friendliness; on the other hand, O's opinion on euthanasia may be viewed as having negative implications for P's attitude toward euthanasia, but as having no implications at all for judgments of his friendliness.

to these characteristics, the assumption that a difference between J_A and J_B reflects a difference in scale value would often be unjustified.

It is sometimes possible to distinguish between scale value differences and weight differences. One strategy is to compare the effect of a third piece of information, C, when it is accompanied by A with its effect when it is accompanied by B. If A has a greater absolute weight than B (i.e., $w_A > w_B$), and if Equation 8-2 is valid, the relative effect of C information should be less when it is accompanied by A than when it is accompanied by B (since its *relative* weight would be less in the former case). However, if the difference between J_A and J_B is a result of a difference in scale values (if $V_A > V_B$), and the weights attached to A and B are the same, then the effect of C information on judgments should be the same regardless of whether A or B accompanies it. Unfortunately, this approach requires a host of additional assumptions, including the assumption that the underlying integration process is, in fact, averaging (i.e., that Equation 8-2 is valid), and that C is not differentially redundant or inconsistent with A and B.

The above considerations point out the desirability of obtaining independent a priori estimates of the parameters of Equations 8-1 and 8-2. While this may often be difficult for reasons implied above, certain strategies are possible. For example, to the extent that the absolute weight of a piece of information (w_i) is a function of its ambiguity or novelty, its value can be estimated from independent measures of these characteristics. Hinkle (1976) employed such a strategy successfully in an application of Equation 8-2 to the prediction of liking judgments based upon personality adjectives. Using the index of ambiguity described in Chapter 5, he found that the ambiguity of adjectives and their normative favorableness did in fact combine functionally to affect judgments of liking in the manner implied by this equation. Moreover, he made accurate quantitative predictions of judgments by assuming that w_i was an inverse function of an independent measure of ambiguity. More critical tests of an averaging model, constructed on the basis of a priori estimates of w_i, also received support, as we shall note presently.

8.2. APPLICATIONS OF ALGEBRAIC MODELS TO SOCIAL INFERENCE PHENOMENA

In the preceding section we analyzed in some detail the formal properties of algebraic models of information integration and the assumptions underlying them. Under conditions in which these assumptions are valid, algebraic models may be a powerful tool in both conceptualizing and describing the manner in which the implications of different pieces of information are combined to arrive at judgments and diagnosing the nature of their effects. Unfortunately, a clear a priori statement of the conditions in which such models are most likely to describe information integration processes has not been attempted. There are, however, some guidelines to use in evaluating their potential applicability. These guidelines are suggested in part by considerations raised in the preceding section and in part by our earlier discussion (in Chapter 2) of the conditions in which script-processing is likely to be invoked (see also Abelson, 1976). As we will see, these considerations lead to the somewhat ironic conclusion that the phenomena to which algebraic models have been most often applied in social psychology (namely, impression formation and interpersonal attraction) are among the least likely phenomena to involve algebraic inference processes outside the unique laboratory conditions in which they have been traditionally studied. After proposing these guidelines, we will review representative research bearing on the applicability of algebraic formulations and evaluate it in light of the considerations we have raised.

Conditions in Which Algebraic Processes Are Invoked: Some General Considerations

In general, algebraic integration processes would seem most likely to be used when both the judgment to be made and the implications of the information presented can be represented numerically along a magnitude scale. In addition, an algebraic process may be used primarily when the judge breaks down the information presented into discrete units and considers the implications of each unit separately, rather than accessing (or constructing) a schema or script for use in interpreting the information as a whole. Several hypotheses seem reasonable as to when those conditions will obtain.

1. Information is more likely to be analyzed into discrete units, and thus an algebraic integration process more likely to be employed, when this information is either (a) of different types; (b) comes from different sources; or (c) concerns different objects or elements. Thus, a piece of visual information about a person's appearance and a piece of verbal information about his personality are more likely to be encoded as separate units than are two pieces of verbal information. Or, two statements concerning the validity of a proposition are more likely to be considered separate pieces of information if they are attributed to two different sources than if they are attributed to the same source. Similarly, two different elements of a situation (e.g., an actor's decision to speak in favor of a particular position and the opinion of persons in general) are more apt to be treated as separate units than are two aspects of the same element (e.g., the actor's decision and his actual delivery of the speech).

2. Information is apt to be analyzed into separate units, and thus an algebraic integration process is more likely, when certain aspects of the information are either inconsistent or have different implications for the judgment to be made. Thus, two adjectives describing a person are more likely

to be treated as separate units if the attributes they describe are unlikely to be found in the same person (e.g., cautious and bold) than if they are commonly found in the same person (e.g., cautious and timid). Moreover, adjectives are more likely to be treated as separate units if their implications for the judgment differ than if they are similar. For example, "friendly" and "dishonest" are more apt to be treated as different units in making a judgment of likeableness than are "unfriendly" and "dishonest." On the other hand, adjectives are less likely to be treated as separate units when in combination they convey a stereotype or schema of a particular type of person (e.g., "beautiful and dumb"; "studious and refined"; "loudmouthed and aggressive") than when they are not likely to convey such a stereotype (i.e., "beautiful and aggressive"; "dumb and refined"; "studious and loudmouthed," etc.).

3. Information is apt to be analyzed into different units, and thus an algebraic inference process is more likely, when the information is presented in a way that artificially distinguishes between the pieces presented, or provides a set to make these distinctions. Thus a detailed verbal description of a person's physical appearance is more apt to be encoded into different units than is a visual description of his appearance (e.g., a photograph) upon which the verbal material is based. Alternatively, a written description of a person's personality attributes is more likely to be encoded into discrete units than an observation of the person's behavior that has implications for these attributes. Instructions concerning how to treat the information presented may also affect how it is unitized. For example, instructions to treat each of a set of adjectives describing a person as "equally important," or to ignore inconsistencies among them, may give judges an implicit set to consider the adjectives as separate entities rather than as a configuration.

4. When a large number of similar judgments are required, and each is based upon a different set of information, a judge is unlikely to put forth the cognitive effort required to form a meaningful script pertaining to each object described, and therefore may resort to more abstract "heuristics" (cf. Abelson, 1976; see Chapter 2 of this volume). Thus, situations in which a judge is asked to infer his liking for each of a large number of stimulus persons in succession, each described by a different set of adjectives, are more apt to invoke an algebraic process than situations in which a judge is asked to evaluate only one or two persons.

The above factors may affect whether an algebraic integration rule of *any* sort is likely to be used. Given that this type of rule is invoked, other factors may determine whether the rule is summative or averaging. As noted elsewhere (Wyer, 1974b), the nature of the rule may depend largely upon socially learned criteria for the judgment to be made. It may also depend upon the inconsistency of the information presented. For example, if one source describes a person as honest and another describes him as deceitful, the judge may assume that the sources cannot both be correct, and therefore may arrive at a compromise between the implications of the two adjectives, perhaps giving relatively more weight to the description he considers to be more valid (i.e., the one whose source is the more credible). On the other hand, suppose the judge learns that two persons, A and B, agree about the value of a strong central government but disagree about the desirability of legalizing marijuana. These two pieces of information could easily both be valid. In arriving at an estimate of A's liking for B, the judge in this case may subjectively "sum" the implications of this information, based upon the assumption that the greater the number of matters on which people agree, the better they are apt to get along.[2]

The above observations become relevant in evaluating the support for algebraic models of social inference processes. The extensive literature bearing upon the validity of algebraic models has been reviewed elsewhere (Anderson, 1974b; Wyer, 1974b), and we will therefore forego a complete discussion of it here. Rather, we will concentrate on a few representative studies that illustrate the conditions in which the models are apt to apply. The discussion will be divided into two sections. First, we will focus upon conditions in which all the information presented is about the same element of a social situation (i.e., an actor, his behavior, another person, etc., as specified in Chapter 1). Then, we will consider the combined effects of information about different elements. In each case, we will evaluate the consistency of the data presented for either an averaging or a summative model, and the assumptions required in order for each model to be applicable. In addition, we will consider the possible reasons for the applicability of these models (or in many instances, their inapplicability) from the perspective outlined above.

Inferences Based Upon Information About a Single Element

Research on the combined effects of information about a single person or object has typically focused upon the effects of a single type of information—personality adjective descriptions—on judges' estimates of their liking for the person described. In a few cases, however, the combined effects of different types of information (e.g., verbal and visual information) have been investigated. Based upon the considerations noted above, one might expect algebraic models to be more likely to apply in the these cases.

---

[2]The latter example seems to run counter to the results of research reported by Byrne and Nelson (1965) that attraction is a function of the proportion of similar attributes and not their number. However, this is not necessarily the case; see Wyer (1974b, pp. 344–347).

Effects of Personality Trait
Information in Judgments of Liking

In a typical experiment on "impression formation," descriptions of hypothetical persons are constructed by combining adjectives in one set, A, with those in a second set, B. Adjectives in each set vary systematically in their normative implications for a stimulus person's likeableness. Judges then estimate their liking for a person described by each combination of A and B adjectives, and these judgments are analyzed as a function of the likeableness of A and the likeableness of B.

In much of the early research reported by Anderson and his colleagues (Anderson, 1962, 1968b), liking judgments appeared to be a nearly linear function of the implications of the component adjectives. That is, there was only a small and often nonsignificant interaction between the A and B adjectives, indicating that the effects of the two sets of information were nearly independent. These data would be consistent with either a summative model (Equation 8-1) or an averaging model (Equation 8-2) in which the absolute weight attached to each adjective in a set was the same (and thus the relative weight of each was constant over all A–B combinations).

In more recent work, however, interactions inconsistent with a summative model have been reported. Perhaps the most definitive series of studies on the issue was conducted by Birnbaum (1974), who obtained consistently divergent effects of A and B adjective likeableness on liking judgments. These effects, shown in Fig. 8.1 for each of three stimulus replications, could not be explained as an artifact of either improper response scaling or improperly positioned stimuli along the response scale. Note from this figure that (a) the effect of the A adjective generally decreases as the normative likeableness of the B adjective decreases; and that (b) the effect of the B adjective generally decreases as the normative likeableness of the A adjective decreases. This general pattern is consistent with an averaging model (Equation 8-2) in which the absolute weight of each adjective is an inverse function of its evaluative implications. (Thus, the large absolute weight of more negative adjectives diminishes the relative weight of the other adjectives presented.)

Unfortunately, the assumption of an interaction between weights and scale values cannot explain all the departures from linearity that have surfaced in adjective combination studies. Wyer and his associates (Wyer, 1974a; Wyer & Dermer, 1968; Wyer & Watson, 1969) have reported several other cases where this assumption inadequately accounts for the way adjectives are combined into judgments. In some instances (see Fig. 8.2), the effect of an adjective in one context differed in direction as well as in magnitude from its effect in other contexts. These reversals are hard for an algebraic model to predict without assuming that the evaluative implications of adjectives (V_i) vary over stimulus combinations.

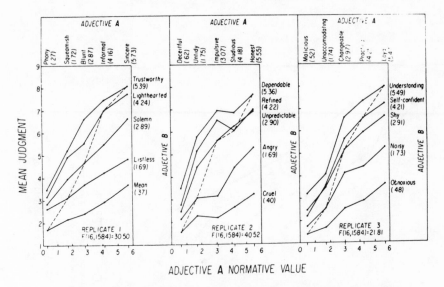

FIG. 8.1.   Mean ratings of likeableness of pairs of adjectives. Normative
values for individual adjectives are listed above and to the right of each panel
(reprinted from Birnbaum, 1974, p. 547).

Indeed, some evidence of these deviations can also be found in Birnbaum's
data shown in Figure 8.1. While these deviations could be spurious, many
appear to be consistent over replications of the experiment. Birnbaum
suggests that in some cases, an adjective with implications for activity or
potency (Osgood, Suci, & Tannenbaum, 1957) may not only contribute to
liking judgments in its own right, but may affect judges' assumptions about
the intensity of the attributes implied by other adjectives. In a sense, they may
serve as "adverbs" that modify these adjectives. For example, a "self-
confident malicious" person may be assumed to be not only more self-
confident, but also more actively malicious, than a "shy malicious" person.
Thus, the first person may be liked less than the second, even though "self-
confident" in isolation is considered a more favorable quality than "shy".

Not all of the deviations from averaging in Birnbaum's data are so easily
explained. For example, note from Fig. 8.1 that a "studious refined" person is
liked less than either an "impulsive refined" person or a "studious
unpredictable" person, even though "studious" and "refined" are both higher
in normative likeableness than either "impulsive" or "unpredictable."
Intuitively, the diminished liking for a "studious refined" person makes some
sense. The description of a person as both studious and refined may elicit a
stereotypic schema or script of a polite but uninteresting grind; it may take
evidence of a bit of impulsiveness or unpredictability to make a studious

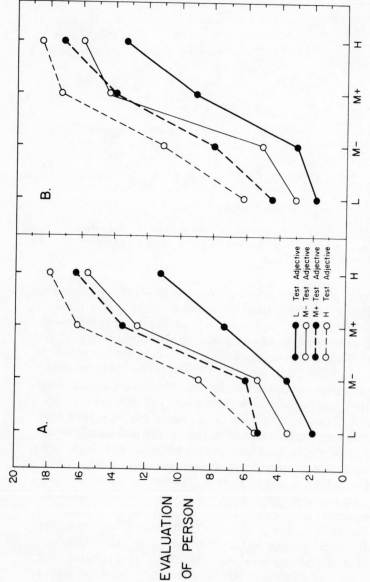

FAVORABLENESS OF CONTEXT

FIG. 8.2. Mean evaluations of persons based on two "context" adjectives and one "test" adjective, (a) reprinted from Wyer and Dermer (1968, p. 10); and (b) based on data from Wyer and Watson (1969).

FIG. 8.2. Mean evaluations of persons based on two "context" adjectives and one "test" adjective, (a) reprinted from Wyer and Dermer (1968, p. 10); and (b) based on data from Wyer and Watson (1969).

person (or a refined person) appear sufficiently stimulating to be likeable. This configural interpretation goes considerably beyond the apparent implications of an averaging model. Indeed, it suggests that the sorts of script-processing we have assumed to exist in more naturalistic situations may sometimes occur in the adjective combination task as well. Such script processing would seem most likely when the combination of adjectives presented is sufficiently similar to the description of a prototypic person the judge has encountered in his previous experience.

Experimental Manipulations of Differential Weighting. The studies described above do not bear as directly on the implications of an averaging model in studies in which the weights attached to each piece of information are manipulated experimentally. According to an averaging formulation, an increase in the absolute weight of one piece of information should decrease the relative weight of information accompanying it, and thus should reduce the impact of the latter information. A rigorous test of these implications was conducted by Birnbaum, Wong and Wong (1976). This study is particularly impressive since essentially parallel results were obtained in two quite different stimulus and judgmental domains. In one study, judges estimated the value of a used car, based upon its blue book value and the estimate of a friend with either high, moderate, or low mechanical expertise. In the second study, judges estimated their liking for persons described by two adjectives, each contributed by a different source who had known the person described for either a single meeting, 3 months, or 3 years. In each case, the manipulation of the source characteristic was assumed to affect perceptions of the source's credibility, and thus the weight attached to the information from him. Data pertaining to the used car study are shown in Fig. 8.3. In the first panel, judgments are shown, pooled over different blue book values, as a function of the source's estimate and his credibility level. As expected, the effect of the source's estimate on judgments increased with source credibility, consistent with the assumption that the credibility of the source affects the absolute weight attached to his expertise. More important, however, are data in the second panel. These data show that, pooled over source estimates, the effect of the blue book value (BBV) decreases as the source increases in credibility. This is consistent with the implications of an averaging model of the sort implied by Equation 8-2, in which the relative weight of one piece of information is an inverse function of the absolute weight of the information accompanying it.

In the second study, the credibility of both sources of information were manipulated independently. Data pertaining to this study are plotted in Fig. 8.4. Each panel of this figure shows liking ratings as a function of the normative likeableness of adjective 1 (low, moderate, or high in likeableness) and the normative likeableness of adjective 2. Each row of panels pertains to a different level of credibility of the source of adjective 1 (source 1), while each

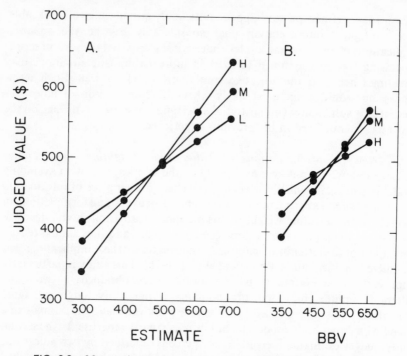

FIG. 8.3.　Mean estimate of car's value as a function of source credibility (L = low, M = moderate, H = high); (a) source's estimate and (b) bluebook value. (Reprinted from Birnbaum et al., 1976, p. 332.)

column pertains to a different level of credibility of the source of adjective 2 (source 2). The effect of adjective 2 on ratings (reflected by the slope of the curves shown in each panel) increases with the credibility of its source (i.e., with the length of time the source has known the stimulus person). More important, it decreases as the source of adjective 1 becomes more credible. Similarly, the effect of adjective 1 (indicated by the difference between the three curves in each panel) increases with the credibility of its own source, but decreases as the source of adjective 2 becomes more credible. Finally, supplementary data (not shown in this figure) indicated that the effect of information from each source was generally greater when it was presented in isolation than when it was accompanied by information from the other source. All of these effects are consistent with the implications of Equation 8-2.

A second aspect of the data in Fig. 8.4 is particularly relevant to the assumption that an initial impression (i.e., V_o) is averaged in with the pieces of information presented. Consider those instances in which both sources are equally credible, and therefore the information from each should be weighted equally. If an initial impression were *not* averaged in with the implications of

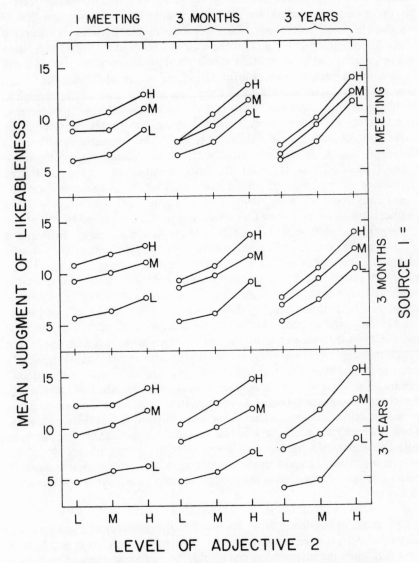

FIG. 8.4. Mean ratings of likeableness as a function of the adjective contributed by the second source, with a separate curve for each adjective contributed by the first source. Each row and column represents a different level of source 1 and source 2, respectively. (Reprinted from Birnbaum et al., 1976, p. 335).

the information presented (in other words, if $w_O = 0$), the combined effects of the two pieces of information presented should be the same regardless of whether the weights attached to them were both high or both low.[3] However, if $w_O > 0$, Equation 8-2 implies that the *relative* weight of the initial impression will be greater, and therefore that the effects of the information presented will be less, when both sources of information are low in credibility than when they are high. Data relevant to this prediction are shown in the upper left, middle, and lower right panels of Fig. 8.4. The effects of both pieces decrease in magnitude as the two sources become less credible (that is, the slope of the curves is less, and they are closer together). These results, considered in isolation, would also be consistent with the implications of a summative model (Equation 8-1). However, the latter model could not account for the interactive effects obtained when the credibilities of the two sources differ. Thus, considered in combination, these data are nicely consistent with the implications of an averaging formulation of the sort proposed by Anderson.

Perhaps the most provocative aspect of the data reported by Birnbaum et al. is that the patterns of results obtained in the two studies are virtually identical. This suggests that a similar process of information integration underlies judgments based upon both types of information. Our earlier speculations about the conditions conducive to averaging processes seemingly imply that averaging should occur in the used car task, but not in the person judgment task. (In the former task, the information consisted of two independent estimates of the car's value, both of which could not simultaneously be correct. This should presumably encourage averaging.) In retrospect, however, the judges' averaging of information in this particular person judgment task may be consistent with task demands. Each adjective in the description was identified as coming from a different source, and was presented with instructions that the sources might differ in their credibility. These factors may predispose judges to consider the implications of each adjective separately, rather than forming an integrated impression of the person described. Judges therefore may process this information in a similar manner to the information in the used car study, as the results of Birnbaum et al. suggest.

Effects of Instructional Set. The strongest support for averaging models that assume invariance in scale value (cf. Anderson, 1965) has generally been obtained when the instructions given subjects predispose them to treat each piece of information as a separate entity. For example, Anderson (1971b) instructed judges to assume "that each adjective had been contributed by a different acquaintance who knew the person well, that each adjective was accurate and equally important, that they should pay equal attention to each adjective, and that some inconsistencies might be expected because different

---

[3]If, in Equation 8-2, $w_O = 0$ and $w_i = w$ for all $i \neq 0$, the equation reduces to $J = \Sigma V_i / n$; that is, J is independent of the value of w.

acquaintances might see different aspects of the person's personality [p. 76]." Instructions used in other studies, while not always as detailed, have been similar in flavor (cf. Anderson, 1965, 1967; Anderson & Clavadetscher, 1976). In contrast, interactive effects that are less easily interpretable on the basis of an averaging formulation (Wyer & Dermer, 1968; Wyer & Watson, 1969; Wyer, 1974a) have usually been obtained under conditions in which judges were simply instructed to form an impression of a person described by the adjectives presented and then to indicate how well they would like such a person, without any further elaboration. These instructions seem less likely to predispose subjects to consider the implications of each adjective separately rather than reacting to the information as a configural whole.

Unfortunately, definitive tests of the effects of these instructional differences have not been performed at this writing. However, some research is indirectly relevant. First, in the aforementioned study by Birnbaum (1974), the judges whose ratings are shown in Fig. 8.1 were in fact instructed in much the same manner as that Wyer has used. In a follow-up study using the same stimuli (Birnbaum, 1974, Experiment 3), subjects were told to consider each adjective as having equal importance and accuracy, and as being contributed by a different acquaintance of the stimulus person. While the general pattern of effects was similar in the two studies, some of the rather marked deviations from simple averaging (e.g., the opposite effects of "impulsive" and "studious" when presented in the context of "refined" vs. "unpredictable") were substantially diminished when the more detailed instructions were used. As we have noted, these deviations may have been the result of a tendency to respond to the information configurally, and this tendency may have been attenuated by the "equal weighting" instructions.

Effects of Manner of Presenting Information. The conditions where algebraic processes are most likely are further circumscribed by Wyer's (1973b) study of grammatical context in which adjectives are presented. Here, judges estimated their liking for persons described by pairs of adjectives that were either (a) simply listed; (b) presented in a sentence connected by "and" (e.g., X is _____ and _____); or (c) presented in a sentence connected by "but" (X is _____ but _____). One adjective in each pair was high in normative likeableness and the other was low. Finally, some pairs of adjectives were inconsistent (as defined in terms of their probability of concurrence in the description of a single person) and other pairs were consistent. Relative to conditions in which they were simply listed, connecting adjectives by "and" increased the influence of the second of two consistent adjectives, but decreased the influence of the second of two inconsistent adjectives. However, connecting the same adjectives by "but" had the opposite effects. These data suggest that substantial differences may occur in the processing of information that is presented abstractly and the processing of information that is presented in a manner more similar to that occurring in everyday conversation.

A Counterintuitive Prediction.   As we have noted, unequivocal tests of algebraic models are difficult without an a priori knowledge of the value of certain parameters underlying the model. However, if an independent estimate of these parameters can be obtained, things simplify considerably. Hinkle (1976) has noted that if an independent estimate of the weight attached to different pieces of information is available, an intriguing implication of Equation 8-2 can be tested. As an example, suppose that, when considered in isolation, each piece of information in one set, A, yields the same judgment as each piece in a second set, B. However, suppose that A information is more ambiguous than B, or for other reasons has a lower absolute weight ($w_A < w_B$). Then Equation 8-2 predicts that the judgment based upon two or more pieces of the ambiguous (A) information will be more extreme than the judgment based upon an equal number of pieces of the less ambiguous (B) information. This may initially seem counterintuitive, since ambiguous information would normally be expected to be relatively less influential (see Chapter 5). However, note that for judgments based upon single pieces of A and B information to be the same despite the lower weight of A, the scale value of A must be *greater* than that of B. Equation 8-2 implies that differences in scale values are more influential than differences in weight when information is combined.[4]

---

[4]To see this, assume for simplicity that $V_O = 0$. Then, the judgment based upon one piece of A information alone and one piece of B information alone would be represented:

$$J_A = \frac{w_A V_A}{w_O + w_A} \quad \text{and} \quad J_B = \frac{w_B V_B}{w_O + w_B}.$$

Substituting the equivalent expressions for $w_A V_A$ and $w_B V_B$ in the theoretical expressions for judgments based upon n pieces of A information (J_{nA}) and n pieces of B information (J_{nB}),

$$J_{nA} = \frac{n w_A V_A}{w_O + n w_A} = \frac{n(w_O + w_A) J_A}{w_O + n w_A},$$

and

$$J_{nB} = \frac{n w_B V_B}{w_O + n w_B} = \frac{n(w_O + w_B) J_B}{w_O + n w_B}.$$

It therefore follows that $J_{nA} > J_{nB}$ whenever

$$\frac{n(w_O + w_A) J_A}{w_O + n w_A} > \frac{n(w_O + w_B) J_B}{w_O + n w_B}.$$

However since $J_A = J_B$, these terms cancel. Simplifying and reorganizing, it can be shown that this inequality will hold only if $w_A < w_B$. In other words, the collective composed of pieces of information with the lower absolute weight will yield the more extreme judgment.

To test the implications of this hypothesis, Hinkle constructed pairs of adjectives that elicited equally extreme liking ratings when presented in isolation, but differed in ambiguity as defined in Chapter 5. As predicted, judges rated persons described by pairs of ambiguous adjectives more extremely (either as more or less likeable, depending upon the favorableness of the attributes described) than they rated persons described by pairs that elicited similar ratings in isolation but were less ambiguous. While other formulations of information integration (e.g., Wyer, 1969a; 1973a) could conceivably account for these findings, several ad hoc assumptions would be required for them to do so. Hinkle's results take on additional importance since they suggest that the weight and scale value parameters in Equation 8-2 may in fact have some relation to the psychological processes underlying judgments. Unfortunately, however, few other examples exist in the literature.

Effects of Information Other than Trait Adjectives

The above discussion has focussed upon the effects of a single type of information (personality trait adjectives). The processes of making inferences based upon other types of information, and the applicability of an algebraic model for describing these processes, may differ from those of concern above. Some possible examples are noted below.

Attitude Similarity.   Byrne and his colleagues have investigated the effects of information bearing upon the attitudinal similarity of a judge and the person he is rating (for summaries, see Byrne, 1969, 1971). This research seems to show that judges' estimates of their liking for the target person are a function of the proportion rather than the number of similar attitudes (Byrne & Nelson, 1965). This finding contradicts the implications not only of a summative model but also of an averaging model that assumes an "initial impression" (V_O) is averaged with the implications of presented information. (Both models imply that judgments will increase in extremity with the number of equally favorable pieces of information presented.) The interpretation of much of this research is somewhat ambiguous, since possible differences over conditions in response scale usage have typically not been controlled (for an elaboration of alternative interpretations of similarity–attraction phenomena, see Wyer, 1974b, pp. 334–347). Nevertheless, Byrne's data suggest that judgments based upon attitudinal similarity involve somewhat different considerations than judgments based upon personality adjectives.

Behavioral Information.   In the typical adjective-combination task, several stimulus persons are rated by each judge. When information about a real person's behavior in a single situation is presented, configural responding is more likely. This possibility is indirectly supported by Aronson, Willerman, and Floyd's (1966) study of pratfall effects. Judges heard an interview with a job candidate whose responses created the impression that he was either extremely competent or extremely incompetent. After the interview, the candidate was offered a cup of coffee by the interviewer, and either spilled the coffee over his new suit or received the coffee without incident. When the candidate had created the impression of being incompetent, the additional information that he spilled his coffee decreased judges' estimates of how well they would like him. However, when the candidate otherwise responded as if he was competent, the information that he spilled his coffee increased liking for him. The directionally different effects of the coffee spill under the two conditions are difficult to explain meaningfully on the basis of either Equation 8-1 or Equation 8-2 without assuming that the evaluative implication (i.e., the scale value) of "spills coffee" differs as as function of its informational context.[5]

It seems likely that in this study, judges may have invoked script processing to predict how they would get along with the candidate. In the case of the otherwise extremely competent candidate, spilling coffee may have created the impression that the candidate was "human," and thus easier to get along with interpersonally than if he had no faults at all. In the case of the incompetent candidate, however, the same behavior may have elicited a vignette of a general buffoon, rendering him less likeable.

When two different types of information about a person are presented simultaneously, and thus the judge is more apt to treat them as different units, averaging processes should be more likely. Although evidence bearing on this possibility is not extensive, it is consistent with this supposition. Perhaps the most interesting study in this category, by Lampel and Anderson (1968), investigated the manner in which verbal and visual information combined to affect judgments. Specifically, female judges estimated the datability of male stimulus persons on the basis of personality adjectives varying in normative likeableness and photographs conveying different degrees of attractiveness. Data in this study were consistent with an averaging model in which the absolute weight of the verbal information is independent of its evaluative implications[6] but in which the visual information is assigned a weight that is inversely proportional to its scale value. In other words, the verbal

---

[5]It would also be possible to describe the results obtained in this study as indicating that the effect of information about the candidate's competence was greater when he spilled coffee than when he did not. This would be consistent with an averaging model if one assumes that "spills coffee" has a smaller absolute weight than "does not spill coffee". However, this does not make much psychological sense.

[6]Although nonsignificant, a close scrutiny of the data reveals that each adjective had somewhat less influence when the adjective accompanying it was negative than when it was positive, consistent with the conclusions drawn by Birnbaum (1974) that negative adjectives have greater absolute weight than do positive ones.

information had relatively more influence when the photograph accompanying it was attractive than when it was unattractive. This suggest that females considered the target's personality attributes when judging his datability only if he was physically attractive; if the target was unattractive, this was sufficient to make him a poor date, and personality factors had much less influence on judgments.

Effects of Information on Other Types of Judgments

The preceding discussion was generally restricted to a consideration of judgments of liking for a person. However, the results of research on other types of social judgments are also reasonably consistent with the notion that averaging processes are likely to be involved when the different pieces of information presented are likely to be treated as separate entities. A study by Oden and Anderson (1971) is representative. Three experiments were run. In one, judges estimated the favorableness of meals on the basis of information about the main course and the accompanying vegetable. In this case, the two kinds of information had nearly independent effects, suggesting that each kind received a weight that was independent of its scale value. In a second study, judges estimated the "badness" of pairs of criminals on the basis of information about the crime committed by each. Here, data supported an averaging model in which the weight of each crime increased with its seriousness. In the third study, judges estimated both the job effectiveness and likeableness of naval officers based upon information about both their scholastic performance and certain personality attributes. In judging liking, both types of information were weighted similarly. In judging effectiveness, however, the weight of the performance information increased as its implications became more unfavorable. This third study thus suggests an instance in which the information presented is weighted differently, depending upon the judgment to be made. All three studies were consistent with the implications of an averaging model. It seems intuitively reasonable to suppose that in each case, judges responded to the information presented as separate pieces rather than as a configuration, and that the process underlying the results obtained was, in fact, averaging.

However, not all research on the combined effects of different types of information can be accounted for by an averaging model unless one is willing to assume that the weights and scale values of the information presented are not independent. In a study by Sidowski and Anderson (1967), judges estimated their preferences for working as a doctor, lawyer, teacher, or accountant in each of four cities. The cities selected were assumed to vary in their attractiveness as a place to live. The effects of location on preferences for working in three of the professions (doctor, lawyer, or accountant) were virtually identical, as shown in Fig. 8.5. However, this effect on preferences

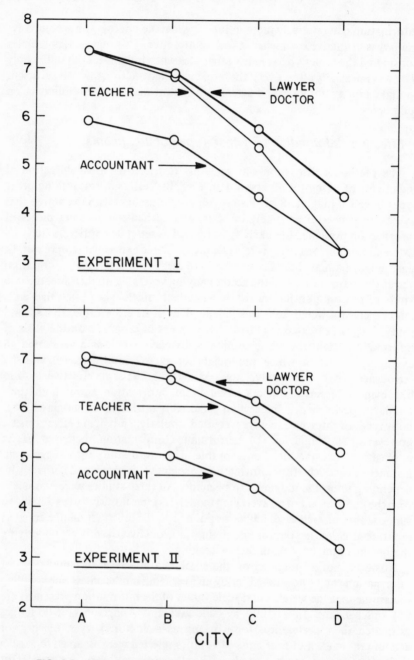

FIG. 8.5. Mean job preferences as a function of occupation and location (reprinted from Sidowski & Anderson, 1967, p. 279).

for working as a teacher differed; specifically, preferences were much more affected by unfavorable locations than by favorable ones. The effect of location on these ratings was not a constant multiple of its effect on preferences for working in other professions. Hence, the results could not be explained simply by assuming that a generally greater weight was attached to location when judging work as a teacher. Rather, one would have to assume that when teaching was evaluated, unlike other occupations, the absolute weight of location was an inverse function of its scale value. Thus, the relation between the weight and the scale value of a piece of information (location) would depend upon the nature of the other information accompanying it (occupation). Moreover, there is an alternative, equally plausible interpretation of the data. Sidowski and Anderson assume that occupation and geographic location are both characteristics with implications along a single judgmental dimension (preference). However, it is equally reasonable to suppose that judges consider different psychological dimensions of judgment when reporting preferences for different vocations, and that the geographical locations have different scale values along each. A similar possibility in another context has been suggested by Higgins and Rholes (1976). Despite this ambiguity, it is important to note that *both* explanations involve configural response processes different from those implied by an algebraic model.

Summary and Conclusions

The results of research in which algebraic models have been applied to judgments based upon information about a single element are frequently consistent with the implications of an averaging formulation of the form of Equation 8-2. However, this seems most typically the case when judges are given either an explicit or implicit set to treat the pieces of information presented as separate units. In many instances, this set may be induced by the type of information and the judgment to be made (as in the case of the used car study by Birnbaum et al. and the studies performed by Oden & Anderson). In other cases, it may be artificially induced by instructional manipulations and the manner in which the information is presented. This latter possibility is of particular concern in the area of person perception, since information about people may not normally be responded to in terms of discrete entities, but rather as a configural whole. Thus, much of the existing support for averaging models may not be relevant to judgments in more naturalistic circumstances. In those circumstances, inferences of liking for a person are likely to depend partly upon factors that are not taken into account in research of the sort described in this section—factors such as characteristics of the perceiver or judge himself, and the similarity of the judge's characteristics to those of the person being judged. These possibilities will be considered more fully later in this chapter.

Inferences Based Upon Information About More Than One Element

When the pieces of information relevant to a judgment concern different aspects of a situation, or in other ways are qualitatively different, their implications are more apt to be considered separately. As we noted earlier (p. 287), algebraic integration processes may be expected on a priori grounds to be more applicable in such instances than in many instances of the sort described in the preceding section. Unfortunately, little research is available in which algebraic models have been formally applied to such inferences. However, two recent studies provide examples of their potential utility. One, by Miller (1976), was concerned with the manner in which different aspects of an actor's behavior, and his personal appearance, combine to affect inferences of the actor's attitude. A second, by Wyer, Henninger, and Hinkle (1977) examined inferences about an actor's opinion (by both the actor and an observer) based upon information about the actor's advocacy of a position to another person, and about the other person's opinion. Both studies are instructive in evaluating the validity and utility of algebraic models with respect to inferences made in actual social situations. We will consider each in some detail.

In Miller's study, observers witnessed an actor deliver a speech either favoring or opposing amnesty. This was done under one of three conditions which were intended to manipulate the actor's responsibility for the content of the speech. In one, *Choice* condition, the actor was ostensibly to choose either position on the issue (pro-amnesty vs. anti-amnesty), to write an essay defending this position, and ultimately to read it aloud. In a second, *Assign* condition, the actor was instructed to write and read aloud an essay either favoring or opposing to amnesty without being given any choice over the position to be advocated. In the third, *Read* condition, the actor was simply handed a prepared essay, either favoring or opposing amnesty and ostensibly written by another person, and was asked to read it aloud. An additional variable in Miller's design was the appearance of the actor. Specifically, in some cases the actor was liberal-appearing (with beard and long hair), thus giving the impression that he might favor amnesty, while in other cases, he was conservative-appearing (no beard and short hair), thus giving the impression that he might oppose amnesty. The availability of the two types of information was varied in a partial factorial design. Specifically, appearance information was always available in choice and assign conditions; however, some subjects under read conditions were able to see the actor, while others could not. In still another condition, only appearance information was available; the actor's behavior in the situation was unknown. In all conditions, judges estimated the actor's personal belief in amnesty after receiving the stimulus information.

While the design of the study was complex, Miller notes that the effects of the informational variables on judgments may be conceptualized easily by applying an averaging model. To see this, first consider behavioral information. In fact, there are three aspects of this information: the actor's *decision* to read and write the essay, his writing of the essay (reflected in the *content* of the essay he has generated), and his *reading* of the essay. It is conceivable that each of these components may have implications for the judgment. That is, judges may infer from the actor's willingness to prepare the essay that he is favorable toward the position to be advocated; in addition, they may infer the strength of his opinion from the quality of the arguments he generates (essay content), and also from the forcefulness with which he reads it. Therefore, assuming for simplicity that the weight of the "initial impression" (w_O) is zero, and applying Equation 8-2, the combined effects of behavioral and appearance information could be represented as follows:

$$J = \frac{w_D V_D + w_C V_C + w_R V_R + w_A V_A}{w_D + w_C + w_R + w_A}$$

where V_D, V_C, V_R, and V_A, are scale values attached to the decision to make the speech, the content of the speech, the actor's reading of the speech, and the actor's appearance, respectively, and w_D, w_C, w_R, and w_A, are the absolute weights attached to this information, respectively. The various components of the behavior were not independently manipulated in this study, and so their implications for the judgment were similar in direction. Therefore, assume for simplicity that $V_D = V_C = V_R = V_B$, where V_B is the scale value of the behavior. The above equation then simplifies to:

$$J = \frac{(w_D + w_C + w_R)V_B + w_A V_A}{w_D + w_C + w_R + w_A}$$

It seems reasonable to suppose that the three behavioral conditions described above affect the weights attached to the decision, speech content, and delivery of the speech. Specifically, under Choice conditions, all three weights (w_D, w_C and w_R) should be greater than zero. Under Assign conditions, however, where the actor has no choice over the position advocated, $w_D = 0$, and under Read conditions, where the actor has no control over either the position advocated or the speech content, $w_D = w_C = 0$). This implies that the overall effect of the actor's behavior will be greatest under Choice conditions and least under Read conditions. However, the effect of the actor's appearance should be least in the former condition and greatest in the latter. In addition, the effect of the actor's appearance should be less when behavioral

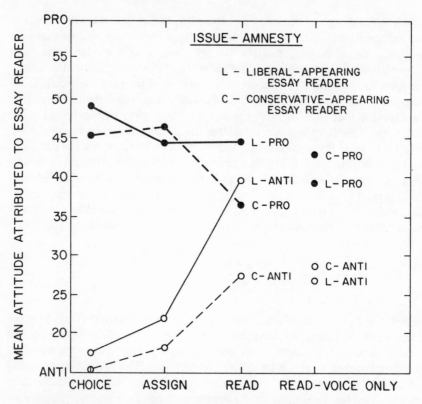

FIG. 8.6.   Mean attributions of attitude as a function of essay direction, constraint level, and target person, including data from voice-only conditions (reprinted from Miller, 1976, p. 331).

information is available (i.e., under Read conditions, where $w_R > 0$) than when it is not (i.e., $w_D = w_C = w_R = 0$). Finally, the effect of the actor's reading the essay (V_R) should be less when appearance information is available ($w_A > 0$) than when it is not ($w_A = 0$).

Results are perfectly consistent with the above hypotheses. Observers' judgments of the actor's attitude are shown in Fig. 8.6 as a function of the position advocated (pro. vs. anti) and behavioral conditions. Clearly, the effect of the behavioral information decreases as the number of relevant aspects of this behavior decreases. However, the effect of the actor's appearance is substantially greater under Read conditions than under conditions in which more behavioral information is available. Finally, the effect of reading the essay was greater under Read–voice-only conditions, in which appearance information was absent ($w_A = 0$), than under Read conditions where the actor's appearance was known.

The Role of Self-Perceptions in Judgments of Others

Miller's study demonstrates the usefulness of an averaging formulation in *describing* the manner in which information affects judgments in role-playing situations. However, the application of this model does not help very much to pinpoint the actual inference processes that may underlie these effects. Perhaps the most intriguing aspect of Miller's data was evidence that the actor's speech affected judgments of his attitude even under Read conditions, despite the fact that the actor had no responsibility whatsoever for the content of the speech. One explanation for this is that a person who reads a speech in a convincing manner (i.e., like someone who believes what he is saying) is attributed an attitude consistent with the advocated position for this reason, regardless of whether he personally wrote the speech. However, there are other possibilities. Yandell and Insko (1977) raise the interesting hypothesis that a person who hears a speech uses himself and his reactions to this speech as bases for judging others and their reactions. Thus, if the listener is himself persuaded by the content of the speech, he may assume that anyone else who has heard the speech (including the speaker) will be similarly persuaded.

To explore these possibilities, Yandell and Insko had observers witness a speaker deliver a speech to a listener, after which they estimated pertinent attitudes of (a) the speaker; (b) the listener; (c) themselves and (d) a person who had not heard the speech. The speaker had no control over either the content of the speech or the position advocated. Judgments of the speaker's and listener's attitudes were affected similarly, indicating that the speaker's actual behavior of delivering the speech was not used as a basis for inferring his attitude. However, both of these judgments were also similar to the observer's self-judgment of his attitude. On the other hand, the observer's judgment of the attitude held by people who did not hear the speech was unaffected. In combination, these data suggest that the speech influenced observers' own attitudes toward the position advocated, and that this effect mediated their judgments of others who had also been exposed to the speech content. The fact that the effect did not generalize to ratings of people who had not heard the speech suggests that judges did not simply project their self-ratings on others. Rather, their use of their self-judgments as a basis for rating others depended upon whether these others had had comparable experiences. These results provide a useful insight into the dynamics of attributions about others in attitude change situations. More generally, they point out that algebraic models, while useful descriptive tools, are at best only a preliminary step in understanding these dynamics. It would of course be possible to interpret Yandell and Insko's results after the fact in terms of the differential weight attached to the actor's behavior in making inferences about oneself and others. However, to do so would have questionable conceptual value, and in some cases would be misleading.

Actors' vs. Observers' Attitude Attributions: Further Considerations

In Miller's study, judgments were made by persons who were themselves not involved in the situation they were observing. It may be unjustified to generalize the implications of these findings to conditions where the judge is a participant in the situation about which judgments are made. We have already noted some contingencies affecting the similarity of actor's self-judgments to judgments of the actor made by others (see Chapters 2 and 5). However, the process of combining this information to arrive at these judgments may also differ.

A study by Wyer, Henninger, and Hinkel (1977) bears on this question, and also on the manner in which behavioral information and information about others' opinions combine to affect judgments of the actor's opinion. In this study, actors prepared and delivered a speech to an unseen audience. The speech either supported a target proposition, opposed this proposition, or pertained to an unrelated control proposition. Moreover, some actors either were led to believe that their audience favored or opposed the target proposition, while others were given no relevant information about the audience's belief. After exposure to a given combination of the above conditions, actors reported their own belief in the test proposition, and also predicted how their audience would judge their belief. The entire scenario was witnessed by a disinterested observer (not the audience), who then also estimated the actor's belief in the test proposition.

The above design enabled the effect of each type of information when presented alone to be compared to its effect when relevant information of the other type was also available. An averaging model implies that in each case, the effect of each type of information on judgments should decrease when information of the other type is added. Data presented in Figs. 8.7 and 8.8 bear upon these predictions. First, consider the effects of information on observers' judgments, which are shown in the third panel of each figure. In each case, the effect of the one type of information was somewhat less when relevant information of the other type was available (pooled over "pro" and "anti" conditions) than when it was not. While these differences were not statistically significant, they are consistent in direction with an averaging model and with the implications of Miller's results. However, the effects of the same information on actors' self-judgments, shown in the first panel of each figure, are clearly *not* consistent with an averaging model. Specifically, the effect of the actor's behavior on his self-judgments is virtually identical, regardless of whether information about the audience's opinion was available, while the effect of the audience's opinion on the actor's self-judgments was non-significantly *greater* when behavioral information was present than when it was absent. These data suggest that different processes

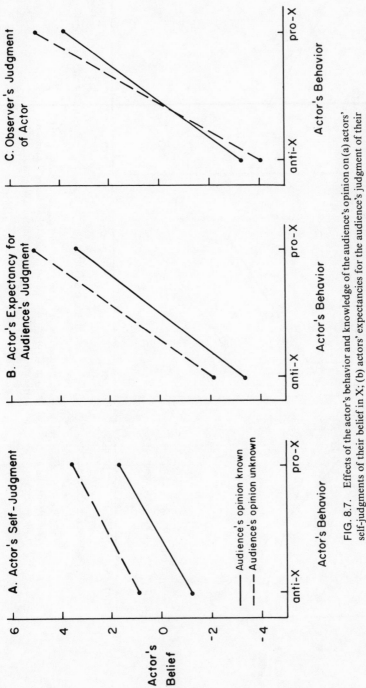

FIG. 8.7.　Effects of the actor's behavior and knowledge of the audience's opinion on (a) actors' self-judgments of their belief in X; (b) actors' expectancies for the audience's judgment of their belief; and (c) observers' judgments of the actor's belief (reprinted from Wyer et al., 1977, p. 209).

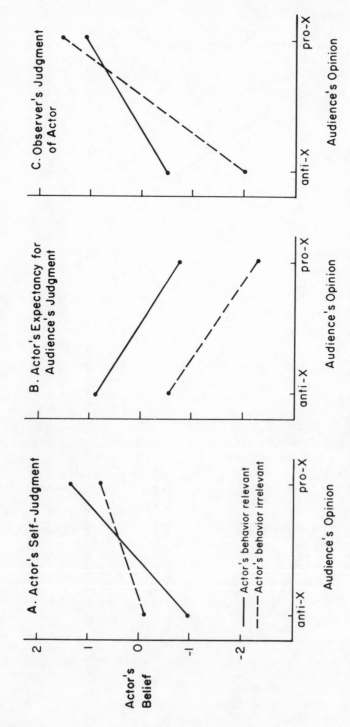

FIG. 8.8. Effects of the audience's opinion and the relevance of the actor's behavior on (a) actors' self-judgments of their belief in X; (b) actors' expectancies for the audience's judgment of their belief; and (c) observers' judgments of the actor's belief (reprinted from Wyer et al., 1977, p. 210).

may underlie an actor's use of information to make self-judgments than underlie others' use of the same information to judge the actor. Moreover, the former processes do not involve averaging.

A second aspect of the data in Fig. 8.7 points out the different assumptions that may underlie the use of information in making different types of inferences. Specifically, the audience's opinion had positive effects upon the actor's self-judgments and also upon observers' judgments of him, but had a negative effect on the actor's expectancy for how the audience would judge his belief. Thus, both actors and observers may take the audience's opinion as an indication of the position considered socially desirable by college students (the subjects used in the study), and may then generalize this opinion to the actor as well. At the same time, the actor may expect the audience to use its own opinion as a standard of comparison in judging, producing a contrast effect of the audience's opinion on the actor's expectancies for how he will be evaluated. Although this doesn't seem too surprising, an interpretation of these data in terms of an averaging model would require the assumption that the "scale value" of the audience's opinion differs not only in magnitude but also in direction, depending upon whether the judge is rating himself or is predicting another's rating of him.

Configural Cues.   A potential difficulty in applying algebraic models to inferences based upon information about several different elements arises when different pieces of information may, in combination, form a configural cue that contributes to judgments independently of the cues provided by each piece of information in isolation. For example, the separate piece of information about the actor's advocacy of a position and the audience's opinion on the issue could in combination be interpreted as a single unit, pertaining to whether the actor agrees or disagrees with his audience. There was no evidence in the study by Wyer et al. that such a cue contributed to judgments.[7]

For example, suppose a judge receives information that a female actor performs well on an achievement task and that her partner, a male, has also succeeded. In this event, P's behavior could be interpreted as "performed well," as "performed at a level similar to her partner," or as "performed at a level likely to receive disapproval from member of the partner's sex." Evidence that such cues may contribute simultaneously to judgments of the actor has been reported by Wyer, Henninger, and Wolfson (1975). This

---

[7]Supplementary analyses of judgments as a function of position advocated by the actor (pro or anti) and the audience's opinion (pro or anti) yielded no significant interactions involving these variables.

research also indicates that these cues may contribute to different degrees, depending upon the attribute being judged and whether the judge is the actor or a disinterested observer. Note that the contributions of the latter two cues could not be predicted from knowledge of the contribution of each type of information (i.e., the actor's sex, the actor's performance, the partner's sex, and the partner's performance) considered separately. This fact does not negate the possibility that an averaging process underlies the inferences made in such situations. However, it points out that when applying a formal averaging model, one must take into account the possibility that the judgment is a weighted average of the implications of configural cues as well as the scale values of each piece of presented information when considered in isolation. This possibility has seldom if ever been recognized in applications of Equation 8-2 and its derivatives.

Some Interpretative Ambiguities

While the research described above provides some evidence for the applicability of algebriac descriptions of inference processes in complex situations, caution must be taken in applying them without a careful a priori consideration of the psychological processes that may underlie the inferences being investigated. Unless this is done, conclusions drawn by applying these models can be misleading.

Research on the effect of an actor's behavior on inferences of his beliefs illustrates these possible ambiguities. Much of this research has been concerned with the effect of offering an incentive to engage in behavior on the judge's perception of the implications of this behavior. For example, suppose an actor is asked to deliver a speech favoring abortion, either voluntarily (for no pay) or for pay of $10. If the actor agrees to do so, this decision may be interpreted as an indication that the actor personally favors abortion. However, this interpretation is more likely when the external incentive for manifesting the behavior is low than when it is high, and thus the actor should be attributed a more favorable attitude toward abortion in the former conditions (e.g., +5) than in the latter (e.g., +1). This tendency has been found in many studies (e.g., Brehm & Cohen, 1962; Calder, Ross, & Insko, 1973).

Alternatively, suppose the actor refuses to deliver the speech. In this case, his refusal may be interpreted as an indication that he personally opposes abortion. However, this interpretation is more likely to be made when he has lost $10 by refusing than when he has lost nothing at all, and thus he should be judged as more opposed to abortion in the high pay condition (e.g., -5) than in the low pay condition (-1). This has also been empirically demonstrated (Darley & Cooper, 1972).

The explanation of each set of hypothetical results described above assumes that the judge's interpretation of the behavior (and therefore the behavior's effect on his judgment) differs under the two incentive conditions. However, suppose we combine the two sets of data in a single 2 × 2 table showing judgments of the actor's attitude toward abortion as a function of the actor's behavior (agrees vs. refuses) and the incentive offered ($10 vs. no pay). These data (see Table 8.1) would suggest that the two variables, behavior and incentive, have independent effects. That is, the actor is judged to be more favorable toward abortion if he agrees to advocate it than if he refuses, regardless of the incentive offered. Moreover, he is attributed a less favorable attitude toward abortion if he has been offered $10 than if he has been offered nothing, regardless of the behavior he has manifested. This independent effect of incentive is not implausible; the amount of pay offered the actor to advocate a position may be interpreted by the judge (either an observer or the actor himself) as an indication of the extent to which the actor is expected to be unwilling to advocate the position voluntarily, and thus of his personal opposition to the position (for an elaboration of this argument, see Wyer, 1974b).

The two alternative explanations of the incentive effects described above cannot be distinguished on the basis of the data in Table 8.1 alone. There are two implications of this analysis. First, unless an actor's behavior is manipulated along with the external incentive for engaging in this behavior, one cannot unequivocally verify that the incentive has affected judgments because of its mediating influence on the interpretation given to the behavior; it may have a direct effect on judgments independently of how the behavior is interpreted. By the same token, results such as those shown in Table 8.1 would not necessarily indicate that judges *do* consider the implications of behavior and incentive independently and combine them in some additive fashion; this could occur even if the incentive information *does* affect the interpretation of the actor's behavior, contrary to assumptions typically underlying the application of a simple algebraic model.

TABLE 8.1
Hypothetical Effects of the Incentive Offered to
Advocate a Position, and Compliance vs.
Noncompliance With This Request, on Attitudes Toward
the Position Advocated

	High Pay	No Pay
Actor complies	+1	+5
Actor refuses to comply	–5	–1

8.3 AN ALTERNATIVE APPROACH

Although the research findings summarized in the preceding sections are often consistent with an algebraic formulation of social inference, many instances occur in which these models seem inapplicable; that is, the models either cannot account for the observed data, or the psychological implications of fitting the model to the data are implausible. The conditions in which an algebriac model is most likely to describe inference processes may be understood through a general conceptualization of the conditions under which judges are likely to analyze available information into separate units and to consider separate implications of each, rather than responding to the information as a configuration. In many instances, as in much of the research on the effect of personality adjectives on liking, the tendency to treat each piece of information as a separate unit may be artificially induced through aspects of the experimental procedure typically used to test algebraic models. In these cases, the methodology may have actually created the phenomena the models are assumed to describe. In other cases, however, where the information presented pertains to different sources, the tendency may exist naturally, even in the absence of methodological artifacts.

The problems we have raised concerning the application of algebraic models to social inference phenomena typically stem from the failure to attend adequately to the assumptions that may underlie judges' use of presented information. A related shortcoming is the failure to take into account the fact that a given piece of information may contribute to judgments in a variety of ways simultaneously, depending upon the configuration of other information accompanying it. In the latter instances, the implications of these configural cues may also be combined algebraically with the implications of separate pieces of information. However, in the algebraic formulations we have discussed so far, there is no way to conceptualize a priori the nature of these cues, nor is there a way to isolate their contributions after the fact.

Fortunately, approaches have been developed that potentially take into account these possibilities, while still retaining many of the more desirable features of an algebraic formulation. Of these, perhaps the most promising is the "subject–verb–object (S–V–O)" model of social cognition proposed by Harry Gollob (1974b). This formulation is of particular value when applied to inferences based upon information about several different elements of a social interaction situation. According to this formulation, the information in such a situation is analyzed into a number of information *cues.* Some of these cues reflect the implications of different pieces of information in isolation, while others reflect the implications of configurations of information. A judge's use of a given cue is presumably based upon a specific assumption the judge makes about the implications of the cue for the particular characteristic to be inferred. Using the methodology suggested by this conceptualization, the independent contributions of these cues to inferences may theoretically be isolated and compared over different situational conditions.

S–V–O concepts and methodology have been used successfully to identify the informational determinants of judgments of an actor's attributes (Rossman & Gollob, 1976; Wyer, 1974b; Wyer, Henninger, & Wolfson, 1975), of his behavior toward another person (Rossman & Gollob, 1976; Wyer, 1974b, 1975b), and of the object toward whom the behavior is directed (Rossman & Gollob, 1976; Wyer, 1974b). This work has addressed theoretical and empirical issues in a variety of areas, including social evaluation and impression formation (Gollob, 1968; Wyer, 1975b; Wyer & Hinkle, 1976), cognitive balance phenomena (Gollob, 1974a,b; Rossman & Gollob, 1976), and attribution (Wyer et al., 1975). In this section we will first present the general approach in some detail and will then demonstrate its potential value in diagnosing inference phenomena.

Description of the Method

Gollob (1974b) notes that the essential features of an interaction involving two persons, P and O, may be conveyed in a single subject–verb–object sentence of the form "$attr_P$ P *verbs* $attr_O$ O," where $attr_P$ is either a positive (p) or negative (n) pole of a bipolar attribute dimension along which P is described, $attr_O$ is a pole of a dimension along which O is described, and the verb is a pole of the behavioral dimension used to describe P's reactions to O. (While the formulation may be easily extended to include elements of a situation other than P, O, and P's behavior, for the moment we will restrict our attention to just these three.) These dimensions may be either bipolar (*kind/cruel, male/female, helps/harms*) or unipolar (*kind/not kind,* or *helps/does not help*). If the values along these dimensioins are denoted p (positive) and n (negative),[8] then any sentence composed of values along the subject, verb, and object dimensions may be characterized simply in terms of this notation. For example, if the subject, verb, and object dimensions are *kind (p)/cruel (n), helps (p)/harms (n),* and *kind (p)/ cruel (n),* respectively, the sentence "kind P harms cruel O" would be denoted *pnn*. Eight sentences may be constructed from values along a given set of subject, verb, and object dimensions. The information contained in each of these sentences often may be analyzed into seven independent cues that a judge might use to make an

---

[8]The use of "positive" and "negative" to denote the poles of a dimension does not, in this context, necessarily carry with it any implications that the characteristics described by these poles are either favorable or unfavorable. When the poles of a dimension do have evaluative implications, it is often convenient to denote the favorable pole by p. However, in many instances the evaluative implications are unclear, if they exist at all.

inference. The use of each cue is hypothetically tied to a particular assumption the judge makes about its implications for the specific judgment to be made.

S–V–O concepts and methodology may be applied in two general types of inference situations. In one, information is available along all three (subject, verb, and object) dimensions, and the judge is asked to infer a general characteristic of the situation described (i.e., its likelihood of occurring, its pleasantness, etc.). In other cases, the judge may be asked to infer a characteristic of a specific element in the situation on the basis of information available about this and other elements (e.g., to infer the kindness of P on the basis of information that P has harmed someone (O) described as unkind). In these latter situations, not all seven cues are relevant to the judgment being made. Therefore, to illustrate the approach under conditions in which all seven cues are potentially relevant, we will initially consider the first type of inference situation.

An Illustrative Example

Suppose a judge is presented each of the eight sentences formed by combining values along the subject, verb and object dimensions described above: *kind (p)/cruel (n), helps (p)/harms (n),* and *kind (p)/cruel (n),* respectively. In each case he is asked to infer the likelihood that the situation described by the sentence would actually occur. Several assumptions may potentially underlie these judgments, each of which would lead to the use of a different informational cue. These assumptions are described below, in each case accompanied by an indication of how to assess the contribution of the cue corresponding to it.

1. and 2. The judge may assume that social interactions involving kind persons are more apt to occur than those involving cruel persons. To this extent, he should judge the four situations (sentences) in which $attr_P$ is *kind* (the sentence, *ppp, ppn, pnp,* and *pnn*) to be more likely to occur on the average than the four situations in which $attr_P$ is *cruel (npp, npn, nnp,* and *nnn).* Moreover, he should judge the four situations in which $attr_O$ is *kind* (*ppp, pnp, npp,* and *nnp*) to be more likely on the average than the four situations in which $attr_O$ is *cruel (ppn, pnn, npn,* and *nnn).* Gollob (1974a,b) has named the informational cues corresponding to these differences *S-bias* and *O-bias,* respectively, to denote the parts of the sentence (subject and object, respectively) from which the information is drawn. (Note: Here and subsequently, the terms "bias" as used by Gollob and "informational cue" are synonymous.)

3. The judge may assume that people are more apt to help others than to harm them, regardless of who these people are. To this extent, the judge should base his judgments only upon P's behavior and thus should judge the

four situations in which P helps O (*ppp,ppn,npp,* and *npn*) to be more likely on the average than the four situations in which P harms O) *pnp, pnn, nnp,* and *nnn*). The informational cue to which this difference pertains is labeled *V-bias*.

4. The judge may assume that people are more likely to behave in a way that is consistent with their general attributes than to behave in a manner inconsistent with their attributes. To this extent, he should judge situations in which kind people help and cruel people harm (*ppp, ppn, nnp,* and *nnn*) to be more likely on the average than situations in which kind people harm and cruel people help (*pnp, pnn, npp,* and *npn*). The cue to which this difference pertains is denoted *SV-bias,* since it is a "configural" cue, defined in terms of values along subject and verb dimensions in combination.

5. The judge may assume that people in a given situation are more likely to be similar in personality than to be dissimilar, regardless of their behavior toward one another. In other words, he may assume that "birds of a feather flock together." To this extent, he should judge the four situations in which P and O are both described as kind or are both described as cruel (*ppn, pnp, npn,* and *nnn*) to be more likely on the average than the four in which the descriptions of P and O differ (*ppn, pnn,npp,* and *nnp*). The cue to which this difference pertains is labeled *SO-bias*.

6. The judge may assume that people are likely to be treated in the way they deserve. To this extent, he should judge situations in which a kind O is helped or a cruel O is harmed (*ppp, pnn, npp,* and *nnn*) to be more likely on the average than the four situations in which a kind O is harmed or a cruel O is helped (*ppn, pnp, npn,* and *nnp*). The cue to which this difference pertains is denoted *VO-bias*.

7. Finally, the judge may assume that the likelihood of people helping one another increases with their similarity, while the likelihood of people harming one another increases with their dissimilarity. To this extent, he should judge the two situations in which a kind P helps a kind O or harms a cruel O (*ppp* and *pnn*), and those in which a cruel P helps a cruel O or harms a kind O (*npn* and *nnp*), to be more likely on the average than the remaining four situations (*ppn, pnp, npp,* and *nnn*). The cue to which this difference pertains, which involves the consideration of values along all three dimensions, is labeled *SVO-bias*.

The seven informational cues described above are summarized in Table 8.2. In each case, the contribution of the cue is inferred from the difference between the mean judgment of the four sentences denoted +1 and the mean judgment of the four sentences denoted −1 in the column to which the cue pertains. In the particular example we have constructed, it seems intuitively likely that the difference corresponding to the contributions of these cues would be positive. In general, however, this is not necessarily the case. For instance, a negative contribution of *VO*-bias in our example would simply

TABLE 8.2
Contrasts Corresponding to Informational Cues Extracted Using S–V–O Methodology

Sentence Type	S-bias	V-bias	O-bias	SV-bias	SO-bias	VO-bias	SVO-bias	Hypothetical Judgment
ppp	+1	+1	+1	+1	+1	+1	+1	8
ppn	+1	+1	−1	+1	−1	−1	−1	5
pnp	+1	−1	+1	−1	+1	−1	−1	1
pnn	+1	−1	−1	−1	−1	+1	+1	4
npp	−1	+1	+1	−1	−1	+1	−1	4
npn	−1	+1	−1	−1	+1	−1	+1	3
nnp	−1	−1	+1	+1	−1	−1	+1	5
nnn	−1	−1	−1	+1	+1	+1	−1	6

suggest that the judge assumes that people are *less* likely to get what they deserve than not. Whether a cue contributes positively or negatively depends primarily upon the somewhat arbitrary designation of the poles of the dimensions involved as *p* or *n*. While the direction of any given cue is used to identify the assumption possibly underlying its use, the degree to which the cue is actually used is inferred from the magnitude of the contrast corresponding to it, independently of sign. The association between the use of an informational cue and the assumption underlying its use must be inferred by the experimenter, but may be validated empirically using other assessment procedures (for example, the judge's self-reports).

The assumptions that underlie the use of different cues are obviously not incompatible; two or more may contribute simultaneously to the judgment being made. In fact, it is clear from Table 8.2 that the differences used to assess the contributions of these cues are orthogonal. Each difference corresponds to one of the seven orthogonal contrasts (main effects and interactions) in a 2^3 factorial analysis of variance of judgments as a function of values along the subject, verb, and object dimensions. The judgment of any sentence i (J_i) may therefore be expressed as a linear function fo the contributions of these cues:

$$J_i = k_S v_{S,i} + k_V v_{V,i} + k_O v_{O,i} + k_{SV} v_{SV,i} + k_{SO} v_{SO,i} + k_{VO} v_{VO,i} + k_{SVO} v_{SVO,i} + k_o \qquad (8\text{-}3)$$

where $v_{S,i}$, $v_{V,i}$, etc. are the values of each cue (either +1 or −1) shown in Table 8.2 for sentence i; k_S, k_V, etc. are regression weights corresponding to the contribution of the cue;[9] and k_o is a constant.

To give a concrete example, suppose a given judge's estimates of the likelihood of the situation described in each of the eight sentences are those

---

[9]The regression weight corresponding to a given cue is equal to half the difference between the mean judgment of sentences in which the cue is positive (denoted +1 in Table 8.2) and the mean judgment of sentences in which the cue is negative (denoted −1).

shown in the last column of Table 8.2. Based upon these data, SV-bias contributes most (k_{SV} = 1.5), followed by VO-bias (k_{VO} = 1.0), SVO-bias (k_{SVO} = .5), and V-bias (k_V = .5), with the remaining cues contributing nothing. These contributions suggest that the judge based his estimates primarily upon the assumption that people are more likely to behave in a manner consistent with their general attributes than to behave in a way inconsistent with these attributes (SV-bias). However, several other assumptions also contribute to lesser degrees. These are the assumptions that people are more likely than not to get what they deserve (VO-bias), that similar people are more likely to help one another than to harm one another (SVO-bias), and that people are generally more apt to help than to harm others (V-bias).

Statistically, the approach described here is simply an application of the general linear model, and as such is hardly novel. However, it often leads to different interpretations of data of the sort obtained in many studies of social inference. For example, while the contrast pertaining to SV-bias is tested statistically as the interaction of subject and verb characteristics in a standard analysis of variance, it is interpreted as psychologically equivalent to a "main effect"; that is, it is postulated to reflect the use of a single informational cue, based upon a single underlying assumption.

The assumptions underlying the use of each cue obviously vary with the particular type of judgment to be made and the particular set of dimensions along which the actor, the object, and the actor's behavior are described. Thus, there is no a priori reason to expect the relative contributions of different cues to generalize over all dimensions of judgment or over all types of information about the elements involved. For example, if judgments were to be made of the pleasantness of the situations described in the preceding example rather than of their likelihood of occurrence, certain of the above assumptions might not apply. And if the subject, verb, and object dimensions were *male (p)/female (n), supports women's liberation (p)/opposes women's liberation (n)*, and *liberal (p)/conservative (n)*, respectively, the assumptions underlying the use of the seven cues, and thus their relative contributions to judgments, would differ considerably from their contributions in the preceding example. Indeed, certain of these cues, if defined in the manner described above, might not be psychologically meaningful. We will elaborate on this matter presently.

Inferences About Specific Elements

S–V–O methodology may also be applied to inferences about one component of a sentence (i.e., the subject, verb, or object) based upon information about the other two. Such applications are more directly relevant to the issues of concern in this paper. Again restricting our considerations to the actor P, the object O, and P's reactions to O, three types of inferences may be defined: *subject* inferences, or inferences of an attribute of an actor from information about the object and the actor's behavior toward the object; *object* inferences, or inferences of an attribute of the object from information about the actor and his behavior toward the object; and *verb* inferences, or judgments of an actor's behavior toward an object based on information about the attributes of the actor and the object. To apply the formulation in each case, inferences must be made pertaining to each pole of the dimension describing the element being judged. Moreover, these judgments must be made at each combination of values along the dimensions describing the other two elements. Then any given inference may be described as a linear function of the informational cues defined in Table 8.2 (see Equation 8-3).

To illustrate this, suppose a judge in our hypothetical example infers both the likelihood that an actor P is *kind (p)* and the likelihood that he is *cruel (n)*, in each case based upon information that P either *helps (p)* or *harms (n)* another person O and that O is either *kind (p)* or *cruel (n)*. These "subject" inferences might be based upon several assumptions, some but not all of which are similar to those described in our previous example:

1. The judge may assume that people in general are more apt to be kind than cruel. To the extent this assumption is made, *S*-bias will contribute to his judgments.

2. The judge may assume that helping is an indication of kindness, and harming is an indication of cruelty. To the extent this assumption is made, the judge should infer P's characteristics from information about his behavior alone, and *SV*-bias will contribute positively to judgments.

3. The judge may assume that "birds of a feather flock together," that is, that people are apt to be similar to others in the situations in which they find themselves. To this extent, P's attributes will be inferred to be similar to O's, and *SO*-bias will contribute positively to inferences. On the other hand, it is also conceivable that characteristics of O may be used as a standard for comparison, and therefore produce a contrast effect; that is, as O appears more kind, P may be judged less kind by comparison. In this event, *SO*-bias would contribute negatively.

4. The judge may assume that help to kind people and harm to cruel people (thus preventing them from manifesting their cruelty) are beneficial to mankind, so that people who manifest this behavior are therefore kind, whereas help to cruel people and harm to kind ones have undesirable consequences, so that people who manifest this behavior are cruel. Or, he may assume that people are apt to be similar to those they help and dissimilar to those they harm. If either assumption is made, *SVO*-bias will contribute positively to inferences. The tendencies to invoke these two alternative assumptions cannot be distinguished without additional information.

TABLE 8.3
Summary of Informational Cues Likely to Contribute to Subject,
Verb, and Object Inferences

Informational Cue	Subject Inference (About P)	Verb Inference (About B)	Object Inference (About O)
S-bias	X		
V-bias		X	
O-bias			X
SV-bias	X	X	
SO-bias	X		X
VO-bias		X	X
SVO-bias	X	X	X

Note: Cues likely to contribute to each inference are denoted by "X" in the column pertaining to the inference.

While other cues (V-bias, O-bias, and VO-bias) could in principle be defined, they are not psychologically meaningful. For example, a positive contribution of V-bias to subject inferences would imply that P is judged *both* more kind and more cruel when he helps O than when he harms O. This would not make much sense. In general, cues that do not involve the sentence component being judged are not psychologically meaningful and should theoretically not contribute to judgments. This notion has been formalized by Gollob (1974b) as the *relevant bias* (cue) *hypothesis*. In fact, the contributions of theoretically irrelevant cues have been found empirically to be small and nonsignificant (Gollob, 1974a, b; Rossman & Gollob, 1976; Wyer, 1975b).

The cues expected to be typically relevant to subject, verb and object inferences are summarized in Table 8.3. This table shows that while certain cues are apt to contribute to only one type of inference, others may contribute to inferences of two or more types. Thus, the S-V-O formulation provides a mechanism for conceptualizing and comparing inferences about different elements of a social interaction in terms of a common set of contributing factors.

The Integration of Informational Cues

Equation 8-3 describes judgments as a linear function of the orthogonal contrasts comprising an analysis of variance of judgments as a function of values along subject, verb and object dimensions. In this equation, $v_{j,i}$ is analogous to the scale value of j as defined in the algebraic models described earlier in this chapter. The contribution of the cue (k_j), as inferred from the magnitude of the appropriate contrast described in Table 8.2, is analogous to the weight of the cue (w). However, it is unclear on a priori grounds whether the weights attached to these cues are absolute (see Equation 8-1) or relative (Equation 8-2).

A related consideration in applying S–V–O methodology concerns the independence of informational cues. Although the contrasts used to infer the contributions of different informational cues are orthogonal, this does not mean that the contribution of each cue is *psychologically* independent of the contribution of others. A judge's tendency to use a given piece of information in making a judgment is very likely to depend upon the amount and type of other information available to him. In fact, when a large amount of information is available, the evidence suggests that a judge will base his inference on only a few cues that he believes to be the most reliable indicators of the characteristic to be judged; moreover, the particular cue that contributes most to his judgment is apt to vary with the dimensions used in presenting information and recording judgments (Gollob, 1974b; Rossman & Gollob, 1976; Wyer, 1974b).

Some insight can be gained into the manner in which different cues are combined to affect judgments by using procedures similar to those described earlier in this chapter. For example, if the contributions of S-bias and SV-bias to subject inferences (k_S and k_{SV} as defined in Equation 8-3) are unaffected when information along an object dimension is added, this would suggest a summative process of information integration. If the contributions of these cues decrease when object dimension is added, but their relative magnitudes (reflected by the ratio k_S/k_{SV}) are unaffected, this would suggest an averaging process of integration. Finally, if the relative contributions of S-bias and SV-bias change when additional information was added, it would suggest a discounting process whereby the new information decreases the attention paid to some but not all other available cues.

Interpretational Considerations

Two related and important considerations should be raised at this point. First, as we noted earlier, not every orthogonal contrast that may be extracted using S–V–O methodology is interpretable as a psychologically meaningful informational cue. For example, it would be hard to interpret the contribution of VS-bias under conditions in which V is the dimension *defeats (p)/loses to (n)* and O is the dimension *honest (p)/dishonest (n)*. (That is, what assumption would lead a judge to infer that actors who defeat honest persons and lose to dishonest persons differ from those who defeat dishonest persons and lose to honest ones?) Contrasts that cannot be meaningfully tied to

TABLE 8.4
Hypothetical Judgments of the Likelihood of
Occurrence of a Situation Involving Persons P and O as
a Function of P's Behavior and Attributes of O

	O's Attribute	
	Kind (p)	Cruel (n)
P helps O (p)	10	8
P harms O (n)	5	7

particular assumptions a judge might make are less likely to contribute significantly to his judgment. On the other hand, a contrast that *is* significant does not necessarily reflect the contribution of the informational cue corresponding to it. Instead, it could indicate that the use of another cue is contingent upon the information accompanying it. (In the example above, the contrast corresponding to VO-bias could mean that the contribution of V-bias, or the weight attached to behavioral information, depends upon whether O was described as honest or dishonest.)

This observation makes salient an implicit assumption underlying the application of S–V–O methodology. That is, the application of Equation 8-3 requires that the contribution of each informational cue to judgments be the same, independent of its context (that is, regardless of the particular combination of values presented along S, V, and O). This assumption is equivalent to the assumption made in early applications of Anderson's averaging model (Anderson, 1965, 1967) that the absolute weight attached to each piece of presented information is invariant over stimulus combinations. As we have pointed out, such an assumption is often invalid under the conditions in which averaging models are often applied (cf. Birnbaum, 1974). However, its validity in applications of S–V–O methodology has not been established.

The failure to establish constancy of contributions of cues over stimulus situations can result in interpretative ambiguities. Suppose a judge is asked to infer the likelihood of occurrence of situations in which an actor (P) is described as either helping or harming another, O, who is either kind or cruel. Hypothetical judgments at each combination of values of these verb and object dimensions are those shown in Table 8.4. Applying S–V–O methodology, the contributions of V-bias, O-bias and VO-bias would be +3, 0 and +2, respectively. This would suggest that judgments are based upon two independent assumptions: that situations where people help others are more apt to occur than situations where people harm others (V-bias), and that situations where people promote socially desirable outcomes (i.e., by helping kind people and harming cruel ones) are more apt to occur than situations where people promote undesirable outcomes (VO-bias). On the other hand, these data might also indicate that judges use only one cue, V-bias, based upon the assumption that people are more apt to help another than to harm him; however, they use this cue to a greater extent when the other is described as kind than when he is described as cruel. This interpretation would be consistent with a weighted averaging model (Equation 8-2) in which the relative weight attached to information about the actor's behavior (V-bias) increases with the kindness of the person to whom this behavior is directed. Although one interpretation may be intuitively more appealing than the other, there is no way to distinguish between them on the basis of the data in Table 8.4 alone.

The above ambiguity is, of course, not a deficiency in S–V–O methodology per se. To the contrary, the methodology helps to make salient plausible interpretations of social inference phenomena that might otherwise be overlooked. The study by Reeder, Messick and van Avermaet (1977) provides a good illustration. Judges read a scenario about a stimulus person (P) in conversation with someone (O) he presumably wished to impress. During the course of the conversation, O expressed a preference for either intellectually oriented or nonintellectually oriented persons. The actor then responded in a manner that was either intellectual or nonintellectual. After reading a scenario conveying one of the four combinations of the actor's behavior (intellectual vs. nonintellectual) and O's attitude (favorable toward intellectualism vs. favorable toward nonintellectualism), judges rated the stimulus person's actual intellectuality, his social perceptiveness, and his trustworthiness.

The authors based their original predictions in this study in part upon the implications of correspondent inference theory (Jones & Davis, 1965). This theory implies that a person's behavior is less likely to be attributed to his general dispositional characteristics if there are extrinsic reasons (i.e., social pressure) to manifest this behavior under the conditions in which it is observed. However, as Reeder et al. point out, this hypothesis assumes that the actor has the ability or skill to respond to the situational demands placed upon him. In the situation described above, a truly intellectual person may be capable of manifesting both intellectual and nonintellectual behavior, while a nonintellectual person is unlikely to have the ability or skill to behave intellectually. Based on this reasoning, the authors predicted that a person who behaved nonintellectually would be attributed less intellectuality if his behavior deviated from situational demands than if it conformed to these demands, whereas a person who behaved intellectually would be attributed high intellectuality, regardless of situational constraints. Judgments, shown in Table 8.5, are consistent with these predictions.

TABLE 8.5

Mean Judgments of an Actor's Intellectuality, Social Perceptiveness, and Trustworthiness as a Function of the Actor's Behavior and the Intellectual Orientation of the Other

	Orientation of Other	
Actor's Behavior	Intellectual	Nonintellectual
Intellectuality		
Intellectual behavior	4.94	5.32
Nonintellectual behavior	2.42	3.85
Social perceptiveness		
Intellectual behavior	4.54	4.06
Nonintellectual behavior	2.47	3.81
Trustworthiness		
Intellectual behavior	5.13	5.97
Nonintellectual behavior	5.24	5.08

[a]Adapted from Reeder et al. (1977).

Results pertaining to judgments of social perceptiveness and trustworthiness are somewhat more difficult to explain on the basis of this reasoning. However, the authors point out another interpretation of their data, the nature of which is similar to that suggested by an application of Gollob's S–V–O formulation. The manipulation of P's behavior may be interpreted as a manipulation of information along the verb dimension *behaves intellectually (p)/behaves nonintellectually (n)*, while the manipulation of the other's attitude may be interpreted as a manipulation of information along the object dimension, *intellectually oriented (p)/nonintellectually oriented (n)*. Moreover, the judgment itself may be conceptualized as a subject inference along the dimension *intellectual (p)/nonintellectual (n)*. Four cues could contribute to these judgments: S-bias, SV-bias, SO-bias, and SVO-bias. The contribution of S-bias cannot be inferred from the data reported, since judgments of both poles of the subject dimension were not obtained in the study. However, if judgments of the "negative" pole of this dimension (nonintellectual) are correlated negatively with judgments of the positive pole, the contributions of the other three cues may be inferred from the magnitudes of the contrasts corresponding to the main and interactive effects of differences along V and O. These contrasts, which are shown for each set of judgments in Table 8.6, suggest that three factors may have affected judges' inferences:

TABLE 8.6
Mean Contrasts Corresponding to Contributions of *SV*-Bias, *SO*-Bias, and *SVO*-Bias, Based on Data in Table 8.5

	Judgments of		
	Intellectuality	Social Perceptiveness	Trustworthiness
Intellectuality of actor's behavior (*SV*-bias)	1.99*	1.16*	.40*
Intellectuality of other (*SO*-bias)	–.90*	–.43*	–.34
Conformity to values of others (*SVO*-bias)	.52*	.91*	–.51*

*$p < .05$

1. The intellectuality of the actor's behavior (*SV*-bias) contributed positively to judgments of his intellectualism, social perceptiveness, and trustworthiness, independently of other considerations.

2. The other's intellectual orientation was used as a standard of comparison in judging the actor's intellectuality and social perceptiveness (and so *SO*-bias had a contrast effect on these judgments).

3. The actor's conformity to situational demands (*SVO*-bias) contributed positively to judgments of his intellectuality and social perceptiveness, but negatively to judgments of this trustworthiness. Perhaps judges assumed that conformity to social pressure is a sign of social intelligence (which is in turn reflected in intellectuality) but also of insincerity, and therefore untrustworthiness.

As Reeder et al. point out, the two alternative interpretations of the findings in Table 8.5 cannot be distinguished on the basis of the judgmental data alone. Additional data would be required that bear more directly upon the assumptions underlying judges' use of the information provided them. However, the example points out the value of S–V–O methodology in identifying possible ambiguities in the interpretation of social inference data.

Empirical Applications

As noted at the beginning of this section, S–V–O methodology has been applied to a variety of social inference phenomena in both real and hypothetical social interaction situations. These applications demonstrate its potential versatility and utility in conceptualizing complex, theoretically interesting inference processes in areas related to person perception and attribution. The reader is referred to the literature summarized earlier in this chapter for detailed examples of this research. However, two recent studies are particularly noteworthy as they demonstrate extensions of the methodology and underlying conceptualization to greater numbers of dimensions and to greater numbers of values along each dimension. Moreover, they bear upon issues raised earlier in this chapter concerning the use of personality trait information to make inferences of liking.

Descriptive and Evaluative Determinants of Liking

One deficiency of most research on the effects of personality trait information on judgments of liking is its failure to take into account the descriptive or denotative implications of this information as well as its evaluative implications. A second deficiency lies in its failure to consider the possibility that inferences of a judge's liking for another may depend upon characteristics of the judge himself. A series of studies reported by Wyer (1975b) attempted to overcome these difficulties.

In Experiment 1, judges inferred one person's liking for another on the basis of adjectives describing each. Sets of four adjectives were selected that, according to normative data (Peabody, 1967), varied systematically in both their descriptive and their evaluative implications. For example, one set consisted of the adjectives *cautious, timid, bold,* and *rash*. Of these, two adjectives (cautious and timid) were similar to one another in denotative meaning, but different from the other two (bold and rash). Within each pair of descriptively similar adjectives, one (e.g., cautious) was evaluatively positive and the other (timid) was evaluatively negative. Thus, each adjective could be represented by a pair of values, one along a descriptive dimension and the other along an evaluative dimension. Other sets of adjectives (e.g., *gay, frivolous, serious,* and *grim; cooperative, conforming, individualistic,* and *uncooperative,* etc.) were selected on a similar basis. To construct stimulus materials, each of the four adjectives in a given set was combined with each of another set of four identical adjectives to form 16 pairs, with one adjective in each pair used to describe a person A and the other used to describe a person B. In each case, judges considered each pair of descriptions and then estimated (a) the probability that A would like B; and (b) the probability that A would dislike B. These judgments were converted to values between 0 and 1. In the S–V–O terms, the judgments made in this situation may be conceptualized as verb inferences based upon information along two subject dimensions, S_D and S_E (pertaining respectively to the descriptive and evaluative characteristics of the adjective describing A) and two object dimensions, O_D and O_E (the descriptive and evaluative characteristics of the adjective applied to B). Given this terminology, seven psychologically meaningful informational cues were expected to contribute to judgments:

1. V-bias—the contribution of this cue reflects the extent to which the judge assumes that a person is more (or less) apt to like someone that to dislike someone, regardless of other considerations.

2. S_DV-bias and S_EV-bias—the contributions of these cues reflect the extent to which A's liking for the object B is assumed to be based upon the descriptive and evaluative implications of the adjective describing A, regardless of the characteristics of the person being evaluated.

3. VO_D-bias and VO_E-bias—the contributions of these cues reflect the extent to which A's liking for B is assumed to depend on the descriptive or evaluative implications of the adjective describing B, independently of characteristics of the evaluator.

4. S_DVO_D-bias and S_EVO_E-bias—the contributions of these cues reflect the extent to which A's liking for B is assumed to depend upon the descriptive or evaluative similarity of the adjectives describing A and B.

Of the seven cues described above, only VO_E-bias is analogous to the factor typically considered in the impression formation research described earlier in this chapter. Moreover, nine additional contrasts could be defined in terms of V and various combinations of S_D, S_E, O_D, and O_E. However, these contrasts are not clearly interpretable as informational cues, and were expected to have little psychological significance. In fact, pooled over stimulus replications, all seven cues expected on a priori grounds to be relevant to inferences of A's liking for B (defined along a scale from 0 to 1) contributed significantly to these inferences: S_DVO_D-bias contributed most ($M = .495$), followed by VO_E-bias (.270), VO_D-bias (.134), S_EVO_E-bias (.105), S_DV-bias (.078), S_EV-bias (0.46), and V-bias (.044). These seven cues accounted for about 98% of the predictable variation in judgments, whereas the other nine contrasts involving V, none of which was significant, accounted for a total of less than 2%.

Two conclusions may be drawn from these data. First, descriptive characteristics of the information presented contributed to judgments of liking independently of the evaluative implications of this information. The descriptive characteristics that contributed positively to liking (cautious, timid, gay, frivolous, cooperative, conforming, etc.) all conveyed attributes that were conducive to congenial interpersonal relations, while those that contributed negatively (bold, rash, serious, grim, individualistic, competitive, etc.) all conveyed attributes that were less likely to lead to positive social relations. Second, by far the greatest contributor to judgments was the descriptive similarity of the adjectives describing A and B. However, the evaluative similarity of these adjectives was also a strong contributor. Finally, characteristics of the evaluator considered separately also contributed to judgments of the evaluator's liking for B. None of these perceiver characteristics is typically taken into account in traditional studies of impression formation.

Determinants of Judges' Own Liking for B. The above data do not of course pertain to judges' own liking for persons. However, it seems reasonable to suppose that similar factors may operate. That is, judges' predictions of their own liking for B may be in part a function of their self-perceptions along judgment-related dimensions, and the descriptive and evaluative similarity of these self-perceptions to their perceptions of the stimulus persons being rated. An investigation of this possibility is complicated by the fact that there are substantial individual differences in self-perceptions along the dimensions involved. However, correlational methods may be used to investigate these matters. While the specific details of the procedures used are beyond the scope of the present discussion, a second study reported by Wyer (1975d, Experiment 2) showed that the informational cues that contributed to judges' own liking for persons were in fact similar to those that contributed to their predictions of others' liking for these persons. The effects of $S_D V O_D$-bias and $S_E V O_E$-bias were particularly pronounced. Thus, while direct comparisons were impossible, there appeared to be considerable correspondence between the factors that judges considered in predicting others' liking for stimulus persons and the cues they used as a basis for their own judgments.

Judgments of Persons Based Upon Several Values Along Each Stimulus Dimension

The preceding analysis was restricted to conditions involving only two values along each subject, verb and object dimension. When there are more than two values along each dimension, S–V–O methodology as we have outlined it cannot be applied strictly. However, the conceptualization underlying it is still valid. Two studies reported by Wyer and Hinkle (1976) exemplify this. The first study was similar in conception to the experiment reported by Wyer (1975b), in that judges were presented adjectives describing A and B and were asked to infer A's liking for B. In this case, however, A and B were each described by a pair of adjectives that varied systematically over several levels of favorableness. The design permitted an investigation of not only the interactive effects of information about the target on predicted liking for this person, but also the interactive effects of information about the evaluator (A). Moreover, the combined effects of subject and object information could be identified. (These effects are of course analogous to the contributions of VO-bias, SV-bias, and SVO-bias as defined previously.)

Of greatest interest were the interactive effects of subject and object information. Two sets of analyses were performed. First, the interactions of each adjective describing A with each adjective describing B, interpreted after eliminating the independent effects of these adjectives, were all reliable. To help interpret these interactions, the adjective pairs describing A and the adjective pairs describing B were each considered as single variables, and a factor analysis of variance (FANOVA) was performed using techniques developed by Gollob (1968). This procedure essentially partitions the overall interaction into a set of interaction factors, each reflecting a relation between the subject and object dimensions as defined on the basis of these factors. The major factor extracted in the analysis was purely evaluative, and of the nature implied by the effects of $S_E V O_E$-bias (cf. Wyer, 1975d; Experiment 1); that is, A was expected to like B more when they were described by evaluatively similar adjectives than when they were described by evaluatively dissimilar ones. However, other reliable factors also emerged, the contributions of which were due to the descriptive implications of the information presented. For example, one factor appeared due to the fact that a listless, talkative person was expected to like noisy people who were either bright or frivolous, but to dislike both self-centered, proud people and discreet, troubled people; however, listless, troubled people and discreet, troubled people were expected to have the opposite reactions. Another factor indicated that informal, argumentative people were expected to like people who were both angry and respectful but to dislike people who were both studious and silent; in contrast, informal, grateful people and unintelligent, prejudiced people were expected to respond in the opposite fashion. These results have some intuitive appeal. More generally, they seem to indicate that judgments of people are based to a significant extent upon idiosyncratic descriptive implications of the configuration of information presented that cannot be captured by considering the evaluative implications alone. This conclusion supports the general interpretation given earlier in this chapter to data collected by Birnbaum (1974) and Wyer (1974b; Wyer & Dermer, 1968).

The second experiment in this series was a more strightforward application of S–V–O concepts. Judges were given an adjective describing a person A (subject information), an adjective describing a person B (object information), and A's liking for B (verb information), and then were asked to estimate their own liking for both A and B. Each type of information was varied over four levels of evluative implications. It seems reasonable that judges' liking for A would be based upon the favorableness of the attributes he is inferred to have from the presented information. One attribute may be conveyed by the adjective describing the judge (subject information). A second may be conveyed by A's liking for B (verb information). That is, A's reaction to B may be a reflection of A's friendliness. A third source of information about A may be the company he keeps (object information). People may infer the likeableness of one person from the likeableness of others with whom he associates. Finally, verb and object information in combination may form a configural cue; specifically, a person who likes good people and dislikes bad people may be seen as having desirable qualities and may therefore receive higher ratings, while a person who likes bad people and dislikes good ones may be seen as undesirable. No other combinations of information appeared to be interpretable as psychologically meaningful informational cues, and so contrasts pertaining to these configurations were not expected. In fact, consistent with expectations, analyses of judges' evaluations of A yielded main effects of subject, verb, and object information, and a verb × object interaction, while all other interactions were unreliable.

Analogous reasoning suggests that judges' liking for B may be a positive function of the adjective describing B, the favorableness of A's reactions to him (an indication of B's general popularity), and the favorableness of the adjective describing A. In addition, the subject and verb information in combination may serve as a configural cue; that is, being liked by good people and disliked by bad people may be assumed to imply favorable attributes, whereas being liked by bad people and disliked by good people may be considered indicative of unfavorable attributes. Consistent with these expectations, analyses yielded significant main effects of subject, verb, and object information and a significant subject × verb interaction, but no other reliable effects.

Discussion

The above studies illustrate the potential value of applying S–V–O methodology to social inference phenomena. The studies make clear that by focusing almost exclusively on the evaluative implications of the information presented about the object of evaluation, past research on informational determinants of liking has ignored many factors that may be as or more important. Descriptive as well as evaluative implications of the information presented must obviously be considered. Moreover, evaluations are affected substantially by characteristics of the evaluator and their similarity to attributes of the object, as well as by characteristics of the object considered in isolation. S–V–O methodology provides a mechanism for identifying the relative contributions of these factors.

While in the above examples the methodology was applied to judgments in fairly abstract situations, it may also be applied to social inference phenomena in actual interaction situations (cf. Wyer, Henninger, & Wolfson, 1975). In such instances, judges are typically exposed to only one combination of informational values. For example, some judges may witness an actor help someone described as kind; others may witness the actor help someone described as cruel, and so on. In each case, judges would be asked to infer the likelihood that P is kind, and also that he is cruel, based upon their observations. Using these procedures, the values along the dimensions to which information pertains are *between-group* variables. Nevertheless, the contributions of informational cues to judgments in these situations may be defined and interpreted in much the same manner as if a within-subject design were used.

S–V–O methodology may be applied with equal facility regardless of whether the judge is a participant in the situation or is a disinterested observer. Consider an experiment in which an actor is asked to deliver a speech either for or against a proposition I to an audience (O) who either favors or opposes the proposition. Suppose further that the situation is witnessed by an observer. Subsequently, both the actor and the observer are asked to report the degree to which the actor personally favors the proposition, and also the degree two which he opposes it. Both judges' estimates are subject inferences along the dimension *pro-I (p)/ anti-I (n),* as a function of information along both a verb dimension *supports I (p)/ opposes I (n)* and an object dimension *pro-I (p)/anti-I (n).* Differences in the contribution of *SV*-bias to inferences by P and the observer would then reflect differences in their tendencies to use P's behavior as an indication of his opinion; between-judge differences in the contribution of *SO*-bias would reflect differences in their use of O's opinion as a basis for inferring P's opinion, and so on. Thus the proposed methodology enables possible differences between observers' judgments and P's self attributions to be analyzed in terms of differences in the contributions of specific informational cues.

Finally, it should be noted that S–V–O concepts and methodology are not necessarily restricted to dimensions describing an actor, his behavior, and an object of this behavior. In fact, information pertaining to any of the elements of a social interaction situation identified in Chapter 1 (e.g., behavioral consequences, situational constraints, et al.) can be analyzed using this methodology. Thus, the general formulation developed by Golob is a very flexible one that has both conceptual and methodological value in understanding social inference phenomena.

8.4 CONCLUDING REMARKS

Algebraic models are potentially useful for conceptualizing and diagnosing the effects of a variety of situational and informational factors on judgments in terms of their mediating effects on both the importance that judges attach to each piece of presented information, and their interpretation of its implications for the judgment to be made (i.e., its scale value). Moreover, the procedures developed by Anderson and his colleagues (Anderson, 1970,

1971a; Birnbaum, 1974) provide insight into some of the factors that affect these judgments. However, despite the apparent success of these models in describing the relation between stimulus characteristics and judgments, some caution should be taken in assuming that they provide valid descriptions of the processes underlying the formation of these judgments. There are undoubtedly many instances in which an algebraic integration rule *is* invoked in making inferences based upon several pieces of information. But the applicability of the rule is often hard to evaluate in any given instance without a clear prior understanding of the psychological referents of the parameters comprising the model, and without a means of assessing the values of these parameters independently of the judgments to which they contribute. Moreover, for algebraic models to have any predictive utility, a clearer a priori understanding must be developed of the conditions in which an algebraic integration process may occur, and, if it occurs, which process (summation, averaging, etc.) it is likely to be. Once these objectives are obtained, however, the continued application of algebraic formulations of social inference judgments may prove productive.

While the general formulation developed by Gollob does not eliminate entirely the interpretative ambiguities surrounding the application of algebraic formulations of social inference, it enables the nature of these ambiguities to be more clearly identified. Moreover, by associating these contributions of different informational cues with specific assumptions underlying the use of these cues, a mechanism is provided for tying model parameters directly to psychologically meaningful aspects of the judge's phenomenology and for validating these links empirically. S–V–O methodology thereby avoids some of the pitfalls of other algebraic approaches in which the psychological referents of model parameters are unclear. The formulation is also able to take into account the potential contributions of configural cues as well as cues defined in terms of a single piece of information about a single situational element. Finally, the S–V–O approach takes into account the possibility that a given piece of information may contribute to judgments in several different ways through its role in several different informational configurations. Of the various algebraic models of inference processes considered in this chapter, Gollob's formulation therefore appears to be the most useful.

9

Generalization Processes

Information about an actor's behavior toward an object may affect judgments of the actor, the object, and the situation in which the behavior occurs. In Chapter 5, we noted that these effects depend upon the judge's assumptions about the generalizability of the actor's behavior to persons, objects, and situations other than those specified in the stimulus information. These assumptions may in turn be affected by the judge's previous experience with the types of elements involved in the situation, and also by aspects of the situation itself that render the behavior more or less likely to occur. While the effects of these assumptions have been discussed in some detail in Chapter 5, the manner in which they are acquired has not been addressed. That is, we have not discussed the cognitive processes that may be involved in deciding whether a generalization is justified on the basis of different amounts and types of evidence that one receives or retrieves from memory. Moreover, we have not considered the extent to which willingness to generalize from knowledge of specific instances depends upon the type of behavior to be generalized and the type of elements entering into it. This chapter is devoted to these matters.

The generalizations we make in everyday conversation (e.g., "college professors exploit graduate students"; "college students smoke marijuana," etc.) are often ambiguous, in that the number of persons and objects to which they refer is not explicit. Nevertheless, we appear to make these statements, and to evaluate statements made by others, with reasonable confidence that we are communicating. Thus, I may take exception to the assertion that college professors favor capital punishment, despite the fact that I know of several who do. At the same time, I may agree with the statement that students smoke marijuana, although I know many who consider it intolerable. Moreover, I may evaluate these propositions differently even though I believe that the proportion of college professors who favor capital punishment and the proportion of college students who smoke marijuana are about equal. My acceptance or rejection of such propositions appears to be governed by certain unstated rules that take into account not only the relative numbers of confirming and disconfirming instances but also the type of relation involved and the elements entering into it.

The acceptance of a generalization about groups of people and objects (college students, professors, marijuana, etc.) may be based upon two types of evidence. One type, *inductive*, pertains to particular instances or subclasses of these groups. A second type, *deductive*, pertains to more general classes to which these groups belong, or alternatively, to attributes of these groups.[1] Thus, information that University of Illinois freshmen smoke Columbian Gold would be inductive evidence in support of the assertion that college students smoke marijuana, since it refers to a particular instance of the relation. On the other hand, information that young persons use mind-expanding drugs would be deductive evidence in support of the same assertion, since it describes a relation between categories to which students and marijuana belong. The use of these types of evidence in evaluating the validity of propositions may differ.

In this chapter, we will first consider the effects of each type of evidence separately. In each case, we will provide a basis for conceptualizing the processes underlying these effects and for identifying the factors that affect them. Our analysis will be based in large part upon the work of Abelson and his colleagues (Abelson & Kanouse, 1966; Gilson & Abelson, 1965l Kanouse, 1971). Then we will consider briefly the manner in which the different types of evidence combine to affect the acceptance of generalizations. Finally, we will discuss the implications of these data for research and theory on social inference processes of the sort considered elsewhere in this volume.

9.1. EFFECTS OF INDUCTIVE EVIDENCE

Theoretical Considerations

As noted above, inductive evidence bearing on the validity of a proposition of the form "As verb Bs" pertains to particular instances, or subclasses, of the subject and object categories described in this proposition. This evidence,

---

[1]The distinction between inductive and deductive evidence, which follows that made by Abelson and Kanouse (1966), should not be confused with a distinction between inductive and deductive *reasoning*. Similar reasoning processes could conceivably underlie the acceptance of generalizations based upon both types of evidence. For example, the conclusion "tribes buy bees" could be inferred syllogistically from either (a) the premises "tribes are primitive societies," and "primitive societies buy bees," or (b) the premises "some tribes are Northern tribes," and "northern tribes buy bees." The reasoning processes underlying these inferences is, of course, a main concern of this chapter.

which may either be retrieved from memory or acquired in the situation where the proposition is being judged, may refer to instances of the subject category that do or do not enter into the relation described, to instances of the object category, or to both. For want of better labels, we will adopt Abelson and Kanouse's (1966) terminology and refer to evidence about instances of the subject category as *subject-specific*, and evidence about instances of the object category as *object-specific*. For example, suppose that altogether there are three types of professors—English, psychology and mathematics—and three types of graduate students—research assistants, teaching assistants and fellowship students. Then three examples of each type of evidence bearing upon the proposition "professors exploit graduate students" are shown in Table 9.1, Cases 1 and 2.

In each set of evidence shown in the table, two pieces of evidence are *confirming* (i.e., they provide support for the generalization) and one is

TABLE 9.1
Examples of Evidence of Different Types and Orientations Bearing upon the Validity of the Generalization "Professors Exploit Graduate Students"

	Case 1: *Inductive, Subject-Specific Evidence*	Case 2: *Inductive, Object-Specific Evidence*
Subcategory description	Altogether there are three kinds of professors: English, psychology and mathematics	Altogether there are three kinds of graduate students: research assistants, teaching assistants and fellowship students
Evidence	English professors exploit graduate students Psychology professors exploit graduate students Mathematics professors do *not* exploit graduate students	Professors exploit research assistants Professors exploit teaching assistants Professors do *not* exploit fellowship students
	Case 3: *Deductive, Subject-Specific Evidence*	Case 4: *Deductive, Object-Specific Evidence*
Criteria for category membership	Professors are educated, absentminded, talkative persons	Graduate students are intelligent, hard-working, beer-drinking persons
Evidence	Educated persons exploit graduate students Absentminded persons exploit graduate students Talkative persons do *not* exploit graduate students	Professors exploit intelligent persons Professors exploit hard-working persons Professors do *not* exploit beer-drinking persons

disconfirming. Nevertheless, the two sets could have different effects upon a judge's willingness to accept the generalization. These differences could result in part from differences in the judge's assumptions about the number of instances to which each piece of evidence refers and also about the number of instances to which the generalization itself pertains. To see this, note that the evidence presented in Case 1 implies that some but not all professors exploit graduate students, whereas the evidence presented in Case 2 implies that professors exploit some but not all graduate students. Suppose the judge assumes that the implicit quantifier of "college professor" in the generalization to be evaluated is more universal (i.e., that it describes a larger proportion of category members) than the implicit quantifier of "graduate students"; more specifically, suppose he interprets the generalization to mean that most college professors exploit some graduate students. Then, he should be more willing to accept the generalization on the basis of the object-specific evidence in Case 2 than on the basis of the subject-specific evidence in Case 1.

This analysis suggests a general hypothesis: factors that affect judges' assumptions about the universality of the implicit quantifiers ("all," "most," "some," etc.) assigned to subject and object categories in a proposition should have predictable effects on the acceptance of this proposition. The question is what these factors may be. Two such factors have been identified: the nature of the relation described in the generalization, and the degree of peceived overlap of subclasses contained in the categories of persons or objects being related. Before presenting data bearing on the effects of these factors, the possible reasons for their effects may be worth considering.

Types of Relations

The relations between persons and objects in social situations are often of two general types. One type describes an overt behavior, or action ("buys," "kills," etc.). The second describes a subjective, emotional or affective reaction ("likes" "fears," etc.). These two types of relations were denoted by Abelson and Kanouse as *manifest* and *subjective*, respectively. It seems reasonable to suppose that judge's assumptions about the number of instances to which a generalization refers, and thus the universality of the quantifiers he implicitly assigns to subject and object categories, may depend upon which type of relation is involved. A subjective relation between two elements ("likes," "dislikes," etc.) may often be a precondition for a manifest relation between them ("buys" or "kills"), but yet may be insufficient to infer the existence of this manifest relation. That is, people may like more things than they buy, or dislike more things than they kill; alternatively, more people like a particular type of object than buy it, and more people dislike a given type of object than kill it. Judges may therefore assume that generalizations about subjective relations apply to a greater number of instances than generalizations about manifest relations. Consequently, they may assign more universal implicit quantifiers to the categories involved in the former generalizations. As a result, a given configuration of confirming and disconfirming inductive evidence may lead to less acceptance of a generalization about a subjective relation between two categories than a generalization about a manifest relation between them.

Two separate studies provide support for the assumptions underlying this hypothesis. Abelson and Kanouse (1966) asked judges to report the minimal evidence of a relation between instances of two categories that would be necessary to justify a generalization of the form "As verb Bs." These estimates were reported along a scale composed of several implicit quantifiers ("all," "most," "some," etc.). Thus, if a judge thought that the statement "tribes buy bees" would be justified if some tribes buy a few bees, he checked the phrases "some" and a "few" along scales pertaining to the subject and object categories, respectively. The above reasoning implies that generalizations about subjective relations (e.g., "tribes like bees") should require a greater proportion of confirming instances to be accepted than should generalizations about overt behaviors ("tribes buy bees"). This was in fact the case.

A somewhat different approach to the problem (Podeschi & Wyer, 1976, Experiment 2) led to similar conclusions. Here, judges read a generalization of the form "As verb Bs" and then, based on this statement, estimated the likelihood that statements containing different combinations of explicit quantifiers ("all" or "some") were true. Response statements were generally judged more likely to be true when the relation described was subjective than when it was manifest, again suggesting that generalizations about subjective relations are regarded as relatively more universal.

Effects of Positivity.   Relations between persons and objects also differ in favorableness (i.e., the evaluative implications of the behavior or feeling described for the person or object toward whom it is directed). If judges have a predisposition to assume that relations among objects are favorable rather than unfavorable (for summaries of this research, see Wyer, 1974b; Zajonc, 1968), they may assign relatively more universal quantifiers to categories involved in favorable relations, with the result that a generalization about these relations is less readily accepted. On the other hand, this same "positivity" bias may lead judges to infer that favorable relations are more likely to hold than unfavorable relations, irrespective of the evidence they have available. While the relative contributions of these two competing effects are hard to predict on theoretical grounds, the latter seems empirically to predominate, as we shall see.

Subcategory overlap (Category homogeneity)

Categories may differ in the degree of overlap of their subclasses, or homogeneity.[2] Thus, the category "graduate students" in our previous example would be homogeneous to the extent that the subclasses "graduate research assistant," "graduate teaching assistant," and "fellowship student" are not mutually exclusive, so that a person could belong to two or more simultaneously.

Assumptions about the overlap of the subclasses comprising a category may affect the influence of inductive evidence concerning these subclasses. Consider the two alternative conditions portrayed in Figure 9.1, which shows Venn diagrams of membership in the categories research assistant (r), teaching assistant (t), and fellowship student (f) under conditions where these subclasses are either mutually exclusive (heterogeneous) or partially overlapping (homogeneous). In each case, there are 30 members of each subclass. Suppose inductive evidence is available that college professors exploit research assistants and teaching assistants but not fellowship students. If there are an equal number of members of each subcategory, and if the implicit quantifiers assigned to the pertinent categories are universal, this evidence would imply that college professors exploit 67% of all graduate students in the heterogeneous case, but only 54% of all graduate students in the homogeneous case. In general, it can be shown that, holding other factors constant, a generalization based upon a given mix of confirming and disconfirming inductive evidence specific to a category will be less readily accepted when the subclasses comprising this category are more overlapping, or the category is more homogeneous.

The homogeneity of a category may also affect the universality of the implicit quantifiers assigned to it in the generalization being evaluated. When members of a category belong to similar subgroups, a judge may infer that propositions concerning this category refer to a greater proportion of its members, and may therefore assign it a more universal implicit quantifier. This also implies that a given amount of confirming inductive evidence will lead to less acceptance of a generalization when the category to which it pertains is homogeneous than when it is heterogeneous.

---

[2]This definition differs from a conceptualization of homogeneity–heterogeneity used earlier by Gilson and Abelson (1965), which was in terms of the diversity of attributes possessed by category members. This distinction is important, since as we will see, the conclusions to be drawn about the effects of "homogeneity" differ from those drawn by the earlier authors. While this may create some confusion among readers who are familiar with the earlier work, no other term seems more suitable for describing the characteristic of concern here.

A. Mutually exclusive subclasses

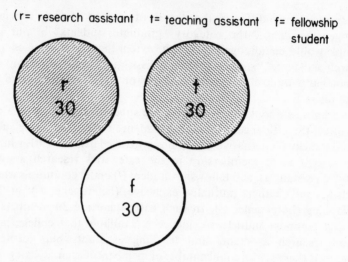

(r= research assistant   t= teaching assistant   f= fellowship student

B. Overlapping subclasses

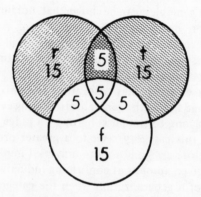

FIG. 9.1.   Implications of inductive evidence for the generalization "college professors exploit graduate students" under conditions in which the subclasses of "graduate student" are (a) mutually exclusive or (b) overlapping. Shaded areas indicate positive instances of the general proposition.

Determinants of Perceived Homogeneity.   The next question concerns the factors that affect judges' perceptions of the homogeneity of a category. One determinant of these perceptions may be the type of elements to which the category refers. For example, judges may have a bias to interpret subcategories of persons as more overlapping than subcategories of nonpersons. This bias may result from the fact that people are simultaneously members of several different groups and occupy several different social and vocational roles. To the extent that judges do perceive person categories as more homogeneous, these categories should be assigned more universal implicit quantifiers than categories of nonpersons. An indication that this is so was obtained in the two studies described previously by Abelson and Kanouse (1966) and Podeschi and Wyer (1976, Experiment 2). In each of these studies, the subject category of the generalizations considered referred to persons ("tribes," "students," etc.), whereas the object category referred to nonpersons ("bees," "classes," etc.). Abelson and Kanouse found that more confirming subject-specific inductive evidence was required to accept a generalization than object-specific evidence. Moreover, Podeschi and Wyer found that statements of the form "all As verb some Bs" were judged more likely to follow from the generalization "As verb Bs" than were statements of the form "some As verb all Bs." Both sets of results suggest that more universal implicit quantifiers are assigned to subject (person) categories than to object (nonperson) categories. If this is true, it has an interesting implication. That is, generalizations about the reaction of a group of persons to a group of objects should be accepted more readily on the basis of inductive evidence that is subject-specific than evidence that is object-specific. This in fact appears to be the case, as the results described below demonstrate.

Empirical Evidence

The preceding analyses outlined and those later in this chapter are theoretically applicable to a consideration of both the effect of new evidence that is presented concerning a proposition of the form "As verb Bs" and to the effects of previously acquired information that a judge retrieves from memory to use in evaluating such a proposition. In the final sections of this chapter, we will consider the applicability of this analysis and results bearing on them to the evaluation of generalizations based upon previously acquired evidence. However, to investigate systematically the effects of the various factors outlined above, it has usually been necessary to control fairly precisely the amount and type of information that subjects consider in evaluating a generalization. For this reason, materials have typically been used in which subjects are explicitly told which subcategories of subject and object classes to consider, and are given explicit evidence concerning the relations among these subcategories. Moreover, materials have been used about which subjects are apt to have relatively few preconceptions. As a result, the research described below may seem to have limited bearing on social inference phenomena outside the laboratory. Nonetheless, the considerations underlying this research, and the results obtained, have implications for the processing of information in more realistic situations, as we shall see.

Two series of studies already mentioned, by Abelson and Kanouse (1966) and by Podeschi and Wyer (1976, Experiment 1; Wyer & Podeschi, 1978) bear directly on the hypotheses outlined above. Similar stimulus materials were used in each set of studies, and the results obtained have generally similar implications. However, since the design of the more recent studies permits a more detailed analysis of the independent and interactive effects of the factors postulated to affect the acceptance of generalizations, only these studies will be described in detail.

Method. The stimulus materials used by Podeschi and Wyer, which were patterned after those used by Abelson and Kanouse (1966), were similar in form to those shown in Table 9.1. However, judges were expected to have little personal interest in the generalizations to be evaluated, decreasing the likelihood that acceptance of these generalizations would be affected by preconceptions about their validity. Four stimulus replications were constructed, each pertaining to a generalization about the relation between a different pair of categories. The subject category of each of the four generalizations referred to persons ("students," "tribes," "foreigners," "urbanites," respectively), whereas the object category referred to nonpersons ("classes," "bees," "American cities," and "magazines," respectively). Three subclasses of each category were selected for use in constructing inductive evidence. (Deductive evidence was also presented in other conditions of the study, and these results are described in a later section of this chapter.) For example, when the subject and object categories involved in the generalizations to be judged were "students" and "classes," respectively, the subcategories of "students" were "freshmen," "sophomores," and "juniors," and those of "classes" were "history," "mathematics," and "English."

For each of the four stimulus replications, four verbs were selected for constructing generalizations. Two of these verbs described favorable and unfavorable manifest relations ("attend" and "disrupt" in the replication described above) and two described favorable and unfavorable subjective relations ("likes" and "dislikes"). Stimulus items representing each possible combination of evidence orientation (subject-specific vs. object-specific), type of relation (manifest vs. subjective), and evaluative implication of the relation (favorable vs. unfavorable), were constructed for each replication. Each item consisted of a statement specifying the three subcategories to which the evidence was specific (see Table 9.1), followed by three pieces of evidence, two of which were always confirming and the other of which was always disconfirming. The items were arranged randomly in a questionnaire. Judges were told to read the information contained in each item and then to rate their agreement with the generalization that followed it (e.g., "students attend classes") along a scale from –3 (strongly disagree) to +3 (strongly agree).

Results. Judges' ratings are shown in Table 9.2a as a function of experimental variables. These data are generally consistent with considerations raised earlier in this section, and with results reported by Abelson and Kanouse (1966). That is, generalizations about manifest relations (i.e., overt behaviors) were accepted more readily on the basis of the evidence presented than were generalizations about subjective relations (affective reactions). Moreover, generalizations were accepted less readily on the basis of inductive evidence when it was specific to person (subject) categories than when it was specific to nonperson (object) categories. Finally, generalizations about favorable relations were accepted more readily than generalizations about unfavorable relations, regardless of the nature of the evidence presented. This could either indicate a positivity bias of the sort postulated by Zajonc (1968) and others, or a tendency for categories to be assigned less universal implicit quantifiers when they are involved in favorable relations than when they are involved in unfavorable ones. (That is, judges may assume that the statement "tribes like bees" pertains to a smaller number of instances than the statement "tribes dislike bees.") Of the two alternative interpretations of this finding, the former seems more plausible.

TABLE 9.2

Mean Acceptance of Generalizations Based upon Inductive Evidence, as a Function of the Type and Evaluative Implications of the Relations Described

	Manifest (Overt) Relations		*Subjective (Affective) Relations*	
	Favorable	*Unfavorable*	*Favorable*	*Unfavorable*
A. Initial experiment[a]				
Evidence specific to persons (subject-specific)	1.02	.55	.60	.12
Evidence specific to nonpersons (object-specific)	1.38	.72	.72	.00
B. Replication				
Evidence specific to persons (subject-specific)	.41	−.38	.16	−.41
Evidence specific to nonpersons (object-specific)	.91	.28	−.06	−.50

[a]Podeschi & Wyer (1976, Experiment 1).
[b]Wyer & Podeschi (1978).

A later study by the same authors (Wyer & Podeschi, 1978) yielded virtually identical results. This study, unlike the first, varied the relative amounts of confirming and disconfirming evidence presented. However, except for this difference and minor changes in the stimulus materials, the design of this study was quite similar to the last. Results of this study, averaged over conditions involving different relative amounts of confirming and disconfirming evidence, are shown in Table 9.2b. The pattern of these results is very similar to that obtained in the earlier experiment. It is perhaps worth noting that in both studies, the orientation of evidence (toward persons vs. nonpersons) had less effect when the generalizations being evaluated described affective reactions (subjective relations) than when they described overt behaviors (manifest relations). This suggests that the predisposition to assign different implicit quantifiers to person and nonperson categories may depend upon the nature of the relation in which they are involved. However, this contingency has not been detected in other studies using this paradigm, so it perhaps should not be taken too seriously.

9.2   EFFECTS OF DEDUCTIVE EVIDENCE

Theoretical Considerations

As we have noted, a generalization about persons and objects may also be evaluated on the basis of evidence about more general classes to which these elements belong. That is, the acceptance of a generalization with the form "As verb Bs" may be based upon evidence that the generalization holds among persons and objects with attributes that serve to define membership in A or B. Thus, suppose that professors are regarded as educated, absentminded, talkative persons, and that graduate students are intelligent, hard-working, beer-drinking persons. Then, Table 9.1, Cases 3 and 4, shows examples of subject-specific and object-specific deductive evidence bearing on the proposition, "professors exploit graduate students."

The effects of deductive evidence on the acceptance of generalizations (like the effects of inductive evidence) are apt to depend to some extent upon judges' assumptions about the number of instances to which the generalization pertains, or alternatively, to the universality of the quantifiers assigned to the categories described. However, an additional factor to be considered concerns the assumptions judges may make about the criteria for membership in these categories. Moreover, in some cases, the process of combining deductive evidence to arrive at judgments may differ from that involved in assessing the implications of inductive evidence. Let us consider these possibilities in more detail.

The Criteria for Category Membership

In the example described in Table 9.1, we characterized professors as "educated, absentminded, talkative persons" and graduate students as "intelligent, hard-working, beer-drinking persons." In effect, these characterizations serve as definitions of the two categories, in that they specify the attributes that serve as a criteria for membership in them. However, the criteria are ambiguous. On one hand, the criteria could be interpreted as *conjunctive* (e.g., as implying that college professors are educated *and* absentminded *and* talkative). In this case, a person would have to possess all three attributes in combination to be a college professor. However, the criteria could also be interpreted as *disjunctive* (as implying that college professors are educated *or* absentminded *or* talkative). In this event, a person would need to possess only one of the three attributes to belong to the category.

The effects of deductive evidence specific to criteria for membership in a category will necessarily depend on the perceived conjunctiveness of these criteria. Suppose that, as in Table 9.1 (Case 3), a judge has evidence that both educated and absentminded people exploit graduate students but talkative people do not, and then is asked to evaluate the generalization that college professors exploit graduate students. If the judge believes that the criterion for membership in the category "college professor" is the conjunction of the three attributes, he is unlikely to accept the generalization, since the single piece of disconfirming evidence is sufficient to render the generalization invalid.[3] On the other hand, suppose the judge believes that the criteria for being a "college professor" are disjunctive. Then the evidence would provide some support for the generalization, since those professors who are either educated or absentminded, but not talkative, *might* exploit students. More generally, the positive effects of confirming deductive evidence should be greater, and the negative effects of disconfirming deductive evidence should be less, when criteria for membership in the category are disjunctive rather than conjunctive. Thus, judges should accept generalizations based on deductive evidence more readily in the former case than in the latter.

The question then arises as to what factors affect judges' assumptions about the nature of the criteria for category membership. Again, one consideration may be whether the category refers to persons or nonpersons. Judges may consider categories of people to consist of overlapping subclasses (i.e., to be homogeneous), but they may also see greater diversity among members of

---

[3]This example assumes for simplicity that the implicit quantifiers assigned to the categories described in each piece of evidence are universal. However, even if this is not the case, the relative differences described in this example would obtain.

their own species than among members of other species. They may therefore be more apt to assume that the membership criteria for a category are disjunctive if the category pertains to persons than if it pertains to nonpersons. Data bearing upon this possibility were obtained by Podeschi and Wyer (1976, Experiment 3). Judges were first given a "definition" of a category (e.g., "tribes are primitive, communal, agricultural societies") and then were asked to estimate both the likelihood that the target category had each attribute comprising the definition (e.g., the likelihood that tribes are primitive societies) and the likelihood that objects with the attribute belonged to the target category (the likelihood that primitive societies are tribes). If judges interpret the criteria for membership in the target category as conjunctive, they should estimate its members to have each defining attribute with high probability. Furthermore, this estimate should be greater than their estimate of the likelihood that an object with the attribute is a member of the target category. However, if they interpret these criteria as disjunctive, the first estimate should not necessarily be much different from the second. If this reasoning is correct, and if the criteria for membership in person categories are assumed to be more disjunctive than the criteria for membership in nonperson categories, the difference between the two judgments described above should be less when categories of persons are involved than when categories of nonpersons are involved. Podeschi and Wyer investigated this possibility for several of the categories used in their first experiment, and found this to be the case.

The above analysis suggests that the effect of deductive evidence on the acceptance of generalization is likely to depend upon the type of category to which the evidence is specific. That is, if subject categories typically pertain to persons, and object categories to nonpersons, generalizations should be accepted more readily on the basis of deductive evidence if it is subject-specific (person-specific) than if it is object-specific (nonperson-specific).

Inference Processes

When a judge either receives or retrieves from memory several pieces of evidence bearing on a generalization, he must combine their implications in order to draw a conclusion about the validity of this generalization. At least two processes might be used.

1. The judge may invoke set-theoretical considerations (cf. Erickson, 1974). That is, he may first estimate the number of instances of the specified relation from the combined implications of the various pieces of evidence, based upon assumptions about the criteria for membership in relevant categories (or, in the case of inductive evidence, the degree of overlap of their subcategories). He may then evaluate the generalization on the basis of this

estimate and his assumptions about the appropriate implicit quantifiers for the categories comprising the generalization.

2. The process may in some instances be algebraic. To borrow an example from Abelson and Kanouse (1966), suppose a judge receives evidence that tribes like buzzing insects and flying insects but not stinging insects, and is then asked to evaluate the generalization that tribes like bees. He may infer that tribes consider "buzzing" and "flying" to be favorable attributes, but "stinging" to be unfavorable. He may therefore sum or average the evaluative implications of these attributes to arrive at an overall estimate of tribes' liking for bees.[4]

This example suggests that algebraic inference processes may be invoked when the evidence presented is deductive and object-specific and the relation to be judged is subjective. In other conditions, an algebraic process seems intuitively less likely. One's subjective reactions to an object may be a composite of one's reactions to the object's individual attributes, but overt behavior (i.e., manifest relations) must typically be directed toward the object as a whole. For example, if bees are defined as buzzing, flying, stinging insects (a conjunctive category definition), it is possible to like them without liking stinging insects in general, provided their other attributes are favorable. However, it is *not* possible to buy bees without buying stinging insects. This implies that a given configuration of deductive, object-specific evidence will lead to greater acceptance of a generalization if the relation described is subjective than if it is manifest. This prediction is important in light of our arguments that in other instances, generalizations about subjective relations will be *less* readily accepted, since the implicit quantifiers attached to categories involved in such generalizations are relatively more universal.

There are nevertheless some reasons to believe that an algebraic process of integrating evidence is more pervasive than the above analysis suggests. We suggested in Chapters 2 and 8 that algebraic processes may be invoked primarily when the information considered in combination is difficult to understand. In many cases, the evidence bearing on a generalization may seem partially inconsistent, and moreover may be partly inductive and partly deductive. In such cases, it may be very difficult for a judge to construe the

---

[4]In Chapter 8, we noted that the process of making evaluative judgments on the basis of personality adjectives may *not* be algebraic except under restricted experimental conditions. However, in the conditions of concern here, the implications of each piece of evidence are likely to be considered as separate groups, and so an algebraic process is more likely. To the extent that the process is nonalgebraic, it is still fundamentally different from the set-theoretic processes postulated under other conditions. Since the research to be discussed in this chapter cannot distinguish between the alternative processes described in Chapter 8, the simpler process will be assumed here for purposes of discussion.

number of instances of the relation implied by the evidence he has available. Therefore, the judge may either discount part of the evidence presented, or may evaluate the implications of each piece of evidence separately and then combine it in some fairly simplistic (e.g., algebraic) fashion.

Empirical Evidence

The considerations outlined above suggest two hypotheses. First, generalizations will be accepted more readily on the basis of deductive evidence if this evidence is specific to categories of persons than if it is specific to categories of nonpersons. Second, the tendency for evidence to have more effect on the acceptance of generalizations about manifest relations than on the acceptance of generalizations about subjective relations (resulting from differences in the implicit quantifiers assigned to categories involved in these relations) may not hold when the evidence is both deductive and specific to the object category; here, a different process may be invoked when the relation is subjective, and thus the effect of the evidence may be greater than it is in other conditions.

Support for these possibilities was obtained by Podeschi and Wyer in the studies described in the previous section (i.e., Podeschi & Wyer, 1976, Experiment 1; Wyer & Podeschi, 1978). In each study, additional conditions were run in which the same generalizations were evaluated, but the evidence bearing on them was deductive rather than inductive. Stimulus items were similar in form to those shown in Table 9.1, Cases 3 and 4. That is, for each category, three superordinate categories (attributes) were selected to use as criteria for category membership. (For example, in instances where the generalization to be evaluated pertained to students and classes, students were characterized as persons who "carry books, sit in classrooms, and do homework," whereas classes were characterized as "informative, formal, challenging situations").

Results of the first study, in which each set of evidence presented consisted of two confirming pieces and one disconfirming piece, are shown in Table 9.3a. Analyses revealed that, as expected, generalizations were typically accepted more readily when the evidence was specific to person categories (i.e., subject-specific) than when it was specific to nonperson categories (object-specific), although a reversal occurred when the relation was subjective and unfavorable. In addition, generalizations were accepted more readily on the basis of object-specific evidence when the relation involved was subjective than when it was manifest. This relation is quite the opposite of that obtained when inductive evidence was presented (see Table 9.2a). This difference is consistent with the conjecture that judges invoke a different integration process in evaluating the implications of deductive evidence about affective reactions to different attributes of an object than they do under other conditions. That is, they simply sum (or average) the subject's apparent

TABLE 9.3

Mean Acceptance of Generalizations Based upon Deductive Evidence as a Function of the
Type and Evaluative Implications of the Relation Described

	Manifest (Overt) Relation		Subjective (Affective) Relation	
	Favorable	Unfavorable	Favorable	Unfavorable
A. Initial experiment[a]				
Evidence specific to persons (subject-specific)	–.08	–.50	–.10	–.50
Evidence specific to nonpersons (object-specific)	–.72	–.97	–.30	–.17
B. Replication[b]				
Evidence specific to persons (subject-specific)	.00	–.72	.03	–.22
Evidence specific to nonpersons (object-specific)	–1.09	–.22	–.72	.56

[a]Podeschi & Wyer (1976, Experiment 1).
[b]Wyer & Podeschi (1978).

evaluations of the object's three attributes to arrive at an estimate of the subject's overall evaluation of the object, and then use this estimate to determine their acceptance of the generalization.

There is a second, indirect indication of this possibility. When judges combine adjectives to arrive at judgments in an impression formation task, they often weight adjectives with unfavorable implications more heavily than adjectives with favorable implications (Birnbaum, 1974; Hamilton & Zanna, 1972; Wyer & Watson, 1969). Therefore, if judges are using a similar process here, they should be more apt to infer that A dislikes B when told that A dislikes two of B's three attributes than they are to infer that A likes B when told that A likes two of B's three attributes. Results of the first study are consistent with this line of reasoning. Specifically, generalizations about favorable relations were typically accepted much more readily than generalizations about unfavorable relations, suggesting a positivity bias similar to that occurring when inductive evidence was presented (cf. Table 9.2). However, an exception occurred when generalizations about subjective relations were evaluated on the basis of object-specific deductive evidence; in this case, generalizations about favorable relations were accepted slightly *less* readily than generalizations about unfavorable ones.

Unfortunately, results obtained under corresponding conditions of the second study (Wyer & Podeschi, 1978) suggest that this interpretation may need to be qualified. Results of this study, averaged over conditions in which different proportions of confirming evidence were presented, are shown in Table 9.3b. These results only partially parallel those obtained in the first experiment. Specifically, the reversal of the positivity bias when object-specific deductive evidence was presented was much greater here than in the first study, and moreover extended to manifest relations as well as subjective ones. It is conceivable that, contrary to initial assumptions, a more complex reasoning process may underlie judgments of manifest relations based upon deductive evidence. For example, if judges are told that tribes destroy buzzing and stinging but not flying insects, they may infer that tribes dislike two of bees' three attributes, and therefore dislike bees; this mediating inference may then affect their acceptance of a generalization about behavior that reflects this affective reaction (i.e., "tribes destroy bees"). While this interpretation is plausible, the reason for detecting the effect in the second study but not in the first remains a mystery.

Additional Considerations

The results described above, in combination with those concerning the effects of inductive evidence, lend reasonably strong support to our conceptualization of the factors that influence the effects of these different types of evidence and the reasons that these effects occur. However, some ambiguities remain. For one thing, in each of the studies described, the type of category (person vs. nonperson) to which evidence was specific was confounded with the position of the cateogry (as subject or object) in the generalization to be evaluated. Perhaps judges are simply biased to attend differently to evidence about the subject of a proposition than to evidence about its object. To this extent, evidence specific to subject and object categories may have different effects regardless of the type of elements contained in these categories. In addition, the hypothesis that the differential effects of deductive evidence result from differences in judges' assumptions about the conjunctiveness of category membership criteria was not directly tested in the studies described thus far.

A subsequent study by Wyer and Podeschi (1978) eliminated these ambiguities. The design and presentation of stimulus materials were similar in most respects to the earlier studies. However, unlike earlier studies, the type of category to which evidence pertained (person vs. nonperson) was manipulated independently of its position as subject or object of the generalization. (Thus in one case, where the categories involved were "scientists" and "apes," the generalization to be evaluated was either "scientists destroy apes" or "apes destroy scientists.") In addition, when *deductive* evidence was presented, judges were given a set to consider category definitions as either conjunctive or disjunctive by connecting the attributes comprising these definitions by either *and* (e.g., "scientists are thinking *and* inquisitive *and* problem-solving persons") or *or* ("scientists are thinking *or* inquisitive *or* problem-solving persons"). When *inductive* evidence was presented, a similar procedure was used to create a set to consider the subclasses as either overlapping ("there are three kinds of scientists: physical *and* social *and* life") or mutually exclusive ("there are three kinds of scientists: physical *or* social *or* life"). This design therefore permitted isolation of the effects of evidence orientation (subject-specific vs. object-specific), type of category (person vs. nonperson), and category definition (conjunctive vs. disjunctive).

Analyses indicated that generalizations were accepted less readily on the basis of deductive evidence when the category membership criteria to which the evidence pertained were conjunctive than when these criteria were disjunctive. Moreover, generalizations were accepted less readily on the basis of inductive evidence when judges were given a set to treat the subcategories as overlapping rather than as mutually exclusive. However, controlling for these factors, acceptance did not reliably depend either on whether the evidence was about the subject or object of the generalization, or on whether it pertained to persons or nonpersons. In other words, when the criteria for category membership were controlled, the different effects of subject-specific and object-specific evidence obtained in previous studies were eliminated.

9.3 RELATIVE EFFECTS OF INDUCTIVE AND DEDUCTIVE EVIDENCE

A final question to be raised concerns the relative influence of inductive and deductive evidence on the acceptance of generalizations. When each type of evidence is presented in isolation, the answer to this question is fairly straightforward. Specifically, if category definitions are more often interpreted as conjunctive than disjunctive, a disconfirming piece of deductive evidence may often be considered sufficient to reject the generalization, while a disconfirming piece of inductive evidence is not. Thus, a given mix of confirming and disconfirming evidence should be less likely to lead to the acceptance of a generalization if the evidence is deductive than if it is inductive. Data presented in Tables 9.2 and 9.3 strongly support this prediction.

When inductive and deductive evidence is presented in combination, a priori predictions become more difficult. Moreover, the results of research investigating these combined effects (Wyer & Podeschi, 1978) are complex and difficult to interpret. Indeed, the primary conclusion to be drawn from these investigations is a negative one: That is, there appears to be no simple rule that subjects use in integrating different types of evidence to arrive at judgments. Set-theoretic, configural, and algebraic processes may all be involved. Moreover, tendencies to discount one or another piece of evidence appear to exist that cannot readily be predicted a priori. Because of the complexity of the results available at this writing, and the difficulties encountered in interpreting them, these results will not be reported here in detail. However, certain aspects of the results may have archival value for persons with particular interest in the problem at hand. To this end, we will describe briefly the procedures used to investigate these matters, and summarize the primary results obtained. The less enthusiastic reader may do well to forego a detailed consideration of these data, and proceed to the final two sections of this chapter.

Method.   The stimulus materials used to investigate the combined effects of inductive and deductive evidence were constructed around the same general propositions used in the first study described in this chapter. However, the actual sets of evidence presented differed in several respects. Three between-subjects conditions were run. If I+ and I– are used to represent confirming and disconfirming pieces of inductive evidence, respectively, and D+ and D– are used to represent confirming and disconfirming pieces of deductive evidence, the configurations of evidence presented in each condition can be represented as follows:

Condition 1:   I+I+I–, D+D+D–, I+I–I–, D+D–D–
Condition 2:   I+D+I–, I+D+D–, D+D–D–, D+I–I–
Condition 3:   D+D+I–, I+I+D–, I+I–D–, D+I–D–

In each case, the evidence was preceded by either a statement of the criteria for membership of the subject or object category to which it was specific, a description of the three subclasses into which the category was partitioned, or both. (Evidence in each set was either all subject-specific or all object-specific.) For example, a set of I+D–D– subject-specific evidence bearing on the generalization "tribes buy bees" was:

Altogether there are three kinds of tribes: northern, central and southern.
Tribes are primitive, communal, agricultural societies.
Northern tribes buy bees.
Communal societies do *not* buy bees.
Agricultural societies do *not* buy bees.

Items in each condition were presented in four 32-item questionnaires, constructed so that stimulus materials were counterbalanced over conditions and each judge was exposed only twice to a given combination of stimulus categories and verb type (manifest favorable, manifest unfavorable, etc.). Judges read each set of evidence and then estimated their agreement with the target generalization along a –5 to +5 scale.

Results.   Two analyses were performed. One investigated the effects of a given piece of disconfirming evidence in the context of different configurations of confirming evidence, and the other investigated the effects of a piece of confirming evidence in the context of different sets of disconfirming evidence. The first analysis was performed on data pertaining to the first two sets listed under Conditions 1–3 described above. This analysis yielded a complex interaction of the type of disconfirming evidence (inductive or deductive), the type of confirming evidence accompanying it (similar to the disconfirming piece, mixed, or dissimilar to the disconfirming piece), the type of relation manifest or subjective), and the favorableness of the relation. Data relevant to this interaction, shown in Table 9.4, suggest the following conclusions:

1. When the disconfirming piece of evidence was *inductive,* generalizations were accepted more readily when the two confirming pieces were either both inductive or both deductive than when they were of different types. This suggests that disconfirming inductive evidence has greater influence when the confirming evidence available is of different types, so that its combined implications are harder to assimilate.

2. When the disconfirming piece of evidence was *deductive,* the acceptance of generalizations about manifest relations increased with the number of confirming pieces of inductive evidence presented. In other words, confirming inductive evidence appeared to override the effect of the disconfirming deductive evidence, whereas confirming deductive evidence did not.

3. The most confusing aspect of the results occurred when the generalization pertained to a subjective relation and the disconfirming evidence was deductive. When the relation was unfavorable (e.g., "hates"), results were similar to those obtained when the disconfirming evidence was inductive. However, when the relation was favorable (e.g., "likes"), the acceptance of generalizations about that relation increased with the number of confirming deductive pieces of evidence presented. This is consistent with the notion that the integration process underlying the use of deductive evidence to evaluate subjective relations is akin to that involved in impression formation tasks, where evaluations typically increase with the favorableness of the attributes of the object being judged. However, the earlier studies reported in this chapter suggest that this tendency exists only when the evidence is specific to the object, whereas here, it generalized to subject-specific evidence as well. Moreover, it is also difficult to explain the failure to obtain parallel results when the judge's relation was unfavorable and subjective (i.e., "hates").

TABLE 9.4

Mean Acceptance of Generalizations Based Upon Disconfirming Inductive and Deductive Evidence, as a Function of the Type of Confirming Evidence Accompanying it and the Type and Favorableness of the Relation to be Generalized[a]

Type of Evidence	Manifest Relation		Subjective Relation	
	Favorable	Unfavorable	Favorable	Unfavorable
Disconfirming inductive evidence (I−)				
Confirming evidence of same type (I+I+)	2.94	2.31	2.47	1.41
Confirming evidence mixed (I+D+)	.91	.12	.62	1.12
Confirming evidence of different type (D+D+)	2.09	1.75	1.87	1.44
Disconfirming deductive evidence (D−)				
Confirming evidence of same type (D+D+)	.75	.84	1.97	1.97
Confirming evidence mixed (I+D+)	1.38	1.44	2.12	.50
Confirming evidence of different type (I+I+)	1.78	1.78	.91	1.59

[a]Reprinted from Wyer & Podeschi (1978, p. 126).

The effect of confirming evidence presented in different contexts was investigated by analyzing the last two stimulus configurations listed under each of the three conditions described above. Two conclusions seem justified on the basis of these analyses.

1. Pooled over the types of disconfirming evidence presented, generalizations were accepted more readily when the confirming piece was inductive than when it was deductive. However, this difference was greater when the evidence was subject-specific than when it was object-specific. This suggests that confirming inductive evidence has more influence than confirming deductive evidence. Moreover, this differential influence is most apparent when the evidence pertains to persons rather than nonpersons.

2. Confirming evidence has greater influence when it was of a different type from the accompanying evidence than when it was of the same type. This may again be a result of judges' difficulty in assimilating the implications of evidence of different types, leading them to process the implications of each piece separately rather than responding to the information configurally.

The pattern of results described above is complex in detail. However, it seems consistent with the general arguments outlined in Chapter 8. That is, judges are more apt to resort to simple heuristic devices for processing information when the implications of the information as a configuration are difficult to assimilate. Thus, when the information presented is of a single type, judges often respond to the information configurally and apply set-theoretic considerations of the sort outlined earlier in this chapter (except when deductive evidence about subjective relations is presented). However, when different types of evidence are presented in combination, judges are apt not to respond to it configurally, and moreover are apt to weight individual pieces of evidence differently than they would on the basis of set-theoretic considerations.

Some insight into the nature of this weighting can be obtained by rearranging the data collected in the manner described in Table 9.5. This table shows the effects of differences in the implications of each type of evidence in the context of different configurations of other evidence.

1. The effect of a given piece of inductive evidence is greater when the other evidence available is of a single type (all inductive or all deductive; $D = 3.68$) than when it is of different types ($D = 2.50$). However, the effect of a given piece of deductive evidence does not depend on whether the other evidence is of a single type or of different types ($D = 2.65$ and 2.88, respectively).

2. The effect of a given piece of inductive evidence is greater when the confirming evidence already available is inductive ($D = 3.48$ for I+I− and I+D− contexts combined) than when it is deductive ($D = 2.70$ for D+I− and

TABLE 9.5

Effects of Inductive and Deductive Evidence upon the Acceptance of Generalizations when Presented in Different Contexts[a]

Context Evidence	Inductive Evidence			Deductive Evidence		
	I+	I–	Difference (D)	D+	D–	Difference (D)
I+I–	2.28	–2.18	4.28	.69	–1.15	1.84
D+I–	.69	–1.63	2.32	1.79	–1.73	3.52
I+D–	1.52	–1.15	2.67	1.36	– .89	2.25
D+D–	1.36	–1.73	3.09	1.38	–1.98	3.36

[a]Reprinted from Wyer & Podeschi (1978, p. 130).

D+D– contexts combined). Similarly, the effect of a given piece of deductive evidence is greater when the confirming evidence already available is deductive (D = 3.44) than when it is inductive (D = 2.05). Put another way, the relative influence of a piece of *confirming* evidence (although not of a piece of disconfirming evidence) is less when additional evidence of the same type is presented than when evidence of a different type is presented.

The reasons for these contingencies are again difficult to understand in detail. However, one thing is clear. That is, the integration processes underlying the use of evidence to evaluate a generalization cannot be simply understood on the basis of either a set-theoretic or an algebraic formulation considered alone. (For an elaboration of the deficiencies of each formulation in accounting for these data, see Wyer & Podeschi, 1978.)

9.4 SUMMARY AND IMPLICATIONS

The series of studies described in this section allow reasonably clear conclusions to be drawn about the effects of different types of evidence on the acceptance of generalizations.

1. Deductive evidence leads to greater acceptance of generalizations when the criteria for membership in the category to which it is specific (subject or object) are interpreted as disjunctive rather than conjunctive. The criteria for belonging to categories of persons are more often assumed to be disjunctive than are the criteria for belonging to categories of nonpersons. As a result, generalizations are accepted more readily on the basis of a given configuration of deductive evidence when this evidence is about a category of persons than when it is about a category of nonpersons.

2. The effect of inductive evidence on the acceptance of generalizations depends upon judges' assumptions about the number of instances to which

the generalizations pertain, and thus upon the implicit quantifiers they assign to the categories involved. Generalizations about overt behaviors are assumed to apply to fewer instances than are generalizations about affective reactions. Consequently, generalizations about overt behaviors are more likely to be accepted on the basis of inductive evidence than are generalizations about subjective reactions. The assignment of implicit quantifiers also appears to depend upon assumptions that judges make about the overlap of the subcategories to which the evidence pertains. That is, when the subclasses of a category are interpreted as overlapping, a more universal quantifier is assigned to the category, and therefore generalizations involving the category are accepted less readily. Categories of persons are assumed to contain more overlapping subclasses than categories of nonpersons. Consequently, generalizations are accepted less readily on the basis of inductive evidence specific to person categories than on the basis of similar evidence specific to nonperson categories.

3. There is a general tendency to accept generalizations about relations that have positive evaluative implications (that is, relations that suggest a favorable reaction by members of the subject category toward members of the object category).

4. The conclusions drawn above apply primarily when judgments are based on assumptions about the number of subject category members and object category members that are related in the manner described in the generalization. When judges evaluate a proposition about a subject's affective reaction to an object on the basis of the subject's reactions to specific attributes of the object (object-specific deductive evidence), this may not be the case. Here, judges may base their inferences on a composite of the subject's apparent affective reactions to each of the object's attributes (cf. Wyer, 1975d; Wyer & Hinkle, 1976). Thus, the orientation of the evidence presented and the relation described in the generalization may affect not only the interpretation of the generalization and specific pieces of evidence bearing on its validity, but also the process of integrating the implications of this evidence.

To the extent that the data reported in this chapter are reliable and our interpretation of them is valid, they have many implications for inferences about persons, objects, and events in social situations of the type we have considered earlier in this volume. Several of these implications, and representative research bearing upon them, are worth noting.

The Impact of Persuasive Communications on Judgments

The indication that the effects of different types of evidence on judgments depend upon both the evaluative implications of the evidence and the type of relation involved is of obvious relevance to belief and opinion change. For example, findings obtained by Abelson and Kanouse (1966) and replicated in the studies reported here (see Table 9.2) suggest that propositions about favorable manifest relations are more readily accepted if relevant evidence is inductive than if it is deductive, whereas propositions about unfavorable subjective relations are accepted more readily if the evidence is deductive than if it is inductive. If these results are generalizeable, communications containing assertions about favorable manifest relations should be more effective if these assertions are bolstered by inductive evidence, whereas communications containing assertions about unfavorable subjective relations should have more effect if these assertions are supported by deductive evidence.

To investigate this possibility, Kanouse and Abelson (1967) constructed messages bearing on two premises from which a conclusion could be drawn on the basis of syllogistic reasoning. One premise pertained to a favorable manifest relation and the other an unfavorable subjective relation. For example, in one case the conclusion, or target proposition, was that current laws against hunting legally protected birds are too strict, and the two premises were that (a) current regulations had produced a large increase in the number of legally protected birds; and that (b) Nebraskan farmers fear an increase in the number of such birds. The persuasive communications consisted of different types of evidence in support of the two premises. In one form of communication, the evidence supporting the favorable manifest relation was inductive (e.g., it indicated that hunting regulations had produced a large increase in the number of Nebraskan crested hawks, a subcategory of "legally protected birds") while the evidence supporting the unfavorable subjective relation was deductive (it indicated that Nebraskan farmers feared an increase in the quantity of government-preserved wildlife). In the other form, the types of evidence supporting these two premises were reversed (it indicated that hunting regulations had produced a large increase in the quantity of government-preserved wildlife and that Nebraskan farmers feared an increase in the number of Nebraskan crested hawks). Thus, the only difference in the two persuasive communications was in the position of the two phrases ("Nebraskan creasted hawks" and "government-preserved wildlife"). Nevertheless, consistent with predictions, judges' beliefs in the target proposition were more strongly influenced by the first type of communication than the second.

Other findings reported in this chapter could be applied in a similar fashion. For example, the data described in Tables 9.2 and 9.3 imply that assertions about persons' favorable reactions to an object (e.g., the proposition that college students like rock music) will be more readily accepted, and thus will have more influence on other propositions, if these assertions are bolstered by either subject-specific inductive evidence (e.g., evidence that college students like many different types of music or subject-specific deductive evidence (e.g., evidence that young, educated persons like rock). On the other hand, the difference would not necessarily hold if the relation to which these arguments pertained was *un*favorable.

The Socratic Method of Belief and Opinion Change

An especially interesting application of the findings reported here is suggested by research in priming effects, and particularly the Socratic method of opinion change described in Chapter 7. That is, once a judge is asked to make an inference, this judgment may then be used as "information" in making subsequent inferences (cf. Carlston, 1977; Henninger & Wyer, 1976; Salancik & Conway, 1975). In the present, context, a judge's acceptance of a generalization may be affected by the sorts of questions he is asked to consider before he evaluates it.

For example, consider the implications of evidence that college professors voted against Gerald Ford and Richard Nixon for the proposition that "college professors dislike Republican presidents." This latter proposition could be inferred from the former through two lines of reasoning. First, since college professors voted against Ford and Nixon, they voted against Republican presidents, and if they voted against Republican presidents, they dislike Republican presidents. Second, since college professors voted against Ford and Nixon, they dislike Ford and Nixon, and if they dislike Ford and Nixon, they dislike Republican presidents. The distinction between these two lines of reasoning is rather subtle. However, the likelihood of accepting the conclusion may differ in the two cases. Note that the first line of reasoning involves making a generalization on the basis of inductive evidence about a manifest relation, whereas the second involves making a generalization on the basis of inductive evidence about a subjective relation. Moreover, recall that generalizations about manifest relations are accepted more readily on the basis of inductive evidence than are generalizations about subjective relations (see Table 9.2, and also Abelson & Kanouse, 1966). Therefore, the first line of reasoning should lead to a stronger belief in the target proposition than the second.

The implications of research on priming effects now becomes apparent. Suppose that two judges are asked to report their beliefs that college professors voted against Ford and Nixon. Then, one judge is asked to report his belief that college professors vote against Republican presidents, while the second is asked to report his belief that college professors dislike Ford and Nixon. Finally, both judges are asked their belief that college professors dislike Republican presidents. The two judges' beliefs that college professors voted against Ford and Nixon may be identical. However, if their interpolated judgments mediated their final ones in the manner suggested, the first judge should accept the target proposition more readily than the second judge.

Evidence supports this hypothesis. Kanouse and Gross (cited in Kanouse, 1971) told judges to assume that a stimulus proposition of the form described above (e.g., "urbanites destroy *Readers' Digests*") was true, and then to make one of the two types of mediating inferences (e.g., that urbanites hate *Readers' Digests* or that urbanites destroy magazines) before inferring the validity of the target proposition ("urbanites hates magazines"). As expected, judges inferred that the target proposition was more likely to follow from the stimulus statement in the second case than in the first. These data not only provide another example of priming effects of prior judgments on subsequent ones, but suggest some intriguing avenues of research on the indirect techniques of social influence.

Attribution Processes: Judgments Based on Behavioral Information

In Chapter 5, we presented a formulation that described the effect of an actor's behavior on judgments in terms of its effects on different mediating assumptions about the generalizability of the actor's behavior to other actors, objects and situations. However, research bearing on the validity of this and related formulations has been limited in two respects. First, the information about generalizability has typically been presented in summary form (e.g., "nearly all (hardly any) persons laugh at the comedian"; see McArthur, 1972) rather than in terms of a series of specific instances (for an exception, see Cordray & Shaw, in press). Thus, little data are available about how configurations of information about specific sets of persons or objects affect judgments. In addition, little attention has been given to the type of behavior involved.

The research cited in this chapter suggests that these factors are important to consider. Moreover, it suggests that an understanding of inferences based on behavioral information requires knowledge of judges' assumptions about generalizeability over different superordinate categories to which the actor or the object of his behavior belongs.

9.5 CONCLUDING REMARKS

The effects of information on the acceptance of generalizations are obviously complex. Many different factors affect the acceptance of generalizations on the basis of a given amount of evidence. Moreover, no single principle adequately describes the process of combining the implications of this information to determine whether a generalization is justified. The process depends very much on both the type of relation being evaluated and the type of evidence bearing upon it.

On the other hand, the phenomena of concern in this chapter embody many of the issues raised earlier in this volume. For example, they reemphasize the need to take into account both configural responses to the information (as implied in this case by the set-theoretic analysis of informational implications) and more elementistic responding, based upon the interpretation of each piece of information separately. Moreover, the phenomena of concern in this chapter have implications for a variety of issues related to social inference, including belief and opinion change, priming effects of information on social judgments, social evaluation processes, and attribution. Thus, while many questions remain unanswered (and many others remain not yet identified) in this area of research, the line of investigation is well worth continuing.

10 Epilogue

We have attempted in this volume to provide an integrative review of the vast literature concerned with, or relating to, social inference. In doing so, we have outlined an approach (perhaps, several approaches, depending on how successful our integration has been) which reflects our convictions about the field, how it can best be understood, and how it can best be studied. In this final chapter we should like to state these convictions over again, explicitly, in order to provide a clearer view of the guiding light which we have tried to follow throughout the preceding text. We shall not at this point justify the various prejudices to which we confess; that justification has been elaborated (and perhaps at times belabored) in the book. Nor shall we try to summarize the contents of earlier chapters or to encompass all the ideas or suggestions therein. Rather, we shall try to explicate our biases and our conclusions, so that this chapter can stand as a general statement of principle.

First, we feel that the whole area of social inference is being studied in piecemeal fashion, owing to the lack of any generally accepted integrative framework. The consequences are twofold. Various subrealms of research (e.g., attribution, impression formation, interpersonal attraction) have been only tenuously interrelated, with areas of overlap obscured by ostensively different foci. And these subrealms, even in combination, fail to exhaust the territory of potential interest to social inference researchers. We attempted in Chapter 1 to identify the prototypical situational elements of common concern to various domains of social inference research, in hopes of providing a framework that will both integrate and illuminate areas of potential concern. Other, possibly better, organizational heuristics might be devised, but the need for some such framework seems fairly evident.

Second, we have emphasized the need for social inference researchers to consider more thoroughly the phenomenological processes involved in social inference making. Many contemporary approaches to the topic (e.g., Kelley's 1967, and Jones and Davis' 1965, attributional models) are essentially stimulus-response approaches, describing the manner in which different informational inputs result in different inferential responses. At the same time, they generally ignore the intermediary cognitive work responsible for such relationships, or provide "as if" formulations of the cognitive processes involved.

Our concern with process leads us to emphasize three specific research areas. First, we are convinced that social cognition follows pretty much the same kinds of rules as other forms of cognition. Although Heider pointed this some time ago, researchers in impression formation and attribution have only recently paid much attention to traditional cognitive research on the mechanics of attention, perception and memory. Second, we feel additional emphasis needs to be placed on the cognitive representations of social information that people actually and spontaneously use. Inference makers may store information along different dimensions, or in altogether different forms, than those commonly assumed and assessed in social inference research. Third, we have proposed that script theory may provide a useful starting point in theorizing about the cognitive processes in which inference-makers actually engage. While we recognize that Abelson's (1976) theory falls short of the kind of comprehensive, empirically verifiable theory we shall ultimately need, it does seem to provide a useful starting point.

These concerns suggest the need to consider more extensively the role of memory (its mechanics, and the resultant representations, including scripts) in social inference processes. A number of social psychologists are now becoming concerned with memory issues (see Chapters 3 and 4), and it appears that the area of "person memory" will become increasingly important in the future. We are naturally delighted with this development.

The formulation we have outlined may be loosely classified as an information processing approach. However, we have not fully embraced an image of human beings as rational, information processors who simply deduce the logical implications of information. In fact, we have taken pains to point out that stimulus information is more than just informative: Such stimuli may have important consequences beyond their direct implications for any kind of inference. Thus, for example, a stimulus cue may stimulate a particular memory, may direct attention towards or away from other cues, or may change the interpretation of other information available. The full range of such effects need to be considered for inference making to be properly understood.

We have partially adopted a configuralist, or Gestalt, view of the effects of multiple pieces of stimulus information. We believe that in many circumstances, such as those likely to prevail in spontaneous, non-laboratory inference processes, separate stimulus cues may not be evaluated separately, and may not be simply averaged to produce an impression. In advancing this position, we wish to emphasize two characteristics of our approach. First, we have tried to present a framework for examining configurations of cues, based upon S-V-O theory (Gollob, 1974a). This framework provides a mechanism for systematically studying, and ultimately predicting, the effects of stimulus cues in combination. It also calls attention to the possibility that different people will tend to focus on different cues in different situations, a complexity that must ultimately be dealt with by inference theorists.

Second, we have not altogether rejected the more particularistic models of inference processing; rather, we have suggested various factors that may determine when one or another kind of processing is likely to occur. Our attention to such models (in, for example, the chapters on combinatorial processes and syllogistic reasoning) reflects our conviction that they provide useful approaches, which can be understood in terms of our current orientation. Yet, as we have previously emphasized, such models are clearly not descriptive of all inference situations, and may in fact be constrained to some very limited kinds of inference tasks.

If this text adequately reflects and justifies these prejudices, without becoming polemical, then it will have succeeded in one very important respect. We also hope the orientation provided will prove useful in integrating admittedly diverse realms of research. And finally, we hope that we have illuminated the directions that we feel social inference theories and research ought to take (or at least, ought to consider taking) in the future.

References

Abelson, R. P. Script processing in attitude formation and decision-making. In J. S. Carroll & J. W. Payne (Eds.), *Cognition and social behavior.* Hillsdale, N.J.: Lawrence Erlbaum Associates, 1976.

Abelson, R. P., & Kanouse, D. E. The acceptance of generic assertions. In S. Feldman (Ed.), *Cognitive consistency: Motivational antecedents and behavioral consequents.* New York: Academic Press, 1966, 171–197.

Abelson, R. P., & Reich, C. M. Implicational molecules: A method for extracting meaning from input sentences. In D. E. Walker & L. M. Norton (Eds.), *Proceedings of the International Joint Conference on Artificial Intelligence,* May, 1969.

Abelson, R. P., & Rosenberg, M. J. Symbolic psycho-logic: A model of attitudinal cognition. *Behavioral Science,* 1958, *3,* 1–13.

Allen, R. B., Ebbesen, E. B., & Bessman, E. *Amount of information in person perception: Evidence for exhaustive memory scanning.* Unpublished manuscript, University of California, San Diego, 1977.

Anderson, J. R., & Bower, G. H. *Human associative memory.* Washington, D. C.: V. H. Winston, 1973.

Anderson, J. R., & Hastie, R. Individuation and reference in memory: Proper names and definitive descriptions. *Cognitive Psychology,* 1974.

Anderson, N. H. Application of an additive model to impression formation. *Science,* 1962, *138,* 817–818.

Anderson, N. H. Averaging versus adding as a stimulus-combination rule in impression formation. *Journal of Experimental Psychology,* 1965, *70,* 394–400.

Anderson, N. H. Averaging model analysis of set size effect in impression formation. *Journal of Experimental Psychology,* 1967, *75,* 158–165.

Anderson, N. H. Simple model for information integration. In R. P. Abelson, et al. (Eds.), *theories of cognitive consistency: A sourcebook.* Chicago: Rand McNally, 1968 (a).

Anderson, N. H. Application of a linear–serial model to a personality impression task using serial presentation. *Journal of Personality and Social Psychology,* 1968, *10,* 354–362 (b).

Anderson, N. H. Functional measurement and psychophysical judgment. *Psychological Review,* 1970, *77,* 153–170.

Anderson, N. H. Integration theory and attitude change. *Psychological Review*, 1971, *78*, 171–206 (a).

Anderson, N. H. Two more tests against change of meaning in adjective combination. *Journal of Verbal Learning and Verbal Behavior*, 1971, *10*, 75–85 (b).

Anderson, N. H. Cognitive algebra: Integration theory applied to social attribution. In L. Berkowitz (Ed.), *Advances in experimental social psychology*, Vol. 7. New York: Academic Press, 1974, 1–101 (a).

Anderson, N. H. Information integration theory: A brief survey. In D. H. Krantz, R. C. Atkinson, R. D. Luce, & P. Suppes (Eds.), *Contemporary developments in mathematical psychology*, Vol. 2. New York: Academic Press, 1974 (b).

Anderson, N. H., & Clavadetscher, J. Tests of a conditioning hypothesis with adjective combinations. *Journal of Experimental Psychology: Human Learning and Memory*, 1976, *2*, 11–20.

Anderson, N. H., & Jacobson, A. Effects of stimulus inconsistency and discounting instructions in personality impression formation. *Journal of Personality and Social Psychology*, 1965, *2*, 531–539.

Anderson, N. H., & Norman, A. Order effects in impression formation in four classes of stimuli. *Journal of Abnormal and Social Psychology*, 1964, *69*, 467–471.

Anderson, R. C., Reynolds, R. E., Schallert, D. L., & Goetz, E. T. *Frameworks for comprehending dicourse* (Tech. Rep. #12). Urbana, Ill.: Laboratory for cognitive studies in education, University of Illinois at Urbana-Champaign, 1976.

Argyle, M., & Dean, J. Eye-contact, distance, and affiliation. *Sociometry*, 1965, *28*, 289–304.

Arkin, R. M., Gleason, J. M., & Johnston, S. Effect of perceived choice, expected outcome, and observed outcome of an action on the causal attributions of actors. *Journal of Experimental Social Psychology*, 1976, *12*, 151–158.

Aronson, E., Willerman, B., & Floyd, J. The effect of a pratfall on increasing interpersonal attraction. *Psychonomic Science*, 1966, *4*, 227–228.

Bartlett, F. C. *Remembering*. Cambridge, England: Cambridge University Press, 1932.

Bem, D. J. An experimental analysis of self-persuasion. *Journal of Experimental Social Psychology*, 1965, *1*, 199–218.

Bem, D. J. Self perception theory. In L. Berkowitz (Ed.), *Advances in experimental social psychology*, Vol. 6. New York: Academic Press, 1972.

Bem, D. J., & McConnell, H. K. Testing the self-perception explanation of dissonance phenomena: On the salience of premanipulation attitudes. *Journal of Personality and Social Psychology*, 1970, *14*, 23–31.

Berscheid, E. & Walster, E. *Interpersonal attraction*. Reading, Mass.: Addison-Wesley, 1969.

Birnbaum, M. H. The nonadditivity of personality impressions. *Journal of Experimental Psychology*, 1974, *102*, 543–561.

Birnbaum, M. H., Wong, R., & Wong, L. K. Combining information from sources that vary in credibility. *Memory and Cognition*, 1976, *4*, 330–336.

Bleda, P. R., Bell, P. A., & Byrne, D. Prior induced affect and sex differences in attraction. *Memory and Cognition*, 1973, *1*, 435–438.

Bower, G. H. Mental imagery and associative learning. In L. Gregg (Ed.), *Cognition in learning and memory*. New York: Wiley, 1972.

Bransford, J. D., Barclay, J. R., & Franks, J. J. Sentence memory: A constructive versus interpretative approach. *Cognitive Psychology*, 1972, *3*, 193–209.

Bransford, J. D., & Johnson, M. K. Considerations of some problems of comprehension. In W. Chase (Ed.), *Visual information processing*. New York: Academic Press, 1973.

Brehm, J. W., & Cohen, A. R. *Explorations in cognitive dissonance*. New York: Wiley, 1962.

Byrne, D. Attitudes and attraction. In L. Berkowitz (Ed.), *Advances in experimental social psychology*, Vol. 4. New York: Academic Press, 1969, 36–90.

Byrne, D. *The attraction paradigm.* New York: Academic Press, 1971.

Byrne, D., & Nelson, D. The effect of topic importance and attitude similarity–dissimilarity on attraction in a multistranger design. *Psychonomic Science,* 1965, *3,* 449–450.

Calder, B. J., Ross, M., & Insko, C. A. Attitude change and attitude attribution: Effects of incentive, choice and consequences. *Journal of Personality and Social Psychology,* 1973, *25,* 84–99.

Cantor, N., & Mischel, W. Traits as prototypes: Effects on recognition memory. *Journal of Personality and Social Psychology,* 1977, *35,* 38–48.

Carlston, D. *The effects of interpolated encoding on the recall of behavior and judgments based upon it.* Unpublished Ph.D. dissertation, University of Illinois, 1977.

Cartwright, D., & Harary, F. Structural balance: A generalization of Heider's theory. *Psychological Review,* 1956, *63,* 277–293.

Chandler, J. P. *Subroutine Stepit. Program QCPE66.* Bloomington, Ind.: Quantum Chemistry Program Exchange, Indiana University, 1965.

Chapman, L. J. Illusory correlation in observational report. *Journal of Verbal Learning and Verbal Behavior,* 1967, *6,* 151–155.

Chapman, L. J., & Chapman, J. P. Atmosphere effect reexamined. *Journal of Experimental Psychology,* 1959, *58,* 220–226.

Clark, H. H., & Clark, E. V. *Psychology and language: An introduction to psycholinguistics.* New York: Harcourt Brace Jovanovich, 1977.

Clore, G. L. *Interpersonal attraction: An overview.* Morristown, N.J.: General Learning Press, 1975.

Clore, G. L., & Gormly, J. B. Knowing, feeling and liking: A psycho-physiological study of attraction. *Journal of Research in Personality,* 1974, *8,* 218–230.

Cohen, C. E. *An information processing approach to social perception: The influence of a stereotype upon what an observer remembered.* Unpublished Ph.D. dissertation, University of California, San Diego, 1977.

Cohen, C. E., & Ebbesen, E. B. Observational goals and schema activation: A theoretical framework for behavior perception. *Journal of Experimental Social Psychology,* in press.

Collins, A. M., & Loftus, E. F. A spreading-activation theory of semantic processing. *Psychological Review,* 1975, *82,* 407–428.

Collins, A. M., & Quillian, M. R. Retrieval time from semantic memory. *Journal of Verbal Learning and Verbal Behavior,* 1969, *8,* 323–343.

Collins, A. M., & Quillian, M. R. Does category size affect categorization time? *Journal of Verbal Learning and Verbal Behavior,* 1970, *9,* 432–438.

Collins, B. E., & Hoyt, M. F. Personal responsibility-for-consequences: An integration and extension of the "forced compliance" literature. *Journal of Experimental Social Psycholgy,* 1972, *8,* 558–593.

Cooper, L. A., & Shepard, R. N. Chronometric studies of the rotation of mental images. In W. G. Chase (Eds.), *Visual information processing.* New York: Academic Press, 1973 (a).

Cooper, L. A., & Shepard, R. N. The time required to prepare for a rotated stimulus. *Memory and Cognition,* 1973, *1,* 246–250 (b).

Cordray, D. S., & Shaw, J. I. An empirical test of the covariation analysis in causal attribution. *Journal of Experimental Social Psychology,* 1978, *14,* 280–290.

Costin, F. The scrambled sentence test: a group measure of hostility. *Educational and Psychological Measurement,* 1969, *29,* 461–468.

Cottrell, N. B., & Wack, D. L. Energizing effects of cognitive dissonance upon dominant and subordinate responses. *Journal of Personality and Social Psychology,* 1967, *6,* 132–138.

Craik, F. I. M. Depth of processing in recall and recognition. In S. Dornic (Ed.), *Attention and performance VI.* Hillsdale, N. J.: Lawrence Erlbaum Associates, 1977.

Craik, F. I. M., & Lockhart, R. S. Levels of processing: A framework for memory research. *Journal of Verbal Learning and Verbal Behavior,* 1972, *11,* 671–684.

D'Andrade, R. G. Trait psychology and componential analysis. *American Anthropologist,* 1965, *67,* 215–228.

Darley, S. A., & Cooper, J. Cognitive consequences of forced noncompliance. *Journal of Personality and Social Psychology,* 1972, *24,* 321–326.

Darley, J. M., & Latane, B. Bystander intervention in emergencies: Diffusion of responsibility. *Journal of Personality and Social Psychology,* 1968, *8,* 377–383.

Dillehay, R. C., Insko, C. A., & Smith, M. M. Logical consistency and attitude change. *Journal of Personality and Social Psychology,* 1966, *3,* 646–654.

Dustin, D. S., & Baldwin, P. M. Redundancy in impression formation. *Journal of Personality and Social Psychology,* 1966, *3,* 500–506.

Dweck, C. S. The role of expectations and attributions in the alleviation of learned helplessness. *Journal of Personality and Social Psychology,* 1975, *31,* 674–685.

Ebbesen, E. B., Cohen, C. E., & Allen, R. B. *Encoding and the processing of person information: Behavior scanning and semantic memory.* Unpublished manuscript, University of California, San Diego, 1977.

Ebbesen, E. B., Cohen, C. E., & Lane, J. L. *Encoding and construction processes in person perception.* Paper presented at American Psychological Association Convention, Chicago, 1975.

Ellsworth, P. C., & Carlsmith, J. M. Effects of eye contact and verbal content on affective response to a dyadic interaction. *Journal of Personality and Social Psychology,* 1968, *10,* 15–20.

Ellsworth, P., & Ross, L. Intimacy in response to direct gaze. *Journal of Experimental Social Psychology,* 1975, *11,* 592–613.

Erickson, J. L. A set analysis theory of behavior in formal syllogistic reasoning tasks. In R. Solso (Ed.), *Theories in cognitive psychology: The Loyola Symposium.* Potomac, Md.: Lawrence Erlbaum Associates, 1974.

Feather, N. T. A structural balance approach to the analysis of communication effects. In L. Berkowitz (Eds.), *Advances in experimental social psychology,* Vol. 3. New York: Academic Press, 1967.

Feather, N. T., & Simon, J. G. Attribution of responsibility and valence of outcome in relation to initial confidence and success and failure of self and other. *Journal of Personality and Social Psychology,* 1971, *18,* 173–188.

Feldman, S. Motivational aspects of attitudinal elements and their place in cognitive interaction. In S. Feldman (Ed.), *Cognitive consistency: Motivational antecedents and behavioral consequents.* New York: Academic Press, 1966, 76–108.

Festinger, L. A theory of social comparison processes. *Human Relations,* 1954, *7,* 117–140.

Festinger, L. *A theory of cognitive dissonance.* Stanford: Stanford University Press, 1957.

Festinger, L., & Maccoby, E. On resistance to persuasive communications. *Journal of Abnormal and Social Psychology,* 1964, *68,* 359–366.

Fishbein, M. An investigation of the relationships between beliefs about an object and attitude toward that object. *Human Relations,* 1963, *16,* 233–239.

Fishbein, M., & Ajzen, I. *Belief, attitude, intention and behavior: An introduction to theory and research.* Reading, Mass,: Addison-Wesley, 1975.

Fishbein, M., & Hunter, R. Summation versus balance in attitude organization and change. *Journal of Abnormal and Social Psychology,* 1964, *69,* 505–510.

Gilson, C., & Abelson, R. P. The subjective use of inductive evidence. *Journal of Personality and Social Psychology,* 1965, *2,* 301–310.

Glass, A. L., & Holyoak, K. J. Alternative conceptions of semantic theory. *Cognition,* 1975, *3,* 313–339.

Gollob, H. F. Impression formation and word combination in sentences. *Journal of Personality and Social Psychology,* 1968, *10,* 341–353.

Gollob, H. F. Some tests of a social inference model. *Journal of Personality and Social Psychology,* 1974, *29,* 157–172 (a).

Gollob, H. F. The *Subject–Verb–Object* approach to social cognition. *Psychological Review,* 1974, *4,* 286–321 (b).

Gouaux, C. *Interpersonal attraction as a function of induced affect and social dependence.* Unpublished master's thesis, University of Texas, 1969.

Greenwald, A. G. Cognitive learning, cognitive responses to persuasion and attitude change. In A. G. Greenwald, T. Brock, & T. M. Ostrom (Eds.), *Psychological foundations of attitudes.* New York: Academic Press, 1968.

Griffitt, W., & Veitch, R. Hot and crowded: Influences of population density and temperature on interpersonal affective behavior. *Journal of Personality and Social Psychology,* 1971, *17,* 92–98.

Hamilton, D. L., & Gifford, R. K. Illusory correlation in interpersonal perception: A cognitive basis of stereotypic judgments. *Journal of Experimental Social Psychology,* 1976, *12,* 392–407.

Hamilton, D. L., & Katz, L. B. *A process-oriented approach to the study of impressions.* Paper read at American Psychological Association Convention, Chicago, 1975.

Hamilton, D. L., & Zanna, M. P. Differential weighting of favorable and unfavorable attributes in impressions of personality. *Journal of Experimental Research in Personality,* 1972, *6,* 204–212.

Heider, F. *The psychology of interpersonal relations.* New York: Wiley, 1958.

Hendrick, C., & Costantini, A. F. Effects of varying trait inconsistency and response requirements on the primacy effect in impression formation. *Journal of Personality and Social Psychology,* 1970, *15,* 158–164.

Henninger, M. *An information-processing approach to the "Socratic effect."* Unpublished M.A. Thesis, University of Illinois at Urbana-Champaign, 1975.

Henninger, M., & Wyer, R. S. THe recognition and elimination of inconsistencies among syllogistically related beliefs: Some new light on the "Socratic effect." *Journal of Personality and Social Psychology,* 1976, *34,* 680–693.

Higgins, E. T., Rhodewalt, F., & Zanna, M. P., Dissonance motivation: Its nature, persistence and reinstatement. *Journal of Experimental Social Psychology,* 1979, *15,* 16–34.

Higgins, E. T., & Rholes, W. S. Impression formation and role fulfillment: A "holistic reference" approach. *Journal of Experimental Social Psychology,* 1976, *12,* 422–435.

Higgins, E. T., Rholes, W. S., & Jones, C. R. Category accessibility and impression formation. *Journal of Experimental Social Psychology,* 1977, *13,* 141–154.

Hinkle, R. L. *The role of stimulus clarity in impression formation.* Unpublished M.A. Thesis, University of Illinois at Urbana-Champaign, 1976.

Holt, L. E. Resistance to persuasion on explicit beliefs as a function of commitment to and desirability of logically related beliefs. *Journal of Personality and Social Psychology,* 1970, *16,* 583–591.

Hovland, C. I. (Ed.) *The order of presentation in persuasion.* New Haven: Yale University Press, 1957.

Insko, C. A., & Schopler, J. Triadic consistency: A statement of affective–cognitive–conative consistency. *Psychological Review,* 1967, *74,* 361–376.

Johnson, M. K., Bransford, J. D., & Solomon, S. K. Memory for tacit implications of sentences. *Journal of Experimental Psychology,* 1973, *98,* 203–205.

Jones, E. E. How do people perceive the cause of behavior? *American Scientist,* 1976, *64,* 300–305.

Jones, E. E., & Davis, K. E. From acts to dispositions: The attribution process in person perception. In L. Berkowitz (Ed.), *Advances in experimental social psychology,* Vol. 2. New York: Academic Press, 1965.

Jones, E. E., Davis, K. E., & Gergen, K. J. Role playing variations and their informational value for person perception. *Jorunal of Abnormal and Social Psychology,* 1961, *63,* 302–310.

Jones, E. E., & Goethals, G. R. *Order effects in impression formation: Attribution context and the nature of the entity.* New York: General Learning Press, 1971.

Jones, E. E., & McGillis, D. Correspondent inferences and the attribution cube: A comparative reappraisal. In J. Harvey, W. Ickes & R. Kidd (Eds.), *New directions in attribution research,* Vol. 1. Hillsdale, N.J.: Lawrence Erlbaum Associates, 1976, 389–420.

Jones, E. E., & Nisbett, R. E. *The actor and the oberver: Divergent perceptions of the causes of behavior.* New York: General Learning Press, 1971.

Jones, E. E., Rock, L., Shaver, K. G., Goethals, G. R., & Ward, L. M. Pattern of performance and ability attribution: An unexpected primacy effect. *Journal of Personality and Social Psychology,* 1968, *10,* 317–340.

Kanouse, D. E. *Language, labeling and attribution.* Morristown, N.J.: General Learning Press, 1971.

Kanouse, D. E., & Abelson, R. P. Language variables affecting the persuasiveness of simple communications. *Journal of Personality and Social Psychology,* 1967, *7,* 158–163.

Kaplan, M. F. Context induced shifts in personality trait evaluations: A comment on the evaluative halo effect and the meaning change interpretations. *Psychological Bulletin,* 1974, *81,* 891–895.

Kelley, H. H. Salience of membership and resistance to change of group-anchored attitudes. *Human Relations,* 1955, *8,* 275–290.

Kelley, H. H. Attribution theory in social psychology. In D. Levine (Ed.), *Nebraska symposium on motivation.* Lincoln, Neb.: University of Nebraska Press, 1967.

Kelley, H. H. Causal schemata and the attribution process. In E. E. Jones, D. E. Kanouse, H. H. Kelley, R. E. Nisbett, S. Valins & B. Weiner (Eds.), *Attribution: Perceiving the causes of behavior.* Morristown, N.J.: General Learning Press, 1971.

Kelley, H. H., & Stahelski, A. J. The inference of intention from moves in the Prisoner's Dilemma game. *Journal of Experimental Social Psychology,* 1970, *6,* 401–409.

Kelman, H. C., & Hovland, C. I. "Reinstatement" of the communicator in delayed measurement of opinion change. *Journal of Abnormal and Social Psychology,* 1953, *48,* 327–335.

Kerber, K., & Coles, M. G. H. *Sources of false heartrate feedback: Cognitive and physiological effects.* Unpublished manuscript, University of Illinois, 1977.

Kosslyn, S. M. Scanning visual images: Some structural implications. *Perception and Psychophysics,* 1973, *14,* 90–94.

Kosslyn, S. M. On retrieving information from visual images. In R. Schank & B. L. Nash-Webber (Eds.), *Theoretical issues in natural language processing.* Proceedings of conference at Massachusetts Institute of Technology, 1975.

Kosslyn, S. M. Can imagery be distinguished from other forms of internal representation? Evidence from studies of information retrieval time. *Memory and Cognition,* 1976, *4,* 291–297.

Kosslyn, S. M., Holyoak, K. J., & Huffman, C. S. A processing approach to the dual coding hypothesis. *Journal of Experimental Psychology: Human learning and memory,* 1976, *2,* 223–233.

Kosslyn, S. M., & Pomerantz, J. R. Imagery, propositions and the form of internal representations. *Cognitive Psychology,* 1977, *9,* 52–76.

Krauss, R. M. *Some truths about lying: Experimental studies of deceptive interactions.* Paper presented at First National Conference on Body Language, City University of New York, 1977.

Krauss, R. M., Geller, V., & Olson, C. *Modalities and cues in the detection of deception.* Paper presented at American Psychological Association Convention, 1976.

Lampel, A. K., & Anderson, N. H.   Combining visual and verbal information in an impression-formation task. *Journal of Personality and Social Psychology,* 1968, *9,* 1–6.

Langer, E. J., & Abelson, R. P.   The semantics of asking a favor: How to succeed in getting help without really dying. *Journal of Personality and Social Psychology,* 1972, *24,* 26–32.

Latane, B. (Ed.), Studies in social comparison. *Journal of Experimental Social Psychology Supplement,* 1966.

Lerner, M. J., Miller, D. T., & Holmes, J. G.   Deserving and the emergence of forms of justice. In L. Berkowitz (Ed.), *Advances in experimental social psychology,* Vol. 9. New York: Academic Press, 1976.

Lerner, M. J., & Simmons, C. H.   Observer's reaction to the "innocent victim": Compassion or rejection. *Journal of Personality and Social Psychology,* 1966, *4,* 203–210.

Leventhal, H.   Findings and theory in the study of fear communications. In L. Berkowitz (Ed.), *Advances in experimental social psychology,* Vol. 5. New York: Academic Press, 1970, 119–186.

Lingle, J. H., Geva, N., & Ostrom, T. M.   *Cognitive processes in person perception.* Paper read at American Psychological Association Convention, Chicago, September, 1975.

Lingle, J. H., & Ostrom, T. M.   *Influences of information availability on cognitive processes in person perception.* Paper read at American Psychological Association Convention, Washington, D. C., September 1976.

Lingle, J. H., & Ostrom, T. M.   Retrieval selectivity in memory-based impression judgments. *Journal of Personality and Social Psychology,* 1979, *37,* 180–194.

Loftus, G. G., & Loftus, E. L.   The influence of one memory retrieval on a subsequent memory retrieval. *Memory and Cognition,* 1974, *2,* 467–471.

Loftus, E. L., & Palmer, J.   Reconstruction of automobile destruction. *Journal of Verbal Learning and Verbal Behavior,* 1974, *13,* 585–589.

Markus, H.   Self-schemata and processing information about the self. *Journal of Personality and Social Psychology,* 1977, *35,* 63–78.

McArthur, L. A.   The how and what of why: Some determinants and consequences of causal attribution. *Journal of Personality and Social Psychology,* 1972, *22,* 171–193.

McFarland, S. G., & Thistlethwaite, D. L.   An analysis of a logical consistency model of belief change. *Journal of Personality and Social Psychology,* 1970, *16,* 133–143.

McGuire, W. J.   A syllogistic analysis of cognitive relationships. In M. J. Rosenberg et al. (Eds.), *Attitude organization and change.* New Haven: Yale University Press, 1960, 65–111.

McGuire, W. J.   Theory of the structure of human thought. In R. P. Abelson *et al.,* (Eds.), *Theories of cognitive consistency: A sourcebook.* Chicago: Rand-McNally, 1968, 140–162 (a).

McGuire, W. J.   Personality and susceptibility to social influence. In E. Borgatta & W. Lambert (Eds.), *Handbook of personality theory and research.* Chicago: Rand-McNally, 1968. (b)

McGuire, W. J.   The nature of attitudes and attitude change. In G. Lindzey & E. Aronson (Eds.), *Handbook of social psychology.* Reading, Mass.: Addison-Wesley, 1968, 136–314 (c).

McGuire, W. J., & Millman, S.   Anticipatory belief lowering following forewarning of a persuasive attack. *Journal of Personality and Social Psychology,* 1965, *2,* 471–479.

Mehrabian, A.   Significance of posture and position in the communication of attitude and status relationships. *Psychological Bulletin,* 1969, *71,* 359–372.

Meyer, D. E., & Schvaneveldt, R. W.   Meaning, memory structure and mental processes. In C. N. Cofer (Ed.), *The structure of human memory.* San Francisco: W. H. Freeman, 1976.

Meyer, D. E., & Schvaneveldt, R. W.   Facilitation in recognition between pairs of words: Evidence of a dependence between retrieval operations. *Journal of Experimental Psychology,* 1971, *90,* 227–234.

Miller, A. G.   Constraint and target effects on the attribution of attitudes. *Journal of Experimental Social Psychology,* 1976, *12,* 325–339.

Miller, G. A. The magical number seven, plus or minus two: Some limits on our capacity for processing information. *Psychological Review*, 1956, *63*, 81–97.

Miller, D. T., Altrusim and threat to a belief in a just world. *Journal of Experimental Social Psychology*, 1977, *13*, 113–124 (a).

Miller, D. T. Personal deserving versus justice for others: An exploration of the justice motive. *Journal of Experimental Social Psychology*, 1977, *13*, 1–13 (b).

Miller, D. T., & Ross, M. Self-serving biases in the attribution of causality: Fact or fiction? *Psychological Bulletin*, 1975, *82*, 213–225.

Mills, J., & Jellison, J. M. Effect on opinion change of how desirable the communication is to the audience the communicator addressed. *Journal of Personality and Social Psychology*, 1967, *6*, 98–101.

Monson, T. C., & Snyder, M. Actors, observers and the attribution process: Toward a reconceptualization. *Journal of Experimental Social Psychology*, 1977, *13*, 89–111.

Mosteller, F., & Tukey, J. W. Data analysis, including statistics. In G. Lindzey & E. Aronson (Eds.), *Handbook of social psychology*, Vol. 2. Reading, Mass: Addison-Wesley, 1968.

Nemeth, C. A critical analysis of research utilizing the Prisoner's Dilemma paradigm for the study of bargaining. In L. Berkowitz (Ed.), *Advances in experimental social psychology*, Vol. 6. New York: Academic Press, 1972, 203–234.

Newtson, D. Attribution and the unit of perception of ongoing behavior. *Journal of Personality and Social Psychology*, 1973, *28*, 28–38.

Newtson, D. Foundations of attribution: The perception of ongoing behavior. In J. Harvey, W. Ickes, & R. Kidd (Eds.), *New directions in attribution research*, Vol. 1. Hillsdale, N.J.: Lawrence Erlbaum Associates, 1976.

Newtson, D., & Engquist, G. The perceptual organization of ongoing behavior. *Journal of Experimental Social Psychology*, 1976, *12*, 436–450.

Nisbett, R. N., & Borgida, E. Attribution and the psychology of prediction. *Journal of Personality and Social Psychology*, 1975, *32*, 932–943.

Nisbett, R. E., & Schachter, S. Cognitive manipulation of pain. *Journal of Experimental Social Psychology*, 1966, *2*, 227–236.

Nygren, T. E., & Jones, L. E. Individual differences in perceptions and preferences for political candidates. *Journal of Experimental Social Psychology*, 1977, *13*, 182–197.

Oden, G. C., & Anderson, N. H. Differential weighting in integration theory. *Journal of Experimental Psychology*, 1971, *89*, 152–161.

Orvis, B. R., Cunningham, J. D., & Kelley, H. H. A closer examination of causal inference: The roles of consensus, distinctiveness and consistency information. *Journal of Personality and Social Psychology*, 1975, *32*, 605–616.

Osgood, C. E., Suci, G. J., & Tannenbaum, P. H. *The measurement of meaning*. Urbana, Ill.: University of Illinois Press, 1957.

Osgood, C. E., & Tannenbaum, P. H. The principle of congruity in the prediction of attitude change. *Psychological Review*, 1955, *62*, 42–55.

Ostrom, T. M. Between-theory and within-theory conflict in explaining context effects in impression formation. *Journal of Experimental Social Psychology*, 1977, *13*, 492–503.

Ostrom, T. M., & Upshaw, H. S. Psychological perspective and attitude change. In A. Greenwald, T. Brock, & T. Ostrom. *Psychological foundations of attitudes*. New York: Academic Press, 1968.

Paivio, A. *Imagery and verbal processes*. New York: Holt, 1971.

Parducci, A. Category judgment: A range–frequency model. *Psychological Review*, 1965, *72*, 407–418.

Patterson, M. L. An arousal model of interpersonal intimacy. *Psychological Review*, 1966, *83*, 235–245.

Peabody, D. Trait inferences: Evaluative and descriptive aspects. *Journal of Personality and Social Psychology Monograph,* 1967, *7* (Whole No. 4).

Peterson, C. R. & Beach, L. R. Man as an intuitive statistician. *Psychological Bulletin,* 1967, *68,* 29–46.

Pichert, J. W., & Anderson, R. C. *Taking different perspectives on a story.* (Tech. Rep. #14). Center for the Study of Reading, University of Illinois at Urbana-Champaign, 1976.

Pittman, T. S. Attribution of arousal as a mediator in dissonance reduction. *Journal of Experimental Social Psychology,* 1975, *11,* 53–63.

Podeschi, D. M., & Wyer, R. S. Acceptance of generalizations based upon inductive and deductive evidence. *Journal of Personality and Social Psychology,* 1976, *34,* 496–509.

Pylyshyn, Z. W. What the mind's eye tells the mind's brain: A critique of mental imagery. *Psychological Bulletin,* 1973, *80* 1–24.

Reeder, G. D., Messick, D. M., & van Avermaet, E. Dimensional asymmetry in attributional inference. *Journal of Experimental Social Psychology,* 1977, *13,* 46–57.

Regan, D., & Totten, J. Empathy and attribution: Turning observers into actors. *Journal of Personality and Social Psychology,* 1975, *32,* 850–856.

Rosch, E. H. On the internal structure of perceptual and semantic categories. In T. E. Moore (Ed.), *Cognitive development and the acquisition of language.* New York: Academic Press, 1973.

Rosen, N. A., & Wyer, R. S. Some further evidence for the "Socratic effect" using a subjective probability model of cognitive organization. *Journal of Personality and Social Psychology,* 1972, *24,* 420–424.

Rosenbaum, M. E., & Levin, I. P. Impression formation as a function of source credibility and the polarity of information. *Journal of Personality and Social Psychology,* 1969, *12,* 34–37.

Rosenberg, S., Nelson, C., & Vivekananthan, P. S. A multidimensional approach to the structure of personality impressions. *Journal of Personality and Social Psychology,* 1968, *9,* 283–294.

Rosenberg, S., & Sedlak, A. Structural representations of implicit personality theory. In L. Berkowitz (Ed.) *Advances in experimental social psychology,* Vol. 6. New York: Academic Press, 1972, pp. 235–297.

Ross, L. The intuitive psychologist and his shortcomings: Distortions in the attribution process. In L. Berkowitz (Ed.), *Advances in experimental social psychology,* Vol. 10. New York: Academic Press, 1977, 174–221.

Ross, L., Lepper, M., & Hubbard, M. Perseverance in self-perception and social perception: Biased attributional processes in the debriefing paradigm. *Journal of Personality and Social Psychology,* 1975, *32,* 880–892.

Ross, L., Lepper, M. R., Strack, F., & Steinmetz, J. Social explanation and social expectation: Effects of real and hypothetical explanations on subjective likelihood. *Journal of Personality and Social Psychology,* 1977, *35,* 817–829.

Rossman, B. B., & Gollob, H. F. Social inference and pleasantness judgments involving people and issues. *Journal of Experimental Social Psychology,* 1976, *12,* 374–391.

Rumelhart, D. E., & Ortony, A. The representation of knowledge in memory. In R. D. Anderson, R. J. Spiro, & W. E. Montague (Eds.), *Schooling and the acquisition of knowledge.* Hillsdale, N. J.: Lawrence Erlbaum Associates, 1977, pp. 99–135.

Salancik, G. R. Inference of one's attitude from behavior recalled under linguistically manipulated cognitive sets. *Journal of Experimental Social Psychology,* 1974, *10,* 415–427.

Salancik, G. R., & Calder, B. J. *A non-predispositional information analysis of attitude expressions.* Unpublished manuscript, University of Illinois, 1974.

Salancik, G. R., & Conway, M. Attitude inferences from salient and relevant cognitive content about behavior. *Journal of Personality and Social Psychology,* 1975, *32,* 829–840.

Schachter, S., & Singer, J. E. Cognitive, social and physiological determinants of emotional state. *Psychological Review,* 1962, *69,* 379–399.

Schank, R., & Abelson, R. P. *Scripts, plans, goals and understanding.* Hillsdale, N.J.: Lawrence Erlbaum Associates, 1977.

Schmidt, C. F. Personality impression formation as a function of relatedness of information and length of set. *Journal of Personality and Social Psychology, 1969, 12,* 6–11.

Schneider, D. J. Implicit personality theory: A reviw. *Psychological Bulletin, 1973, 79,* 294–319.

Schvaneveldt, R. W., & Meyer, D. E. Retrieval and comparison processes in semantic memory. In S. Kornblum (Ed.), *Attention and performance IV.* New York: Academic Press, 1973.

Shaver, K. G. *An introduction to attribution processes.* Cambridge, Mass.: Winthrop, 1975.

Shepard, R. N., & Metzler, J. Mental rotation of three-dimensional objects. *Science, 1971, 171,* 701–703.

Sherif, M., & Hovland, C. I. *Social judgment.* New Haven: Yale University Press, 1961.

Shoben, E. J. The verification of semantic relations in a same–different paradigm: An asymmetry in semantic memory. *Journal of Verbal Learning and Verbal Behavior, 1976, 15,* 365–379.

Sidowski, J. B., & Anderson, N. H. Judgments of city–occupation combinations. *Psychonomic Science, 1967, 7,* 279–280.

Smith, E. E., Shoben, E. J., & Rips, L. J. Structure and process in semantic memory: A featural model for semantic decisions. *Psychological Review, 1974, 81* 214–241.

Snyder, M., & Ebbesen, E. B. Dissonance awareness: A test of dissonance theory versus self-perception theory. *Journal of Experimental Social Psychology, 1972, 8,* 502–517.

Spiro, R. J. Remembering information from text: The "state of schema" approach. In R. C. Anderson, R. J. Spiro, & W. E. Montague (Eds.), *Schooling and the acquisition of knowledge.* Hillsdale, N.J.: Lawrence Erlbaum Associates, 1977.

Storms, M. Videotape and the attribution process: Reversing actors' and observers' point of view. *Journal of Personality and Social Psychology, 1973, 27,* 165–175.

Streeter, L. A., Krauss, R. M., Geller, V., Olson, C., & Apple, W. Pitch changes during attempted deception. *Journal of Personality and Social Psychology, 1977, 35,* 345–350.

Swenson, C. H. *Introduction to interpersonal relations.* Glenview, Ill.: Scott, Foresman, 1973.

Tannenbaum, P. H. The congruity principle revisited: Studies in the reduction, induction and generalization of persuasion. In L. Berkowitz (Ed.), *Advances in experimental social psychology,* Vol. 3. New York: Academic Press, 1967, 271–230.

Tesser, A. Thought and reality constraints as determinants of attitude polarization. *Journal of Research in Personality, 1976, 10,* 183–194.

Tesser, A., & Conlee, M. Some effects of time and thought on attitude polarization. *Journal of Personality and Social Psychology, 1975, 31,* 262–270.

Tesser, A., & Cowan, C. L. Some effects of thought and number of cognitions on attitude change. *Social Behavior and Personality, 1975, 3,* 165–173.

Tesser, A., & Cowan, C. L. Some attitudinal and cognitive consequences of thought. *Journal of Research in Personality, 1977, 11,* 216–226.

Tesser, A., & Leone, C. Cognitive schemas and thought as determinants of attitude change. *Journal of Experimental Social Psychology, 1977, 13,* 340–356.

Tesser, A. Self-generated attitude change. In L. Berkowitz (Ed.), *Advances in experimental social psychology, Vol. II.* New York: Academic Press, 1978, 290–338.

Thibaut, J. W., & Kelley, H. H. *The social psychology of groups.* New York: Wiley, 1959.

Triandis, H. C. Exploratory factor analyses of the behavioral component of social attitudes. *Journal of Abnormal and Social Psychology 1964, 68,* 420–430.

Tulving, E. Episodic and semantic memory. In E. Tulving & W. Donaldson (Eds.), *Organization and memory.* New York: Academic Press, 1972.

Tversky, A. & Kahneman, D. Availability: A heuristic for judging frequency and probability. *Cognitive Psychology, 1973, 5,* 207–232.

Upshaw, H. S. The personal reference scale: An approach to social judgment. In L. Berkowitz (Ed.), *Advances in experimental social psychology,* Vol. 4. New York: Academic Press, 1969.

Upshaw, H. S. Social influence on attitudes and on anchoring of congeneric attitude scales. *Journal of Experimental Social Psychology,* 1978, *14,* 327–339.

Valins, S. Cognitive effects of false heart-rate feedback. *Journal of Personality and Social Psychology,* 1966, *4,* 400–408.

Valins, S. Persistent effects of information about internal reactions: Ineffectiveness of debriefing. In H. London & R. E. Nisbett (Eds.), *Thought and feeling: Cognitive alteration of feeling states.* Chicago: Aldine, 1974.

Walster, E. Assignment of responsibility for an accident. *Journal of Personality and Social Psychology,* 1966, *3,* 73–79.

Walster, E., Berscheid, E. & Walster, G. W. New directions in equity research. *Journal of Personality and Social Psychology,* 1973, *25,* 151–176.

Ward, L. B. Reminiscence and rote learning. *Psychological Monographs,* 1937, *49* (Whole No. 220).

Warr, P. Inference magnitude, range, and evaluative direction as factors affecting relative importance of cues in impression formation. *Journal of Personality and Social Psychology,* 1974, *30,* 191–197.

Wason, P. E., & Johnson-Laird, P. N. *Psychology of reasoning: Structure and content.* Cambridge, Mass.: Harvard University Press, 1972.

Waterman, C. K., & Katkin, E. S. Energizing (dynamogenic) effect of cognitive dissonance on task performance. *Journal of Personality and Social Psychology,* 1967, *6,* 126–131.

Watts, W. A., & Holt, L. W. Logical relationships among beliefs and timing as factors in persuasion. *Journal of Personality and Social Psychology,* 1970, *16,* 571–582.

Weiner, B., Freize, I., Kukla, A., Reed, L., Rest, S., & Rosenbaum, R. M. *Perceiving the causes of success and failure.* Morristown, N.J.: General Learning Press, 1971.

Wolfson, M. R., & Salancik, G. R. Observer orientation and actor–observer differences in attributions for failure. *Journal of Experimental Social Psychology,* 1977, *13,* 441–451.

Woodworth, R., & Sells, S. An atmosphere effect in formal syllogistic reasoning. *Journal of Experimental Psychology,* 1935, *18,* 451–460.

Wyer, R. S. The effects of information redundancy on evaluations of social stimuli. *Psychonomic Science,* 1968, *13,* 245–246.

Wyer, R. S. A quantitative comparison of three models of impression formation. *Journal of Experimental Research in Personality,* 1969, *4,* 29–41. (a)

Wyer, R. S. The prediction of behavior in two-person games. *Journal of Personality and Social Psychology,* 1969, *13,* 222–238. (b)

Wyer, R. S. Information redundancy, inconsistency and novelty and their role in impression formation. *Journal of Experimental Social Psychology,* 1970, *6,* 111–127 (a).

Wyer, R. S. The quantitative prediction of belief and opinion change: A further test of a subjective probability model. *Journal of Personality and Social Psychology,* 1970, *16,* 559–571 (b).

Wyer, R. S. The effects of outcome matrix and partner's behavior in two-person games. *Journal of Experimental Social Psychology,* 1971, *7,* 190–210.

Wyer, R. S. Test of a subjective probability model of social evaluation processes. *Journal of Personality and Social Psychology,* 1972, *22,* 279–286.

Wyer, R. S. Category ratings as "subjective expected values": Implications for attitude formation and change. *Psychological Review,* 1973, *80,* 446–467 (a).

Wyer, R. S. The effects of information inconsistency and grammatical context upon evaluations of persons. *Journal of Personality and Social Psychology,* 1973, *25,* 45–49 (b).

Wyer, R. S. Further test of a subjective probability model of social inference. *Journal of Research in Personality,* 1973, *7,* 237–253 (c).

Wyer, R. S. Changes in meaning and halo effects in personality impression formation. *Journal of Personality and Social Psychology,* 1974, *29,* 829–835 (a).

Wyer, R. S. *Cognitive organization and change: An information-processing approach.* Potomac, Md.: Lawrence Erlbaum Associates, 1974 (b).

Wyer, R. S. Some implications of the "Socratic effect" for alternative models of cognitive consistency, *Journal of Personality*, 1974, *42*, 399–419 (c).

Wyer, R. S. Direct and indirect effects of essay writing and information about other persons' opinions upon beliefs in logically related propositions. *Journal of Personality and Social Psychology*, 1975, *31*, 55–63 (a).

Wyer, R. S. Functional measurement analysis of a subjective probability model of cognitive functioning. *Journal of Personality and Social Psychology*, 1975, *31*, 94–100 (b).

Wyer, R. S. The role of probabilistic and syllogistic reasoning in cognitive organization and social inference. In M. Kaplan & S. Schwartz (Eds.), *Human judgment and decision processes.* New York: Academic Press, 1975 (c).

Wyer, R. S. Some informational determinants of one's own liking for a person and beliefs that others will like this person. *Journal of Personality and Social Psychology*, 1975, *31*, 1041–1053 (d).

Wyer, R. S. Effects of previously formed beliefs on syllogistic inference processes. *Journal of Personality and Social Psychology*, 1976, *33*, 307–316 (a).

Wyer, R. S. The role of logical and nonlogical factors in making inferences about category membership. *Journal of Experimental Social Psychology*, 1977, *13*, 577–595.

Wyer, R. S., & Dermer, M. Effects of context and instructional set upon evaluations of personality-trait adjectives. *Journal of Personality and Social Psychology*, 1968, *9*, 7–14.

Wyer, R. S., & Goldberg, L. A probabilistic analysis of the relationships between beliefs and attitudes. *Psychological Review*, 1970, *77*, 100–120.

Wyer, R. S. & Hartwick, J. Information retrieval, syllogistic reasoning and social inference. In L. Berkowitz (Ed.) *Advances in experimental social psychology*, Vol. 3. New York: Academic Press, in press.

Wyer, R. S., & Henninger, M. The effects of reporting beliefs on the recall of belief-related propositions. Unpublished manuscript, University of Illinois, 1978.

Wyer, R. S., Henninger, M., & Hinkle, R. An informational analysis of actors' and observers' belief attributions in a role-playing situation. *Journal of Experimental Social Psychology*, 1977, *13*, 199–217.

Wyer, R. S., Henninger, M., & Wolfson, M. R. Informational determinants of females' self-perceptions and observers' perceptions of them in an achievement situation. *Journal of Personality and Social Psychology*, 1975, *32*, 556–570.

Wyer, R. S. & Hinkle, R. L. Informational factors underlying inferences about hypothetical persons. *Journal of Personality and Social Psychology*, 1976, *34*, 481–495.

Wyer, R. S. & Podeschi, D. The acceptance of generalizations about persons, objects and events. In R. Revlin & R. E. Mayer (Eds.) *Human reasoning.* Washington, D. C.: V. H. Winston, 1978, 101–138.

Wyer, R. S. & Polsky, H. Test of a subjective probability model for predicting receptiveness to alternative explanations of individual behavior. *Journal of Experimental Research in Personality*, 1972, *6*, 220–229.

Wyer, R. S. & Schwartz, S. Some contingencies in the effects of the source of a communication upon the evaluation of that communication. *Journal of Personality and Social Psychology*, 1969, *11*, 1–9.

Wyer, R. S. & Srull, T. K. The processing of social stimulus information: A conceptual integration. In R. Hastie, T. Ostrom, E. Ebbesen, R. Wyer, D. Hamilton, & D. Carlston, *Person memory: The cognitive basis of social perception.* Hillsdale, N.J.: Lawrence Erlbaum Associates, in press.

Wyer, R. S. & Watson, S. F. Context effects in impression formation. *Journal of Personality and Social Psychology*, 1969, *12*, 22–33.

Yandell, B. & Insko, C. A. Attribution of attitudes to speakers and listeners under assigned-behavior conditions: Does behavior engulf the field? *Journal of Experimental Social Psychology*, 1977, *13*, 269–278.

Yavuz, H. S. & Bousfield, W. A. Recall of connotative meaning. *Psychological Reports*, 1959, *5*, 319–320.

Zajonc, R. B. Cognitive theories in social psychology. In G. Lindzey & E. Aronson (Eds.), *Handbook of social psychology*, Vol. 1. Reading, Mass.: Addison-Wesley, 1968, 320–411.

Zanna, M. P. & Cooper, J. Dissonance and the pill: An attribution approach to studying the arousal properties of dissonance. *Journal of Personality and Social Psychology*, 1974, *29*, 703–709.

Zanna, M. P. & Cooper, J. Dissonance and the attribution process. In J. Harvey, W. J. Ickes, & R. F. Kidd (Eds.) *New directions in attribution research*, vol. 1. Hillsdale, N.J.: Lawrence Earlbaum Associates, 1976.

Zanna, M. P., Higgins, E. T., & Taves, P. A. Is dissonance phenomenologically aversive. *Journal of Experimental Social Psychology*, 1976, *12*, 530–538.

Zimbardo, P., Cohen, A. R., Weisenberg, M., Dworkin, L., & Fireston, I. Control of pain motivation by cognitive dissonance. *Science*, 1966, *151*, 217–219.

Zuckerman, M. Use of consensus information in prediction of behavior. *Journal of Experimental Social Psychology*, 1978, *14*, 163–171.

Author Index

Subject Index